T0303935

COLLECTED STUDIES SERIES

Cosmographers and Pilots of the Spanish Maritime Empire

To the memory of
Helen Wallis, OBE, FSA
friend and colleague over forty years.

Ursula Lamb

Cosmographers and Pilots of the
Spanish Maritime Empire

VARIORUM
1995

Published by
Ashgate Publishing Limited
Wey Court East
Union Road
Farnham
Surrey, GU9 7PT
England

Ashgate Publishing Company
110 Cherry Street
Suite 3-1
Burlington
VT 05401-3818
USA

ISBN 0-86078-473-8

British Library CIP Data
   Cosmographers and Pilots of the Spanish Maritime Empire
   (Variorum Collected Studies Series: 499)
   I. Title II. Series
   387.50946

US Library of Congress CIP Data
   Lamb, Ursula
   Cosmographers and pilots of the Spanish Maritime Empire
      p. cm. — (Variorum Collected Studies Series: CS499)
   Includes bibliographical references (p.   ) and index.
   ISBN 0-86078-473-8 (cloth : alk. paper)
   1. Navigation—Spain—History. 2. Cosmography. 3. Nautical
   astronomy—History. 4. Spain—History, naval. I. Title. II. Series:
   Collected Studies: CS499.
   VK87.L36 1995   95–15395
   623.89'0946—dc20   CIP

Transferred to Digital Printing in 2012

ISBN 978-0-8607-8473-9

Printed and bound in Great Britain
by Printondemand-worldwide.com

COLLECTED STUDIES SERIES CS499

VARIORUM

CONTENTS

PART III

This volume contains xv + 267 pages

PUBLISHER'S NOTE

The articles in this volume, as in all others in the Collected Studies Series, have not been given a new, continuous pagination. In order to avoid confusion, and to facilitate their use where these same studies have been referred to elsewhere, the original pagination has been maintained wherever possible.

Each article has been given a Roman number in order of appearance, as listed in the Contents. This number is repeated on each page and quoted in the index entries.

INTRODUCTION

The essays of this collection, written over a span of forty years, were presented in varying contexts. They tell a cohesive story which is not apparent when only the detail of any one single piece is considered. From the whole emerges an interpretation of some of the problems of Spain's navigation upon the expansion of her empire across the Atlantic ocean. My interest began with the accidental discovery in 1964 of the manuscript of a book on cosmography by a Spanish author in a collection of Italian poetry in the Bodleiean library. The *Libro* aroused my curiosity about the author, Pedro de Medina. I found that as a cosmographer, he was in the company of many fascinating individuals who were involved in the theoretical aspects of Spain's maritime traffic to her Indies. That is, together with the pilots, they were charged with the interpretation of the new Atlantic world, to fix its outline, and to chart the routes across the ocean with the help of stars, the constant guide of travelers. Put crudely, they had to find out where was what and how to get there. My search for further material on transoceanic traffic resulted in the eventual discussion of four more cosmographic manuscripts, calling attention to their value for maritime history. They are by now all published.[1]

It so happened that the second half of the twentieth century saw a revival of maritime history, because of its international aspects, subsequent to World War II. Under the sponsorship of UNESCO, and the editorship of Michel Mollat, a *Colloque Internationale de l'Histoire Maritime* met periodically in a variety of cities after 1957, to discuss advances in the field of maritime discoveries and history. My first contacts with scholars in the field were through that organization. I attended several meetings, in Paris, on a cruise of the eastern Mediterranean, and in Varna, Bulgaria, which had a program on

---

1. Ursula Lamb, *A Navigator's Universe: The Libro de Cosmographia of 1538 by Pedro de Medina*, translated and with an introduction by Ursula Lamb, Monograph Series of the Society for the History of Discoveries, University of Chicago Press, Chicago, 1972 (article I). Alonso de Chaves, *Quatri Partitu en Cosmografía Practica y por Otro Nombre Espejo de Navegantes*, Paulino Castañeda Delgado, Mariano Cuesta Domingo and Pilar Hernandez Aparício, (eds), Instituto de Historia y Cultura Naval, Madrid, 1983 (article II). Juan de Escalante de Mendoza, *Itinerario de Navegación de los Mares y Tierras Occidentales*, Museo Naval, Madrid, 1985. Also: Manoel de Andrada Castel Blanco, *Instrucción al Rey*, edited and published by P.E.H. Hair, *To Defend Your Empire and the Faith*, Liverpool University Press, Liverpool, 1990; and Baltasar Vellerino de Villalobos, *Luz de Navegantes*, with an introduction by María Luísa Martín-Merás Verdejo, Jefe de Investigación del Museo Naval, Madrid, 1985 (article XIII).

port cities. This goes to show that the themes of the meetings determined what kind of material could be treated. For the Varna meeting, a graduate student, Gary Miller, had prepared a collection of facsimile maps of the area which could not be presented in Varna, nor printed in Vienna. But the material would have been very helpful to the story of 'Puerto de Caballos', published under joint authorship with Gary Miller.

In 1960 at a meeting in Lisbon, began a series of celebrations under Portuguese auspices of the Portuguese discoveries, and three of the meetings organized under the auspices of the *Agrupamento* (now *Centro*) *de Estudos de Historia e de Cartografia Antiga* and at three of those meetings I presented papers. The main sponsors were Luís de Albuquerque, Armando Cortesão and Avelino Teixeira Da Mota. This organization arranged periodic meetings and published the proceedings, i.e. talks given by an international roster of scholars, in an impressive series of *separatas*, and a separate list of edited texts over the years. It is still publishing, numbers by now having risen to over 250. This organization, after the deaths of Teixeira Da Mota and Cortesão, proceeded under the guidance of Luís de Albuquerque. It attracted the cooperation of Brazilian scholars, under the leadership of Max Guedes, director of the *Serviço de Documentação Geral de Marinha* of Rio de Janeiro, and led to *International Reunions of Historians of Nautical Science and Hydrography* in Bahia, Rio, Portugal (Coimbra, Lisbon and Sagres) and in Greenwich. In the latter place (1980) it was decided to agree on a constitution for the *International Reunion of Nautical History and Hydrography*, to meet regularly and alternately in Portugal and America.

Of the papers I presented at those meetings only one suited the content of this collection. North American interest in discovery history, including nautical science, resulted on the occasion of the Lisbon celebration of 1960 in the founding of the *Society for the History of Discoveries* by John Parker, Wilcomb Washburn, and Svevolod Slessarev. The society publishes an annual periodical, since 1969, called *Terrae Incognitae* with a bibliographical listing of the year's publications in the field. Three of my papers appeared in that periodical. The society also circulates a triannual newsletter. In 1981, I was asked to deliver the Eva G.R. Taylor lecture. My talk was delivered at the Royal Geographical Society in London under the auspices of the Royal Institute of Navigation. Two more lectures were given on special occasions, one at the University of California and another at Imperial College, London.

This summary of my odyssey through the waters of international scholarship explains the apparent lack of connection between topics and treatment as mentioned above. It is hoped however, that the knowledge of these organizations which made it possible for me to meet seasoned scholars will demonstrate the ample range of opportunities available.

'The cosmographies of Pedro de Medina' (no. I, 1966) was the first study which caught the interest of friends of Professor Rodriguez Moñino who, among other things, was an expert on sixteenth-century bibliography. It introduced me to the subject of cosmographers and pilots of the Spanish maritime empire, and my path went on, directed toward more documentation about the texts on early nautical science. 'The '*Quatri Partitu*' by Alonso de Chaves' (no. II, 1969) was another manuscript, not unknown, but never published in its entirety, and accessible to me only in part during a visit to Spain in 1967. This practical handbook for sailors therefore reappears in 'The teaching of pilots' (no. VIII, 1993), where its content and use are discussed on the basis of an edition of the whole work, published by the Museo Naval in 1985.

The following three articles (nos. III, IV, and V) document my search for the manner in which an understanding of the new geographic and hydrographic environments were established in Spain. The progression from one finding to the next necessitated a certain amount of repetition as the essays were read to different audiences. Cumulatively, they establish a path of knowledge through social institutions which were available to make decisions about the truth of competing statements of facts or theories. This is after all the initital requirement made of the new knowledge: that its hypotheses be proven to be true by consistent records and repetitive results, while applications of experience with scientific phenomena alone, useful though they may be, do not constitute science.

The next article, 'The cosmographers of Seville' (no. VI, 1976), invites the reader into the midst of all the various constituents of society concerned with maritime problems in thought and deed. None of the institutions were designed to attest to scientific truths. These stories of conflict among scientists are chapters preceding the 'scientific revolution', in so far as the role of experiment for verification was anticipated by very few experts, rarely practiced, and only sporadically understood. The proceedings of litigation showed that *péritos desapasionadas* (disinterested experts) respected information from any reliable source. Competition showed the contradiction of means and ends in pursuit of scientific truth, and the *junta* confirmed the need for multiple and consistent records, for integrity and reliability as well as skill. In all these cases a moral dimension goes along with purely scientific requirements for telling the truth.

'The Sevillian lodestone' (no. VII, 1987) shows how circumstance helped or hindered the advance of knowledge. 'The teaching of pilots' (no. VIII, 1993) presents wider social references as well as more specific ones. They discuss who was concerned with what issues in gathering and interpreting the facts of the new geographic and hydrographic world and its position with regard to the universe.

II

In a second part this wider reference leads to more specifics about practical problems, with which the cosmographers and pilots had to deal. 'Nautical scientists and their clients' (no. IX, 1985) is an amplification of article VII. 'Dos huellas científicas del tratado de Tordesillas' (no. X, 1973) is a unique cosmographic consideration of two practical problems: firstly, the organized transplant of spices to the Spanish Indies, which would have put the spice production and marketing wholly under Spanish control; and secondly, a late application of a grid of map coordinates to the projection of hypothetical political organizations over unexplored terrestrial space. This is the last instance of a division of this kind and of such size, cast over unexplored though inhabited regions. Professor Demetrios Ramos of the Casa de Colón in Valladolid helped me with this paper.

The next piece 'Puerto de Caballos, Honduras' (no. XI, 1986) shows the involvement of entrepreneurs, colonists, and royal officials, along with cosmographers and pilots in a problem resulting from the length of the Atlantic link. It tells how the flow of information, or lack of it, and the conflicting bases of judgement, influenced the choice of a port for the Honduras fleets. The story is unusual for the long time span that this scheme stayed alive, and for the variety of interests involved.

'The silver masters' (no. XII, 1978) describes the origin and functioning of middlemen concerned with the security of shipments. They were put under the orders of the captain and masters and considered part of the naval personnel.

'Advice to the King' (no. XIII, 1967 and 1981) on fleets of the Atlantic proffers a minute description of the traffic, and suggestions to the King concerning the routing of the 'Carrera de Indias' by Juan de Escalante de Mendoza. This is joined to the presentation of a pamphlet concerned with Spain's nautical routes in the South Atlantic by Manoel de Andrada Castel Blanco (1988), a talk here reconstituted, in order to complete the Iberian shipping routes in the Atlantic.

III

The essay titled 'Argos and Polyphemus' (no. XIV, 1992) is somewhat set apart from the concerns of the rest. Delivered as one of a series of lectures in celebration of the Quincentennial of the Columbian voyage of 1492, it is an attempt to look at what happened when the surface of the terraquaeous globe was expanded by two thirds within just thirty years. Once the oceans entered into the western record, experience with time and space led to new concepts of distance and duration, and there were different impacts on governance. Comparing this with a similar sudden and very large expansion of space and time in our day of moon landing and satellites, leads to a more precise understanding of the discovery period. The enormous difference of circumstance does not prevent a clearer focus directed to the prior experience.

Spanish maritime traffic had lost most of its exploratory characteristics well before the end of the sixteenth century. A reprise of the theoretical aspects of naval concerns, under direct supervision of the crown, became effective again in the eighteenth century. There is much material on that phase of maritime history, the founding of the naval school, the evolution of its curriculum, the establishment of the observatory of San Fernando etc. It was realized that the historical data assembled during the early phases of the imperial enterprise could still be useful, and a dual approach to regaining Spain's preeminence on the seas was to be directed to history as well as to the future. The collection and publications of the past, and the revitalization of a scientific center for naval affairs (formerly the Pilot Major's Office), led to the establishment of the Spanish Hydrographic Office, and *Depósito Hidrográfico.* Martín Fernández de Navarrete was involved in both enterprises, collecting and publishing the sources, and supporting the scientific naval office: 'Martín Fernández de Navarrete clears the deck' (no. XV, 1980). When the French invasion of Madrid, caused the director of the *Depósito*, Felipe Bauzá, to flee, first to Cádiz, and then to exile in England in 1823, Navarrete accepted the 'interim' directorship of the Hydrographic Office in Madrid, counting on the return of Bauzá. 'Felipe Bauzá: Spanish Hydrographer' (no. XVI, 1981) is built on the correspondence between Navarrete and Bauzá. A final essay 'Early plans for lithographic reproduction of maps' (no. XVII, 1990) shows the vitality of the Spanish hydrographic enterpise in one aspect, the experiments with lithographic printing, which at the time of Navarrete, were on a par with what was done elsewhere.

URSULA LAMB

Tucson, Arizona
December 1994

LIST OF ILLUSTRATIONS

Study I
Portrait of Pedro de Medina: Museo Naval, Madrid.
Title page of Pedro de Medina, *Libro de Cosmographia*, Collection of Western Manuscripts. Bodleian Library, Oxford.

Study II
Title pages '*Comienca el Libro*' and '*Libro Quarto*' and extract of transcription of *Padrón Real*: Alonso de Chaves, *Quatri Partitu en Cosmographia Practica y por Otro Nombre Espejo de Navegantes*, Paulino Castañeda, Mariano Cuesta Domingo and Pilar Hernandez Aparicio (eds). Instituto de Historia y Cultura Naval Madrid, Museo Naval 1983.

Study VIII
Pages of *Tractado de la Sphera* ... and schematic rendering of celestial sphere: Hieronymo de Chaves, *Tractado de la Sphera que Compuso el Doctor Sacrobusto*, Sevilla, 1545. Museo Naval, Madrid.
Title page of *Chronographia* and drawing of Capricorn: Hieronymo de Chaves, *Chronographia o Repertório de los Tiempos* ... , Sevilla, 1561. Museo Naval, Madrid.

Study XI
'Sierras questan sobre puerto de caballos...'; 'Nombre de Dios': Baltasar Vellerino de Villalobos, *Luz de Navegantes*, facsimile edition, introduction and commentary by María Luísa Martín-Merás Verdejo. Jefe de Investigación del Museo Naval, Madrid. Europa Artes Gráficas, Salamanca, 1990.

Study XIII
Routes of the Carrera de Indias; 'S. Domingo de la Isla Española'; and 'La Havana', ibid.
Andrada's Atlantic: Manoel de Andrada Castel Blanco, *Instrucción al Rey*, unique copy, undated, on deposit at the Dr William's Library, London; translation, introduction and notes by P.E.H. Hair, *To Defend Your Empire and the Faith*. Liverpool University Press, 1990.
Taking the height of a star ... : Juan de Escalente de Mendoza, *Itinerario de Navegación de los Mares y Tierras Occidentales*, introduction by Robert Barreiro. Salamanca, 1985.

The author has made every effort to trace all copyright holders, but if any have been inadvertently overlooked, please contact the author via the publishers to make any necessary arrangements at the earliest opportunity.

ACKNOWLEDGEMENTS

I thank Harold B. Johnson for suggesting that a collection of my maritime studies be gathered for publication. Dr John Smedley of Variorum invited me to submit them, and I am grateful to him and his editor, Mrs Ruth Peters, for their care and patience during the production process.

Acknowledgement for permission to reproduce the articles in this volume is gratefully made to the following: Editorial Castalia, Madrid (I); the editors of *Centro de Estudos de Historia e Cartografia Antiga*, Lisbon (II, IX, XV); David Buisseret, *Terrae Incognitae*, Detroit (III, V, VII); Magdalena Mora, *Revista de Occidente*, Madrid (IV); the Regents of the University of California (VI); Professor Eduardo L. Ortíz, Imperial College, London (VIII); the editors of *Segundas Jornadas Americanistas*, University of Valladolid (X); Christiane Villain-Gandossi, CNRS, Aix-en-Provence (XI); Professor Dr Jürgen Schneider (XII); *Journal of Navigation*, Royal Institute of Navigation, London (XVI); the editor of *Revista da Universidade de Coimbra*, Coimbra (XVII).

I would also like to thank Professor Norman J.H. Thrower of the University of California, Los Angeles, and Eduardo L. Ortíz of Imperial College, London, for an invitation to present a paper on a special occasion. The authorities of the Museo Naval in Madrid gave generous permission to make use of illustrations from its publications. For the portrait of Pedro Medina from the museum's collection, I am obliged to María Luísa Martín-Merás Verdejo and to Lola Higueras of the editorial and research staff. They gave generously of their time and advice for my projects. Their help and friendship are invaluable to me. I thank Professor Paul Hair of the University of Liverpool for his permission to reprint the map of the routes of Manoel de Andrada from his edition of the *Instrucción al Rey*.

Pedro de Medina
By courtesy of Museo Naval, Madrid.

I

THE COSMOGRAPHIES OF PEDRO DE MEDINA

T H E presence of a handsome Manuscript by the cosmographer Pedro de Medina in an unexpected place marked the beginning of this study. During a search through the Western Manuscript division of the Bodleian Library I was suddenly intrigued by an item which seemed unrelated to the lists of titles in which it appeared. The final section of the *Canonici Italiani* Manuscripts contains six Spanish items of poetry and among them entry No. 243 a «*Libro de Cosmographia por Pedro de Medina.*» Upon my call for it from the stacks, there appeared a handsome quarto size manuscript, bound in blue velvet covered wood boards, and fastened with two metal clasps in typical sixteenth century fashion. [1] It is written in a clear printed hand and much care has been lavished upon the setting of the text and upon the accompanying drawings.

Pedro de Medina was known to me as the author of the first great textbook on navigation, the *Arte de Navegar,* which was published in 1545, was many times translated, and used well over a hundred years. [2] Moreover the series of *Clásicos Españoles,* brought out by the Consejo Superior de Investigaciones Científicas in Madrid, prints the non-scientific works of Medina with a prologue by Ángel González Palencia as its first volume. Since the *Canonici* catalogue suggested that the *Cosmographia* was an unpublished manuscript, and in view of the status of the author, an inquiry appeared promising.

The *Libro* manuscript had reached the Bodleian from a Venetian source, the collection of a Jesuit, not further identified by the compiler of the *Canonici* catalogue, the Conde Alessandro Mortara. This gentleman was a reader in the Bodleian

---

[1] Irving A. Leonard, *Books of the Brave,* (New York, 1949), p. 225.
[2] Julio F. Guillén, *Europa aprendió a navegar en libros españoles.* (Barcelona, 1943). p. 11-12. Medina's tables were used in 1689 by captain Alonzo de León in Texas during a survey and search for La Salle. E. P. Arneson, «The early art of terrestrial measurement and its practice in Texas.» *The Southwestern Historical Quarterly,* XXIX, oct. 1925, p. 83.

I

Library who spent the year 1852 in making the catalogue in Oxford.[3] From Pulido Rubio's book on the Pilot Major[4] it appears that during the early years of the scientific work of the Casa de Contratación, there was no central deposit for papers which were allowed to circulate freely — with the exception of the Padrón Real or master map—. So, for instance, it was five years after the death of the cosmographer Alonso de Santa Cruz in 1567 before his papers were catalogued. Among them was a «description of all of Spain with part of the coast of Africa» by Pedro de Medina, lost since the dispersal of the papers.[5] Other such lost works are frequently cited, and it is therefore quite possible that here and there some of them re-appear.

My first inquiries into the matter of a Medina cosmography established that a manuscript called *Suma de Cosmographia,* of 1561 by Pedro de Medina is preserved in the Colombina Library in Sevilla. An edition of 200 facsimile copies was printed in 1947 by the Diputación Provincial of Sevilla, upon the suggestion of D. Luis Toro Buiza. In the preface by the admiral of the Spanish fleet, D. Rafael Estrada, one reads that this manuscript is regarded as the last unpublished work of the Maestro Medina. It was probably after 1947, therefore, that another manuscript by Medina, called *Suma de Cosmographia,* formerly of the Gayangos collection, reached the Biblioteca Nacional in Madrid. A comparison of the three manuscripts shows that they are not identical but are distinct and seperate works. I had meantime set about to translate the Oxford *Libro,* when an unusual occurence brought forth yet another unpublished manuscript cosmography by Medina. It is called *Coloquio de Cosmographia* and forms part of the distinguished private collection of works on nautical subjects assembled by Mr. Henry C. Taylor. He was exhibiting a selection of his books and manuscripts in the Beinecke Rare Book Library of Yale University and among them this *Coloquio de Cosmographia* which is dated in the colophon as made in 1543. It also seems to be unknown to bibliographers.

There are now four manuscript cosmographies known to exist which cover the productive years of the Maestro Pedro de Medina as cosmographer. This fact somewhat changes the kind fo discussion which was at first indicated on the basis

[3] Mortara was a friend of the curator of manuscripts, Dr. Wellesley, who bought the MS copy of the catalogue in 1852 and arranged it for publication in 1864. The Conde was a noted collector who lavished unsual care on the catalogue making it a model of complete reference. Sir E. Craster, *History of the Bodleian Library,* 1845-1945. Oxford, 1952, 92.

[4] Pulido Rubio, *El Piloto Mayor,* Escuela de Estudios Hispano Americanos, (Sevilla, rev. ed. 1950), Chapter IX.

[5] Alonso de Santa Cruz, *Crónica de los Reyes Católicos,* edición y estudio por Juan Mata Carriazo. (Sevilla, 1951), 2 vols. vol. I p. cxxvi. As to the papers which were gathered, «los papeles que se recogieron por fallecimiento del cosmographo Alonso de Santa Cruz en 1572,» see also Martin Fernández de Navarrete, *Disertación sobre la Historia de la Náutica,* (Madrid, 1846), p. 162.

of only one new manuscript. There still is no reason to translate more than one of them because their content is quite similar, and any of them might serve for a discussion of all. [6] Two of the works are dated and the other two are not. Attempts at dating those two will be helped by a brief summary of the life of the author.

A statement in the colophon of one of his books, the *Regimiento de Navegación* which he published in 1563, says that the author is seventy years old. He was therefore born in 1493, and he died probably in 1567. The place of his birth has not been established with certainty. Sevilla and the town of Medina could both claim him as a son, and neither with certainty. [7] Pedro de Medina mentions that as a member of the noble household of Medina Sidonia, which his parents served, he visited many towns belonging to the ducal family. [8] Eventually Pedro de Medina became tutor to a son of the house, the young Juan Claros de Guzman, count of Niebla. It is known that Medina had graduated from a University, and Angel Gonzalez Palencia argues convincingly though without documentary proof in favor of Sevilla. Medina's interest and systematic study of the art of navigation and associated sciences date back 26 years from 1544 which means he started in 1518, at the age of 25. [9] There is no way of confirming his whereabouts at that time. His pupil to be, D. Juan Claros, [10] was born in 1519, and sometime thereafter Medina combined his interest in navigational matters with his tutorial duties. By 1538 he had taken Holy Orders. His young pupil may have challenged him to present the world around him in a more comprehensive fashion than the Maestro's own interests in the latest navigational information at the ports of San Lucar, Sevilla, or Cadiz, would have led him to consider. But it is certain that Medina's mathematical training, his wide reading, the availability of the splendid ducal Library, and his experience of being a member of a great household, made him aware of the role of cosmographical knowledge in government. At the age of 43, widely traveled, deeply read, and scientifically trained, he sought an appointment as royal cosmographer from the Emperor.

An attempt will now be made to identify the Bodleian Manuscript as Medina's first literary work and first cosmography. Mention of a *Libro de Cosmographia* appears in the royal cedula of 1538 which was published by José Toribio

---

[6] A translated edition and extensive commentary is in an advanced state of preparation.

[7] Luis Toro Buiza, «Notas biográficas de Pedro de Medina», *Revista de Estudios Hispánicos,* July 1935, pp. 31-35.

[8] A. González Palencia, ed., *Obras de Pedro de Medina* (Madrid, 1944), Prologue for this and other biographical data.

[9] Archivo General de Indias, Justicia, Leg. 1146, Ramo II.

[10] Who died in 1556 at the age of 37 Toro Buiza, *op. cit.,* p. 35.

Medina in his *Biblioteca Hispano Americana*. [11] On December 20th of that year the Emperor issued a cedula which says that upon proof of competence submitted to the Consejo de Indias, Pedro de Medina is granted a license to function as cosmographer of the Casa de Contratación. The important point in the document is the mention - among the proof of competence submitted - of a *Libro de Cosmographia*. The distinguished Chilean bibliographer J. T. Medina, knew of the existance of the *Suma de Cosmographia* in the Colombina Library and therefore thought that the Maestro had returned to the book on Cosmography of 1538 in 1561, the date of the Columbina *Suma,* and that this work was therefore identical with the *Libro* of the cedula of 1538. With the discovery of the Bodleian copy it is no longer necessary to guess about the *Libro* submitted in 1538, which is clearly the Oxford Ms directed to the Emperor Charles V even though undated. [12]

With his license to make and sell instruments and «things necessary to navigation» (charts), Medina settled in Sevilla, in order to follow his new profession. He was also soon thereafter licensed to examine pilots and to cooperate in the making of the *Padrón Real* or master map of explorations kept by the Casa de Contratación. [13] Exposed to the ignorance around him, the Maestro set about to write his great textbook, the *Arte de Navegar*. This is the work with which his name is identified in the history of nautical literature of all the countries in the West. In the year 1543 when he presented the first draft of this work, he also found time to write the *Coloquio de Cosmographia*, our second manuscript. [14]

The *Coloquio* looks hastily though conscientiously done, like a copy by memory of the Libro of 1538, but it has in addition the regiments of the north star and of the sun. Such new regiments Medina appears to have submitted separately to the Consejo de Indias already in 1538 because they are specifically acknowledged in the royal cedula of that date. [15] The *Coloquio* tables appear identical with the tables of the *Arte de Navegar,* except for small corrections, and the use of Arabic numerals throughout. Colors are used to distinguish the columns of figures, rather than Roman numerals as appear in the *Arte*. The *Coloquio* has one other very interesting feature. This is a paragraph and figure drawn by a different hand on the last page. Its subject is the «altura del norte» converted into distances in leagues for each rhumb of the windrose. The anonymous author

---

[11] José Toribio Medina, *Biblioteca Hispano Americana*, 1493-1810, (Santiago de Chile, 1878), 2 vols., I pp. 192-193.
[12] Libro de Cosmographia en que se declara una descripcion del mundo dirigida a la S. M. del Emperador don Carlos nuestro señor, fecho por pedro de medina cosmographo.
[13] José Toribio Medina, *loc. cit.*
[14] Coloquio de Cosmographia fecho entre el Magnº senor comendador pedro de benavente e pedro de medina maestro de la navegacion cosmografo de su magestad. Col. Henry C. Taylor, at Yale University.
[15] See above note 11.

says that it seems that the Maestro Pedro de Medina who wrote this book had intended

> «to present a short account to the senor comendador buenavente of the materials which he discusses in it ... but ... had somehow omitted a discussion (memoria) and demonstration of the number of leagues which each of the winds counts on its rhumb for each degree.»

It is true that in the prior text Medina does allude to that problem and that the lack of discussion was an oversight. The expert and anonymous emendation of this manuscript is worth consideration together with the story of the *Arte de Navegar* which is told is another document. [16] It seems that the manuscript of that book circulated among the cosmographers and pilots of Sevilla quite freely in 1543 and was criticized by Diego Gutierrez and other pilots who asked that it not be licensed for printing. But its utility was defended by other cosmographers and friends of Medina. A royal order requested that the critics meet with the author and, in view of the usefulness of the book, correct it for publication. Accordingly chapters were distributed and taken home by them, amended and initialled, to be eventually incorporated into the *Arte de Navegar*. The *Coloquio*, a contemporary of the *Arte*, appears to have likewise circulated. That it stems from the times of heated controversy between the pilots and cosmographers is illustrated by a passage from the additional note mentioned above which says that, since it appears to have been the intent of the author to discuss the matter amended «this addition is made by a respectful friend of the said Pedro Medina and not because he (Medina) lacks the knowledge...» [17] One may further reflect that the *Coloquio* of 1543 was the product of frustration over the *Libro* held up in the Consejo de Indias and the *Arte de Navegar,* stalled in the Casa de Contratación. It may have been a matter of policy to present an influential friend, the comendador Pedro de Benavente with proof of Medina's vision and of his skill.

Between the making of the *Coloquio* and the *Arte de Navegar* in its first presentation of 1543, [18] and the next dated Cosmography there elapsed eighteen years. This time span was filled out with many literary labours. Medina found that the ignorance of his countrymen concerning the sea and newly discovered lands lagged only shortly behind their lack of knowledge about Spain and her past. In 1548 he brought out the «first guide to Imperial Spain» called *Libro*

---

[16]   Archivo General de Indias, Justicia 1411 Ramo II case between Medina, Diego Gutiérrez and other cosmographers.
[17]   Coloquio, Col. Henry C. Taylor.
[18]   Renewed attempts to prevent its sale in 1546 failed. A. González Palencia, *loc. cit.,* and note 9.

I

de Grandezas y Cosas memorables de España. [19] A moral tract entitled *Libro de la Verdad,* of 1555, was followed by the *Crónica de los Duques de Medina Sidonia* in 1561. This is the year when he also wrote the *Suma de Cosmographia.* There are later editions of abbreviated versions of his *Arte de Navegar,* called *Regimiento de navegación,* starting in 1552 which were approved by the Pilot major, Alonso de Chaves and sold under the license for the *Arte.* The last edition of a *Regimiento* newly licensed and bearing testimony of Medina's work upon it, was published in 1563.

One must now inquire where the undated *Suma de Cosmographia* of Madrid fits in. This work has two distinguishing features: One is a map, not included in the other Cosmographies, and the other is the use of pasted prints of sculptured figures and of verses accompanying them. It is the handsomest of the cosmographies but it has no dedicatory preface. The printed hand in the text is that used by Medina but there are curious misspellings which make one doubt that he wrote it, except for the title page. Although the drawings appear the same it contents as the ones in the other manuscripts they are infinitely better made and very heavily gilded. The map is a piece of fancy even allowing for the picturesque approach rather than a scientific one. It seems unlikely that Medina had much to do with it because the heavy distortion involves the north-African coast which was presumably known to him. There is one river drawn on the map which flows from somewhere in the west of France to the north of Greece all across Europe. There are no other rivers. Outlines are very distorted and illustrative devices, - little trees all over Africa - enhance the looks of the map but do not remedy the lack of precision. Most probably the work was a presentation copy for some patron's library, similar to the «lost» six figures concerning the Universe for which he was paid by his patroness the Duchess in 1567. [20] The Madrid *Suma* is the only book that opens with illustrations of no cosmographical significance, but represents an introduction to Medina's ideas concerning man's place in the Universe which he demonstrates in his non-technical works. There are three engravings of women in classic garb the first facing right under the legend: time coming, the second en face, under the heading: present time, and the third, turning left, under the label, time passed. There appear two additional figures pointing out of their frame to a clock drawn in the margin with a verse written above. [21]

---

[19]   So called by Ángel González Palencia, *La Primera Guia de la España Imperial,* (Madrid, 1940).
[20]   Luis Toro Buiza, *loc. cit.*
[21]   The figures have a mark LS. They could be the sybils of a flemish engraver, Lambert Sustris, see No. 1915 of Francois Bulliot, *Dictionaire des Monogrammes* (Munich, 1833), II, p. 249. Ulrich Thieme und Felix Becker, *Allgemeines Lexikon der bildenden*

The dating of the first three cosmographies is certain: the *libro* made in 1538, the *Colloquio* dated 1543, and the *Suma* of Sevilla, written in 1561. This leaves the question of date for the Madrid *Suma* awaiting further evidence.

A curious fact, considering the eminence of the author, is that none of the cosmographies were ever published during Medina's life time. With regard to works one and two, the *Libro* and the *Coloquio*, the explanation is straightforward. One was part of an application directed to the Emperor, and had fulfilled its purpose by the license of 1538. Moreover, publication rights would have had to be sought by protracted negotiation. In his new work with the pilots, the *Arte* was closer to Medina's heart. The *Coloquio* was written for a specific patron at a time when the *Arte* was still held up by the authorities. Concerning the Colombina *Suma*, the Almirante Estrada speculated that it was not published because it was too old-fashioned, and that its content no longer interested people eighteen years after Copernicus and the consequent changes in astronomy. It might be suggested rather, that the specific nautical information in the *Colombina Suma* is neither sufficient for a sailor, nor quite simple enough for a landsman. In the fifteen sixtieth the technical interest of sailors had got away too far from the casual interest of the general public. Far from Copernicus' theory preemping the field, authors were aware that the lay expert was officially discouraged from acquiring tools which might make him able to learn scientific secrets. Publication of cosmographical material was the exception rather than the rule for Spanish authors. [22] The Madrid *Suma* would appear to be a late work, general in content, beautiful in excecution, and possibly commissioned.

Künste von der Antike bis zur Gegenwart. (Leipzig, 1907-1950), 37. vols. XXXII, p. 314-316, Sustris = Zutman? (1515/20) Amsterdam, died, 1568.

[22] C. Fernández Duro, *Algunas Obras desconocidas de Cosmographia y de Navegación, pertenecientes a la Academia Real de la Historia* (Madrid, 1893) who speaks of 26 such *mss* before 1600, and the famous *Itinerario* by the admiral Juan de Escalante y Mendoza.

LIBRO DE COSMOGRAPHIA

En que se declara una discripçion del
mundo, dirigido ala S. M. del enpe
rador don Carlos nuestro señor

fecho por pedro de medina cosmog
espho

Title page of *Libro de Cosmographia* by Pedro de Medina
Collection of Western Manuscripts, Bodleian Library, Oxford.

II

THE QUATRI PARTITU EN COSMOGRAPHIA
BY ALONSO DE CHAVES — AN INTERPRETATION

The subject of this paper is the manuscript entitled: «*Quatri Partitu en Cosmographia*» by Alonso de Chaves (1), which is on deposit in the Library of the Royal Academy of History in Madrid. It consists of 150 folios but the text is not complete in all sections, i.e. the table of content refers to parts for which only a title or even a blank page appear in the manuscript. Some selected passages of this book and a brief description were published by Cesareo Fernandez Duro in 1895 (2). There exists an unpublished translation into English of part four in the Yale Historical manuscript collection made by Edward Luther Stevenson in 1929, and reference to it appears in several modern works (3).

My acquaintance with the book came about because of a concern with the pilot-examinations run by the *Casa de Contratación* in Seville and with the literature which might reflect the content of the curriculum offered to student pilots. An attempt will be made to show that this document was the depository of the material taught in Seville, especially to the pilots of the *Carrera de Indias* and that it stands poised on the dividing line between

(1) Full title of the manuscript, Quatri Partitu en Cosmographia pratica i por otro nóbre llamado Espeio de Navegantes: Obra muy utilissima i cópendiosa en toda la Arte de Marear i mui neccesaria i de gran provecho en todo el curso de la navegaciõ, principalmente de Espana. Agora nuevamente ordenada y compuesta por Alonso de Chaves cosmographo Dela Magestad Cesarea del emperador y Rei delas espanas Carlo quinto Semper Augusto:

Dell collegio dela compa de Jesus de Monsorio, Real Academia Biblioteca de la Historia, MS 9-14-1 2791.

(2) Cesareo Fernandez Duro, «De algunas obras desconocidas de Cosmografía y Navegación y singularmente de la que escribió Alfonso de Chaves a principios de siglo XVI». Reprint, *Revista de Navegación y Comercio*, Madrid, 1895, 46 pp..

(3) Literary estate of Edward Luther Stevenson in the Yale Historical Manuscript Colletion.

improvisation and organization of both scientific teaching and practices. In addition, the manuscript contains the earliest preserved example of part of a *Padrón Real*, which was the central product of the Casa's most important scientific enterprise.

Certainly the author of the *Quatri Partitu* was representative of the cosmographic establishment. Alonso de Chaves was born before the beginning of the sixteenth century and died in his nineties in 1599. He spent his entire productive life time as a cosmographer in the service of the Casa de Contratación at Seville. His work was well enough regarded by the crown to have him put in charge of the examination of pilots and of charts in 1528, and to bring him the title of Royal Cosmographer. He was a member of the Junta appointed to serve with Hernando Colón charged with the compilation of a *Padrón Real* in 1529. During the absence of the Pilot Major Sebastian Cabot, on his expedition to the La Plata, the scientific work of the Casa fell upon the cosmographers Diogo Ribeiro and Alonso de Chaves. Upon the death of Ribeiro in 1533 Alonso de Chaves alone was for a while in charge of teaching and the examination of charts and instruments. In 1552 he was made Pilot Major, and he took over the *cátedra* of Cosmography eventually succeeding his own son. Alonso de Chaves took part in all aspects of the training and examination of pilots which he had by and large developed, writing a précis about the practices he established in 1556. The crown allowed him to retire only when he was over ninety, despite his earlier requests to be pensioned, and he was granted a degree of grudging recognition which was exceptional in an epoch of notorious royal ingratitude. So much suffices to establish the pivotal role of the author of our manuscript in the cosmographic enterprise of the Casa de Contratación. It is the contention of this paper that the *Quatri Partitu* deserve a comparable place.

The four parts of the manuscript contain a summary of practical knowledge for the professional pilot, that is; the text is ample and precise in the numeration of observed and recorded fact, it is limited in explanation to what is useful for an understanding of the phenomena with which pilots have to deal, and it is careful in instructions for the making and use of instruments and the conduct of ships.

The book set a pattern for later *Artes* by bringing first the *calendarios* which became routine in all similar texts. Part two of the book concerns nautical instruments and brings instructions for their use. The instruments given are: compass, chart, maritime astrolabe, quadrant, ballestilla, lead and line and sand clock. There are also tables of scales and measures in use among cosmographers. Part two presents the sixteenth century concepts of the universe in terms of Ptolomeic astronomy and Aristotelian physics as commonly presented in cosmographies of the epoch. It also contains a record of eclipses from 1539-1560, with tables adjusted for the meridian of Seville. There is another table for the «miles contained by each degree of longitude with reference to each parallel of latitude starting from the equinox». In this chapter the controversy over the sixteen and seventeen-mile degree of longitude is mentioned. Book five of this part is the unusual one which was printed by Fernandez Duro in 1895 along with other selected excerpts from the work which are the only ones ever to have been published. This section discusses all extant information available to sailors for predicting the weather. The material is collected from ancient authors as well as from pilot observations. As many data are applicable to weather inland as are useful at sea. The most significant contribution of this passage is therefore the importance it attaches to the observation and repeated record of phenomena and not to their nature. Fernandez Duro used the text for a discussion of mariners rhymes about wheather from the point of view of literary, historical, and ethnological interest, which, however, does not make the point above.

The Third Part discusses the basic problem in navigation of how to know where the ship is and how to steer from there to the desired port. This section presents the problem of compass declination (so called by Chaves and not variation), which was then at the center of scientific debate. Book two of Part Three contains a discussion of currents and tides. Chaves' interpretation of the origin and nature of ocean currents persuaded him that there would have to be an open northern passage from Atlantic to Pacific and that a solid and permanent separation of the oceans could not be assumed nor was there knowledge enough to deny this theory, he said. His treatment of tides is thorough and does not appear in such detail in any of the later Spanish *Artes*. It contains an analysis of tidal flow as observed on various coasts and an explanation based upon the phases of the moon. In addition there is the precise description of an instrument designed to tell the state of the tide at any latitude at any time. This description is not illustrated and I have not found the instrument mentioned among those carried by Spanish pilots of the carrera. Tides were no major problem of the Caribbean and for practical pilots the experience with the amplitudes of tides in various latitudes and of the peculiarities with tidal currents in estuaries, bays and straits, was more than a match for an instrument which merely counted time. The difference between the theoretical satisfaction and the use of instruments for the carrera pilots which was a major battle ground between cosmographers and pilots at this time in Seville (4), stands nowhere better revealed than in the design and subsequent obscurity into which this «instrumento general de mareas» was allowed to fall.

The Third Book of Part Three brings discussion about what to do in a shipwreck. Here from the first, Alonso de Chaves is more practical than for instance Pedro de Medina. The latter advises the drowning sailor to remember the year, month, day, and hour of the accident in order to establish his location, while Chaves advises the man to shout, and to find a plank or

---

(4) URSULA LAMB, «Science by Litigation: Compass and Chart before the Law, 1545-46» paper read before the Society for the History of Discoveries, Bloomington ILL. October 1965, to be published in *Terrae Incognitae*, No 1.

barrel to hold onto. If this sounds trivial, it is characteristic of the attitude of first things first, which is so refreshing a characteristic of the manuscript.

Under six additional headings Chaves brings the vocabulary used to describe ships and their parts and the men who serve in them, officers crew and their duties. This passage was published by Fernandez Duro and has led to characterize the manuscript as a vocabulary or nautical dictionary (5). There is furthermore included a chapter on the conduct of warfare at sea. This early modern discussion superceded the statment concerning naval war in the «Siete Partidas» of Alfonso the Wise (Partidas II, Títulos 24 and 25, ley XXLV; and Título XXV, leyes 1-14). Chaves' chapter is the first to discuss the use of firearms at sea and treats the tactics of naval warfare by squadrons on the open sea. (Coastal defense had been discused by Mosén Diego de Valera on comission by the Catholic Kings in 1497). Chaves initiated the teaching of the *cátedra* of naval war and artillery which was to be founded in the Seville School in 1576 and whose first incumbent was Andrés de Espinosa.

The Fourth Part, properly called «espeio de navegantes» is a *derrotero* describing the way to and from the Indies, that is as in a mirror looking from two sides. The derrotero consists of an alphabetic list of place names which are given their «alturas y leguas» i.e., position, and distance and direction to the nearest ports of reference. It is the contention of this paper that the *derrotero* of Chaves is in fact as close an approximation to the earliest *Padrón Real* as has yet been encountered. This interpretation rests upon the sequence in which the padrones were manufactured and upon what Chaves says about Part four in his manuscript. In résumé the *derrotero* seems to be the Indies section of the book which Chaves used for the examination of pilots and charts before the «visita» to the Casa de Contratación by the licenciado Suarez de Carvajal in 1540. From internal data, the manuscript can be said to be closset to the year 1539. Fernandez Duro places it between 1520 and 1539 because those are the years of the *aureo número*. But church festivals are given only for the year 1540 and eclipses from the year 1539. Stevenson placed the Ms in 1537 because he added a year to the order by the crown to make a *Padrón Real* at the end of 1536 when papers were to be newly gathered together for the purpose (6). His reference is Oviedo y Valdés. There certainly was in use for examinations a *Real Padrón* in January 24th, 1540, when Pedro de Medina was given access to it by cedula. In October of that year an order was given that all charts had to be based upon the *Padrón,*

---

(5) H. C. WOODBRIDGE, «A tentative bibliography of Spanish and Catalan Nautical Dictionaries, Glossaries and Word Lists», *The Mariner's Mirror*, 1951, vol. 37, p. 64.

(6) This is also the year when the cosmographer Santa Cruz was to be furnished with all the data concerning the Padrón Real for his *Islario*. See the edition of Santa Cruz by F. Mata Carriazo.

GONZALO FERNANDEZ DE OVIEDO Y VALDES, *La Historia general de las Indias*, Madrid, 1851-1855, 4 vols.; vol. 2, p. 114 alludes to the map «painted» by Alonso de Chaves, 1536.

and the appointment of the Junta by Carvajal for a revision of the *Padrón* dates from the same year. It is probable that the manuscript by Chaves was not published because its information, particularly in part four, was superceded and not because it was censored.

As for the manufacture of the *espeio* Chaves says: «that it is due to the author» qual asismismo hordeno y compuso con sola su industria y trabajo el dho Alonso de Chaves Cosm. de S.M. Cesarea. La cual obra es aprovada por los otros cosmographos de su magestad y conforme a voto y parecer de los sabios y experimentados pilotos que navegan». The text by Chaves is practically a copy of the emperor's instructions to Suarez de Carvajal that he should bring together the most outstanding cosmographers and the most experienced pilots in order that they might pool their knowledge and compile and sign the corrected Padrón. It is safe to assume then that the *espeio* dates no earlier than 1536 when the data were gathered for Chaves, and 1540 when revision was about to begin.

The manuscript of the *Quatri Partitu* contains therefore a part of a document which has been very elusive despite much search. When used in conjunction with the depositions by Faleiro, Sebastian Cabot and other pilots in the famous legal quarrel between Pedro de Medina and Diego Gutierrez, (1545-46) one might get an exact idea of the state of geographic knowledge and the controversies concerning specific points in the mid sixteenth century. If the *espeio de navegantes* of the *Quatri Partitu* can indeed be regarded as the earliest survival of a *Padrón Real*, it overshadows the rest of the manuscript in importance.

But exclusive discussion of this Part Four or of any other separate part of the manuscript does not do justice to the whole. The manuscript is unlike other Spanish texts a comprehensive record of both the *Arte* and *Oficio de la Mar*. Its instruction is reflected in a manuscript which comes as close to an actual transcript of a pilots examination as I have found excerpted in the *Apuntes para una Biblioteca Científica Española del siglo XVI* by Felipe Picatoste, (p. 348). Other works just cite categories of subject matter but that manuscript brings sample answers, including misleading ones (as to what is longitude and latitude and whether under the Arctic pole they could be found by the compass).

In addition to the extensive coverage of disciplines, the manuscript also refers to a wide geographic area. Mention is found of places on the North Sea coast as well as of Mediterranean ports. Tides are discussed with reference to northern latitudes and local practice of correcting the compass, *(aguja de corujo)* is mentioned. The manuscript thus calls to mind that while shipping to the Indies was eventually concentrated in two fleets each year, the port of Seville was choked with European coastal traffic all year round. This is a good corrective for historians of the *Carrera de Indias* or of *the Portuguese imperial roteiros*, or of the exclusive study of European shipping in isolation from each other. Chaves took for his province all the sea lanes which crossed the oceans — even if the *espeio* proper is limited to the Atlantic routes. This versatility has many implications. Foremost among them is that he accepted facts from whatever quarter they came. Through this manuscript breathes a freedom of inquiry in naval matters which was to survive the freedom to publish for some time. The work on this aspect and others raised, however, is all to be done, and so is the analysis of the entire manuscript in the light of time place and circumstance of its writing and of the audience which it was meant to reach, as well as of its place in contemporary literature. I thought it justifiable to present research under way rather than conclusions to this distinguished audience as long as acquaintance with the *Quatri Partitu* is not general among scholars.

DISCUSSÃO

R. A. SKELTON. — For the exploration and mapping of North America in the second quarter of the XVI century, the *derrotero* of Chaves is a significant document, which was cited by Harrisse only at second-hand through Oviedo, and abstracted by Phelps Stokes and Ganong from an (unpublished) transcript of F. C. Wieder. It is to be hoped that, even if we must wait for a critical edition of the whole manuscript, the *derrotero* may be published in full, perhaps separately, as soon as possible.

A. TEIXEIRA DA MOTA.—Devemos estar gratos à autora pelo exame que fez do invulgar escrito de Alonso de Chaves e por nos ter mostrado a grande importância e significado de que se reveste. Fazemos votos porque possa em breve ser totalmente publicado, para melhor conhecimento das artes e ciências do homem do mar em meados do século XVI. Neste momento vem-nos ao espírito, pela sua afinidade com a de Alonso de Chaves, a obra de um tratadista náutico português coevo, o P.e Fernando Oliveira, cujos trabalhos constituem uma verdadeira enciclopédia marítima, já que neles se ocupa de arte de navegar, cartografia náutica, construção naval, organização da vida a bordo e arte da guerra no mar. O cotejo entre os dois tratadistas deve permitir úteis conclusões sobre as semelhanças e diferenças nas técnicas marítimas de portugueses e castelhanos, e aproveitamos este momento para anunciar que a Secção de Lisboa do Agrupamento de Estudos de Cartografia Antiga trabalha na edição da «Árte Náutica» do P.e Fernando Oliveira, estando já concluída a sua tradução para português.

A autora salienta muito justamente o interesse da obra de Alonso de Chaves, para o melhor conhecimento da organização e actividade da Casa de Contratación de Sevilha, no campo da náutica e cosmografia, nomeadamente no respeitante às funções do piloto-mór e cosmógrafos e às questões de ensino e respectivos exames. Também neste campo se afigura que poderá ser muito significativa a comparação entre o que se passava nestes domínios na Casa de Contratación, de Sevilha, e nos Armazéns da Guiné, de Lisboa, já que também era nestes que se centralizava a admissão e exame de pilotos, o seu ensino e a elaboração da «carta padrão d'el-Rei», percursora lusitana do «padrón real». Assim, apontamos que em 1559 e 1592 foram promulgados em Portugal «regimentos do cosmógrafo--mor», cujo estudo temos em curso, os quais lançam muita luz sobre a importante questão do ensino e exame de pilotos, estando ligados aqueles dois regimentos os nomes prestigiosos de Pedro Nunes e João Baptista Lavanha.

Em conclusão, o estudo de Ursula Lamb é da maior oportunidade e abre-nos importantes perspectivas para o melhor conhecimento de questões que têm andado um tanto esquecidas.

W. WASHBURN. — The Society for the History of Discoveries of the United States intends to publish a new editon of Pedro de Medina à *Cosmographia* edited by Ursula Lamb who discusses the training and examination of pilots and the legal questions relating to the licencing of pilots in her introduction to the book.

F. MADDISON. — Can you give a discription of the instrumento general de mareas? How did it work?

U. LAMB. — The discription of the *instrumento general de mareas* comes in two parts. One: a description of the manufacture of a circular tide-table which consists of four concentrically mounted wheels which move inside one another. Across the face of the wheels moves a «cuadrante» of 90°. Two: gives several examples of the use of the instrument at various times and latitudes. I did not at first realize the importance of the appearance of the instrument, and my notes are limited to part one and are sketchy. Part two would explain some ambiguity in what appears etched on the wheels, since in my notes two wheels have the zodiac marked on them. I cannot get a microfilm and one will have to wait for publication in Spain before the instrument will take its proper place in the literature.

R A. SKELTON. — Are there any places mentioned on the North American continent in Part four?

U. LAMB. — The derrotero does have points on the North American continent indicated from Baccalaos to Florida — which is the entire coast. Yale University has a transcript and translation into English of the derrotero in manuscript which was made by E. L. Stevenson in 1929. This work was based upon a fotocopy made on plates at that time from a copy of the Derrotero in the Palacio Real at Madrid. Stevenson thought the other three parts of the *Quatri Partitu* were lost. The foto copy is in the manuscript section of the New York Public Library.

COMIENCA EL LIBRO PRIMERO DELO QUATRI PARTITU EN COSMO GRAPHIA PRATICA·I·POR OTRO NŌBRE LLAMA DO ESPEIO DE NAVEGĀTES.

Partesceste primero libro enlos partes principales Y cada vna enciertos Capitulos

¶ La parte primera deste primero libro trata detodo lo tocante alas festimidades quela sancta madre yglia tiene y manda guardar atodo Xpiano sopena depecado/ordinaria menteen cada vnuno.

Diuidesesta primera parte enquatro Capitulos quesesiguen.

¶ Capitulo primero tracta del Calendario Romano y segund el vso dela sancta iglia de Seuilla

¶ Capitulo Segundo trata del circulo lunar o Aureo nummero Perpetua mente

¶ Capitulo tercero tracta Del circulo Solar y Letra dominical perpetua mente

¶ Capitulo quarto trata Delas fiestas mouibles Perpetua mente yconlos otros preceptos ordinarios Concernientes aesto

TRATADO. I CAPITVLO

primo Jncipit ∞ ∞ ∞

Primum querite regnum dei. Dize la diuina escriptura. yenotra parte finitum sapi entie timor Dominj donde por estas dos auctoridades la sacra escriptura nos amonesta yensena que ante todas cosas Deuemos procurar yquerer el reyno de dios yque el Princi pal fundamento y principio de mi sabiduria sea amar y temer adios nuestro Senor guardan do sus mandamientos ylos otros Diuinos preceptos aquela sancta iglia mi madre nos obliga que debemos guardar y honrrar sopena depecado asi como son los Diuinos offici os y preceptos que por ella son establecidos y las otras festimidades Delos sanctos bienaue nturada quella solenniza ycelebra por todo el ano y por tanto me parescio queante todas cosas deuia tomar por fundamento y principio dela presente obra tractar y declararlas reglas y ordenamientos qlasant ... e iglia tiene enel guardar y celebrarlas festin

Title page of Book I of the *Quatri Partitu ...* by Alonso de Chaves
By courtesy of Museo Naval, Madrid.

LIBRO QVARTO·DELA COS MOGRAPHIA·PRA TICA·Y MODERNA·LLA MADO·ESPEIO DENAVE GANTES·

hordenado y compuesto por Alonso De chaues Cosmographo dela sacra cessarea y catholica y Real magestad del emperador Carlo quinto semper augusto.

Title page of Book IV of the *Quatri Partitu* ... by Alonso de Chaves
By courtesy of Museo Naval, Madrid.

3. Puerto Rico, 18½ grados.

Está al oeste-noroeste de la punta del Loquillo, dista 16 leguas.
Está al este de la punta de Ayala, dista de ella 24 leguas.

Este Puerto Rico tiene tales señas que para ir a él de la banda del este tiene una sierra la más alta que hay en toda aquella costa del norte, y tiene una blanca tierra y no hay otra tal en aquella costa, y en pasando la sierra y la tierra blanca está luego el puerto. Tiene este puerto a la entrada del norte de él, por la banda del oeste, a un cuarto de legua, unas tres isletas cerca de tierra, y entre ellas y la tierra pueden salir navíos, mas la entrada ha de ser por la banda del este, arrimándose a un morro que allí está y guardándose de una baja que tiene, y así será la entrada a medio freo. También se han de aguardar de arrimarse a la tierra por la banda del este de este puerto, porque tiene 7 leguas antes bajos que salen media legua a la mar, y cuando quisieren llegar al puerto verán luego el monasterio alto, que está sobre el puerto, y aquél han de llevar por guía para entrar en el puerto, el cual es el mejor que hay en esta isla y mayor.

Extract transcribed from the *Padrón Real*, describing the coast of
Puerto Rico with information on distance, direction and state of anchorage
By courtesy of Museo Naval, Madrid.

III

SCIENCE BY LITIGATION: A COSMOGRAPHIC FEUD

The geographical discoveries of the sixteenth century upset the European world picture fashioned in the Middle Ages. After Columbus' return, the rapid accretion of new information about man's environment required a drastic reshaping of ideas. In the new world, radical changes in individual lives—from the building of the Portuguese trade empire, from the Spanish conquest of America—made attempts to alter one's life by one's own efforts, or to reach an actual terrestrial goal, seem far more feasible than ever before. Experiment came to seem preferable to miracle, evidence to belief, change itself to the status quo. In varying degrees, practical problems were approached scientifically and observed regularities in natural phenomena began to be put to predictive use, for instance in the charting of a ship's course by stellar observation.

Anticipated in the example above is the fact that transoceanic shipping, which opened the road to the new worlds, depended in large measure upon the use of regular observations of the movements of stars, of winds and tides, for fixing positions at sea and on land and for mapping the coasts. Nautical science, the guarantor of safe passage around the globe, was therefore the first discipline which developed an international group of lay experts whose work ranged from the total reshaping of ideas concerning the universe to the charting of the oceans and the design of nautical instruments. The men concerned with this work were the pilots and cosmographers, the latter in charge of all scientific information concerning the description of the physical universe. It is no wonder that over this range of information and speculation disagreement should be frequent and issues complex. What is of special interest, however, is that the scientific issues are complicated by the fact that the men involved belonged to a world in which natural science in the modern sense was not a recognized concept. The cosmographic feud over the "two-scale chart" and the "corrected compass," which is the subject of this paper, affords an intimate look at the process of the evolution of scientific thought in the living tissue of the environment in which it took place.

In the sixteenth century the nature of scientific truth was not yet distinguished from that of any other kind. Scientific endeavor only gradually revealed a new intellectual discipline leading to truths which differed in content, method, and use from previous knowledge. The process of sorting out scientific knowledge from the truths of theology, magic, or poetry required a long time. Science was in the first instance recognized in its application, and establishing the merit of scientific theory and hypothesis among laymen was a slow process.

From one of the noisiest and most celebrated lawsuits among cosmographers in the sixteenth century, the startling fact emerged that doing justice to scientists was not the same as defining truth in science. Among questions raised were whether secrecy or publication would better foster scientific knowledge, whether demonstration was the exclusive method of proof in science, and whether the control of science was better entrusted to an individual, an office, or an institution. This important debate of intellectual exploration took place in the midst of the hurly-burly of Seville, the busiest port in Christendom, where impassioned controversies engaged the expert practitioners of the art and science of navigation before the Casa de Contratación (Colonial Office in control of Commerce, shipping, and finance). This litigation is fittingly part of the age which J. H. Parry has called the "Age of Reconnaissance."

Since the appointment in 1508 of Amerigo Vespucci to the post of Pilot Major attached to the Casa de Contratación, Spanish business with her Indies had greatly expanded. It had become necessary to appoint a cosmographer or official registrar of geographic information, brought in by returning pilots, to license charts which were sold to the pilots and to train them for transoceanic voyages. The Pilot Major and Royal Cosmographer developed a master chart *(Padrón)* of all the coastlines "discovered," i.e., of those points which had been reconnoitered and described by *derrota* (dead-reckoning) or *altura* (latitude fixed by star sighting). Since 1528 an instrument maker had been associated with the scientific office to supervise the construction of compasses, astrolabes, and *ballestillas* (Jacobs-staffs). The Pilot Major and the cosmographers were also responsible for examining and licensing pilots and masters and for checking the soundness of their instruments on outgoing ships. Pilots were required to carry their own charts and to correct and amend them on their voyages. Observations were then registered with the Pilot Major upon the pilots' return, and if seconded by others or apparently reasonable the observations were incorporated into the Padrón.

The staffing and regulation of the scientific branch of the Casa was the work of the Consejo de Indias, which advised the king and drew up legislation for colonial government. It also functioned as court of appeal in cases referred to it by the Casa de Contratación in Seville. In 1543, the Pilot Major was Sebastian Cabot and the Cosmographer Major Alonso de Chaves. Associated with them were a number of experts, licensed by the King for one or several of the following tasks: the making of charts for specific routes and coastlines, the fabrication and sale of instruments, the calculation of regiments (nautical tables), and the examination of pilots and masters. Of no immediate concern to the legal controversy under discussion are the men who dealt with the construction and arming of ships, although they were also part of the scientific establishment. The work of these experts and the key product of their collaboration, the master map or Padrón, were periodically reviewed by a visitor delegated by the Council of the Indies.

To the pilots and cosmographers, the *visitación* by the Council of the Indies was an opportunity to get a hearing, and the *visitador* was empowered to settle disputes between them as best he could while in Seville, or to initiate legislation in the Council of the Indies. Over the years there had evolved a set of rules which defined and governed the rights and duties of the Pilot Major, the Royal Cosmographers, and their aids, mainly in response to disputes and requests originated in Seville.

The Pilot Major's establishment has been regarded as Europe's first technical college, dealing exclusively with the development and application of scientific knowledge to the furtherance of navigation necessary to the empire. The frequent disputes among members of the staff, a faculty of scientific experts, have, therefore, two aspects of interest: one, the gradual development of science as a new intellectual discipline; the other, the relation of science to other issues, among them the role of patriotism in scientific argument, the effect of secrecy upon the growth of knowledge, and the meaning of social status and moral character of scientists for the advancement of their discipline. The lawsuit to be discussed sheds some light on both the nature of science as it was then discerned, and the development of science as affected by elements outside its discipline.

The story of the suit over the "two-scale chart" is based in the first instance upon documents from the Archivo General de Indias, *Sección Justicia, legajo* 1146, containing the papers collected in Seville to be presented on appeal before the Council of the Indies. The papers are not chronologically ordered or numbered, but comprise a great variety of documents: copies of *cedulas*, original depositions (some in the handwriting of the parties of the suit), and notes by the secretaries concerning judicial decisions. There are two main phases of the hearings in Seville: August to November, 1544, and January to February, 1545. The case then went before the Council of the Indies; documents for this period, scattered in various deposits, are less complete. Along with the legal action went official decisions about the subject matter of the hearings.[1]

The oldest conflict in terms of the lawsuit had arisen in 1540 between the Pilot Major, Sebastian Cabot, and Alonso de Chaves, the Cosmographer Major of the Casa de la Contratación, when the revision of the Padrón was checked by the *visitador* sent by the Council of the Indies, the *licenciado* Caravajal. His report to the Council of the Indies resulted in the confirmation of the provision that all charts for sale in Seville must be made directly from the Padrón, and he added a penalty of 50,000 maravedis for violation. Caravajal had failed at first to get an agreement among the members of the junta appointed to declare their opinion on the revision of the Padrón, and had made a special appeal to get the necessary signatures. The lawsuit argued the question of whether or not this appeal had been backed by a threat of force. Sebastian Cabot soon denounced the Padrón as faulty, and a subsequent *visita* in 1544 of an *oidor* (judge) of the Council of the Indies, D. Gregorio López, did not manage to get any better agreement on the chart, although

---

[1] Documents from the Archivo General de Indias, Justicia, legajo 1146, Ramo 2, have been published in various books. José Toribio Medina brings several in his *Biblioteca Hispano-Americana, 1493–1810* (Santiago de Chile, 1898) 2 vols. The documents relating to Cabot are to be found in his *El Veneciano Sebastian Caboto al Servicio de España* (Santiago de Chile, 1908) 2 vols., I, 358–387, 518–519, 553–554; Gonzalez Palencia published the major Medina texts in his edition of Medina's works: *Obras de Pedro de Medina*, Clásicos Españoles, vol. 1 (Madrid, 1946). José Pulido Rubio brings the texts of the two Chaves, Alonso and Hieronymo, and several parts from other testimony in his *Piloto Major* (Madrid, 1923 and 1950). These works will be cited as Pulido Rubio I and II respectively. The second edition is much enlarged, but does not bring the texts appended to the first. The case treated here is found in general outline in the second edition, pp. 265–269, 400–414. The documentation can be found on pp. 484–530 which brings selected transcripts. The entire proceedings can only be pieced together from the original legajo cited above which has no consistent pagination and in additional documents from *Sección Contratación* especially Leg. 794 (A): "Sancho Gutierrez con los pilotos y maestres". This is another case but has some relevant data.

in fact Cabot suggested alterations of the Padrón only in "two or three places." In his capacity as examiner of the pilots concerning their routes, Alonso de Chaves was therefore in conflict with Sebastian Cabot, the Pilot Major, in charge of the Padrón.[2]

This conflict over the Padrón between the Pilot Major and the Cosmographer Major was connected to another over instruments and the making and sale of charts between the licensed cosmographers Pedro de Medina and Diego Gutierrez. As Diego Gutierrez received his main support from Sebastian Cabot, so Pedro de Medina was associated with Alonso de Chaves. In fact the conflict between Diego Gutierrez and Pedro de Medina was the one which led to the litigation before Casa and Council in the years 1544–1546.

The Maestro Pedro de Medina had received a royal license, to make and sell charts and instruments for the Indies route to the pilots of Seville, in the year 1538.[3] He was a highly educated mathematician and literary man, well connected at court through the Dukes of Medina Sidonia, whom he had served as a tutor. In 1543 he was forty-six years old, experienced in the scientific lore of the Indies from his years of residence in the harbor town of San Lucar de Barrameda. He had built instruments, made charts, and drawn up nautical tables which, when published later, received international acclaim. Upon beginning his work in Seville he had been shocked to find that instruments currently on the market in Seville, made by Gutierrez, were faulty and regiments unreliable. This so disturbed him that he addressed a memorandum about it to the Council of the Indies. His appointment was, in part, based upon receipt of his complaints and the Council's hope that he might be able to apply his criticism usefully in Seville. Upon his arrival there, he was warmly welcomed by the Cosmographer Major, Alonso de Chaves, who called upon him to examine the pilots and who seconded his attempts to get an official hearing for irregularities in the conduct of business by the Pilot Major.

Sebastian Cabot could not stay aloof from the quarrel of Pedro de Medina and Diego Gutierrez, since it involved his scientific competence and his monopoly over the chart and instrument market, which had brought considerable profit to him and to Gutierrez. Probably Diego Gutierrez drove Cabot to denounce Chaves, the Cosmographer Major, but in any case Cabot joined Gutierrez when the latter took his denunciation of Pedro de Medina before the judges of the Casa de Contratación who constituted an admiralty court in colonial affairs.

---

[2] Sebastian Cabot, born in 1479, was the son of Giovanni Caboto who under his father's tutelage became an explorer of international renown. He entered the service of the Spanish crown in 1518 and was the last of the Pilot Majors who themselves went on voyages of discovery. He had powerful friends and made legions of enemies in a stormy career. By 1543 he had been re-installed as Pilot Major and was resident in Seville. This law suit was one of the many in which he was engaged. Alonso de Chaves, a Spaniard from Trujillo, was not a sailor but a cosmographer employed in Seville since 1528. He was the author of the earliest complete nautical dictionary or Mariner's Mirror which covered both *arte* and *oficio* (practice and theory) of navigation. It was called: *Quatri partitu en cosmografia pratica i por otro nombre llamado espeio de navegantes*, written between 1520 and 1538, vide C. Fernandez Duro, *De algunas Obras desconocidas de cosmografia y de navegación* (Madrid, 1895). Chaves rose steadily in his profession, being put in charge of the Padrón or Master Chart, at the Casa de Contratación in Seville in 1536. He was a man of even temper, great learning and respected by everyone, referred to in the law suit by a crown official as a *persona despasionada y perita* . . .

[3] J. T. Medina, *Biblioteca*, I, 194–195 brings the license of 1538 and a supplementary provision (Instruction to give Medina access to the Padrón) of 1539.

Diego Gutierrez had been active in the manufacture of charts and instruments following Nuño García de Torreno from 1511 and thereafter.[4] He befriended Sebastian Cabot when Cabot appeared in Seville in 1521 and they became friends and *compadres*.[5] With Cabot's support he received a license to make and sell instruments on May 21, 1534.[6] His son Sancho also received a comprehensive permit in 1539 to "produce and sell charts, compasses, astrolabes, quadrants, cross-staffs, regiments, and all other instruments necessary for navigation to the Indies, both East and West."[7] The Gutierrez family, father and three sons, operated an extensive business, often buying instruments to resell for licensing from the Pilot Major. Into this situation of scandalous abuse of privilege, which cut out all other license holders, walked Pedro de Medina, newly licensed cosmographer, who arrived with his *cedula* of 1538 and submitted a chart for license to the Pilot Major. For many years no such independent application for license had reached Sebastian Cabot directly without going through the hands of Gutierrez. Even the process of manufacture had been made difficult for Medina because he had not been given access to the Padrón, upon which all charts on the market had to be based. But he had copied a chart currently for sale to pilots and made by Gutierrez.

When Medina presented his work for licensing, the monopoly of the industry held by Sebastian Cabot and the Gutierrez family was seriously endangered. The Pilot Major therefore persuaded the cosmographers and some of the pilots of the Casa, whom he rarely consulted otherwise, to turn down Medina's work on grounds that the chart did not conform to the Padrón, but he never mentioned that Medina had been denied access to it, and testified that his regiments were also inaccurate.[8] Upon this report from the Casa de Contratación to the Consejo de Indias, inquiry was made by the court and the Council regarding the truth of charges against Medina's work. This attack could not be allowed to go unchallenged by Medina if he wanted to continue functioning as cosmographer. He had to defend himself and, in answer to the denunciation, he addressed a petition to the crown to be heard. A hearing before 150 people resulted in his being given access to the Padrón, but otherwise things went on as before; as a result Medina addressed a *Memorial* to the Council of the Indies pointing out in detail the irregularities in the Pilot Major's office and the defects in the products of the Gutierrez family. He suggested an unbiased inquiry by a group of highly trained and neutral experts before the court and the Council of the Indies into the illegal monopoly over the Padrón and the chart market and the sale of unreliable instruments. This *Memorial* to the Council caused the suit brought by Sebastian Cabot and Diego Gutierrez against Pedro de Medina and Alonso de Chaves.[9]

The relationship of the stray facts and scientific assumptions found in the papers of the suit to the great advance in the science of navigation during the century can be

---

[4] The document says: "Nuño Gutierrez," which appears to be a misspelling. The license for chart making was given to Diego Ribero and to *Nuño Garcia de Torreno*.
[5] J. T. Medina, *Sebastian Caboto*, I, 354.
[6] Archivo General de Indias, Contratación, 5784, Libros de toma de razón, Libro I, fol. 57 v.
[7] Pulido Rubio, *Piloto Mayor*, II, 309.
[8] J. T. Medina, *Sebastian Caboto*, I, 363.
[9] Pedro de Medina, *Obras*, ed. A. Gonzalez Palencia, Appendix to the Prologue, XLV.

studied in modern works.[10] A more pertinent reason for the brief and intermittent mention of scientific matter in this paper is the fact that it played only a brief and intermittent part in the proceedings to be described. Moreover, the learned men among the witnesses were themselves well aware of the state of imperfection of their science. They were on safest ground when purely astronomical facts were under discussion, because there was a standard of accuracy which had been achieved in the compilation of regiments (solar and lunar tables) and the engraving of instruments to which professional cosmographers could aspire. The problem without a satisfactory solution had to do with the compass, that "extra pair of eyes which enabled a pilot to see in the dark of a cloudy day or in a starless night."[11] Controversy over this had arisen with the discovery, during Atlantic voyages, that the needle pointed away from north first in one direction and then in another (norestar and noruestar). Magnetic "variation" (declination) had been earlier noted in the Mediterranean and northern shipping lanes. The variation thus far observed, however, differed in degree, but not in direction. The reversal in direction only occurred on the way across the Atlantic Ocean beyond the Azores, where the needle was said to point true north.[12] This phenomenon of deviation posed a number of questions: exactly where did the reversal take place, how large was the deviation at different points, how could it be allowed for in the making of the compass and of charts? And what were the reasons for it? In this order, practical men approached the problem.

Diego Gutierrez had two answers: he manufactured compasses by permanently "correcting" them, i.e., by setting the wires $\frac{1}{2}$ point to the east of north so that when the needle pointed to magnetic north the compass fly indicated approximately true north. This appeared to be common practice among the Portuguese pilots on the northern routes and is reported to be in use on the coasts of Galicia to this day.[13] Gutierrez also manufactured charts according to a scheme which would take account of the effects of compass variation in the North Atlantic. He adopted the "double-latitude scale." This was meant to reconcile the astronomically observed latitude of places with their position as plotted by compass bearing, that is, Gutierrez manufactured charts with latitudinal scales which were capable of adjustment for correction of magnetic variation. The method

---

[10] D. W. Waters, *The Art of Navigation in England in Elizabethan and Early Stuart Times* (New Haven, 1958); E. G. R. Taylor, *The Haven-Finding Art* (London, 1958); A special analysis of the cosmographic ideas of Pedro de Medina is found in Rafael Pardo de Figueroa, *Regimiento de Navegación . . . Crítica* (Cadiz, 1867); A general survey of Renaissance ideas on cosmography and mathematics is Marie Boas, *The Scientific Renaissance, 1450–1630* (London, 1962), and Thomas S. Kuhn, *The Copernican Revolution* (Harvard University Press, Cambridge, 1957). In Spanish consult: Salvador Garcia Franco, *Historia del Arte y Ciencia de Navegar* (Madrid, 1947), 2 vols., by topic; and for a short survey: José-M. Millás Vallicrosa, "Nautique et Cartographie de l'Espagne au XVIe siècle" in Colloque Internationale de Royaumont, 1–4 Juillet, 1957, *La Science au seizième siècle*, pp. 29–47.
[11] Garciá de Céspedes, *Arte de Marear* (Madrid, 1606) p. 73.
[12] Waters, *op. cit.*, p. 25, note I on authorities.
[13] Pedro de Medina, *Suma de Cosmographia*, ed. Rafael Estrada (Sevilla, 1946) Intro. p. 21: called *Agujas de Corujo*, and so called by some pilots in their answers to the lawyer's questions in Medina's suit. A. G. I. Justicia, 1146, Ramo 2, testimony of Diego Sanchez Colchero, the needle is set: "a la media quarta del norte quarta al nord-este." *Ibid.*, Cristobal Cereço de Padilla says such compasses were in use in "Flanders, Portugal, France, and Genoa." For an explanation see Waters, *loc. cit.*, for a recent discussion: José Mariá Martínez Hidalgo Terán, *Historia y Leyenda de la Aguja Magnetica* (Barcelona, 1946). Figure on p. 149. Garcia Franco, *op. cit.*, I, 53–54; Pulido Rubio, *Piloto-Mayor*, II, 482.

is described by H. Winters in the article on "The Pseudo Larador and the Oblique Meridian" in the following way:

> In this scheme, according as the deflection underlying the map was an easterly or westerly one, so the latitudinal scales were raised on the right or left as circumstances required. In Gutierrez' map the latitudinal parallels are not constructed by joining corresponding degrees although a few of the parallels, tropics, and the equator are indicated as fixed lines. They are not raised on the left or the right, but arranged in two sections within which they range parallel with each other in parallel lines but on a reverse plan, the left part being higher than the right.[14]

This practice is referred to throughout the legal papers as the two scales or *dos graduaciones*. It was a scheme which led to compounded error when paired with Gutierrez' compasses, which had been "corrected" for variation. For many sailors astronomical sailing was still astrological sailing with the virtue of the compass outdoing its exactness.[15] The production of such charts and instruments had a wide variety of consequences, which were really the matter *sub judice* in 1544–1546. The charts and instruments approved by the Pilot Major soon monopolized the market, which was supplied by Diego Gutierrez and controlled by Sebastian Cabot. To the scientifically minded this situation was a dangerous development which, if left to continue, would seriously injure the progress of nautical science. Furthermore, the denial of independent production and of scientific supervision by the cosmographers diminished their reputation for competence in the eyes of the pilots. From this fact resulted the loss of income and prestige for the cosmographer. Political interests, which were dependent upon the most accurate information for the correct definition of boundary lines, were also reflected in the suit. These facts represent a large reservoir of ill will and resentment among the cosmographers. The *Memorial* by Medina addressed to the Council of the Indies prompted Sebastian Cabot and Diego Gutierrez to file an ordinary suit of law against Medina and Alonso de Chaves.

The procedure in civil cases in the several courts of Spain varied considerably with the locality. It is possible, however, to present the sequence of legal steps in this suit which appears to fit a general pattern. A suit began with a complaint brought before the judges, in this case before the Casa de Contratación. They had first to decide whether to accept the case. They therefore invited a rebuttal by the accused, who had the right to plead for annulment of the charges. Upon denial of this annulment and acceptance of the case, arguments were heard from A against B, answers from B to A and rebuttal by A to B. B then pleaded for annulment on the basis of incompetence of the court to deal with the matter. The court overruled this plea and formal hearings of witnesses were then arranged by both sides to be held within a given period of time. Each party was asked to present a list of questions which their *procurador* was to ask of a list of witnesses before the judges.

---

[14] H. Winter in *Imago Mundi*, vol. II, 19, 55–61, this text. He also discusses the attempts of the Reinels, Falero, and Santa Cruz in coping with the problems of the chart and of magnetic variation.

[15] Guy Beaujean and Emanuel Poulle, "Les origines de la navigation astronomique aux XIVe and XVe siècles." *In Colloque Internationale de l'Histoire Maritime, Le Navire*, pp. 103–119, Paris, 1957; A. Texeira da Mota, "L'Art de Naviguer en Mediterranée du XIIIe au XVIIe siècle et la Création de la Navigation Astronomique dans les Oceans." *Ibid.*, pp. 127–140, p. 139. Also comments by P. Chaunu, p. 150 and A. M. Godinho, p. 151.

There was no cross-examination, but the parties were allowed to use the same witnesses. No deviation from the prepared questions was permitted, so that the effectiveness of the testimony depended in large part upon the nature of the questions put by the *procuradores*. Each witness was asked his name, age, occupation, and address, as well as his relation to the party for whom he testified. Upon completion of the hearings, the judges of the Casa handed down their decision which could be, and in this case was, an appeal before the Council of the Indies. The councillors in Valladolid, where the court resided at that time, had submitted to them the papers of the entire proceedings. They could hear the *procuradores* from the two sides and invite special testimony on their own initiative, which they did. Their decision was final.

The first deposition before the judges is dated August 19, 1544. In this text Medina appears an unwilling participant in a lawsuit which was unwelcome to him because he understood that scientists are trained to look for a single truth, whereas judges are presented with points of view by the opposing parties. He therefore reiterated his suggestion that the Pilot Major's office be subjected to an expert examination.[16] But once challenged before the judge, he filed a specific charge about mistakes in the charts and instruments of Diego Gutierrez, mistakes in the regiments of the Pilot Major, and the collusion between them to control the market. When the proceedings began, Medina had to be called from Cadiz where he had gone "for his health" so that by the time of his first statement the preliminary hearings were in full swing. The usual procedure was followed: depositions were taken from one party and the text referred to the opposition in order that reply be made within a specified term, from twenty-four hours to three days. Sometimes, however, longer periods were allowed between challenges and response of "one part to the other and the other to the other," as the secretary put it. In the exchange of depositions the grounds of the debate between the two parties was gradually defined. Challenged with regard to his privileges, Alonso de Chaves produced the only document, a *cédula*, or royal order to the officials of the Casa de Contratación, instructing them to insist that all charts should be made according to the Padrón.[17]

On August 21 appeared the first deponent not belonging to either party of the suit. This was Pedro Mexia, who up to then had been on the judges' panel as *teniente de contador de la Casa de Contratación*. Mexia had been a member of the junta of experts employed in the construction of the Padrón of 1536 with Chaves, and its revisions under the *licenciados* Caravajal and Gregorio Lopez. Mexia held an appointment as cosmographer. He was a writer of distinction, a chronicler, and a learned man. He was asked because of his special knowledge, and in spite of his sitting on the bench, to answer one specific question: whether Gutierrez' charts conformed to the Padrón. On August 28 in a one-page statement he said they did not, and added that the method of construction used by Gutierrez was erroneous.

---

[16] Pedro de Medina, *Obras*, ed. Gonzalez Palencia, Appendix to the Prologue.
[17] *Colección de D. Juan Bautista Muñoz*, Real Academia de la Historia, XC, p. 105v brings the earliest text of July 12, 1512, addressed to Juan de Solís and Juan Vispuche [sic]; Chaves produced the order of the Licenciado Caravajal of 1544, the text of which is not included in the legajo.

Immediately Diego Gutierrez lodged a protest saying that Mexia was prejudiced and should be removed from the panel. On the following day, Mexia swore to his impartiality with the same gesture of putting his hand on his heart as Gutierrez had used in denouncing him the day before, but declared himself challenged and withdrew from the bench. The case then proceeded with three judges. Mexia's name is missing from their list, but he was again heard from as witness for the opposing party. On August 26, Medina told the judges that Francisco Falero, the great Portuguese cosmographer, was in town. The Maestro was still trying to have his complaints considered by experts even before the Casa judges in Seville, but at this time nothing came of it. On September 23, the judges decided to accept the case for trial. The following day, Pedro de Medina appealed to them to annul the proceeding because the scientific substance of the dispute could not properly be subject to the decision of "any ordinary judge." He asked once more for a hearing before experts, called by the Council of the Indies not as a court but as an administrative body. The judges of the Casa found this decision outside their competence and denied Medina's request *(que no ha lugar por ser de sentencia interlocutoria)*, but he was allowed a transcript of the proceedings so far and advised of his right to appeal. On September 27, conforming to common practice, he filed his complaint in the form of a brief summary of his *Memorial*.

Cabot and Gutierrez had in the meantime petitioned for a *cuarto plazo de tres meses*, that is, a recess of three months in order to prepare their questionnaires for witnesses. Meantime the Maestro betook himself to court at Valladolid to see that his grievances did not remain bogged down in the legal tangle in Seville and that the Council of the Indies might be made properly aware of the deteriorating situation there. The judges of the Casa had granted Cabot and Gutierrez their request for a recess with the proviso that Medina be informed at his address at the *"Callejuela de la mar* where he is said to live," but was not to be found. On October 9, Gutierrez' request was repeated and granted with the proviso that an edict should be written and proclaimed by town crier. This was done. Medina was cried for at Las Gradas, the business center of Seville, and at the doors of his *posada*, and the edict was nailed up on the doors of the Audiencia on November 8, 1544, instructing him to answer either in person or by *procurador*.

At this point in the proceedings developments begin to take place at two different levels. The law case in Seville could not be stopped, but Medina's warnings concerning irregularities in the Pilot Major's office had fallen on receptive ears. No one cared about damaged egos, but everyone cared about the loss of ships and the malfunction of the vital navigation office. Considering that the Emperor was not in Spain, the response by the Council of the Indies to Medina's plea was rapid. On November 5, a royal *cédula* was addressed by the crown and the Council of the Indies to the president and the judges of the Casa in Seville. It appears to be directly built upon the complaints presented by Medina and Chaves, enumerated as so many indictments of neglect of duty on the part of the gentlemen addressed. They are instructed to obey and enforce the provisions applicable in the strictest form, both with regard to the Padrón as model for charts, and concerning the examination of pilots and instruments. In addition there is a request to speed up taking all depositions in the law case before the Casa to within thirty days of receipt of the order. These were then to be forwarded after an additional two weeks allowed for copy and verification.[18]

The recess in depositions, however, did not slow the rising of tempers. In December, Gutierrez went before the judges of the Casa to accuse Medina and Chaves of tampering with the evidence, that is, of falsifying his instruments and regiments. He gave the following details: that "a three and an eight are similar, and so are a nine and a six, and that anyone who wanted to injure him could change one number into the other." When he brought his instruments to the Casa, he said, they had at first been approved by Mexia and Falero. Medina's story was that he, Francisco Tello, and Alonso de Chaves had acquired three regiments by Gutierrez which, when compared, proved to differ from each other. Chaves then told the judges that the Padrón had been tampered with and that spots had appeared on it and similar spots on the Gutierrez charts.[19]

This accelerated the proceedings at two levels. The Council of the Indies had commanded, even while final hearings were under way in Seville, that the contestants in the suit, all cosmographers, and selected pilots be called together to deliberate concerning the state of the Padrón, and that they together, opponents in a bitter dispute as they were, should bring it up to date. Their depositions should then be forwarded without delay to the Council in Valladolid. The two famous documents that resulted, the depositions (pareceres) of Sebastian Cabot and of Francisco Falero, together with other statements, give precise information of the state of cartographic knowledge in 1545.[20] Differences of opinion among chartmakers were evident.

Meantime the testimony in answer to Cabot's and Gutierrez's questionnaire was given from the beginning of January to February 22, 1545, before the judges of the Casa in Seville. The papers were duly forwarded to the Council of the Indies, but a judicial decision was not handed down by the Seville judges, who wrote that they "could listen only to what one party said and what the other party said." In Valladolid, the Council of the Indies acted with speed on the administrative level. Two cédulas were forwarded to Seville, one dated February 22 instructing the judges to abide by the rule that all charts were to be copied from the Padrón, and the other of March 9, addressed to Diego Gutierrez, enjoining him from selling instruments without examination by the Pilot Major. Gutierrez and Cabot felt themselves injured and decided to lodge an appeal. On April 4 they appointed Sebastian Rodriguez to act as their procurador in Valladolid before the Council of the Indies. This phase of the hearings produced one exceptional new piece of testimony, the statement by Francisco Falero.[22] The other parties reworded their previous depositions, but did not alter their argument except by elaboration or emendation.

There is an additional piece of literature bearing upon this stage of the conflict:

[18] J. T. Medina, *Sebastian Caboto*, I, 376.
[19] This by-play—because it is completely without scientific substance—has not been discussed in the literature. A. G. I. Justicia, 1146, Ramo 2.
[20] J. T. Medina, *Sebastian Caboto*, I, 371–373 (Falero, *Pulido Rubio, Piloto Mayor*, I, 482–487; in context this belongs here, it is undated and probably belongs to the appeal, I, 482–487). Also Sancho Gutierrez, *Ibid.*, II, 526–528.
[21] Texts in reverse order in J. T. Medina, *Sebastian Caboto*, I, 376 and 377.
[22] Pulido Rubio, *El Piloto Mayor*, II, 482–487, as given above. It is doubtful that Falero was in Seville because the document appears to be addressed to the Council of the Indies and not to the Casa de Contratación. It is in his own hand and there is no countersignature by a secretary.

the *Coloquio sobre las dos graduaciones que las cartas de Indias tienen.* This manuscript, found in the Escorial Library, is by an anonymous author and was published by Fernandez Duro, who attributed it to Hernando Colón.[23] Other writers have ascribed it to Juan Valdés or other contemporaries. Pulido Rubio suggested that it might be the work of either Pedro de Medina or Hieronymo de Chaves, the son of Alonso. I believe that the case for Medina can be strengthened. The *Coloquio* is a dialogue between *Teodosio* and *Fulgencio.* It refers to a *pleito* or legal case over the double-latitude scale before the Council of the Indies, and it mentions two *cédulas* issued (presumably those of February 22 and March 9, 1545) which are "currently disobeyed." *Teodosio* states that the Padrón is more than ten years old, a statement which led Pulido Rubio to date the piece as late as 1548.[24] But the date for the "completion" of the Padrón, considering its many corrections, is somewhat arbitrary, and in this case appears to refer to the Chaves revision of 1536.[25] The arguments of *Teodosio* are almost exactly like Medina's in his texts before the courts. The choice of *Teodosio*, a Greek author of a work on the *sphere* (in the Portuguese sailor's tradition associated with Sacrobosco)[26] and *Fulgencio* (Fabius Fulgentius Planciades), a fifth-century African writer of bombastic prose about obscure and absurd mythology mixed with fact, has the taste of the scholar about it, and both Hieronymo de Chaves and Medina were scholars. Hieronymo's testimony lacks the circumstantial evidence about the stages of the legal quarrel, and this fact points to Medina and not to Hieronymo de Chaves as author of the tract. Moreover, Medina had written two previous dialogues; as for temperament, Hieronymo sounded very confident indeed in his plea before the Council, but used only principle and not specific evidence for this argument.[27] This may have led the crown to include him with his father among people *desapasionadas y peritas.* Whoever its author, there is no doubt that the *Coloquio* is a piece of special pleading for Medina and Chaves, written during the time when the appeal of the case between them and Cabot and Gutierrez was before the Council of the Indies. It enlivens the debate considerably and confirms the sequence of events.

The case proceeded through May of 1546, when the last provision concerning one of its points was made. No record of a final judgment has been encountered. A brief discussion of the case need not therefore take account of the timing, which is of interest only to show that the Casa de Contratación and the Council of the Indies were simultaneously aware of the quarrel among the new men, the cosmographers upon whom so much depended. While the parties fought in the court of the Casa, the Council expected them to collaborate as experts. There was no one else to arbitrate in these battles of experts,

---

[23] C. Fernandez Duro, *Disquisiciones Nauticas* (Madrid, 1877–1882), 6 vols., IV *Arca de Noé*, pp. 508–525.

[24] Hernando Colón died in 1539.

[25] Dates for the Padrón which are of interest here, 1529 (Colón); 1536 (Alonso de Chaves), 1540 *visita* of Caravajal, 1544 visita of Gregorio Lopez (1553 Chaves and Medina appointed to a junta on the Padrón at court).

[26] E. G. R. Taylor, ed., Roger Barlowe, *A Brief Summe of Geography*, Hakluyt Series II, LXIX (London, 1922), appendix II. There is a Spanish copy of Theodosius in a sixteenth century copybook in the Col. Muñoz, Academia Real de la Historia, A71, vol. 44, Num. p. 604.

[27] J. T. Medina, *Sebastian Caboto*, I, 373–374, on the Padrón. Other testimony in A. G. I. Justicia, 1146, Ramo 2.

[28] In later years Chaves himself did not re-examine either pilots or instruments thoroughly for each voyage but at that time, twenty years in the future, the Carrera de Indias was better established.

and it was to the credit of the administrators in Valladolid that they saw this, and did not judge, but only questioned.

A closer look at the content of the litigation takes one back to Seville, where Chaves and Cabot fought over the privileges and duties of the Pilot Major as against those of the Cosmographer Major. Sebastian Cabot was supposed to examine regularly the instruments and charts carried by all pilots, and publicly to examine the pilots for licensing, that is, before a panel of cosmographers and pilots. The Padrón was to be kept up to date with the help of the logs of the returning pilots. Chaves said that the Padrón stayed uncorrected because the pilots did not give proper data to the cosmographers: "they did not know how to collect them." He added that Sebastian Cabot knew nothing of regiments. As for the examinations of pilots, he states that they should be held on feast days and not on working days in order to enable pilots and cosmographers to attend, as provided in the instructions. The instruments should be checked for each voyage, and the examination should be in the Casa. As for instruments, the Pilot Major should review them all and not allow Diego Gutierrez to pass on them.

Among the arguments before the court, those concerning the Padrón have been presented most recently by Pulido Rubio. Of interest here are some additional data concerning the making of it, and how allegedly Cabot and Gutierrez disagreed with the others, Pedro Mexia, Alonso de Santa Cruz, Francisco Falero, and Alonso de Chaves. The Padrón was made in the house of the *Mariscal* Diego Cavallero, and Pedro Mexia remembered that Cabot had objected only to the eastern areas of the maps which were drawn in by *derrotas* and not by *alturas*. Falero said he remembered lots of disagreement as they went along, but none at the end. What really mattered were of course the continuing corrections which were to take place. Among the noted pilots who testified were Diego Sanchez Colchero *(el viejo)*, Gerónimo Rodriguez, Franciso del Barrio, who said he had sailed with Gutierrez' charts on the de Soto expedition, and Tomé de la Ysla. These pilots all agreed on the uselessness of the Padrón, saying they were well aware of it because "they are pilots and they understand something of the art of going to sea."[29]

The irregularities of Cabot's conduct in handling the Padrón and in keeping data from the cosmographers were proved, and they were not new. When Alonso de Santa Cruz was working on his royal commission to make the *Islario General* in 1536, he complained bitterly about the fact that the pilots did not bring him data.[30] The reason may well have been the incompetence of several pilots to gather them. The *Coloquio* tells of three returning pilots asked to give their data who "made their points on the chart, one showing 100 leagues, the other giving 45, and the other appearing to have sailed over land."[31]

As for examinations, Cabot stated that the *portero* did not find the pilots and cartographers at home. He had no powers to enforce attendance. As for the locale where the examinations were supposed to be held, the Casa de Contratación, Cabot said that

---

[29] "Y se le entiende alguna cosa del arte de marear." But Falero said that his brother Ruiz made the charts for De Soto and "con una sola graduación", A. G. I. Justicia, 1146, Ramo 2.

[30] *Alonso de Santa Cruz, Crónica del Emperador Carlos V*, ed. J. de Mata Carriazo (Seville, 1951), suspects that the crown deliberately commissioned Santa Cruz to do the *Islario*, at a time that Sebastian Cabot needed watching.

[31] Fernandez Duro, *op. cit.*, p. 513.

at the time of Juan Vespucci and de Solis the Pilot Major had been entitled to hold them in his house. He claimed this right too. He "proved" his scientific knowledge by saying that when he had sailed to the La Plata and back, he had lost his instruments on the voyage and had made new ones. All of his witnesses testified to the fact that he was indeed a splendid sailor.

Gutierrez was much more vulnerable to attack than Cabot, and he had mainly to contend with Medina. This was best done by attacking such work of Medina's as would not get Gutierrez himself into trouble. Instead of the Padrón, on which indeed Medina had not worked, he chose a chart which was no longer available except in the memory of some who said they had seen it. Even so, he could not keep Medina from a countermove concerning the principles of chart-making which led to an indictment of Gutierrez' instruments as well. The belated attack on Medina's *Arte de Navegar*, and provisions concerning it from the Council of the Indies, close his testimony.

The only circumstantial evidence concerning Medina's chart was given by Hieronymo de Chaves, the twenty-one-year-old son of Alfonso. Hieronymo was a trained cosmographer headed for a bright career. He remembered Medina's chart, which had been censured as "not made in accordance with the Padrón." This he reported had been said in his father's house, and he recalled telling it to D. Bernardino de Mendoza, to whom the chart had been offered. There was some hearsay testimony about the chart, but no one recalled actually having seen it except for the *alguacil* of the Casa who testified that he remembered that it had been put into a certain box *de hoja de manila*. On such testimony no case against Medina could be built; Gutierrez, however, left himself open to arguments regarding the principles of chart-making.

Here at least the litigants had an honest difference of opinion. The partisans of the multilatitude scale—for they testified to two or more latitudes—describe the makers of the Padrón as inexperienced theoreticians: "They have not sailed." Their own practical knowledge paid, it was argued, because the pilots could understand their charts and make trips safely. The position taken by Medina and Chaves was that no one could understand the two-latitude scheme, and that Gutierrez exploited the pilots' fear in the basest fashion by persuading them that only his charts were safe. Medina said that the losses of ships were not due to the charts made according to the Padrón. Indeed, he had participated in the raising of a ship which went down just before the bar at San Lucar in 1542. Both sides could produce enough lost ships without convincing each other, or anyone else, of the reason for the losses. The pilots differed about causes also, but they characterized Gutierrez' charts as uniformly certain and true.

To this testimony Diego Gutierrez added that the Padrón was simply no good, merely a theoretical product without relation to the facts brought to him by the pilots after their voyages. He said that he and Sebastian Cabot had signed the Padrón of the *licenciado* Caravajal, which carried 150 signatures, only after the latter had suggested that in any jury, to get unanimity, some one had to compromise and to submerge differences. He implied he had been compelled to sign, though this was promptly denied by the other members of that junta. All the pilots, however, supported Gutierrez in his claim that the Padrón was useless. Franciso del Barrio said it was the work of the devil, others admitted that even after they had been compelled to submit charts according to the Padrón for license, they would throw them overboard and sail with an old one if they could get hold of it. Gutierrez' claim that the charts after the edict of 1540 did not sell seems to have been justified. He said that this was the reason that he and the Pilot Major returned to the old pattern of the double-latitude charts.

Medina tried to show the faults of Gutierrez' scheme by a long dissertation about the nature of the sphere, which has only one set of longitude and latitude lines.[32] Hieronymo de Chaves added that Gutierrez' charts gave the latitudes of some places correctly on both sides of the Atlantic, but that for the middle there was no chart at all, with multiple equators, tropics, and even poles (therefore Pole-Stars).[33] He added that if he were only allowed to demonstrate it, the truth would be obvious.[34] In sum, Medina's party stated that Gutierrez' charts were irrational in plan, incorrect in detail, and dangerous in use. With this judgment Pedro de Mexia and Francisco Falero agreed.

Then came the chance for Medina to complain about the instruments made by the Gutierrez family. This raised the temperature of the proceedings because of the harshness of the indictment and the number of people involved. Medina said that Gutierrez' instruments were inaccurate because Gutierrez did not know anything about them; that he did not understand a regiment and could not engrave an astrolabe or mark a cross-staff. As for compasses, he said that Gutierrez' attention to them was that of a physician who, upon encountering a man with one dislocated arm, proceeded to restore him by dislocating the other. This rather startling argument was very clever, considering that the "sky man" (an imagined figure with arms stretched at full length in the stellar sky) was a popular device for telling time among sailors. More learnedly, Chaves added that from very small mistakes on an instrument, very large mistakes resulted in practice. Medina said that Gutierrez was illiterate and dishonest about it, that he knew neither Latin nor even Romance (Spanish), that he bought patterns from others and copied them; that he abused the privileges of the Pilot Major by trafficking in licenses and was furthermore in collusion with the Pilot Major to defraud the pilots. Alonso de Chaves supported these charges, adding that the Pilot Major was aware of the situation; that the Gutierrez father and his three sons, Diego, Sancho, and Luis, worked on instruments independently, though only Sancho was licensed among the sons; and that Luis did not even work under his father's roof but had his own shop and his own son and a niece working for him. When instruments finally reached the Pilot Major for licenses from the Gutierrez, in Medina's pithy phrase, *si errados vienen errados se van*, if they come faulty, so they go.

Cabot and Gutierrez answered in characteristic fashion. The Pilot Major said that he had to approve and examine only the state of the instruments and not their origin. Also, he was not required to make regiments, but to examine them. Gutierrez said that all instruments leaving his house were approved and checked by him personally and that

---

[32] This is based upon Medina's manuscript cosmographies of 1538 and 1543. See U. Lamb, "The Cosmographies of Pedro de Medina" in *Homenaje a Rodriguez Moñino, Estudios de Erudición que le ofrecen sus amigos ó discipulos Hispanistas Norteamericanos* (Madrid, 1966) 2 vols., I, 297–303.
[33] Garcia Franco, *op. cit.*, I, 53. Waters, *op. cit.*, pp. 67ff.
[34] Marie Boas, *op. cit.*, p. 30, on mathematics by public demonstration; challenge and defense as a common method of proceeding in the sixteenth century.

he was no ironmonger, carpenter, or painter, but that he gave out the patterns and checked the results, which it was his duty to do as cosmographer making instruments. Thus far then, everyone stood by his charges.

The only remarkable addition to previous testimony was Francisco Falero's. He in tact brings to the case disinterested expertise which throws into relief the absurdity of frying scientific truth by ordinary law. He discussed the state of nautical science and showed the way in which it had to move. As to the first, his judgement was devastating: he simply asserted that most data on the Padrón were unreliable because every man had had his own means and methods. He suggested the Padrón be treated like a house which, though finished, must be torn down because the foundations were wrong: *porque falsamente fundado*. The projection of a global sphere upon a plane chart falsifies the relations between latitude and longitude, he pointed out; and with the best of equipment and good will, he declared, many of the problems involved were as yet beyond immediate solution. He suggested that a government-sponsored research ship, manned by the most competent men and equipped with the best instruments, be sent out on an exploring expedition over the ocean routes to compile the necessary data for reliable charts. He referred to instruments made by himself for taking latitude more correctly and he suggested magnetic variation as a possible solution to the problem of longitude. Here was a scientist and sailor speaking from experience and without reservation, simply because he was a disinterested witness. Falero's testimony bore out Medina's contention that truth in science was not a proper subject for judicial decision.

The last subject to be taken up in the suit was Medina's book the *Arte de Navegar*. This resulted in a rather meaningless sequence of orders and counterorders from the Council of the Indies which did not encumber the road to fame for this great book. After a simultaneous prohibition of its circulation and an order to have the book investigated by the cosmographers of the Casa, given on the same day, November 27, 1545, a license was granted to Medina to have the book printed on December 16, 1545; it was immediately seen through the press in Valladolid. Opinions contrary to it were meantime forwarded from Seville to Valladolid by the Gutierrez faction. A new junta was appointed, in April 1546, to look over the book—a book which was selling well and had been three months in print, and which moreover had been corrected by the same people and its parts initialled in 1543. The brief spell of prohibition in 1546 while the junta met did not, then, stop the work on its way to international acclaim.

A decision of the legal case has not been found in any records. Laws were repeated and practices resumed in violation of them, except for the multilatitude chart. Its manufacture was definitely halted, though not as soon as ordered, because the *cédula* of February 22, 1545, had instructed the officials of the Casa not to force pilots to change charts immediately, but to wait until they could be trained to use the ones according to the Padrón. With the defection of Cabot from Spanish employment, the Gutierrez family lost a powerful friend. Diego died in 1554, and was succeeded by his son Diego, who also obtained a license. In 1553, Medina was called to court as a member of a cosmographic junta to give expert opinion. When the crown gave up hoping for the return of Sebastian Cabot from England, Alonso de Chaves was made Pilot Major. In 1552

Hieronymo de Chaves was installed as the first incumbent of a chair of cosmography in the Casa de Contratación. This marked a new maturity of the subject, but it also ended both the intimacy of collaboration and the collision of theoreticians and practical men which had begun with the appointment of Alonso de Chaves in 1528.

It appears from the record that the prolonged litigation had neither an overwhelming immediate impact—except for stopping the charts with the double latitude scale—nor a measurable long-range effect upon the Pilot Major's office. But regardless of the limited consequences of judicial decision in the case, the legal debate brought out ideas people held about the nature of truth in science and about the rights and duties of scientists. These arguments had a powerful influence upon the development of scientific disciplines and the social role of a new group of lay experts which was carving out a special place for itself.

The participants in the dispute tell us much about the social orientation of the scientist litigants. The party of cosmographers, Chaves, Medina, and Mexia, appeal to traditional powers. They deal with the crown, Council and judges in familiar terms: God and his laws, society and its ways, and science and its discipline all support them in their fight. Aside from technical conflict over the interpretation of the scientific problem, Alonso de Chaves and Pedro de Medina produce the following arguments: that Gutierrez' manufacture and Cabot's negligence and complicity violate royal orders and injure royal power, that they damage the prestige of the Padrón; that greed, stupidity, ignorance, the faulty construction of instruments, misunderstanding of principles of chart construction, and the disorderly tampering by unskilled pilots with evidence challenge the very laws of astronomy, both scientific and divine, and push the North Star off its heavenly position.[35]

The Pilot Major, Sebastian Cabot the Venetian, and Diego Gutierrez were men of wide experience but "unlectured in schooles" or "unlettered in bookes" of the new international artisan-artist-expert group who appealed not to tradition, so often wrong or inapplicable, but who built their case on the expediency in a given situation and upon the baser instincts of human nature. In general terms they asserted their rights regardless of the consequences for sailors. Concerning the opposition in court, they argued that the wild speculations of mere theorists, lack of practice and experience at sea, unwarranted assumptions both about the nature and the capabilities of men, snobbishness, and the

---

[35] Chaves and Mexía were in fact asked for their opinion by the crown and open their statements thus: "Digo que vuestras mercedes me mandaron que diese mi parcer." Pulido Rubio, *El Piloto Mayor*, II, 498 and 504 respectively. Some other quotes from the testimony of Alonso de Chaves: "Y demas de esto el dho Diego Gutierrez y el dho piloto mayor no han cumplido el mandamiento de v. mag. antes lo an quebrado"; "puesto caso que el padrón estoviera errado devieran él (Gutierrez) y el piloto mayor dar delo razón a vra mag."; "inventando cosa tan mala e falsa; ensenandoles (los pilotos) falsa doctrina." *Ibid.*, p. 489; "por tanto v. mag. mui umilmente suplico que en todo . . . provea q conviene al servicio de dios e de vra. mag. . . . e bien utilidad de la navegacion pues es cosa q tanto importa a todos los que navegan, . . . que destruyen y falsean la astrologia, geometria y cosmografia." *Ibid.*, p. 406; for Hieronymo de Chaves: J. T. Medina, *Sebastian Caboto*, I, 373–374: "e visto no solo falsedades y confusiones pero hasta muchos quimeras y falsas ficciones; los pilotos no saben leer; no solamente carecen de arte pero aun de principios della; por estas cartas se concluye haber infinitos (polos) son sacadas de la postura do dios las crio." Mexía says, Pulido Rubio, *op. cit.* II, 506, that the instruments are made by: "hombres que carecen de los fundamentos que se requieren por la fabrica;" and "presumo y usando de falsos instrumentos como este seguira gran daño." And concerning the two scale chart he suggests "que las rompe." A. G. I. Justicia, 1146, Ramo 2.

stubborn refusal to distinguish a workable compromise from a theoretical argument, contributed to the loss of ships, goods, and men.[36] All of these arguments were the terms chosen for an appeal by one party to privilege limited by duty, and by the other to power motivated by greed.

A review of the scientific debate shows a lack of an autonomous terminology of science and a confusion of reference. In this lawsuit scientific truths are subjected to the requirements of politics, economics, dogma, and law, among other disciplines. The *licenciado* Caravajal, *visitador* of the junta of cosmographers in 1540, believed truth in science was reached by consensus. If all cosmographers were to sign the Padrón, that seemed to one faction to make it right. Diego Gutierrez changed his charts to suit the pilots because it was profitable, and therefore defended measuring the value of science by the extent of preference expressed in the market place. Sebastian Cabot said that in his activity he obeyed the law and suggested that science was limited by legality. Pedro Mexia said that Gutierrez' charts did damage to the crown's claims, implying that in this case scientific truth was not politic.[37] The two Chaves and Medina said that interference with the God-given and reasonable design of the universe and the arbitrary doctoring of instruments was, among other things, immoral and unorthodox. In Falero's text alone appear the elements and sequence of tests of scientific truths: observation, description, experiment, deduction, and prediction. Some of these criteria appear occasionally throughout, but their interdependence and independence from the qualifying terms above was far from granted. In 1545 it was necessary not only to get things right, get them to work, in the modern sense; it was also necessary to create a conception of truth in science by scientific method for scientific ends.

The main contribution to science thus came from the Portuguese cartographer, Francisco Falero, and it was the use of a consistent scientific terminology toward which he, Alonso de Chaves, and Pedro de Medina had pointed in their works, but which among the multiple attacks upon them they could not preserve.[38] The achievement of the Maestro Medina and his party was to win support for the idea that science is a search for truth and not for justice, and that a court of law is not the proper agency for the control of science. The minor controversy over the *Arte de Navegar* brought out Medina's firm belief in progress by cooperation amongst scientists.[39] The conflict over the Padrón raised the issue of monopoly control by the Pilot Major and the damage this could do to the

---

[36] Expediency: In the absence of Cabot and of Gutierrez the licensing was left to Juan Gutierrez, a secretary of the Casa, himself unlicensed. Question VI of the *Pedimiento y Parecéres de Pilotos*, A. G. I. Justicia, 1146, Ramo 2, deals with lost ships. Most sailors confirm that Cabot has the legal right to license any instrument he sees fit. Many say that the makers of the Padrón are not sailors but only astrologers who know nothing of the sea. The crown was aware that there was a difference between licensing the charts for sailors and having them used.

[37] Mexía in his testimony states the danger to Spanish rights; also Sanchez Colchero: "... si con las dichas dos graduaciones se retruera el dho Diego Gutierrez en el, este diera tierras de las de la demarcación de Castilla a Portugal." A. G. I. Justicia, 1411, Ramo 2, Parecer de Colchero, on question XIII.

[38] That the problem of personality in scientific dispute persists with undiminished vigor can be seen for instance in a passage from Rudolph Virchow, *Selected Essays, Disease, Life and Man* (Stanford, 1958), p. 77. "If only people would finally stop finding disagreement in the personal characteristics and external circumstances of investigators."

[39] Ursula Lamb, *A Cosmographers Universe, Pedro de Medina's Libro de Cosmographia, 1538*. (Forthcoming, University of Chicago Press), chapter II.

progress of knowledge. By implication the trial raised the issue of access to knowledge by anyone qualified—that is, by foreigners—and it cast sidelights upon the question of the duty of scientists in the political arena, relevant when boundaries in the Pacific came to be drawn. The texts of the lawsuit are therefore capable of sustaining a much broader inquiry into intellectual and social history than the concentration on the scientific content permits.

IV

La nueva ciencia
geográfica

*(Una víctima del sistema de concursos. Premios españoles
para la solución de los problemas de la longitud)*

Nos importa saber dónde estamos, sobre el globo terráqueo, si
queremos ir y regresar de un lugar a otro. A medida que
recorremos mayores espacios sobre el planeta, nos interesa más
y más saber dónde está cada lugar y a qué distancia de todos los
otros. A esos datos, inequívocos, los denominamos latitud y
longitud geográficas desde que medimos la distancia con una
unidad básica a partir de cualquier punto, y esas denominaciones
no plantean hoy problemas a nuestra tecnología ni provocan
discrepancias conceptuales pero, esta concordancia respecto
a los puntos del globo, la han logrado gradualmente la investigación y la exploración geográfica. En este artículo presento
algunos aspectos de la exploración emprendida para determinar
la longitud.

Hoy se acepta generalmente que la ciencia tiene la clave
del conocimiento de la naturaleza. Una descripción científica
es válida con referencia a circunstancias sometidas a reiteradas
pruebas y, con ellas, se apoyan teorías que autorizan un cierto
grado de predicción. El hombre de ciencia nos dice que, dentro
de una serie de circunstancias, un fenómeno previsto se pro-
ducirá. Cuando semejante predicción es avalada por otros
científicos, queda reconocida la certidumbre de tal proposición.

El hecho de que cualquier profano pueda escribir un párrafo
como el que antecede, certifica la universalidad del consenso

otorgado a una auténtica proposición científica y el modo de alcanzarla. No se entendía esto así, ni podía estar reconocido cuando los hombres, a todo riesgo, comenzaron a sacar partido, con sus presentimientos, de los acontecimientos naturales sobre los cuales está fundada la civilización.

En la España del siglo XVII, hablando en términos generales, las ideas que entrañaban predicción quedaban sometidas a la Iglesia y la explicación de los fenómenos observados se buscaba originariamente en la tradición ancestral o clásica; la experiencia venía sugerida, cuando no por el sentido común, sin él, con frecuentes recursos a la magia, blanca o negra. Luego casi de repente, en el transcurso de una generación, los descubrimientos geográficos de tierras y mares ignorados, nos proporcionaron nueva información acerca de la naturaleza del mundo, a medida que llegaba a Europa cada barco a su regreso de un viaje por el océano. Estos hechos, de necesidad indispensable para la recusación de las suposiciones, entonces en boga, concernientes a la naturaleza se fueron acumulando a paso acelerado en Lisboa y en Sevilla. En esas ciudades, las escuelas de Pilotos Mayores y Cosmógrafos fueron el depósito oficial de todas las noticias científicas geográficas, hidrográficas y astronómicas recibidas con cada cuaderno de bitácora, cuyos datos acumulados y analizados servían para formular teorías y para concebir y proseguir experimentos. Se diseñaban y probaban nuevos instrumentos, y fue establecido el cargo de Cosmógrafo Real, que tuvo encomendadas todas las disciplinas del arte de navegar: matemáticas, astronomía, cartografía e historia natural del mar, y en especial, el trazado de líneas costeras y rutas marítimas.

Dado que la historia de la ciencia prefiere tratar de las ideas certeramente encaminadas a resolver un problema que admite solución, se ha desentendido casi en absoluto del tema de la longitud geográfica tal y como se abordaba en el tiempo y lugar de nuestro estudio: la España de los Habsburgos hasta Felipe IV. Los problemas referentes a la longitud eran prácticamente irresolubles con los instrumentos de aquella época, y no podría registrarse ningún experimento científico que constituyese el eslabón indispensable para descubrir «la longitud». Historiadores de los fenómenos sociales se han limitado a considerar el tema en lo que tiene de curioso, o eventualmente lo relacionaron con la vida de algún hombre, o les sirvió para aportar hechos económica o políticamente significativos. Estas aproximaciones dejan inédita una parte importante de nuestra historia,

164

a saber: de qué manera la ciencia infructuosa precedió con sus pasos a la disciplina científica tal y como lo caracteriza someramente el párrafo inicial.

El trabajo de los cosmógrafos comenzaba en la interpretación de datos escuetos y avanzó, en primer lugar, por la vía de la confrontación de opiniones contrapuestas, teniéndolas presentes, así como a los diversos modos de resolver esas divergencias. La gradual definición de la naturaleza y los adelantos de la ciencia natural se fueron alcanzando, sin embargo, por medio de organismos estatuidos para esclarecer otras aspiraciones intelectuales o materiales cuestionables; tales como los tribunales de justicia, donde lo justo se separaba de lo injusto, la plaza del mercado, de donde lo barato desalojaba a lo caro, y la corte real, en donde se premiaba a la mejor solución dada a un problema planteado entre competidores.

o   o   o

Los archivos de la Casa de Contratación de Sevilla y del Consejo de Indias nos transmiten casos de este género. Controversias entre científicos sobre la construcción de brújulas y trazado de cartas de marear fueron llevadas ante el tribunal de la Casa de Contratación y ellas atestiguan que la «Ciencia por litigio» [1] no define la verdad por vía científica. Las pruebas de viabilidad de instrumentos, rutas, etc., que no podían repetirse exactamente, aún no bien definidos y estimados tan solo por su «costo-eficiencia», separan una de otra la teoría y la práctica [2]. La ciencia por competición se ocupa del problema de determinar y medir la longitud geográfica y en este artículo se pretende sacar a la luz la trascendencia de aquellos litigios con respecto al progreso de la ciencia misma.

El problema de la longitud hízose crítico cuando la necesidad de fijar puntos de referencia y trazar meridianos sobre la superficie del globo terráqueo vino a ser acuciante con la circunnavegación del mundo, las demandas de nuevos territorios y la necesidad de garantizar un tráfico transoceánico en gran escala. A mediados del siglo XVI, la determinación de la latitud era ya una cuestión de pericia que dependía de la habilidad del observador, de la precisión de sus instrumentos y la solvencia de sus tablas, pero el problema de la longitud no era tan manejable porque el cambio de posición en el globo terráqueo hacia el Este o el Oeste, o a través de un meridiano, no alteraba la aparente altitud de los astros. El orto y el ocaso aparentes tendrían lugar, más temprano si caminamos hacia el Este y, a la inversa, más tarde hacia el Oeste, con lo cual la longitud únicamente puede establecerse mediante referencias a la hora local. El desplazamiento, cruzando los meridianos, iguala, por lo tanto, el tiempo transcurrido de veinticuatro horas con la rotación de la tierra en un día, o sea, el ciclo completo de veinticuatro horas con la circunferencia de 360 grados. Así lo entendieron varios investigadores de la cuestión de la longitud, y dedicaron sus esfuerzos a conseguir mejores medios para averiguar y mantener la hora correcta. Los problemas de la longitud serían de observación y registro, de comprobación por repetición, y de proyección del dato sobre un planisferio, y fueron reconocidos y definidos con diversidad mucho antes de anunciarse las recompensas; el camino hacia la solución utilizable de alguno de ellos fue indicado no más tarde del año 1513, y luego con la clara sugerencia de una cronometración anunciada en 1530, y con la aproximación loxodrómica a los problemas de la proyección utilizada por Mercator en 1569. La primera junta que atacaría el problema de determinar la longitud en el mar, sirviéndose de la clasificación de los once métodos de Santa Cruz, fue celebrada en 1555.

Se desprende de lo que antecede, que las fechas de asentamiento de la auténtica solución de los problemas relativos a la longitud nada tienen que ver con los concurrentes al premio. Y nos importa más recordar que las aportaciones de aspirantes a la recompensa del rey no fueron las únicas tomadas en consideración. Si los límites en cuanto al tiempo no pueden ser rígidos, también son fluctuantes las fronteras del tema de la competición. Resultados de experimentos y sugerencias marginales llegaron al certamen, y no dejó de atenderse con interés a cuestiones nada afines con el tema del premio. Muchos asuntos irrelevantes se entremezclaron con los papeles pertenecientes a la columna vertebral de mi documentación, reunidos en un legajo del Archivo General de Indias (Patronato, 262), titulado «La aguja fixa». Esta expresión atestigua que la idea de un polo magnético pudo ser fundamental en muchas de las proposiciones concurrentes. El repertorio utilizado por Gould y Thrower nos basta para establecer el total de las sugerencias[3].

A. *Métodos terrestres*
1. Variación de la brújula.
2. Señales sonoras. No utilizado en la competición española.

B. *Métodos celestes*
1. Eclipses de los satélites de Júpiter.
2. Ocultamientos de las estrellas por la Luna.
3. Eclipses y fenómenos similares.
4. Paso de la Luna por el meridiano.
5. Distancias lunares.
6. Cronómetros. No incluidos en la competición de que tratamos.

El patrocinio de la Ciencia por la Corona fue generoso en tiempos de Carlos V, cuando los cosmógrafos eran gratamente acogidos en la corte, y los matemáticos y artífices de instrumentos obtuvieron empleos y recompensas. Felipe II y sus cortesanos vivieron en un ambiente amistoso para con los científicos, con su contribución a numerosos proyectos que cuajaron en el departamento de Pilotos Mayores de Sevilla y en los consejos de estado (cuestiones de fronteras), y guerra (artillería y fortificaciones). Cuando estaba Felipe en Flandes, en 1548, alguien de su séquito, un noble llamado Juan Rojas de Sarmiento [4], llegó a ser discípulo de Gemma Frisius, y habiéndole interesado la obra de Mercator, publicó un libro [5] sobre astrolabios y el planisferio, en cuya parte cuarta (*Liber IV De Dimensionibus*) toca los problemas de la longitud. Se conserva correspondencia sostenida entre Felipe II y el duque de Alba el año 1577, en la cual el Duque solicitaba el patrocinio real y fondos para establecer una cátedra de matemáticas en la Universidad de Lovaina que incluiría las disciplinas de geografía, cartografía, y que alentaría la construcción de instrumentos [6]. Cuando Felipe II, tras la anexión de Portugal, visitó Lisboa, pidió noticias del nivel en que estaban allí las ciencias naturales, incluyendo las matemáticas, la cartografía, la fortificación y la artillería, y adoptó la propuesta de Juan de Herrera, su arquitecto y asesor en tecnología, para fundar una real academia de ciencias en Madrid. Convenció a Juan Bautista Labanha, el famoso hombre de ciencia portugués, para que aceptase la primera cátedra, en la capital de España, con una retribución anual de 400 ducados más «casa y botica»; y Labanha, según parece, iniciaría sus tareas docentes en enero de 1584. El resultado de tal actividad fue la creación de una especie de cámara de compensación, próxima a la corte, para la información científica, y como apertura de conductos por los cuales llegaran las ideas a conocimiento de hombres que podrían encontrar quien les escuchara, y así se diera base, uso y rendimiento a sus proposiciones. Pero así como, ante nuestra retina, el rendimiento de la comunidad científica española crece como una tela de araña, concuerdan autoridades tales como Rey Pastor y Picatoste en situar la cumbre de la labor creadora de España un cuarto de siglo antes (año 1560). El auténtico triunfo de la empresa marítima de España unido al del imperio de Portugal produce la ilusión de una misión cumplida. La labor científica que había desempeñado un papel vital en aquel feliz desarrollo, fue estimada únicamente por su utilidad. Pero en cuanto los científicos, liberados de las viejas restricciones de pensamiento y armados con hechos nuevos, comenzaron a ser una amenaza para las ideas tradicionales, empezó a causar temor un trabajo que desde entonces quedaría vigilado y restringido a las tareas «útiles». Con todo, bajo Felipe II, la visible actividad científica teórica alentada en la corte, confirma el refrán según el cual «En la vida privada de los reyes, no son los gustos gustos, sino leyes». Bajo sus sucesores Felipe III y Felipe IV, la Academia fue deteriorándose y, finalmente, desaparecería (1624). El ofrecimiento de generosas recompensas a la solución acertada del problema de la longitud es un signo de decadencia, más bien que de progreso, en cuanto reto lanzado a los problemas insolubles con los medios y conocimientos entonces disponibles. Esto lo entendieron bien los competentes hombres de ciencia partícipes en el certamen; pero no así los patrocinadores.

Junto a la limitación de la curiosidad intelectual que significa el ofrecimiento del premio, contemplaba la Corona la solución que menos comprometiera su superioridad en la navegación oceánica. Después de todo, medir una longitud no era otra cosa que fijar la situación de un punto en la superficie del globo. Así como las rutas de navegación podrían aún mantenerse «en secreto», habría de aprovechar a todos los estados la localización de puntos concernientes a acuerdos internacionales, tales como ciertas costas e islas o el trazado de «líneas de amistad» (1559) en el Atlántico, y, si es verdad que un método para determinar la longitud podría facilitar el descubrimiento de rutas, tales como el paso septentrional de Este o de Oeste y por eso los consejeros de estado se inclinaron más bien a «guardar el secreto», por otra parte, era científicamente más factible hallar la longitud cerca del ecuador, donde la extensión de un grado podría acordarse ateniéndose a un patrón internacional. El conflicto, real o imaginado, entre el reto políticamente deseable y las tentativas por atraer talentos internacionales que trabajaran en la solución del problema, era, por lo tanto, un factor en el desarrollo de la investigación. Algunos partícipes en el certamen, con la intención de prestigiar sus proyectos, se atuvieron a la tendencia heredada que prefería las ventajas del conocimiento secreto —tendencia derivada probablemente de la intervención sacerdotal en los misterios del culto—.

Bajo los dos primeros Habsburgos prefirieron los científicos alcanzar la atención y el patrocinio de sus trabajos, ganando la simpatía de algún amigo o pariente que les prestase oído y, a ser posible, les facilitase la obtención de empleos o recompensas. Tal fue, en efecto, el caso de Colón, y, en empresas semejantes cual la bomba de barco metálica, de Diego Ribeiro, o la del barco de ruedas de paletas, experimentado en aguas de Málaga por Blasco de Garay, bajo el patrocinio de la Corona. El ofrecimiento de premios a la solución de un problema específico no carecía de precedentes. Casos de este tipo tenemos en las curas medicinales y en la arquitectura. Pero el certamen abierto por Felipe II, en 1598, para el problema de la longitud fue el precursor de los que con idéntico objeto convocaron los gobiernos de Venecia, Holanda, Francia e Inglaterra. La índole de la tarea, la talla del patrono, la cuantía del premio y el curso de la competición, hacen de este concurso español el primero de una serie y no el último de una vieja tradición.

Es probable que la idea de un concurso de premios naciera en la Academia de Madrid, aunque yo no he encontrado ningún anuncio original. El documento más antiguo que he podido consultar está fechado en 1603, e invoca el pago de unas cantidades prometidas en 1598. Toda la literatura secundaria coincide en señalar la fecha de 1598, sin mencionar base documental [7].

El grueso de la documentación española, por inferencia, parece confirmar el anuncio efectivo de recompensas para la solución del problema de la longitud. De todos modos, la más temprana promesa de pago, antes citada, aparece en un concurso que adjudica premio de compensación a un científico, en pugna con otro, una vez comprobada la veracidad de sus afirmaciones. Las órdenes de pago están extendidas el 2 de septiembre de 1603 a favor del doctor Arias de Loyola, antiguo cronista mayor de la Corona y de un contrincante suyo, Luis de Fonseca, y ascienden a «6.000 ducados de renta perpetua y 2.000 de por vida» [8]. Ello representa una cuantiosa recompensa regia del trabajo, en aquel tiempo, aunque no alcanza, ni con mucho, la generosidad de las mercedes dispensadas a los amigos corte-

sanos; por ejemplo, a validos tales como el duque de Lerma,
que recibió, una tarde, 5o.ooo ducados cuando el Rey tuvo
noticia de que la flota de Indias había llegado sin daño. El
premio antedicho puede compararse, favorablemente, con las
retribuciones asignadas a los trabajos de Labanha y Herrera,
y con los sueldos de los funcionarios en Sevilla y Madrid, de
quienes se esperaba que ganasen estas sumas en el desempeño
corriente de sus tareas [9]. Tan importantes como el premio en
dinero eran los privilegios anejos al real patrocinio: la ventaja
de vivir en la corte, y la posibilidad de asegurar el porvenir
de la familia [10]. Por otra parte, abundan las quejas concernientes
al costo de la vida cerca de la corte y a los viajes de ida y
vuelta a Madrid.

Las sumas abonadas en realidad las registra, en parte,
Fernández Duro [11] y, al parecer tienen poca relación con el
resultado, o los méritos, del trabajo propuesto. Donaciones,
asignaciones, subsidios y promesas de donativos en los mismos
términos que los de Fonseca y Arias, se acumulan entre los
años 1612 a 1626 en la colección de documentos de Fernández
de Navarrete, publicada por su hijo Eustaquio. En estos documentos leemos que, de hecho, Luis de Fonseca recibía dinero,
en pago de un trabajo incompleto o mal ejecutado y basado en
pretensiones insustanciales, con mayor frecuencia que su contrincante el doctor Arias, quien, a su vez, reclamaba la suma
máxima, de las que aparecen registradas. Una persona, cuyo
trabajo en el tema de la longitud merece menor atención (Ferrer
Maldonado), obtuvo un subsidio de 4o ducados mensuales en
tanto realizaba sus observaciones, con la promesa de 5.ooo si
solucionaba el problema por medio de la «aguja fija» (agosto
de 1615) [12].

Si nos fijamos en la talla del patrono y en la naturaleza del
premio ofrecido a los aspirantes resulta obvia la necesidad de
buscar un atajo a través del laberinto documental, de índole
miscelánea.

El material que he revisado se presta a un examen más
ceñido de los datos separados por materias: 1) la duradera
pugna entre dos contendientes en la cual las condiciones y la
cuantía del premio están puntualizadas; 2) la participación
internacional en el certamen; 3) el atractivo de cuestiones
extravagantes; 4) la reacción pública ante los avances revelados
y, por último, una breve ojeada a la investigación científica de
un problema abordable.

La contienda más larga, que duraría años, y la más áspera

en lenguaje, la sostuvo Luis de Fonseca Coutinho, portugués favorecido por don Duarte, infante de Portugal, contra su compatriota el científico Juan Bautista Labanha, y contra el doctor Arias de Loyola, español, en tiempo atrás cronista de la corona de Castilla. Esta pugna se mantuvo desde el año 1602 al 1612, en el que Fonseca se retira, y hasta que en 1632 Arias renuncia.

La reorganización general de las tareas científicas en España, subsiguiente a la muerte de Alonso de Chaves [13], trajo consigo al principio, algunos nombramientos incoherentes dado el personal disponible. Tal es el caso del doctor Arias, matemático y geógrafo, que ocuparía el cargo de *Cronista Mayor de Indias*, «por sus muchos servicios». Rara vez se encuentra un hombre tan inepto en la tarea encomendada, y tan obligado a fracasar en sus esfuerzos. En 1596 fue depuesto por «no haberse aplicado bien el doctor Arias, en lo de la historia» [14]. Libre para dedicarse a menesteres que le interesaran más ofreció, en 1603, revelar soluciones sigiladas, concernientes a la longitud, al primer piloto mayor Rodrigo Zamorano y a sus dependientes en Sevilla. El Rey le concedió 600 ducados a condición de que Labanha o Guillermo de Céspedes participaran en el conocimiento de la fórmula. Desde que los proyectos de Luis de Fonseca concernientes a la longitud estuvieron apadrinados por Labanha en la corte, y discutidos en la Academia de Madrid, nada sucedió hasta 1609, fecha de una primera opinión opuesta a los trabajos de Fonseca. Los datos los había reunido Hernando de los Ríos Coronel, piloto matriculado, con sus expertos compañeros, en experiencias realizadas utilizando los instrumentos de Fonseca en una travesía de ensayo entre Manila y Nueva España, en 1607-1608, o, según dice el texto, «en un viaje de Filipinas al Puerto de Teguantepeque».

El 9 de mayo de 1609, Arias solicitó audiencia una vez más para exponer «cinco proposiciones», y, de nuevo, se encontró el camino bloqueado por una investigación acerca de la obra de Fonseca. En otras palabras, mientras que las propuestas e instrumentos de este se examinaban en la teoría y la práctica, los proyectos de Arias quedaban pospuestos. ¿Para qué ensayar dos proyectos prometedores, si estaban fundados en premisas similares, sirviéndose de las variaciones de la brújula, y de adelantos en la observación del cielo, por medio de astrolabios y de tablas astronómicas recientemente compuestas y corregidas? Así ocurre con las proposiciones de ambos competidores. El 8 de julio de 1610, la junta examinadora decretó que en el caso de ser insatisfactorios los trabajos de Fonseca, el doctor Arias recibiría una pensión perpetua de 6.000 ducados y 2.000 ducados de por vida. El día 22 del mismo mes y año, el doctor Arias expuso que llevaba ocho semanas en la corte con una verdadera solución para la reforma y perfeccionamiento de la navegación y para la corrección de la brújula, así como para establecer el auténtico meridiano, y que, entre tanto se había ofrecido a un tal Fonseca, portugués, 6.000 ducados, etc., y que por lo tanto si él, Arias, probaba que las declaraciones de Fonseca eran falsas, a él, Arias, deberían darle 12.000 ducados.

Sin embargo, posiblemente, sin que Arias lo supiese, en ese otoño de 1610 fueron sucediéndose las cosas. El 7 de septiembre fue convocada una junta en Madrid a tiempo de que el célebre Labanha pudiese asistir personalmente [15]. Los demás miembros fueron: Pedro de Ledesma; el secretario Pedro de Valdés; el licenciado Juan de Cedillo, matemático famoso; Antonio Moreno, por entonces profesor de cosmografía en Sevilla; Diego de Molina; también Luis de Fonseca, don Alonso de Flores y cuatro pilotos sevillanos, de los cuales «uno cayó enfermo y no pudo acudir». Tal fue la junta en la que Fonseca, uno de los miembros, aparecía como contendiente, sometiendo a comprobación sus tres brújulas [16].

Labanha pudo informar de que los resultados obtenidos con la brújula de punto fijo, durante un viaje experimental a Goa contorneando Africa, habían sido buenos, según atestiguaban los capitanes Pedro de Silva y Constantino de Menelao y varios de sus pilotos. Este diestro testimonio fue aprobado por todos, con excepción de Pedro Valdés y los tres pilotos de Sevilla que consideraban insuficientes las pruebas y proponían como prueba necesaria un viaje a las Indias españolas, navegando en dirección Oeste, y bajo la inspección de los castellanos, y no de los portugueses.

Labanha no fue tan afortunado en los resultados de la «brújula de este a oeste», ensayada en tierra entre Madrid y Lisboa, dado que las observaciones fueron hechas por Fonseca mismo, y las pruebas llevadas a cabo entre Madrid y El Escorial por Hernando de los Ríos [17] correspondían a distancias demasiado cortas para demostrar algo. Sugirió, pues, nuevos ensayos en tierra sobre distancias mayores, y con dos brújulas de comprobación mutua. La «aguja regular del norte al sur», por consiguiente, se iba a someter a otras pruebas por un grupo que encabezaba don Diego Brochero, «caballero con mucha experien-

cia en estos menesteres», según Navarrete (p. 32) [18]. Brochero
celebró una junta en su casa de Lisboa y parece que accedió muy
gustoso a ensayar cualquier idea. Son sus propias palabras:
«con las observaciones que se han hecho estos días, es cosa mila-
grosa lo que sería alcanzado en lo que ha. Espero en Dios que
en tiempos de V. S. se ha de descubrir cosa tan importante para
la navegación; querría que este buen hombre de Fonseca estu-
viese guardado en algodones, por que no se nos muera» [18 a].
Otros equipos de expertos deberían salir de Sevilla, y se pro-
yectaba asimismo un recorrido desde Barcelona a Valencia.
Labanha insistió en que se aplazasen las pruebas hasta que él
sin riesgo, pudiera intervenir, esto es, sin miedo a que le detu-
vieran en España antes de rematar su propia tarea de trazar
un mapa de Aragón.

Armando Cortesão [19] examina la exposición llevada a cabo
por intersección de los rayos azimutales, y apoyada en deter-
minaciones de la latitud en diversos puntos, y Labanha sugiere
necesarias mejoras en el utillaje y en los métodos. Avanzado el
año, Hernando de los Ríos dio cuenta de los resultados de las
pruebas, en otro viaje de ida y vuelta a Méjico, cuya consecuencia fue el pleno reconocimiento de la buena calidad de la brújula
ordinaria de Fonseca, instrumento bien construido y manejado
habitualmente por los expertos. La de este a oeste y la de norte
a sur ideadas por Fonseca, causa determinante del premio,
con promesa de nuevas ayudas y resultados revolucionarios,
se consideraron completamente inútiles. De los Ríos, al someter a examen un cuaderno de bitácora con lecturas separadas
hechas por los observadores, dijo: «no vale todo nada». Contra
este dictamen, Fonseca reaccionó manifestando que «cuando
yo se las di (las brújulas) yo mesmo no las había entonces aca-
bado de comprender, y por esa causa no le di reglas ni regimiento alguno».

A continuación Arias encontró un amigo poderoso, el conde
de Lemos, que estaba al corriente de estas cuestiones y conocía
los trabajos de hombres tales como Galileo, y las posibilidades
de proyectos distintos de los de Fonseca. Lemos propuso la adjudicación de 10.000 ducados a Arias y el finiquito de los experimentos de Fonseca, que requerirían la construcción de veinte
o treinta brújulas sin que se hubiese demostrado su valor efectivo. Como Fonseca, junto con sus compañeros miembros de la
junta, por propio interés, había jurado guardar el secreto y es
de suponer que Arias hiciera lo mismo, aunque insinuando su
solución, se puede imaginar que el asunto no proseguiría de

acuerdo con los supuestos de cualquier ensayo científico experimental razonable. Se puede imaginar un fenómeno paralelo en la carrera emprendida entre fabricantes de drogas, en busca de datos, en nuestros días. Fonseca, postergado, se refugia detrás de Labanha, que pide se le permita proseguir sus trabajos, insinúa grandes promesas, y respalda sin reservas a su compatriota. Arias se negó a revelar la «tercera» proposición, concerniente a su investigación encaminada a averiguar la altura de la estrella polar a cualquier hora del día o de la noche, una observación de la bóveda celeste dedicada a determinar la longitud. Y pide una gratificación extraordinaria por su «secreto» que rebasaba el campo de la recompensa ofrecida a Fonseca. Durante los meses subsiguientes, continuaron las pruebas de este entre Sevilla, Madrid y Cádiz. El premio lo tenía a su alcance. Los documentos que siguen, sin más interés científico que casi toda la colección, revelan dos nuevas briznas de información. Una: de donde habría de sacarse el dinero en tiempos de moneda terriblemente devaluada y de irresponsabilidad fiscal. Los 6.000 ducados de pensión perpetua quedaban separados en tres lotes de 2.000, cargados respectivamente sobre la *avería* o tasa náutica recaudada principalmente en Sevilla, sobre la tesorería real de España y sobre la de Portugal que pagaría, además, la libranza de los 1.000 ducados de la *ayuda de costa*. Fonseca ofrecía ahora un instrumento novísimo, el llamado «compás vertical», hasta entonces jamás visto, y sobre ello existe una orden de pago por valor de 1.000 ducados, fechada en agosto de 1610 y otra de 600, en septiembre del mismo año.

El otro material interesante se refiere a las pruebas de sus brújulas, efectuadas entre 1610 y 1612. La «aguja vertical», probablemente similar a otro modelo de astrolabio, montado sobre una brújula adecuada para leer la diferencia entre el polo magnético y el polo celeste, habría de ensayarla el mismo Fonseca, en una travesía de las islas Canarias a la Tercera y en la ruta de regreso a Lisboa. De este modo se eludía cómodamente el problema de la navegación por la parte occidental de la ruta de Indias, donde estaban comprobadas las variaciones de la brújula. Nuevos experimentos, en tierra, fueron aceptados de acuerdo con este plan propuesto por Labanha. El mismo había trazado las instrucciones y hasta diseñó los instrumentos, ateniéndose a indicaciones de Fonseca. Este «librito» de Fonseca fue presentado en Sevilla, cuando el mismo Labanha se negaba a dirigir las pruebas, por causa de otros compromisos.

Y así prosigue la historia de la demanda de *ayuda de costa* hecha por Fonseca, y de su «indisposición» para viajar, de sus responsabilidades domésticas y su negativa a embarcarse en la flota de Indias. Como recurso final, su recusación (ante el poderoso Labanha) de los peritos nombrados para probar sus instrumentos. Antonio Moreno, notabilísimo piloto y cosmógrafo, lamentaba con amargura: «que se me haga este agravio y que me haya mandado venir a que padezca detrimento en mi onra y reputación siendo como soy hombre noble y haviendo venido aquí con tanto deseo de servir al Consejo en esta ocasión».

Transcurre todo este tiempo con la pugna entre Fonseca y Arias, quien no perdía la oportunidad de señalar las dilaciones del portugués, ni dejó de quejarse por la pérdida de tiempo resultante de haber retenido su propio «secreto» en la solución del problema de la longitud. El antagonismo entre estos dos hombres amargó sus vidas. Parece, por ejemplo, que alguien, en Lisboa —un «loco», según los archivos— ofrecía ocultamente 2.000 ducados como precio del «secreto». Cuando, por último, fue invitado Fonseca a presentarse personalmente en Sevilla, con sus instrumentos, para pasar a las Indias o, por lo menos, a Canarias, rehusó sencillamente incorporarse a la expedición de 1612, alegando su «avanzada edad» y los cuidados de su «casa y hacienda» [20].

La retirada de Fonseca daría, al fin, una compensación a Arias. Esta historia tiene, en cierto modo, un paralelo en los ensayos fracasados —aunque se efectuaron menos pruebas en tierra— con la interferencia de otros competidores, principalmente Río Riaño y Van Langeren, y con las poderosas maniobras del favorito duque de Lerma, dada la influencia sobre los miembros de la Junta de Guerra. La muerte de Labanha, en 1624, acortaría el interés de los experimentos científicos. Arias pondría en ridículo nuevos proyectos, tales como la utilización de los eclipses de los satélites de Júpiter, y, finalmente, fue desterrado de la corte en 1632 no sin proclamar con énfasis que una corte extranjera le había ofrecido, por su invención, un millón de ducados en «oro de oro» —alusión esta, despectiva, a la devaluación de la moneda española—.

Pasando de estos dos destacados contrincantes ibéricos a los concursantes extranjeros, encontramos en primer lugar, a un tal «Banlangren», así denominado en los manuscritos españoles, un contemporáneo bien relacionado con especialistas en náutica flamencos que tenían la categoría de un Tansen y un White —llamado Juan Blanco—. Aquel Michael Florenzio Van

Langeren, o Florencio Langreno [21], estaba al corriente de la obra de Galileo, con quien pudo tener contacto [22]. Van Langeren gozaba fama internacional como astrónomo y se puso su nombre a una montaña de la Luna; un contemporáneo suyo muy distinguido, Giovanni Bautista Riccioli, cita, con frecuencia, en sus escritos sobre astronomía, una *Selenografía Langretina o Lumina Austriaca Philipica*, publicada en 1645. Van Langeren consiguió de la regente de Flandes, doña Isabel, que escribiese a España, solicitando que se le recompensara, de la misma manera que a Fonseca y Arias, a fin de que revelara sus secretos acerca de la navegación de este a oeste. «En Villete del 28 de Febrero de 1632, el Señor Juan Osbaldo de Brito dice que por el Consejo de Flandes se consultó a S. M. la proposición del dho Miguel Florencia que viene con él y está aquí y resolvió se viese en la Junta de Guerra de Indias y se viese con toda brevedad, si era la misma del doctor Arias de Loyola; y que aunque se hallaze no ser en todo punto la misma se informase de qué provecho sería el premio que se le podría prometer». Cuando se le notificó que Van Langeren recibiría una suma igual a la mitad del premio en metálico prometido a Arias, expuso sus quejas, pero le respondieron: «Hemos aprestado que se contente con eso...», y su réplica fue una «representación del gran agravio y ynjusticia que recivirá» y puso el caso en conocimiento de su favorecedor, el duque de Osuna.

Aunque Van Langeren volvió a España bajo los mejores auspicios, no le faltaron enemigos, o contrincantes en España y en Flandes. Arias fue quien en Madrid intentó probar que las ideas de Van Langeren habían sido robadas a Galileo y, además, que serían inoperantes. En cuanto a esto, Van Langeren había añadido a la observación de los satélites de Júpiter la utilización de las manchas de la Luna, y lo cierto es que su tesis no carecía de interesantes sugerencias, aunque ninguna fuese viable en la mar. Ya en 1629 le había atacado un colega holandés en un folleto titulado *La longitud mal fundada*, y Florencio se quejaría, diciendo que este folleto «va por el mundo incitando a bien y a mal los oidores de los curiosos y además de que muchas personas de calidad van informadas de mis proposiciones por varios caminos como sucede de ordinario en las cortes...» Se conserva una carta en la que anuncia su inminente partida, en viaje de regreso a Flandes, por falta de apoyo financiero en España [23].

Tenemos también una breve referencia a la participación de Galileo en estas investigaciones acerca de la longitud geográfica, incluso en los concursos de premios. Se dice que mantuvo tratos con España entre 1616 y 1632. Su idea era utilizar las lunas de Júpiter, y se puso en contacto con el embajador toscano en Madrid, conde Orso Delzi. En una carta del rey al duque de Osuna, fechada en Madrid, el 28 de enero de 1620, se menciona un folleto de Galileo, probablemente entregado al embajador. Pero del folleto no se encuentra rastro [24]. Las negociaciones de Galileo con la corte española quedarían cubiertas por la adversidad de su arresto domiciliario, la carencia de libertad bajo la Inquisición, y por su decaída salud y su pérdida de vista [25]. Junto a Galileo, el más eminente de los competidores extranjeros, figura Jean Baptiste Morin, distinguido matemático francés, que se sirvió de la astronomía kepleriana en sus tablas, teóricamente válidas, pero consideradas inaplicable para los navegantes. Ni Galileo ni Morin aparecieron por Madrid. En cambio vino otro francés, Jean Maillard, quien recibiría dos subvenciones sucesivas para «estudiar la longitud», una en 1614 y otra en 1625, una vez perfeccionados sus utensilios durante el viaje a Honduras de la flota de Indias [26]. Benito Escoto, noble ciudadano genovés, aunque se llamara Escoto, y buen conocedor del lejano Oriente, llegó a la corte española bajo el patrocinio del padre Aliaga, confesor del rey. Otros muchos españoles, y algunos portugueses, además de Fonseca, también se presentaron solicitando apoyo. Entre ellos, el famoso Simón de Oliveira quien, al final, reconocía, con tristeza y de acuerdo con el gran Labanha, que el sistema de «computo» esto es, de observación y cálculo, mediante el empleo de los instrumentos ordinarios por pilotos experimentados, era, hasta ahora, el más seguro en las medidas de la longitud en el mar.

Todos estos hombres, honrados y formales contrincantes, estaban respondiendo a uno de los mayores retos en la ciencia de su época. La obra de muchos de ellos quedó sin fruto por la desviada dirección de sus esfuerzos y el defectuoso enfoque resultante de las condiciones estipuladas en la adjudicación de recompensas. Si las tareas de los partícipes en los concursos científicos se nos figura que fueron abortivas, tampoco deberíamos olvidar la magnitud de los talentos puestos en juego para comprobar proyectos ilusorios en pruebas inútiles, entre expedientes devastadores de tiempo y viajes, o en agrias y estériles polémicas con los jueces nombrados al efecto. Entre los miembros de las juntas reunidos con periodicidad figuran los ingenios más distinguidos de la época. Comenzando por Juan de Herrera[27], arquitecto del rey y su consejero en diversas materias científicas, encontramos una reclamación suya que alude a su oferta de planes para la solución de algunos aspectos del problema, con el diseño de nuevos artificios. En 1573, Alonso de Toledo y Juan López Velasco habían recibido seis de esos aparatos para que los ensayara Menéndez Avilés, y el mismo Herrera se dolía de no haber recibido ni los 2.000 ducados de pensión vitalicia por su trabajo, ni los honorarios devengados en su asistencia a las juntas. Ni siquiera los 200 ducados de *ayuda de costa* que tenía reconocidos, puesto que los instrumentos se construían a sus expensas. Lamentaba también el verse obligado a examinar «muchos malos proyectos», en especial durante la ausencia de Labanha. Este, igualmente, reclamaba; se negó a ensayar los instrumentos de Fonseca, después de haberles dedicado tanto esfuerzo, pero persistía en dar apoyo a las pretensiones de su compatriota. Céspedes y Zamorano, que habían sido pilotos mayores, y, con ellos, los expertos de la Casa de Contratación y los pilotos experimentados, que por ser tan poco numerosos como perentoriamente necesarios, apenas podían salir de Sevilla sin que se notara su falta. Antonio Moreno, el cosmógrafo y muchos profesores de matemáticas, como Juan de Cedillo (de Toledo) y otros de Salamanca y Alcalá[28] estaban pendientes de las llamadas de la corte. Y siendo el problema de la longitud, a la vez teórico y práctico, con él habrían de enfrentarse quienes lo conocían y estudiaban desde la cubierta cabeceante de un barco en ruta, mientras otros esperaban un día claro en algún lugar entre Madrid y El Escorial. Si las actas de aquellas sesiones aparecieran alguna vez, valdría la pena leerlas.

Otra notable peculiaridad del sistema es que muchos de los competidores defendieron sus propios proyectos formando parte de la junta. Así lo observamos en el caso de Fonseca. Y Herrera y Labanha vieron utilizar su labor, ignorada al adjudicarse el premio[29]. Jerónimo Ayanz (Mayans) era un competidor que presentó un libro acerca de la cuestión y al mismo tiempo juzgaba los trabajos de los demás, y, al parecer, Andrés del Río Riaño, está en el mismo caso con una obra suya, titulada: *Tratado de un instrumento por el cual se conocerá la nordestación o noroestación de la aguja de marear navegando...*, de la cual posee un ejemplar un particular, en Nueva York. Este libro contiene el mejor dibujo de un compás con astrolabio, probablemente similar a la «aguja vertical» de Fonseca, que permite comparar el norte de la bóveda celeste con el norte magnético[30].

178

Otro famoso competidor, precoz pero serio, el cosmógrafo Jaime Juan (1583) es digno de mención porque combina la presentación de su obra y sus instrumentos con la de un horóscopo favorable para el rey. Pasó a Méjico, y allí hubo de leer una conferencia sobre la longitud, en relación a Sevilla, establecida con un error de 14 grados: distancia nada corta aun para aquel tiempo [31].

Irritantes, en realidad, resultan los fraudulentos y obstructivos proyectos, con su osadía difícil de igualar. El personaje más famoso en la lista de pícaros es Lorenzo Ferrer Maldonado, el de los estrechos de Aniano, cuyo descubrimiento denunciaba en 1588. El documento que le concierne merecería ser citado palabra por palabra [32]. Baste mencionar aquí que el rey dicta una *cédula* en 1615, que ofrece a Ferrer Maldonado 3.000 ducados «de oro de Velmillar» como pensión vitalicia en recompensa de: 1) Una brújula fija; 2) Otra con variación, para hallar el punto fijo; y 3) Un instrumento para marcar una línea del meridiano, en la mar; es decir, Ferrer Maldonado hacía un mucho de muy poco, aun cuando Navarrete, al restaurar el texto original de una mala copia, todavía se las arreglara para sacar de estas tres ofertas cuatro [33]. Labanha propuso que los viajes para ensayar estos ingenios podrían hacerse con dos expertos portugueses y otros dos españoles, dedicados a la observación en ambas travesías: una a las Indias Orientales y otra a las Occidentales. Ferrer Maldonado pidió 5.000 ducados por el viaje a las Indias Orientales solamente. Figuran registrados dos pagos a su favor, uno de 40 ducados mensuales, por el viaje de 1616, y otro de 200 ducados por la construcción de algunos instrumentos de observación. Ferrer Maldonado es uno de los más pintorescos personajes de esta historia y autor de una *Imago Mundi*, en 1620, justificadamente famosa, en parte por su combinación de lo imaginado con lo cierto. Esta mezcolanza ganaría relieve después de morir Juan Bautista Labanha, en 1624, cuando la cátedra de matemáticas de la Real Academia se extinguía, y toda la compañía quedaba sometida a la supervisión del Colegio de Jesuitas. Las cátedras de artillería, y todas las de ciencias exactas fueron suprimidas, sin sustitución alguna. Puede imaginarse que en semejante ambiente la labor científica en España no había de mejorar.

La reacción popular frente a los concursos de premios y a la política aneja tuvo repercusión en España entera. La acusan obras de Lope de Vega y de Cervantes. Lope de Vega había sido discípulo de Labanha y estuvo seriamente interesado en

Matemáticas, materia de buen tono. En dos de sus comedias, *La Dragontea* y *El Vellocino de Oro*, refleja su expectación de una respuesta popular a los problemas náuticos y a las disquisiciones sobre la longitud geográfica. Cervantes satiriza el apoyo indistinto prestado a proyectos alucinadores sobre el tema, en su *Diálogo de los Perros*. En una conversación famosa, el matemático dice: «Veintidós años ha que ando tras hallar el punto fijo; y aquí lo dejo y allí lo tomo, y pareciéndome que ya lo he hallado y que no se me puede escapar en ninguna manera, cuando no me cato, me hallo tal lejos dél que me admiro...»

En España, ocasionalmente, siguieron apareciendo proposiciones fantásticas. Entre ellas una del padre Miravete (1737), uno de los más pertinaces abogados de la valía de proyectos suyos, que, afirmaba, «guardan la llave de oro», y están presentados en una obra titulada: «*La más preciosa Margarita del Océano, en cuyo fondo gira un fijo punto*, perla verdadera que identifica el de una ciencia náutica, que manifiesta el uso práctico de la brújula, hasta hoy mal entendida...» Este y otros trabajos similares, con los cuales asediaba a los reales consejos, a los particulares y a la Corte, le valieron una reprimenda del marqués de la Victoria, en el prólogo a una de las cartas «que escribe el padre Juan Olvido, mínimo piloto y matemático...» con esta cuarteta:

> Padre, la cosmografía
> que aborta su Reverencia,
> como la explica, es demencia;
> como la piensa, manía [34].

Otro crítico sugiere: «que confiese que es tonto y que debe aver años que le ayan vuelto el juicio, si alguna vez lo ha tenido» [35].

En cuanto a Inglaterra, nos refirió muy bien Robert Gould la historia del mismo asunto en su libro *The Marine Chronometer*; y el verdadero «Descubrimiento de la longitud», subtitulado «Observaciones sobre el uso de cronómetros para determinar la longitud en el mar, 1530-1770», publicado por Norman Thrower en *Navigation*, vol. V, núm. 8, 1957-59. Esta es en gran parte, por supuesto, la historia de los relojes Harrison. La Academia Francesa, que aún esperaba otra solución, se vio obligada, cuando anunció otro premio, en 1767, a definir de nuevo el significado de la longitud y a explicar lo que se entendía por «la longitud calculada, que se toma a bordo», todo en aras del progreso de un problema insoluble al cabo de trescientos años.

Ello nos hace recordar la oferta de un millón de dólares por el invento de un escudo contra la gravedad, debido a Roger Babson, en 1932.

En Inglaterra, a la vez que la Board of Longitude (por 12 Ana, cap. 15) juzgaba los trabajaos de Harrison y Tobías Mayer [36], examinaba proyectos increíblemente estúpidos. Uno de ellos el del perro herido, cuya pata se estiraría a bordo de un barco cuando alguien en Inglaterra sumergiese una venda en el agua. Esto estaba basado sobre la teoría de Digby que postulaba la curación de una herida aplicando un vendaje al arma que la causara, y no a la herida misma. Siendo así se podría comprobar la hora, a cualquier distancia. El deán Swift dispararía contra dos notabilidades serias, aunque equivocadas, Whiston, de Cambridge, y Ditton, una bárbara *Ode for Music on the Longitude*, incluida en cualquier edición de sus obras completas, y en la que, aún en nuestros liberales tiempos, encontramos palabras demasiado fuertes. Estoy haciendo nada más que unas alusiones a un tema explorable y, en cierto modo, estudiado por los historiadores literarios. Los historiadores sociales no han mostrado tanto interés por la reacción del pueblo ante las primeras discusiones científicas, ante los concursos y demás cosas análogas.

Las conclusiones de este examen sumario parecen reforzar la sospecha inicial de que los premios dados a la solución de determinados problemas son inoperantes para aproximarse a las verdades que explora la ciencia. Como vehículo conducente a los problemas científicos, la competencia en concursos es útil, si llega a atraer la atención del público; apreciar el hecho de que tenga dudoso valor para los adelantos científicos y escasos efectos en la conciencia de los científicos, no deja de ser interesante en cuanto difiere inequívocamente de lo que acontece en la arquitectura y otras artes, en deportes, etc. En estas ramas, con frecuencia, el patrocinio, aun limitado a una tarea singular, sabido es que alentó el desarrollo de talentos con resultados excepcionales. La satisfacción, aliciente capital del concursante, que pretende resolver un problema importante y ser reconocido entre sus iguales, es un aliciente capital en todas las contiendas de este tipo. Especialmente interesante es, sin embargo, en sentido inverso el peso que los mismos científicos concursantes otorgan a sentimientos de orgullo por la labor realizada por ellos y, a menudo, oficialmente despreciada (Galileo), o a tareas aclamadas por el mundo de la ciencia, y fundadas, sin embargo, en supuestos erróneos (Fonseca, Ferrer

Maldonado) [37]. Esta diferencia se advierte, al cabo de siglos, con igual claridad que si los documentos estuvieran recién escritos. Leyéndolos hacemos una experiencia conmovedora; diríase que nos muestran los valores que hacen vivir a los hombres.

Este trabajo quiere mostrar, con la ayuda de un ejemplo —el esclarecimiento de la longitud geográfica— el modo en que la ciencia, como fuente de conocimiento de la naturaleza, comenzó a contender con el dogma en la tradición clásica y en el folklore de la España del siglo dieciséis. Cuando los fenómenos naturales científicamente determinados fomentaban la prosperidad y el poderío, se ensayaban teorías y prácticas científicas ante los tribunales de justicia, en la plaza del mercado y mediante premios del monarca. Sin asamblea ni tribunal alguno designado para juzgar los conocimientos científicos, la ciencia fue desarrollándose a pesar de tales ensayos, más que por su causa. Por esta razón el progreso de la ciencia, en cuanto disciplina, no está reconocido en estas fuentes. Sin embargo, la tarea de dar cuerpo al conocimiento de las llamadas ciencias naturales recorrería una fase de importancia en la España de los Habsburgos. Cara tuvo que pagarse la exploración de una ruta intelectual que sus sucesores podrían seguir más cómodamente, hacia meridianos hasta entonces indeterminados.

NOTAS

[1] Ursula Lamb, «Science by Litigation: A Cosmographic Feud», *Terrae Incognitae*, I, Amsterdam, 1969, pp. 40-48.

[2] A. de Smet, «Louvain et la Cartographie Scientifique dans la première moitié su XVe siècle» *Janus*, Leiden, 1967, vols. 3-4, pp. 219-233, expone la división de la práctica y la teoría entre Leiden y Amsterdam. También, Ursula Lamb, «Advice to a King: The Representation of Juan Escalante de Mendoza». Ensayo leído en la *Society for the History of Discoveries*, de la Universidad de Minnesota, noviembre 1969.

[3] Rupert J. Gould, *The Marine Chronometer*, Londres, 1923, ref. 3; J.W. Thrower, «The Discovery of Longitude at Sea, observations on carrying time keepers for determining longitude at sea, 1530-1770», *Navigation*, vol. V, número 8, Winter 1957-58, sin paginación, en nota. Estos autores no consideran el admirable examen de los errores textuales de la edición publicada en 1921 de la obra de Santa Cruz, *Libro de las Longitudines*, por Mata Carriazo de la *Crónica de los Reyes Católicos*, Alonso de Santa Cruz, 2 vols., Sevilla, 1951, pp. CLI-CLXII.

182

⁴ Felipe Picatoste y Rodríguez, *Apuntes para una Biblioteca Científica Española del siglo XVI*, Madrid, 1891, p. 27. El padre del citado Juan Rojas, matemático famoso, ostentaba el título de marqués de Poza.

⁵ Martín Fernández de Navarrete, *Biblioteca Marítima Española*, 107-8, 2 vols., Madrid, 1851, II, 292-293. Juan Rojas de Sarmiento, *Comentarium in Astrolabium, quod planisferium vocant... 1551*. En El Escorial se guardan también instrumentos ideados por él.

⁶ Con referencia a Lovaina véase: A. de Smet, «Leuven als Centrum van den Wetenschappelijke Cartografische Traditie», *Acta Geographica Lovaniensia*, vol. V, 1967, pp. 97-116.

⁷ Rupert J. Gould, *op. cit.*, p. 12. Según esto, la convocatoria de un concurso con premio, abierto por Holanda, parece haber sido posterior, es decir, una copia del certamen español, como expone Rupert Gould.

⁸ *Colección de Documentos Inéditos para la Historia de España*, 112 vols., Madrid, 1843-95, vol. XXI, pp. 116-117.

⁹ La cuestión de los salarios es un tema de estudio sumamente curioso acerca del cual no he hallado referencia. Tan solo datos incompletos y cifras que no pueden informarnos sino en parte. Los miembros del Consejo de Indias recibían 266 2/3 ducados al año y *ayuda de costa* y, algunos, alojamiento gratuito. El cosmógrafo y piloto mayores ganaban 300 ducados. Pero en sus historias personales figuran continuas peticiones de dinero aparte del salario y tenían derecho a una serie interminable de gajes. Pueden encontrarse algunos datos en el libro del doctor don Angel de Altoaguirre y Duvale y don A. Bonilla y San Martín, editores, *Indice general de los papeles del Consejo de Indias*, vol. 1, Madrid, 1923, pp. 180-86. Ferrer Maldonado, Juan Mayllard y Luis de Fonseca.

¹⁰ Papeles del doctor Arias: Archivo General de Indias, Patronato, 262: «La aguja fija».

¹¹ C. Fernández Duro, *Disquisiciones Náuticas: Los ojos en el cielo*, Madrid, 1885, pp. 125-126.

¹² *Colección de Documentos Inéditos para la Historia de España*, XXI, p. 144, 19 enero 1616; A. G. I., Patronato, 262.

¹³ El desastre de la Armada Invencible, la decadencia de la empresa científica del Piloto Mayor y la escasez de pilotos españoles deben tenerse también en cuenta.

¹⁴ Ernesto Schäfer, *El Consejo Real y Supremo de las Indias*, 2 vols., Madrid.

¹⁵ Labanha emitió su veredicto el 29 de setiembre. Su propia labor aparece registrada en Frazaõ de Vasconcelos, «Subsidios para a Historia da Carreira da India no Tempo dos Filipes», *Boletim Geral do Ultramar*, 1968, número 10, p. 34.

¹⁶ En Lisboa fue convocada otra junta que presidió el marqués de Castel Rodrigo. José Pulido Rubio, *El Piloto Mayor*, edición de 1950, Sevilla, páginas 760 ss., expone el ensayo efectuado por Moreno.

¹⁷ Tampoco pudo sentirse satisfecho Antonio Moreno con las realizadas por De los Ríos entre Sevilla y Cádiz.

¹⁸ Don Diego Brochero de Paz y Amaya, fallecido el 20 de julio de 1625, fue llamado «ornamento de la milicia naval, hombre de corazón, cabeza privilegiada, superintendente de armadas, infatigable trabajador, alma de las reformas iniciadas en las armadas». C. Fernández Duro, *Armada Española*, 8 vols., Madrid, 1895-98, vol. IV, pp. 7, 9, 29.

¹⁸ᵃ Colección Navarrete. Vol. XVII, vols. 120, 128.

¹⁹ Armando Cortesaõ, *Cartografia e Cartógrafos Portugueses dos Séculos XV e XVI*, Lisboa, 1935, 5 vols., vol V, p. 65.

²⁰ Resulta interesante una reacción contemporánea frente a Fonseca. García de Silva y Figueroa, *Comentarios*, 2 vols., Madrid, 1903-5, vol. I, pp. 92-98, vol. II, pp. 190-94, dice de Fonseca y «otros hombres charlatanes y noveleros ... del todo idiotas y sin algún ingenio, ... habían siempre en el mundo engañado y persuadido de variedad de negocios ... han sido tenidos y estimados por valores enteros y prudentes...» Debo esta referencia y otras varias a C. R. Boxer.

²¹ Michael Floris van Langeren falleció en 1625; nacido en Arnheim, fue el tercer hijo de Arnold Florentius. Véase A. J. van den Aa, *Biographisch Woordenboek der Nederlanden*, Haarlem, 1852, 78 vols., vol. 10, p. 30. En cuanto a la familia Van Langeren de grabadores y cartógrafos, Raymond Lister, *How to Identify Old Maps and Globes*, Nueva York, 1965, p. 79.

²² *Documentos Inéditos para la Historia de España*, vol. XLVII, pp. 339-40.

²³ Real Academia de la Historia, manuscritos varios, 9-3559.

²⁴ *Documentos Inéditos para la Historia de España*, vol. XLVIII, pp. 339-40. Para una visión general, D. W. Walters, «Galileo y la Longitud: Contribuciones Fundamentales a un Problema Fundamental», *Physics*, Florencia, 1964. No incluye la correspondencia.

²⁵ Véase J. J. Fabié, *Galileo Galilei, His Life and Works*, Londres, 1903, p. 373. Según parece, los Estados Generales, en 1636, votaron un crédito para regalar una cadena de oro a Galileo como recompensa por su trabajo dedicado a la longitud. Cuando, en 1638, le fue llevada a Italia la cadena, ya estaba ciego, y se dice que pasó sus manos sobre ella, pero rehusó aceptarla porque no podía seguir trabajando en el caso.

²⁶ Esta flota de «tierra firme» la relacionan erróneamente con la «armada suiza». Gould, *op. cit.*, p. 12, notas.

²⁷ Respecto a Herrera y a Labanha, podrá verse la obra de George Kubler, *Portuguese Architecture, 1550-1700*, Wesleyan Press, proyectada para el otoño de 1971. Debo agradecimiento a este autor por su información acerca de Labanha. En cuanto a los instrumentos ideados por Herrera, véase Archivo General de Indias, Patronato, Leg. 259, Ramo 58.

²⁸ Fernández de Navarrete, Martín: *Historia de la Náutica*, en la *Biblioteca de Autores Españoles*, vol. LXXXIII, p. 417. Trata de la creación de cátedras científicas por Felipe II.

²⁹ Armando Cortesão y A. Teixeira da Mota, *Portugalliae Monumentae Cartographicae*, Lisboa, 1960, 5 vols., vol. IV, pp. 65, 75. Trata de las tablas de amplitudes del sol compuestas por Labanha. Este determinó con suma precisión la longitud de las Molucas el año 1611.

³⁰ Se incluyen las críticas de Río Riaño a la labor de Fonseca.

³¹ E. Schäfer, «El Cosmógrafo Jaime Juan», *Investigación y Progreso*, año X, núm. 1, Madrid, 1936, pp. 10, 13.

³² E. Navarrete, *op. cit.*, documento núm. 12, pp. 141-144.

³³ A. G. I. Patronato, 262.

³⁴ Fernández Duro, *Disquisiciones Náuticas. Ojos en el cielo*, p. 121.

³⁵ Museo Naval, MS 1406, fol. 80.

³⁶ Eric G. Forbes, «¿Quién descubrió el modo de determinar la longitud en el mar?», en *Sky and Telescope*, enero de 1971, pp. 4-6. Mayer compuso nuevas tablas solares y lunares, y Harrison construyó cuatro relojes, p. 6. «El invento de Harrison había hecho practicable el método del cronómetro (como se le denominó luego), pero no útil generalmente, en tanto que las tablas de Mayer permitían que el sistema de las lunares generalmente resultara útil pero no practicable, a la vez que la precisión de este último método apenas alcanzaba la mitad del primero.»

³⁷ Peter B. Medawar, *The art of the soluble*, Londres, 1967.

IV

ABSTRACT

Science by Competition: the Problem of Longitude

When choices have to be made as to the right or wrong, the better or worse, or any other pair of qualities, there are a number of social mechanisms to help the process. In the sixteenth century, science was not yet a concept with its own terms of reference and a search for a mechanism, which could be trusted to judge the truth of science, resulted in an attempt to adapt the extant forums of public debate. The courts of law, discussed as a forum for science in 'Science by litigation', found the search for justice to differ from that for scientific truth. This paper shows that the mechanism of a public competition, which rewarded advantage, turned out to be another forum unsuitable to science.

The problem of longitude was how to measure it and how to project it on a globe. The measure of longitude was a theoretical and practical enterprise. Men building and handling instruments confronted those who drew up stellar regiments and who posited the length of a latitudinal degree measured in miles. A *junta* of 1566 had considered the problem and found it insoluble except by some timing mechanism, as yet beyond the competence of watch makers, or the use of stellar reference (the moons of Jupiter) which depended on the use of instruments at sea.

It is probable that the suggestion for a public competition to solve the problems originated with the Royal Academy of Mathematics in Madrid and the proclamation of it is variously dated. Announced by Philip II, the first records of funds in support of travel to the court and recompense for instruments submitted, date from the time of Philip II in 1598 and continue under Philip III and IV.

The four sets of data considered were: 1) the longest lasting feud between two rival competitors during which the terms, the amounts of the prize and support for the work were defined; 2) the international participation in the competition and the imitation thereof in Venice, Holland, France and England; 3) the judges, their work and opinions; and 4) public reaction to the proceedings as they became known and the attraction to a lunatic fringe.

The proposals are by and large for compasses of special design, some corrected for declination, others combined with an astrolabe, the so-called 'vertical compass'. The papers in the Archivo General de Indias are filed under 'La Ajuga Fixa' (the fixed compass, illus.).

The Dutch Florencius Van Langeren was a most prominent figure invited to Madrid. Galileo was in touch with the Spanish ambassador but did not go to Madrid. Among the judges were Juan de Herrera, Juan Bautista Labanha, two Pilots Major, and the mathematician Juan de Cedillo – Spain's greatest scientific talents. All of them lamented the enormous waste of time spent on useless projects.

A mountebank who obtained funding was Ferrer de Maldonado, he of the straits of Anian, discoverer of the mouth of a transcontinental waterway on the North American west coast. Public interest is recorded in the works of Lope de Vega (*La Dragoneta* and *El Velocino de Oro*) and of Cervantes (*Dialogo de los Perros*). A final piece of delusion, as late as 1737, entitled '*La preciosa margarita ...*', which turned around a fixed point in the center of the earth, was dismissed by the Marqués de la Victoria in a doggerel: 'Padre, with all due deference, cosmography aborted by your reverence, as you explain it is bad, and as you conceive it is mad.'

The terms of a competition, which required the demonstration of the advantage of one theory or method over another, could not reflect any progress in science because of the basic insolubility of the problem. The criteria to judge relative advantage, because it was safer, easier, cheaper, more convenient, more reliable, were equally incapable of 'solving the longitude'.

V

THE SPANISH COSMOGRAPHIC JUNTAS
OF THE SIXTEENTH CENTURY

This study of the Spanish cosmographic juntas is directly related to two of the papers which I have read before the Society of the History of Discoveries. One was called "Science by Litigation", dealing with the problems of the compass and maritime chart, and the other, entitled "Science by Competition", treated the problem of determining longitude.[1] An alternative title for this paper on the Spanish cosmographic juntas might be "Science by Consultation". All three studies are inquiries into the social mechanism by which the work of the cosmographers, their theories, their experiments and accomplishments, found room in a world of inherited ideas and traditional practices of navigation and relevant branches of science.

The inquiry is germane to the history of the discoveries because the spectacular advance of scientific speculation and the growing opportunities for experimentation in sixteenth century Spain were by and large based on information coming from the newly discovered lands, seas and societies, and upon the challenges to tradition posed by it. This needs no demonstration. Cosmographers of any distinction had to come to terms with the expanded environment and the data from the broadened field of observation made available by the voyages of discovery and exploration.

My inquiry concerns experiences with the social mechanisms available to the cosmographers of the sixteenth century to define the nature of their knowledge (technological and scientific), to get opportunities for their work and recognition for their results. The first two articles showed how the nature of the new knowledge was tried in the wrong forums, that is to say, scientific knowledge cannot be judged as to its validity or truth in a court of law, nor can competition lead to the solution of an as yet insoluble problem or one for which neither the intellectual nor the experimental apparatus has been devised. This paper sets out to describe another mechanism, that of the variously constituted juntas used by the Spanish crown to tap the reservoir of scientific intelligence for practical purposes, that is, it deals with science applied and with the feedback from this into theory and experiment. Again, the relations between the conceptual basis of science and the use of experimental results are seen to be interdependent and it becomes clearer that the social mechanism which promotes the one does not necessarily benefit the other.

---

[1] *Terrae Incognitae*, I, 1, 1969, pp. 40–57; The second paper was published in Spanish "La Nueva Ciencia Geográfica (Una victima del sistema de concursos. Premios españoles para la solución de los problemas de la longitud.)". *Revista de Occidente*, May 1972, No. 110, pp. 162–183.

It will be noted that each article in this series of three covers successively a longer time span and draws on a larger complex of events. The examples chosen for my present argument may appear arbitrary, but the topic of the Iberian cosmographic juntas vastly exceeds the limits of an article and selections were made for illustration. A more ample discussion of the subject forms part of the study of sixteenth century Iberian cosmographers which I have under way.

V

I will examine the makeup and the mechanism of procedure, the issues, the decisions, and the effect upon the development of science of these ad hoc committees of experts. For this purpose I have looked at the following examples of cosmographic concerns: (1) the question of demarcation and the problem of the Moluccas; (2) the continuing revision of the master map or Padrón Real; and (3) inquiries concerning the scientific aspects of running the Carrera de las Indias, that is, the make and use of navigational instruments, including charts.

I

The first problem of the line of demarcation came to the forefront when Columbus returned with news of a possible western approach to the riches of the East. This inspired diplomatic moves by Spain and Portugal in direct negotiation and before the Holy See resulting in the famous series of Papal Bulls. In these documents appears the concept of a line of demarcation. The treaty of Tordesillas between Portugal and Spain in 1494 was a step toward a scientific as well as political determination of the line in the Atlantic Ocean at 370 leagues west of the Cape Verde Islands. Many aspects of the treaty of Tordesillas were the subject of a week-long conference of Spanish and Portuguese scholars in 1972. It was one of a series of "Jornadas Americanistas" under the auspices of the *catedrático* for Latin American History at Valladolid D. Demetrios Ramos. Of greatest interest to me for my present subject was the paper by Luís de Albuquerque of Coimbra concerning the technical difficulties of applying the decision. He was supported by Avelino Texeira Da Mota of Lisbon who, in an illustrated lecture, discussed the cartographic evidence.[2] Both of these papers showed how much can still be gained from a systematic study of the documentation by stripping off the interpretative accretions. Albuquerque laid to rest the tradition of prejudice assumed to have motivated the cosmographers in favor of their respective employers for reasons of patriotism or greed. There was in fact a large area of agreement between them. Albuquerque defines the issues as three: (1) that the line of demarcation be a division of the globe from pole to pole; (2) that a mixed commission locate and determine it on the charts; and (3) that, because astronomical means would not suffice, a mixed commission be sent to sea, made up of navigators and mariners, i.e., composed of men versed in theory and men with experience at sea. The difference so often discussed between $16\frac{2}{3}$, and $17\frac{1}{2}$ or more leagues per degree on the equator and the fixed distances at the tropics, was not a matter of conviction on the part of the cosmographers but an hypothesis which had back of it the different traditions of practicing navigators of Spain and Portugal.

The difficulties with the line of demarcation come under two headings: false assumptions concerning the circumference of the earth (Ptolemy: de situ orbis), and the impossibility of measuring distances at sea accurately. Albuquerque examined the texts of the "Regiment of Leagues" by Jayme Ferrer,[3] The Catalan cosmographer commissioned to fix the line by the Catholic Kings. He quotes him as saying, ". . .que para entender la regla y plática susodicha [which is measured by singladura (a day's sail)] es menester que

[2] *El Tratado de Tordesillas y su proyección.* 2 vols., Valladolid, 1973 and 1974. (Vols. III and IV of the "Series Americanista" of El Seminario de Historia de America, Universidad de Valladolid: Primer Coloquio Luso Español de Historia Ultramarina.) Luis Mendonça de Albuquerque, pp. 119–136, A. Texeira Da Mota, pp. 137–148.
[3] Luis Mendonça de Albuquerque, "El Tratado de Tordesillas: Las Dificuldades tecnicas da sua aplicacão rigorosa", Publicaçao Num. LXXXIII, Junta de Investigacoes do Ultramar, Coimbra, 1973, especially p. 8: O regimen das leguas.

sea cosmographo, aresmetico y marinero, y quien estas tres sciencias no habrá, es impossible la pueda entender. . . ." This puts into sharp relief the separate disciplines needed and of reference between them which was to lead from the practice of consulting one expert to the calling of juntas of scientists.

From 1495 to 1524 the Spanish and Portuguese kings called on committees of experts on several occasions in pursuit of their primary goal, to secure the way to the Spice Islands. King Ferdinand during his two regencies called two councils, one at Toro in 1505 and another at Burgos upon his return from Naples in 1508. These dealt with the projection of an exploring expedition via the west which required secrecy because it might violate the clauses of Tordesillas. While the Spanish king was thinking about a northwest passage to the Moluccas, the Portuguese reached Malacca via the east in 1511, and the importance of exploration with its stress upon commercial considerations turned their interest once more to scientific concerns in order to ascertain the line of demarcation. There is no doubt that King Ferdinand projected the demarcation to the Far East as is implied in the instructions to Solís which show his grasp of the notion of an antimeridian in that year of 1512. They read ". . .que luego iría a Celán para ver si estaba en parte que pertenecia a España y de ahí a la isla del Maluque. . .que cae en los límites de nuestra demarcación e tomareis posesión della por la corona real destos reinos".[4] It is known that the practical approach at this time came to nought as Solís put himself in touch with the Portuguese ambassador Mendes Vasconcellos and Ferdinand had to suspend his search which was clearly in violation of Tordesillas, ". . .hasta que comunique con el Rey de Portugal my hijo en lo que toca a aquella navegación. . .".

For the year 1515 we have a set of documents printed by Fernandez Duro and J. T. Medina[5] which are *pareceres* or expert accounts concerning the location of Cape St. Augustin of Brazil. Four of these are dated on the same day and were to be brought to the king by Andrés Morales from Seville to the court, where he presumably was to give his own opinion orally. The people represented are Sebastian Cabot, Juan Vespucci, Juan Rodriguez Serrano, Hernando Morales, and Nuño García. This testimony has so far interested Brazilianists, but it is also of note as one of the earliest juntas of scientific experts confronted by one question which they were to answer before judges in Sevilla and under oath. The problem arose over the imprisonment of four Portuguese sailors in la Española for having presumably entered the Spanish zone by making a landfall at Cape St. Augustin. The question asked of the witnesses was, Where is the Cape with respect to the line of demarcation?

The papers make one suspect that many more experts were consulted because of the repeated plurals, mention of the presence of "otras personas" or "we were called" "to answer in the presence of all", etc. The opinions preserved are probably only the ones forwarded to the crown because of their importance. Of the witnesses testifying, only one had ever been to the Cape. Juan Rodriguez Serrano remembers that he had been sailing a "certain number of leagues from the Canaries, and from there to the island of Santiago which belongs to the Cape Verde Islands in a southeasterly direction without change for several days" "because we were becalmed", until he made a landfall "a little north, 5 or 8

[4] Ramón Ezquerra, "Las Juntas de Toro y de Burgos", see above *El Tratado de Tordesillas*, pp. 148–170.
[5] Boletín de la Sociedad Geográfica, Madrid, 1884, vol. XVI, pp. 25–30; José Toribio Medina, *El Venetiano Sebastian Caboto al Servicio de España*, 2 vols., Santiago de Chile, 1908, I, pp. 27–29; also in *Gavetas da Torre do Tombo*, vols. 6, 8, 9 bring the relevant documentation for the Molucca debate from that Archive.

leagues from the Cape" which he then rounded, proceeding "toward the southeast a certain number of leagues without any further change". Serrano was very young at the time, he says, and did not know anything about navigation ("Yo era mancebo y no se me entendía nada de las alturas.").

The conflict among the witnesses concerns a chart made by Andrés Morales, famous as author of the first Padrón Real (Royal Pattern Map) who had been with Columbus on his third voyage. His chart was based upon data brought by the first pilots who had reached the Cape and upon later information. Morales says that even though he had never been at the Cape he had reached the mouth of the Rio Marañon and run the coast from there. Since he realized the grave contradiction concerning the location of the Cape, the King "should have it verified and marked", "Que su Alteza debe mandar que se vea e se sepa lo cierto e se límite e se pongan señales en los dichos terminos." He was supported by Hernando Morales, the aforementioned Serrano and Juan Vespucci. Juan concluded that there was no other way than to seek out the place and mark it as suggested by the others. Nuño García agreed to this eminently scientific suggestion, making clear that he felt an accusation of prejudice in behalf of either power because a cosmographer had been employed by one or the other was most unfair and out of order. Contradictory opinions were not expressed "maliciosamente". He also said meantime Amerigo should be believed, "se debe dar crédito a Amerigo", until he be proved wrong. But such an exploration did not get organized then, nor have I found any record of what happened to the Portuguese prisoners in Santo Domingo.

From these papers it emerges quite clearly that the cosmographers possessed the three characteristics isolated by Norman W. Storer in *The Social System of Science* (New York, 1966) as typical of scientists: (1) their disinterestedness; (2) their organized scepticism as to the acceptance of data as well as hypotheses; and (3) their "communality". In this case, to illustrate: politics did not motivate them; they called for verification of dubious estimates; and they respected facts from whatever source. Even so political a man as Sebastian Cabot is all scientist on this occasion. One can clearly see in this junta of 1515 that scientific knowledge and the use of scientific results are separate concerns, and that is what the Spanish crown learned from it.

Once the Spice Islands had been reached by other powers -- Portugal had reached Malacca in 1511, the *Victoria* returned to Sevilla in 1522 -- political obligations and commercial interests of the Iberian crowns were in immediate and serious conflict over the control of production and the distribution of the spices. Correspondence between the Iberian rulers led to the junta of Victoria in January of 1524 which set up a joint commission of three astronomers (astrólogos), and three pilots from each power to define the line of demarcation, and of three lawyers from each side to negotiate the terms of legal possession. The junta so-called of Badajoz, after the Spanish town to which the representatives first adjourned after the opening on the bridge over the Cayas river which was on the border, later met in Yelves on the Portuguese side of the river for equal time-spans during the two months of meetings. Negotiations actually began on the borderline, lasting for three days from April 11 when the nine representatives and their assistants, secretaries, etc., in full regalia and with great ceremony held forth on the bridge where, according to the text, there was no suitable accommodation ("no hay lugar aparejada para ello").

The failure of this meeting, which lasted two months, to reach agreement on anything, whether political, legal, commercial or scientific issues, is well known, and the junta of Badajoz has been denounced as a sterile subject ever since Jean Denucé gave his masterful account of the problem of the Moluccas in 1911.[6] Documentation concerning it is very rich, however, and still worth another look. The descriptive material for social history has rarely been used except for a stray remark or paragraph and nothing can be done here except to mention the fact. A glance at the scientific pursuits shows that the gathering met a high mark of interest for cosmographic concerns. In that respect it had the potential for one of the great scientific occasions of the century. One is compelled to ask why it did not become one instead of merely registering the fact.

The Portuguese were to bring to it the latest observations concerning their routes to the Far East via the Cape of Good Hope and places in the Far East. This material, so far jealously guarded by the Portuguese crown, must have been awaited with bated breath by the Spanish delegation who, in turn, were expected to bring their practical expertise and the log of Magellan and El Cano to help resolve the theoretical and practical problems of the line of demarcation. So much for the documentary base of the conference as scheduled. The participants were recruited from the most experienced members of the cosmographic profession and from the ranks of practiced navigators. It looked as though the most advanced theories would be considered together with the latest data and, in friendly confrontation, astronomers, mathematicians, geographers and navigators would deliberate to resolve the problem of the Moluccas.

That things would not turn out that way became obvious from the start. At the opening ceremony of verifying the credentials of the delegates, held on the bridge over the Cayas, the Portuguese lawyers insisted on the withdrawal by Spain from its delegation of Simon de Alcazaba, the only Spaniard who had ever been in the East with the Portuguese, though he was now in Spanish service, also of Diogo Ribeiro and Juan Vespucci. The Spanish lawyers thereupon were ordered to demand the recall of all Spaniards now in Portuguese service, naming two: el bachiller Maldonado and Bernardo Pérez.

These acts politicized the negotiations beyond repair. In fact, the Spanish cosmographers put the Spice Islands 3° east of the line of demarcation and the Portuguese 43° west of it. This was too great a distance to be negotiated without a comprehensive factual base, and that in turn depended upon available records and the best trained men to interpret them. The Portuguese scientific delegation was made up of Simão Fernandez, Lope Homen, and Tomas de Torres, and had its strength in the documentation they brought. Though the king kept globes and charts under tight control, they brought two globes and many charts with them. One of the globes, giving few coastal points but an *itinerario* which proved the Moluccas in the Spanish zone, was immediately withdrawn, as were some of the charts, once Hernando Colón, following his instructions, had pointed this out. It may be presumed that the question at issue was the projection of a chart taken from a globe and the Portuguese cosmographers had brought their data in good faith, but the kings were interested in advantage and not in fact. The strength of the Spanish delegation rested in their men. Hernando Colón, Tomas Durán, and Dr. Salaya

[6] Jean Denucé, "Magellan: La question des Moluques et la première circumnavigation du globe", Académie Royale de Belgique, Classe de Lettres et des Sciences morales et politiques et Classe des Beaux Arts. *Mémoires*, Deuxième Serie, vol. IV, Brussels, 1908–1911, Sept. 1911, pp. 391–403: "Dernières expéditions espagnoles aux Moluques, la junta de Badajoz et la fin de la querelle des Moluques". I have just received the program of the II Coloquio Luso Espanhol de Historia Ultramarina held in Lisbon in 1973. This conference was largely devoted to the Junta at Badajoz and associated problems. I was to receive the *actas* before submitting this paper but publication seems now to be delayed for at least six months. I have kept to the obvious sources and refer the reader to the appended page of the talks which will be published.

were joined at times by Sebastian Cabot, Diogo Ribeiro, Alonso de Santa Cruz, and Sebastian El Cano, who are mentioned by name. Other pilots came and went or sent in their *pareceres*. It was an impressive pyramid of talent, but the Spanish crown had learned from the junta of 1515. This was not a meeting for science but for the use of scientific opinion, and it was ordered that scientific deliberations of the Spanish delegation be held in secret and opinions before the mixed commission be unanimous: "in order that you may be resolute and concerted in your arguments and answers which are in our favour you shall speak with once voice". "Y con una boca hableis todos." It was therefore the withdrawal of documentation by the Portuguese and the immobilization of expert opinion on the Spanish side which undercut the deliberations and sabotaged one of the potentially great conferences of science.

What has characterized the literature about this meeting is the reaction to the prevailing feeling of the failure, frustration and recrimination which the negotiators encountered. Instead, it might be worth noting the dispassionate tone of the Portuguese experts as against diplomats, the policy of their king, as well as the repeated advice from all cosmographers to sponsor further exploration, to join efforts in reconnaissance and to withhold judgment until the facts were in. The junta of Badajoz showed the idea which scientists had of themselves and the experience they acquired with the use made of their knowledge. They accepted into their ranks anyone with information, regardless of affiliation or origin of the paycheck, judging the quality of the work. This orientation was challenged by the lawyers. Free and open submission of all available data had to be limited by the Portuguese crown and freedom of discourse was prohibited by the Emperor. Badajoz thus became indeed the scene of a sterile exercise.

The sequel to Badajoz was the sale to Spain of the Moluccas at Zaragoza in 1529. Among the five clauses of that agreement there was one which raised the possibility of reopening the scientific question regarding the location of the Spice Islands and the line of demarcation. To such a meeting each power was again to send nine delegates, but this time no lawyers were to be included, giving way to three pilots from among those who would then have been in the Islands. So experience was to be reinforced and separated from other issues.

The question of lines of demarcation remained alive and many cosmographic opinions are extant concerning them, but a formal junta of experts to consider specifically the Moluccas was called only in 1566 by Philip II upon the occasion of the return of Legazpi from the Philippines. This event had raised the issue of whether to proceed, or rather how to proceed, with colonization. Its members were Alonso de Santa Cruz, Pedro de Medina, Sancho Gutierrez, Fr. Andrés de Urdañeta, cosmographer companion of Legazpi, and Jieronymo de Chaves. Their *pareceres* are all dated October 8, 1566, and are depositions of opinions expressed in a meeting. They were paid various sums for their attendance which reflected the distances which each of them had to travel to Madrid. Urdañetas' *parecer* is well known because it contains his pioneering return log from Manila to Acapulco which was to become the standard route of the Manila Galleon.

The experts were asked two questions: on which side of the line of demarcation lay the Moluccas, Philippines and Cebú; and whether they were within the borderline of the Spanish domain as defined in the purchase agreement of Zaragoza where the *raya* had been laid down $17°$ east of the Moluccas. From this it can be seen that the inquiry was not alone for a scientific definition but called for an interpretation of the clauses of the sale. This appeared to prepare the approach suggested in the treaty of Zaragoza, but when Medina and Santa Cruz understood what was asked of them, having testified that the demarcation favored Spain, they returned the following year to give another opinion (on July 16 and 17, 1567) to say that to testify to the legal aspect of the clauses of the sale was none of their concern as cosmographers. King Philip II did not take up the question in an open conference with the Portuguese. A Portuguese *paracer*, solicited by King Manuel from Dom João de Castro, has been recently republished,[7] and it had apparently been seen by Urdañeta when he was in Lisbon. It is undated but presumed to have been written before 1541, and it is most notable in our context for the resigned note of the author to have to repeat an opinion despite a lack of new data.

The juntas and *pareceres* on the line of demarcation and the Moluccas show clearly and in a modern context the conflict between what scientists do and what use or abuse can be made of that. By the highest level of government, the crowns and the Royal Council of Castile and the Indies, the best-informed experts were consulted concerning their knowledge so it could be applied to problems as stated by diplomats on behalf of power and profit to be derived from the spice trade. They were not given the whole problem stated as such, a choice of formulating their role in the solution of it, or suggestions concerning policy.

II

The interest of the crown and the scientists coincided more closely in the matter of the Padrón Real or master chart. This was purely a Spanish product in charge of the Pilot Major and Cosmographer Major of the Casa de la Contratación at Sevilla. The Padrón consisted of a large wall map and of a book of charts of considerable size covering specific routes. A description of the whole survives in a bill sent to the crown by Andrés García de Céspedes in 1596 which may be regarded as typical if not equal of earlier versions.[8] At issue here is the fact that it was a joint product. From the time of Vespucci and Hernando Colón, repeated meetings of experienced pilots, navigators, and cosmographers were held to correct the charts on the basis of information which had meantime reached the Casa. Each pilot was by law required to submit his log upon return from a voyage and to indicate discoveries concerning their routes. A general overhaul in assembly was eventually ordered for January each year for three days, but the sessions were to last as long as necessary in order to get agreement on all the changes to be made. Upon this corrected Padrón all new charts in use by pilots had to be based. The problems of the juntas were how to get information and how to reconcile differences. The first is illustrated by the many complaints, orders and repeated admonitions to the pilots to bring their data to the Casa. The frequently less articulate, less trained, and unknown of the mariners who were the backbone of the Carrera de las Indias turned to the chart makers and instrument makers such as the Gutierrez family. These pilots did not like to defend their findings before a sceptical Pilot Major, a theoretician-Cosmographer and a whole assembly of rival pilots. The next problem was how to achieve agreement, and the accepted method was by majority vote. The Bishop of Lugo, Suarez de Carabajal,[9] the visitador of the Casa de la

---

[7] A Fontoura da Costa, *Tratado da Sphera. . .*, Lisbon, 1940, pp. 113–121. My avoidance of the substance of the discussion is due to the republication of D. João de Castro's texts, not available to me as yet, by Armando Cortesão and A. Texeira Da Mota. See also A. Cortesão, "D. João de Castro e o tratado de Tordesillas" in *El Tratado de Tordesillas*, above pp. 93–102. Luis de Albuquerque has written about the theoretical work of D. João on several occasions. For his latest contribution see appended program: Dia 28 de setembro.

[8] Archivo General de Indias Patronato, 262, Ramo 2.

[9] José Pulido Rubio, *El Piloto Mayor*, Sevilla, sec. ed. 1950, p. 496, text on procedure of D. Juan Suarez de Carabajal.

Contratación from the Consejo de Indias, was the one who suggested that in any assembly individual opinion has to give way to majority vote at some time for the good of the whole. His Eminence was no scientist.

The meaning of these gatherings for an analysis of what science has to cope with under a system of team research, which is a burning topic today, has not been explored by historians. The July, 1973, issue of the periodical *R/D, Research and Development* has an article by Michael Auber of the Physical Science Division of the Stanford Research Institute entitled "The 'Bridge-scientist' and his role". He stresses that advance in science is stimulated by thinking across disciplines which is, of course, best represented by a team. Certainly a junta on the Padrón was a team made up of navigators, cartographers, cosmographers, mathematicians, astronomers and instrument makers. Auber works out two types of organization corresponding to two stages of a joint project. The first, or interdisciplinary, team functions at the stage of conceptualization and preliminary planning; the other, or multi-disciplinary, stage sets the course for translating a project into practice under the management of a leader who assigns specific tasks to subteams. This rather crass adaptation of one part of an interesting article shows up the problems of the juntas of the Padrón. Conceptualization and execution were never consciously separated in the meetings. It would have involved a systematic follow-up on points of disagreement, instead of a vote, to consider the issue settled. The lack of a clear definition of roles in a meeting of experts is now seen to hamper results. It was an important factor in the unsatisfactory results of the Spanish juntas and the surprising fact is that so much progress was made despite the handicap. This feature has been neglected by historians but the problem, though not defined, was obvious to the Spanish crown and we next consider other mechanisms for access to and use of scientific information, the *Memorial* and the *Interrogatorio*, or the petition and the questionnaire.

III

It was the privilege of all subjects of the Spanish king to memorialize the crown. Many pilots and cosmographers individually wrote unsolicited *memoriales* to the king and Consejo de Indias. Among the instances of collective appeal there survives one set of papers concerning the *derrota* and timing of the ships of the Carrera de las Indias useful for illustration. These issues were under continued discussion during much of the sixteenth century. The *memorial* in point was presented by two pilots in 1572 who were sent by a self-constituted junta of forty who appended their signatures on the last page. Some of the points raised by them had been presented to the crown in two *memoriales* by Juan Garcia Hermosilla and associates in 1558 and 1566. They had suggested that the *flota* should make its trading stop on the Honduras coast instead of at Nombre de Dios. They recommended Puerto Caballos and Truxillo as the better stopping points with clean sand, a protected position, etc., and Fonseca del Mar on the Pacific instead of Panamá.[10] The junta of pilots and masters had been assembled under the auspices of the Universidad de Mareantes, a sort of trade union of mariners. The response of the crown was a receipt and an *interrogatorio* asking for more information.

---

[10] Martín Fernández de Navarrete, *Colección* MSS in the Museo Naval Madrid, vol, V, Flotas, 1556: 1074 and 1077; 1560: 1077, documents by Juan García de Hermosilla. This is a long story which is now being studied by several scholars who are putting together the story of Caribbean routes, among them Richard Boulind of the John Carter Brown Library and Paul Hoffman of Louisiana State University.

So, while a *memorial* called attention to a problem or set of problems, it was frequently followed up by an *interrogatorio*, that is, a request for more information. The most characteristic example of one of these available to me is a questionnaire (entitled "Memorial") grounded in complaints about the neglect of affairs in Sevilla by the officials of the Casa de la Contratación. There survives a set of printed questionnaires, addressed to the pilots of the Casa, which contain the answers right on the pages[11] and reflect the interests of the crown's agents, the Pilot Major, García de Cespedes, and the visitador from the Consejo de Indias, Pedro Ambrosio de Ondáriz. These men wanted to know what could be done by the Casa's technical experts to improve matters and so they asked: how to correct the Padrón, i.e., where did it need correction; whether the charts should also be amended; and whether the instruments should be changed, the astrolabes as to size and the compasses with respect to correction for variation.

The answers written and scribbled right onto the printed sheets range in length from a few saying, "It is so", "I agree to what is said", "I say yes", to several appended pages.

I have not found these papers explored (in my admittedly limited search) for the geographic material in them. It appears that true observation of many coastal points led one pilot, Hernando Marqués, to the conclusion that from Santo Domingo to Mari Galante many points were not properly marked and were consistently off by $1/3°$ (too low), influencing as well the position of coastal points on the Tierra Firme coast. In reading I caught the idea that some pilots felt an entire part of the chart should be rotated and for that all points east of Santo Domingo would have to be newly ascertained with respect to their exact position. This would have been a project of vast proportion. The men who suggested such major revision appeared to have little hope for it, and they agreed that the relocation of individual points would not suffice but only prove upsetting to the pilots. Such a survey would be too costly, they said, and a consistent error would be preferable. As for the size of instruments, their recommendation was also not to disturb a working compromise: let those who are curious carry a bigger astrolabe; let a larger instrument -- which would give more precise results -- be used on land, but just don't think it can be used at sea. Those who care about the compass could carry several, and maybe everyone should carry two (as required by rule -- though not of different design). In the meantime, the medium-sized one designed by Nunes and carried by Urdañeta would serve well. The overall impression is that, except for some outstanding talents and some cantankerous characters, the reaction to the questions asked was: Let well enough alone.

But that is not the whole of the text. The questionnaire did not ask but gave a chance to the pilots to tell what really concerned them, namely, to describe the currents in the Caribbean and the shifting sandbanks and coastal hazards encountered. These matters led to happy testimony of the practical men. The word *experience* carries the day, and he who has none of it should not be taken seriously. Let the men gather experience with the complicated currents and seasonal vagaries of wind and weather while estimating the position of their ships, teach them to watch for shallows and sandbanks and by all means these should be entered on the charts. In sum, it was the unasked question which really seemed close to the hearts of the pilots.

What happened to this information? Was it ever acted upon? Or did it, like so many answers to that most sophisticated set of questionnaires which is one of the glories of

---

[11] Archivo General de Indias. Indiferente General, 2005, Junta de Maestros y Pilotos, 1563.

Spain in the sixteenth century, the *relaciones geographicas*, just stay in dustry drawers? Céspedes, remaining as Pilot Major to 1597 or just another year, did prepare a whole new Padrón, which is not preserved, and a set of charts, but there was no response to the questionnaire as such.

I could not help but reflect that during this time of 1597 morale at the Casa de la Contratación was very low. The enterprise of England had taken the spotlight from the Carrera de las Indias which, with increased cargoes, became a freight-carrying line no longer in the forefront of navigational experiments. Was the *visíta* of Ondáriz and the attempt of Céspedes allowed to go forward simply as a gesture to the pilots to make them feel that someone was listening to them? The questionnaire would have the virtue of defusing rebellious complaints while bringing in possibly useful information, and mostly it would prevent the kind of open confrontation which more often than not had ended in fruitless brawls. One can imagine, however, the increase in frustration on the part of the pilots after the brief and pleasant feeling of having had their say. It is rather typical for the time and place of Spanish affairs.

What this questionnaire proves is that scientific results cannot be regarded as an "as is" or to stand equal to revealed truths, subject at most to interpretation but never to basic challenge. The scientists among the men were those who saw the need for experiment and further search to find better answers. Today the instrument of the questionnaire is a favored tool of modern technology assessment, this newest profession which explores the transition from individual perspectives on a subject to group consensus on its impact. The *New Scientist* of May, 1973, devoted a whole issue to "Technology Assessment: A Route Through Chaos", dealing, among other things, with the offices now being organized for it by various European nations. For the purposes of seeing what happened with the Spanish juntas on the Padrón as well as with the techniques of *memorial* and questionnaire, it seems that the main difficulty was the failure to formulate a series of proposals relating to short medium and long-term projects as related to their consequences. The juntas were deprived of a choice of direction or projection. A piecemeal correction of the Padrón or master chart could surely have been devised over a span of years as it came about by happenstance, but more economically and more systematically. However, in the Spanish system the members of the juntas and the consultants were only asked to state, This is so now. Deprived of the *should, would, might*, or *will be*, all they could arrive at was: Let well enough alone. They were deprived of the dimensions of time and of intent.

IV

Two examples will show the effect of this. One of them, from my point of view the most majestic enterprise nearly co-terminal with the empire upon which the sun never set, was the observation of a lunar eclipse of October 17, 1584. Astronomers do not consider this an important event. What makes the enterprise remarkable is the sponsorship and the execution. Preparations were made under the auspices of the Royal Academy of Mathematics in Madrid and the Royal Council well enough ahead of time to supply observers in Antwerp, Venice, Sevilla, Toledo, Madrid, and Mexico City with identical instructions for an "instrumento", i.e., a uniform-sized sheet containing a half circle of the same radius, to register the sightings. The papers in the AGI are the ones for Mexico City.[12] I know of the others only through documentary notice. Jayme Juan was the astronomer who went to Mexico City and helped observe the eclipse in the palace of the archbishop.

[12] Archivo General de Indias, Mexico, Mapas y Planos, 34, to be published.

The results were insignificant, yet the junta qualifies for more than a footnote in the history of science. It represents a solid bid by Spain's scientists to have anticipated the scientific revolution as identified by Kuhn. In the eminence of the sponsorship this event even softens the accusation that there never was any sponsorship for science in Spain made by, for example, Pedro Laín Entralgo in the *Revista de Occidente* (August–September, 1973). In its thoroughness and in its geographical scope the observation was extraordinary. This example of pure science might justify the title which Don Ramón Carande suggested for my article on the longitude when it was translated into Spanish. I had called it "Science by Competition", there being no single word for peaceful competition in Spanish. D. Ramón suggested calling it "Science in Diapers". Charming as this sounds, I found the reservations of my editor concerning its dignity less persuasive than my own, which were based upon the conviction that too much entered into the story of longitude to fit the topic. With respect to the lunar eclipse, however, I would find the title appropriate. But like babies, new scientific ideas need not only credentials of origin to join the legitimate line, but a chance to grow. While royal sponsorship and professional cooperation were present in 1584, a future was not granted to science nor to the sponsoring institution, which folded in 1624. The vast geographic extent of Spanish sovereignty was a coincidence of its political interests which were of a practical and not scientific nature. Even the public echo of this event and the popularity of the academy are deceptive, for what people are interested in is what science can work, not what scientists do, as J. R. Ravetz has put it. Theoretical science was no longer found useful enough in Spain after 1584.

A last series of juntas shows that in practical matters there was also to be a slowdown. I am referring to the plans for the discovery of the Islands of Gold and Silver, or Islas Rica de Oro y Rica de Plata. The protagonists of this scheme were Hernando de los Ríos and Sebastián de Vizcaíno. In order to solicit support they suggested many purposes: to explore the California coast; to search out hideouts of pirates in the Pacific; to find a convenient watering point for the Manila Galleon; to find, explore, and settle the reputedly rich islands; to reconnoiter the Pacific at a higher latitude more systematically than heretofore; etc. Juntas were held in Mexico, then in Madrid and then in Mexico again in the years 1609–1611. The project was advocated by Vizacaíno for a start from Acapulco, and de los Ríos wanted to begin at Manila. The Viceroy of Mexico called together the experts he could find, as did the Concejo de Indias in Madrid. The lure of the islands was the oldest one: to discover, conquer and possess new lands.

What defeated this enterprise was that the crown wanted too many contradictory results from too small a project. If building ships was possible in Manila, manning them was cheaper in Acapulco. If distances were favorable to Manila, the need to reconnoiter the California coast would do two jobs at once. Greediness for practical concerns precluded useful results. Scientific progress in seventeenth century Spain was hampered in its technical progress as it had been stalled in its theoretical aspects already at the time of Céspedes and Ondáriz.

Conclusion

This is, of course, the usual dismal picture which has relegated the story of Spanish science and technology to map study and the pursuit of the curious and rare. Yet I found that contemporary Europeans considered the cosmographers of sixteenth century Spain important, their reputation to be enviable, and their work significant. Spanish cosmographic books were read and translated and used over a long span of time. The cosmographers were mature men knowing what they were about. From the Casas in Sevilla and Lisbon a scientific orientation toward natural phenomena was spreading over an imperial canvas of a world reconnoitered. The participants in the search for knowledge came from all classes, ranging from a ship's boy to the emperor. The problems considered reached from those of the constitution of the stellar universe to the design of ship's tackle. The social bonds between men of the sea were international at a time of growing nationalism. What one is looking at is a major story and it has to do with discovery and the scientific consideration of natural phenomena. But its importance lies not in the theories of science or in the chronology of results. It lies in the social problems of science and scientists, or in putting history into science rather than write history of science.

The contention of my papers is that to the history of science as knowledge about nature and as chronology of successful experiments there must be added the story of formulation and presentation of scientific problems and the application of scientific results as well as the repercussion upon progress due to it. Scientific problems and results had to be filtered through certain social mechanisms which have been described. They are much in the forefront now. Litigation, though not the road to truth in science, has been mined for its adversary procedure as useful in advising the United States government in a statement by James B. Conant.[13] Competition, though equally remote from scientific solution, is visible in the game of grants which is being played in Washington, and the functioning and use of ad hoc expert advisory groups described in sixteenth century Spain do entitle that history to be considered a legitimate part of the history of science in the wider sense.

In other words, the Iberian scientists worked singly at the construction of a conceptual base and a collection and collation of data, but they faced the problem of making their work accessible through available social channels which are only now being studied.

The scientific revolution began when like-minded men preferred traveling the channels of communication between each other represented by the printed word, and connecting nascent scientific associations, to following the sluggish drift of public opinion. They abandoned the upstream work to enlighten the ignorant and to persuade the powerful and to learn from other creative men. The divergence of flow of interest was not that between the two cultures of C. P. Snow, between scientists and humanists. But at that time, it was a split between the old *vita contemplativa* and the *vita activa* of the conquests. Theorists and practical men no longer depended upon one another because there was enough information to occupy the scientist and enough new riches to challenge the entrepreneurs.

Spain's contribution to science before the scientific revolution was access to law and to the court and mainly to its conciliar system, of expert advice, social debate and manifold decisions which pervaded her body politic. The foundation of the University of Alcalá and of the *cátedras* of science in the Casa de la Contratación and at the Royal Court had a common origin in the response to the new environment of the discoveries. But they lost their influence when they left everyday problems because they found inadequate social mechanisms to present their ideas to society at large and failed to develop them to address a common purpose. As long as we must survive in societies, the sixteenth century history of Spain offers a look at the origins of some current problems and shows how their solution was aborted.

[13] Harry Woolf, ed. *Science as a Cultural Force*, Baltimore, 1964. p. 26.

APPENDIX

Program
II COLÓQUIO LUSO-ESPANHOL DE HISTÓRIA ULTRAMARINA
Lisboa, 25–29 de setembro de 1973 Junta de Investigacões do ultramar.

DIA 25 DE SETEMBRO

18 h: Sessão inaugural, sob a presidência de Sua Excelência o Presidente da República, Almirante Américo Deus Rodrigues Thomaz, e com a presença de Suas Excelências o Embaixador da Espanha e os Secretários de Estado da Administração Ultramarina e da Instruçao e Cultura, na Aula Magna do Instituto Superior de Higiene e Medicina Tropical.

Discurso do Dr. Justino Mendes de Almeida, Presidente da Junta de Investigações do Ultramar, e do Prof. Dr. Ciriaco Pérez-Bustamante, Reitor honorário da Universidade Internacional Menéndez Pelayo e Presidente honorário do Instituto Gonzalo Fernandez de Oviedo.

Após a sessão, inauguração, no mesmo edificio, de uma exposição bibliográfica de obras da Junta de Investigações do Ultramar relativas a história e outras ciências humanas.

20 h: Recepção oferecida por Sua Excelência o Embaixador da Espanha.

DIA 26 DE SETEMBRO

9 às 12,30 h e 15 às 19 h: sessões de trabalho, com a apresentação das seguintes comunicações:

Dr. RAMÓN EZQUERRA ABADIA: **La idea del antimeridiano.**

Dr. LUIS FILIPE REIS THOMAZ: **Malaca e Maluco.**

Dr. ARMANDO CORTESÃO: **As mais antigas cartografia e descrição das Molucas.**

Dr. ANTÓNIO DA SILVA REGO: **As Molucas em principios do século XVI, 1511–1521.**

Dr. FRANCISCO MENDES DA LUZ: **Portugal na época de Magalhães.**

Dr. JOÃO DA GAMA PIMENTEL BARATA: **Os navios da época de Magalhães: técnicas de construção.**

Coronel ROLANDO A. LAGUARDA TRIAS: **Las longitudes geográficas della membranza de Magallanes y del primer viaje de circumnavegación.**

Dr. DEMÉTRIO RAMOS PÉREZ: **Magallanes en Valladolid: la capitulación.**

Dr. FRANCISCO MORALES PADRÓN: **Las instrucciones para el viaje de Magallanes.**

Dr.ª MARIA LOURDES DIAZ-TRECHUELO: **La organización del viaje magallanico: financiación, enganches, acopios e preparativos.**

Comandante A. TEIXEIRA DA MOTA: **A contribuição dos irmaos Rui e Francisco Faleiro no campo da náutica em Espanha.**

Comandante JOSÉ LUIS MORALES. **La derrota de Magallanes-Elcano.**

Comandante MAX JUSTO GUEDES: **A armada de Fernão de Magalhães e o Brasil.**

Dr. LEANDRO TORMO SANZ: **El mundo indigena conocido por Magallanes en las Islas de San Lazaro y su muerte.**

Dr. JOSÉ IBAÑEZ CERDÁ: **La muerte de Magallanes.**

Dr. ALFONSO F. GONZÁLEZ GONZÁLEZ: **La dispersion de la escuadra magallanica. El problema del regresso a las costas americanas.**

DIA 27 DE SETEMBRO

8 h: Partida para a excursão ao Alentejo, com visitas a Elvas, Vila Viçosa (almoço) e Évora (jantar).

DIA 28 DE SETEMBRO

9 às 12,30 h e 15 às 16,30 h: sessões de trabalho, com a apresentação das seguintes comunicações:

Dr. ANTÓNIO ALBERTO BANHA DE ANDRADE: **Sentimentos de honra e direitos de justica na viagem de Fernão de Magalhães.**

P.e FRANCISCO LEITE DE FARIA: **Relações impressas sobre a viagem de Magalhães anteriores a 1550.**

Comandante ROBERTO BARREIRO-MEIRO: **El Estrecho y el Pacifico en la cartografia del siglo XVI.**

Drs. LUIS DE ALBUQUERQUE e RUI GRAÇA FEIJÓ: **Os pontos de vista de D. João III na Junta de Badajoz-Elvas.**

Dr. LUÍS DE MATOS: **Em torno de António Maldonado e da questão das Molucas.**

Dr. FRANCISCO SOLANO PÉREZ LILA: **Navios y mercaderes nela rota occidental de Especieria.**

Dr. CIRIACO PÉREZ-BUSTAMANTE: **La expedición de Ruy Lopez de Villalobos a las Islas del Pacifico.**

V

Dr. ALBERTO IRIA: **As Ilhas Molucas no Arquivo Histórico Ultramaríno.**
Dr. JUAN PÉREZ DE TUDELA: **Repercusiones en el Atlantico delos viajes a las Molucas.**
Comandante MAX JUSTO GUEDES: **Teoria versus prática-a costa brasileira na cartografia espanhola, 1540.**

17 h: Recepção oferecida por Sua Excelência o Ministro do Ultramar no Jardim e Museu Agricola do Ultramar.

DIA 29 DE SETEMBRO
11 h: Sessão de encerramento, sob a presidência da Sua Excelência o Ministro do Ultramar, na Aula Magna do Instituto Superior de Higiene e Medicina Tropical.
Discursos do Prof. Dr. Luis Suarez Fernandez, Director-Geral de Universidades e Investigação, e do Comandante A. Teixeira da Mota, director da Secção de Lisboa do Agrupamento de Estudos de Cartografia Antiga.
12 h: Partida para a excursão à zona Estoril-Cascais-Sintra, com almoço cm Cascais.

VI

Cosmographers of Seville:
Nautical Science and Social Experience

Cosmographers worked in Europe before the great Discoveries, but they were in greatest demand when the New World was new, and they were called upon literally to take its measure, fix its image, and to comprehend and explain its nature. Their numbers were always small. When eventually institutionalized, their disciplines were astronomy, mathematics, applied physics, the technology of shipbuilding, naval armament and war, cartography and textual description. The art of navigation as practiced by them in Seville concerned all aspects of ships and their use which are subject to rule based upon observation and deliberate response to it.[1]

What one can say about the cosmographers collectively is that they were a mobile group of experts often found working outside their country of origin, and that they were remarkably versatile. Their origin could be humble, but their ranks included nobles both as practitioners and as pupils. In a time of growing nationalism the cosmographers were an international group, able to change loyalties and to command favors and pay raises from their patrons when their work was needed. The remarkable leveling of social differences, unusual during the early sixteenth century, is shown in the ad hoc councils of experts assembled in the cosmographic juntas by the Spanish crown. As a social group the cosmographers were closest to Renaissance artists, and were granted a degree of social mobility which was not found in other professions.

The stages upon which their new experience and ideas confronted old methods and notions were institutions of public life, mainly of government. How these acted as filters through which intelligence of the New World reached the Old has been the subject of a sequence of inquiries. The best way to explain what I mean is to review very briefly what I have found so far. Ample records left by the cosmographers illustrate that sixteenth-century Spain was a litigious country, increasingly administered by lawyers.[2] The true and false of anything was equated with the just and unjust and in case of conflict recourse was had to the law. A phenomenon of the social climate, this interchange of terminology had an important effect upon the development of science, upon the understanding of scientific information, projection, and experiment, and upon investment policy in technology. A court of law is the wrong forum for the advancement of science[3]; this experience was first recorded in a modern context with reference to nautical science in Spain in the sixteenth century, and it is a subject newly become relevant.[4]

Another trace left by the cosmographers was at the center of power: the Spanish court. There, under imperial and later royal sponsorship, cosmographic work was patronized throughout the sixteenth century. A high point of the patronage was reached by the offer of a prize for the best solution of the problem of longitude. Rewards went to the socially well-connected, the articulate compromisers with fact, or favorites ahead of the cautious, realistic, and busy practitioners of the cosmographic profession. The royal court was a limited forum for the advancement of nautical science, and royal patronage distorted the choice of scientific priorities which would have been made by the experts.[5]

A further brief study concerning the Spanish cosmographic juntas of the sixteenth century might have been called "Science by Consultation."[6] The critical conflict in the advance of scientific ideas and practices was the struggle between leadership and consensus—leadership based upon authority, trust, power, force, or argument, necessarily restrained by the consensus exacted from a variety of experts. The cosmographic juntas represent the social mechanism of Spain's conciliar government with respect to science. Decisions by the crown concerning the New World should not be judged without referring to the juntas and the use or neglect of their resolutions. How joint deliberation works has been a problem throughout history, and the cosmographers of Spain left

Cosmographers of Seville

a record worth exploring, especially today in an era of scientific decision.[7]

I now propose to look at the cosmographic offices and their holders. I have chosen three institutions which were intimately concerned with the *carrera de las Indias*, or convoy routes across the Atlantic:[8] the *Casa de Contratación* in Seville, the *Consejo Real y Supremo de las Indias,* and 'the Royal Academy of Mathematics in Madrid.

In this narrative there is no "first" and no "last"; for convenience the appointment in 1508 of the first Pilot Major of the *Casa de Contratación* in Seville, Amerigo Vespucci, may serve as a beginning[9] and the folding of the Madrid Academy in 1624 as an end.[10] The Pilot Major was responsible for the entire technical control of navigation of the *Casa.* He served as teacher and examiner for pilots, and for instruments and charts. He was also in charge of the *Padrón Real* or master map, begun by Juan de la Cosa and elaborated by Fernando Colón. The first Cosmographer Major in charge of instruments was Diogo Ribeiro (1523), and in 1528 Alonso de Chaves was appointed to teach and examine pilots and to test instruments and charts—which had to correspond to the *Padrón Real.* In 1552 a *cátedra* of nautical science was added, and Chaves' son Hierónymo was put in charge. The examination of pilots was for specific routes, *Tierra Firme, Nueva España,* and the *derrota* to Honduras.[11] Pilots studied nautical science and the use of charts, regiments, and instruments. The Pilot Major, cosmographers, and expert pilots gave the examinations; and instruments were tested and licensed at stated times and regular intervals by the Pilot Major and cosmographers and, upon approval, sealed for each voyage. The *Casa* was also the only official deposit of the ships' measure and its code. Every book tells us and the record shows that the charts and instruments were made, the pilots were examined, the revisions of the *Padrón* and modifications of routes and regiments were debated and instituted—but frequently not in the way the provisions stated.

While the categories of work were being defined, actually more people worked on the problems of the *carrera* than three posts could take care of. An original group of experts had been drawn to the *Casa* and obtained royal titles as cosmographers with the rights to examine pilots and to act in other capacities in the preparation of fleets or in going out with ships for reconnaissance. First, there were four Portuguese appointees—the two Reinels, father and son, and the two brothers Faleiro, Francisco serving until late in the 1560's. Pilot Major Sebastian Cabot, of Venetian origin, was a knowledgeable cosmographer active in Seville to 1547. Then there were the two Chaves and the family Gutiérrez, of whom three held official appointments: Diego the elder and his son

Diego *el moço* and Sancho, while Luís Gutiérrez worked under their supervision. Also licensed royal cosmographers were Pedro de Medina, Pedro Mexia, and the famous Alonso de Santa Cruz. This embarrassment of talent led to mutual interference and the notorious lawsuits and complaints to the *Consejo de las Indias*, but in the mid-1560's death began to take care of the problem. With the appointment of Domingo de Villaroel as cosmographer in charge of instruments, this phase ended.

Alongside the pressure on the rules of the *Casa* to accommodate royal cosmographers with their special commissions, the abuses of holding multiple offices and of nepotism developed. The Chaves and Gutiérrez families monopolized the business in the late 1550's, and Rodrigo Zamorano united all three scientific appointments of the *Casa* in his person despite repeated legislation forbidding this. He was *catedrático* of cosmography from 1575 to 1613, cosmographer in charge of instruments and charts from 1579 (without pay), and Pilot Major from 1586 to 1596 and again from 1598 to his death in 1620.[12] Zamorano also placed a son in the *cátedra de cosmografía*; moreover, he lectured at the same time on mathematics and nautical science at the University of Salamanca.

The same men served in various capacities and offices of the scientific branch of the *Casa de Contratación,* sometimes alongside members of their families. They were indispensable to the lifeline of the empire, and their varied skills reflect those expected from the men aboard ships, whose versatility for improvising in any situation marks the age of reconnaissance.

If the cosmographers' scientific work under various office titles was often interchangeable, their role in the *Casa* had been intended to prevent what actually happened—as in the case of Zamorano: as Pilot Major he could determine a route for the *Padrón*, of which he had charge as Cosmographer Major, to be followed by every pilot whom he had taught and examined as *catedrático*. He was a Pooh Bah as regards his powers to approve and disapprove the work of others. He exercised considerable power over Seville's chart and instrument market and a certain control over the *oficios de mar de la carrera de las Indias*. The possibility of abuses occurred practically simultaneously with the creation of the offices: it was to some extent unavoidable. The ambiguity inherent in the state of the nautical sciences required multiple skills from its cosmographers but restricted them to single and separate applications. Rules of the office also limited their activites in the open market.[13]

Multiple office holding and privileges sought for family connections created an institutional problem of restricted input which was aggravated by tightening the prohibition against foreigners. This so drastically diminished the chances of careers or advancement for cosmographers that after 1596 Seville no longer held an attraction for them.[14]

Cosmographers of Seville

The fate of the *cátedra de cosmografía,* introduced at the height of scientific activity and reconnaissance under the auspices of the *Casa,* reflects this course of events. Hierónymo de Chaves, himself the *cátedra's* first incumbent, requested a reduction in the required curriculum from one year to three months in 1555, after holding his position for two years. In 1565 it was reduced to two months and in 1568 these were to include feast days so as not to cost too many working days.[15] More dramatic was the reduction of requirements for the examination. The glory of Spain's scientific literature, its vernacular textbooks on navigation by which "Europe learned to sail," were wasted on its own pilots.[16] No more could be expected from them than that they could read the regiments or nautical tables, mark their charts and sign their names. Meantime the requirement for practical experience remained six years, though a concession was made for a year spent without going on a voyage if no opportunity was available.[17]

There is repeated proof of the lack of examined pilots. Ship owners petitioned for permits to put unexamined seamen in charge of their vessels. Within an entire convoy from Mexico in 1584 it was difficult to find one examined pilot for the flagship let alone two for each ship, or a pilot and a master, as required by law.[18] The 1580's and 1590's were the years of greatest scarcity of pilots in sixteenth-century Seville, and apparently the cosmographers also looked elsewhere for opportunity and reward.

This brief survey has led me to the following conclusions: 1) The definition of function for the various cosmographic offices or *cargos* does not reflect the way cosmographers actually worked. 2) The intent of the definition was to get the maximum benefit from scientific work directed toward specific goals such as safer and faster traffic, larger capacity of the fleets, and the use of less manpower. 3) The extent of the discrepancy between the definition of the job and the work actually done indicates a measure of health in the system's ability to solicit and to take advantage of scientific contributions for the solution of nautical problems. Repeated attempts to give procedure a better theoretical fit had specific reasons for failure, and the result was corrosion and corruption in the institution. The separation of intent from implementation in the Pilot Major's office became a major cause for the decay of Iberian cosmography.

The statutes of the *Consejo Real y Supremo de las Indias* (1524) provided two posts for cosmographers which were, however, not immediately filled. The *Consejo* was, of course, vitally interested in the problems of the *carrera* which was in the care of the scientific staff of the *Casa,* but apparently supervision was left to individuals, commissioned intermittently for specific tasks, who were to maintain liaison with the experts and judges in Seville.

Until the *visíta* to the *Consejo* by Juan de Ovando (1567-71), the *Consejo* supervised the cosmographic activities of the *Casa* in Seville via periodic *visítas* and liaison between scientists and experts called to Madrid.[19] In the mid-1590's complaints about the Pilot Major's office in Seville to the *Consejo's* cosmographer, Ambrosio de Ondériz, were getting so bad that he was appointed to check on the *Casa*. He died before he could finish the work, and was succeeded in this mission by Juan García de Céspedes and Luis Jorge de Barbuda, royal cosmographers. Céspedes—staying on as Pilot Major—made a new *Padrón* and six special charts. He wrote new regiments and a text on chart-making and sent out printed questionnaires to pilots about their opinions regarding charts and instruments. He designed globes, tested instruments, and made models of them.[20] After two years of whirlwind activity at the *Casa de Contratación* he returned to Madrid, leaving the scientific office in Seville breathless, relieved, and in the charge of Zamorano, who was reappointed Pilot Major by the judges. These gentlemen opted for continuing business as usual, considering their new charts and Céspedes' instruments sufficient for their purposes. The glorious days of the *Casa* as a center for scientific excitement were over as the *Consejo* reduced contact with the day-to-day work in Seville. Although the *Consejo* continued to call ad hoc juntas of cosmographers, including Seville's experts, especially about the problem of longitude, there was no longer an important group of cosmographers working together who could draw the attention of the *Consejo* to nautical problems.

The appointment which most distinguished the cosmographic work of the *Consejo Real y Supremo de las Indias* was that of the *cosmógrapho-cronista*. The format of the *crónica mayor* of the Indies, the official chronicle, was introduced by Juan de Ovando during his *visíta,* since the *Consejo* lacked systematic and complete information concerning the dominions it was appointed to administer. He obtained for the cosmographer Juan López de Velasco the title *cosmógrapho-cronista* of the *Consejo* and had him gather all information obtained over a span of the preceeding 20 years. Velasco's great *Geografía y descripción universal de las Indias*, finished in 1574, became the first statistical portrait of the New World. It contained information concerning harbors and other matters useful for the *carrera*, which was among the reasons why its contents was regarded as privileged and the work was not licensed for publication.

The *crónica* of Velasco is a mirror of the New World envisioned by Juan de Ovando when he fashioned his famous instructions for the *relaciones geográficas*.[21] To the textual description and quantitative assessments in the *relaciones* were to be added cartographic representations according to rules which accompanied them. Though several people played a part in the evolution of the *relaciones*, Ovando introduced the technique of the periodic questionnaire to the *Consejo de las Indias*, and Velasco, its cosmographer, was the first to put it to use. In the contemporary practice of European colonial government, the *relaciones geográficas* represent a first appearance of a systematically constructed and periodically amended factual base, an indispensable aid to policy makers. Quantitative analysis had thus far been reserved to bankers, military men, and the Church. The purpose of this information was to give the *Consejo* an alternative base for decisions which heretofore had to depend upon rival claims by its colonial administrators. The *relaciones* represent an innovation compared to preceding and contemporary censuses with respect to three associated elements which must be taken together—their scope, their evolution, and their institutionalization— which were the reasons for their lasting into the nineteenth century. The first true heirs of the *relaciones* were to be the U.S. Coast and Geodetic Service together with the U.S. census.

This view of the *relaciones* as a comprehensive model of the New World is in harmony with the geniuses of the builders of the Escorial. It was equalled by the simultaneous commission given to Velasco to collect and order all legislation then in existence concerning the Indies.[22] The problems of enumeration, depiction, and explanation, so much with us in our multimedia world, were foreshadowed in the literature of the cosmographers of the Indies. Progress in cartography and the quantitative assessment of natural and social phenomena can be described as two impacts the New World had on the Old, and the cosmographers of the *Consejo de las Indias* were the people who registered them in their work.[23]

The Philippine Academy of Mathematics, opening its doors to students on 1 January 1584, presents yet another setting for nautical science in Spain in the sixteenth century.[24] When Philip stayed in Lisbon as the new king of Portugal from 1581 to 1583, he was greatly impressed with the scientific talent he found there and he raided both Lisbon's and Coimbra's scientific establishments. His architect, Juan de Herrera, had advised him that the best nautical scientist, who would be able to reconcile the discrepancies between the Castilian and Portuguese charts with respect to the Line of Demarcation, was João Bautista Labanha.[25] So Philip named him to the first chair of his new academy. He was joined by Ondériz, Luis Jorge de Barbuda, Julián Ferrufino, Juan Cedillo Diaz, Pedro Rodrigues Muñoz, and other luminaries of the epoch. They decided to render classical scientific texts into the vernacular and then to produce their own texts. Thus a whole library of works on mathematics, cosmography, and military and nautical science in all its branches issued from the *cátedras*. While the work of translation centered on the classics, the Copernican theory was freely debated, and Cristóbal de Rojas wrote the first treaty in Spanish on artillery and fortification. Among the students were many nobles and men at court who cultivated the sciences: el Conde de Puñorostro D. Francisco Arias de Bobadilla, el Marqués de Moya D. Francisco Pacheco, D. Ginés de Rocamora, Antonio de León Pinelo, and D. Bernardino de Mendoza, lately ambassador to France and England.[26] D. Ginés de Rocamora y Torrano was a representative for the city of Burgos in the *Cortes* of Castile who attended classes in Madrid and then upon request of his friends set himself up as a teacher of mathematics and of "the sphere."[27]

Nautical problems of the *carrera de las Indias* and of the Manila Galleon had meantime been taken up in the New World. A famous and popular text on the art of navigation, the *Instrucción nautica*, was published in Mexico by the *Oidor*, Diego García de Palacio, in 1587, and the viceroys of New Spain and of Peru sponsored voyages of reconnaissance duly staffed with knowledgeable pilots and cosmographers.[28] The metropolitan orientation of the personnel of the Madrid academy also explains why the institution soon favored the study of artillery and the requisite mathematics and physics over its cosmographic concerns. Ondériz was dead, and Labanha left Spain for Flanders on a genealogical commission. The military nature of research for securing the naval link with the empire ranked increasingly above either reconnaissance or experimentation in the later Habsburg regime and in 1624 all that was left of the academy was absorbed by the *Colegio Imperial*, a Jesuit institution.[29]

The history of the academy has not yet been written. Its contributions appear under the proper rubric in the history of science, mathematics, physics, astronomy, and mechanics—or wherever its scientists added to the intellectual ferment which produced the scientific revolution. Insofar as their excellence made them notable, the cosmographers of the academy were absorbed into the non-Spanish story, and the rest has been forgotten. The paradox is that the scientific work, most advanced in content and sophistication and precursor of later European academies and scientific societies, responding to the cosmographic problems raised by Spain's vast dominions, has been totally neglected because it had no sequel. The direct contributions of the academy were inspired by the new source of speculation and experiment: the nautical link and the delimitation of the Spanish empire which it was the intent of the crown to define, maintain or improve. The failure of the academy, its lack of sequel, is in part due to the divorce from its source of inspiration: the nautical sciences and the New World. The cosmographic concerns of the academy were scattered instead in "safe" mathematical speculations. Information from Seville, such as the extraordinary *Itinerario* of Juan de Escalante, a gathering of experience in Atlantic navigation of the *carrera* over many years, was not allowed to be published.[30] Moreover, the limitation of foreign contacts under the later Philips tore the net of international correspondence. The cosmographers were thus cut off not only from their source of problems, but also from the stimulation they received in the exchange of experience and ideas with their foreign colleagues.[31] The link with Seville which was the origin of the academy has been completely ignored by those who lament the institution's passing, ascribing it exclusively to the Jesuits. They did indeed deal the final blow, but I believe that the collapse of the link to Seville ranks as an important cause for the barrier to Spanish advance in science.

CONCLUSIONS

In response to demands for improving the nautical link with the New World, the first public lay institution in Europe for science and technology came into being in Seville. Its success made a routine of adventure. This was the achievement of the cosmographers who staffed the scientific offices of the *Casa de Contratación* and who advised the *Consejo* and the crown. Their accomplishments have so far been assessed with respect to the individual contributions to various scientific disciplines which constitute a most obvious "blunted impact" on European scientific thought by the naval link of the Iberian empires.

But if one looks to history for the answers "which the past gives to successive futures," in Leonard Krieger's words,[32] then one is struck by the role which social experience played in this story. It influenced the choice of problems raised by the Discoveries and Conquests as well as the conditions for their solution. As Michael Baxandall[33] in a recent book has called attention to the social experience of painters in fifteenth-century Italy to explain its bearing upon style and therefore a vital aspect of art, so can the nature and role of successive forums for science, created in response to the demands of the maritime link with the New World, shed light on two problems which are newly with us: the role of social restraint in shaping the physical sciences, and in evolving the scientific professions.[34]

NOTES

1. The current state of research on the subject is best reflected in the following publications: *Boletim internacional de bibliografia luso-brasileira*, Fundação Calouste Gulbenkian (Lisbon), "Bibliographie des grandes routes maritimes," which from vol. 9:2 (1968) to vol. 14:1 (1973) covers the nautical literatures of Germany, Denmark, France, Poland, USA, Spain, Greece, Great Britain; *Recueils de la Société Jean Bodin pour l'histoire comparative des institutions* (23 vols. Brussels 1972); Publications of the Agrupamento de estudos de cartografia, Junta de investigações do Ultramar (Lisbon: *Série separata*, irregularly since 1961, over 80 articles by now; *Série memórias*, since 1963; Armando Cortesão, *Cartografia e cartógrafos portugueses dos séculos XV e XVI* (2 vols. Lisbon 1935); Armando

Cortesão and Avelino Teixeira da Mota, *Portugaliae monumenta cartographica* (6 vols. Lisbon 1960-62). I am especially obliged to A. Teixeira da Mota of Lisbon for his untiring support and much bibliographical information. Armando Cortesão and Luis de Albuquerque of Coimbra have also been prompt with answers and most liberal with advice and help. See also Huguette and Pierre Chaunu, *Séville et l'Atlantique (1504-1650)* (8 vols. Paris 1955-59); *Colloques internationaux d'histoire maritime* (Paris 1956-62); *El tratado de Tordesillas y su proyección*, Segundas Jornadas Americanistas, Valladolid, 1972 (2 vols. Valladolid 1973).

2. Richard L. Kagan, "Universities in Castile 1500-1700," *Past & Present* 49 (1970) 44-71, and his *Students and Society in Early Modern Spain* (Baltimore 1974); Juan Linz, "Intellectual Roles in Sixteenth and Seventeenth Century Spain," *Daedalus* 101 (1972) 59-108.

3. Ursula Lamb, "Science by Litigation, A Cosmographic Feud," *Terrae Incognitae* 1 (1969) 40-57.

4. John Maynard Smith, *New Scientist* 63:911 (1974) 476: "It does not seem to me that the method of advocacy helps in understanding science."

5. Ursula Lamb, "La nueva ciencia geográfica. (Una víctima del sistema de concursos. Premios españoles para la solución de los problemas de la longitud)," *Revista de Occidente* 110 (1972) 162-183.

6. Ursula Lamb, "The Spanish Cosmographic Juntas of the Sixteenth Century," *Terrae Incognitae* 6 (1974) 51-62. This is a mere pilot study.

7. For instance, John D. Bernal showed "how a conclusive result could be obtained from a number of individually inconclusive observations." See J. G. Crowther, "John Desmond Bernal, An Appreciation," *New Scientist* 51:770 (1971) 666, quoting Sir Lawrence Bragg about the "peculiar genius of Bernal in the strategy of science." Such possibilities were apparently visualized in the Spanish juntas.

8. José Pulido Rubio, *El piloto mayor . . .* (ed. 2 enlarged, Seville 1950) 452 ff, gives a list of *oficios* of the *carrera* and coast guard.

9. *Ibid.*, Appendix I to Part I, "Titulo de Piloto Mayor para Amerigo Vespuche," 460-464.

10. Martín Fernández de Navarrete, *Obras*, Biblioteca de Autores Españoles 75-77 (3 vols. Madrid 1954-55) 3.363-364.

11. Eventually examinations were sought in the Canary Islands (Archivo General de las Indias, Patronato 261, Ramo 10) by the Piloto Mayor del Juzgado de las Indias, Isla de las Palmas; and finally the Buenos Aires route was added as examination subject for the *carrera*.

12. Pulido Rubio (n. 8 above) 670, 679, 681, 682, Ch. III.

13. *Recopilación de leyes de los reynos de las Indias* (4 vols. Madrid 1681) Ley III, Titulo XXIII, Libro LX strictly prohibits the sale of instruments and charts by the Pilot Major and cosmographers of the *Casa*. Since the aim of the legislation was, however, to promote creative work and not to stifle it, they were allowed to make globes, charts and instruments for sale outside of Seville, always barring the use of *derrotas* and other information reserved to the *carrera*, a nearly fatal restriction; Archivo General de Indias, Indiferente General, 1957, Libro IV fol. 241V, 4 Dec. 1591.

14. Domingo de Villaroel was the last of the foreign cosmographers at the *Casa*. He settled down to live with a Florentine colleague in Bordeaux where he did a thriving business in the sale of instruments and charts which he designed. Pulido Rubio (n. 8 above) 693-694. The problem of the contribution of foreigners to the work of the *Casa* is a major topic which I am still working out. Considering the feelings of mutual dislike, an instruction by the Spanish king that Portuguese pilots teach Spaniards in 1612 shows the desperate situation in Spain. I find a number of foreign cosmographers working throughout the Habsburg regime, usually on royal commissions, but no longer named to the offices in either the *Casa* or the *Consejo*. José Frazão de Vasconcelos, *Subsídios para a história da carreira da India no tempo dos Filipes* (Lisbon 1960) 9.

15. Arch. Gen. Indias, Indiferente General, 1967, Libro XVI fol. 312, 25 Feb. 1568. *Ibid.*, 28 March 1568, Aranjuez, fol. 358V, answer by the judges.

16. Julio F. Guillén y Tato, "Europa aprendió a navegar en libros españoles," Contribución del Museo Naval de Madrid a la *Exposición nacional del libro del mar* (Barcelona 1943).

Cosmographers of Seville

17. José Veitia Linaje, *Norte de la contratación de las Indias occidentales* (Seville 1672; Buenos Aires 1945) Lib. II, Cap. XII, 9.

18. Luís Navarro García, "Pilotos, maestres y señores de naos en la carrera de las Indias," *Archivo Hispalense* 2a época, 46-47 (1967) 240-295. On 276 it refers to "la flota de Don Domingo de Alcega a Nueva España . . . Arch. Gen. Indias, Contratación, 5780." In Chaunu (n. 1 above) 3.372, there appears the "Armada y Flota de Nueva España, Capt. General Diego de Alcega, Départ de la Vera Cruz, 16 mai 1585." Alcega is further identified by Ernst Schäfer in his *Índice de la colección de documentos inéditos de las Indias* (2 vols. Madrid 1946) 1.13.

19. Ernst Schäfer, *El Consejo real y supremo de las Indias* (2 vols. Seville 1935-47) 1.118.

20. He also furnished the room of the *Cátedra* in the Alcazar with three large tables, one small one, and three benches. Arch. Gen. Indias, Patronato, 262, Ramo 2, Céspedes, contains the whole list of his expenses and activities.

21. Richard Konetzke, "Die 'Geographischen Beschreibungen' als Quellen zur Hispanoamerikanischen Bevölkerungsgeschichte der Kolonialzeit," *Jahrbuch für Geschichte von Staat, Wirtschaft und Gesellschaft Lateinamerikas* 7 (1970) 1-75; Erwin Walter Palm "Estilo cartográfico y tradición humanista en las Relaciones Geográficas de 1579-1581," in *Atti del XL Congresso internazionale degli Americanisti, Roma, Genova, 1972*, International Congress of the Americanists, Proceedings, 1972 (3 vols. Genoa 1974) 3.195-203; *Handbook of Middle American Indians* 12, Guide to Ethnohistorical Sources, Part 1, ed. Howard F. Cline (Austin, Tex. 1972) has the latest survey of the *relaciones*.

22. *Recopilación de leyes* (n. 13 above) to serve as a base for future governments. José de la Peña y Cámara, "La copulata de leyes de Indias y las ordenanzas ovandinas," *Revista de Indias* 2:6 (1941) 121-146; Juan Manzano y Manzano, "La visita de Ovando al Real Consejo de las Indias y el código ovandino," in *El Consejo de las Indias en el siglo XVI*, Primeras Jornadas Americanistas, Valladolid, 1969 (Valladolid 1970) 111-123.

23. One aspect of special interest to me which this paper gives me no chance to explore is the relationship between the method of description and representation of intent. In the arts and philosophy this problem is of current interest. With respect to geography see H. C. Darby, "The Problem of Geographical Description," *The Institute of British Geographers, Transactions and Papers* 30 (1962) 1-14. M. Salmon, "Representation and Intention in Art," paper read to the Philosophical Society of Philadelphia (Oct. 1974), to be published in the *Philosophical Quarterly*, discusses Nelson Goodman's *Languages of Art* (Indianapolis 1968) and his critic Paul Ziff in *Philosophical Review* 80 (1971) 509-515; see also Ernst H. Gombrich, *Meditations on a Hobby Horse* (London 1963), especially "Expression and Communication," 56-70.

24. The scattered information concerning the academy is still being assembled. I have not found any modern work on it. Interest in the academies of the sixteenth century has concentrated on Italy, France, and England, while Spain would bear out points made by these investigations and would strengthen the argument of the need for liaison between the artisan-artist engineers and the courtiers. See Joseph Ben-David, "The Scientific Role: The Conditions of its Establishment in Europe," *Minerva* 4 (1965) 15-54, bibliographical note 52.

For the institution see: José Augusto Sánchez Pérez, *Las matemáticas en la Biblioteca del Escorial* (Madrid 1929). Most important for the nautical aspects of the story: Navarrete, *Obras* (n. 10 above) 3.355-388; José Fernández Montaña, *Felipe II el Prudente, rey de España, en relación con artes y artistas, con ciencias y sabios* (Madrid 1912) 341, gives a *cedula* of 31 January 1584 addressed to Diego Corzana, paymaster of the Alcázar of Madrid, to pay 22,500 maravedis to the "rectora y Beatas de Santa Catalina de Sena" for the rent of a house "which has been taken for us, located in la Puerta de Balnadu where mathematics are taught." In the following pages appear documents concerning individual mathematicians and cosmographers.

25. George Kubler, *Portuguese Plain Architecture: Between Spices and Diamonds, 1521-1706* (Middletown, Conn. 1972). See also Cortesão, *Cartografia* (n. 1 above) 294-356, and Francisco Marques de Sousa Viterbo, *Trabalhos náuticos dos portuguezes nos séculos XVI e XVII* (2 vols. Lisbon 1898-1900); Picatoste and Navarrete also have short biographies.

26. Navarrete, *Obras* (n. 10 above) 3. 361. Antonio de León Pinelo, the famous jurist

VI

who became *cronista mayor de las Indias* in 1658, was a student of Juan Cedillo Diaz when he made the "new Nautical and Geographic plan for the use of navigation." León Pinelo himself wrote on the problem of longitude and compiled writings he referred to as "Oceano Universal," among other titles. These manuscripts have not been published nor have they survived intact. Antonio León Pinelo, *El gran canciller de las Indias,* ed. Guillermo Lohmann Villena (Seville 1953) Ch. v, especially cxxxviii-cxxxix.

27. Agustín González de Amezúa, *Andanzas y meditaciones de un procurador castellano en las Cortes de Madrid de 1592-1598* (Madrid 1945) 143. Ginés de Rocamora y Torrano, *Sphera del Universo* (Madrid 1599) is marked "Vendese en el Palacio." It contains a dedicative sonnet to the author by Lope de Vega.

28. C. R. Boxer, "Portuguese and Spanish Projects for the Conquest of Southeast Asia, 1580-1600," *The Journal of Asian History* 3 (1969) 118-136, esp. 132-134.

29. Navarrete, *Obras* (n. 10 above) 3.417 ff.

30. The Itinerario of *Escalante* survives in various manuscripts. The Museo Naval has the maps which were drawn for it. Admiral Julio Guillén had planned to publish an edition of this great work which has been printed from an uncorrected copy by Fernández Duro in *Disquisiciones Náuticas* 5 (Madrid 1880) 415-515.

The policy of secrecy could be absurdly counterproductive as when the biography of a religious who worked in the Philippines contained a "roteiro" of her voyage. The book, *Perfecta religiosa . . . la vida de la Madre Gerónima de la Asunción . . .,* was printed in Puebla, Mexico in 1662. The Council of the Indies ordered that the roteiro and description of Manila be deleted from the copies remaining for sale. The result was that the printed pages were sold as a separate booklet and without the burden of the life of the "perfecta religiosa." Ursula Lamb, "Some Books Relating to Colonial Latin America," *The Yale University Library Gazette* 42 (1967) 19.

31. The continued interest of data from the *carrera* for scientists and cosmographers is proven by the work of Pedro Porter, who wrote extensively on problems of longitude, stellar observations and instruments. He sailed as admiral of the Indies fleet. He and Ruesta found their audience in Madrid and not in Seville. For documentation, Museo Naval, MS 119; Navarrete (n. 10 above) 3.3; Pedro Porter y Casanate, *Reparo a errores da la navegación española,* ed. W. Michael Mathes (Madrid 1970). For an admirable summary see Ricardo del Arco, "El Almirante Pedro Porter y Casanate, explorador del Golfo de California," *Revista de Indias* 8 (1947) 783-844.

32. Leonard Krieger, "The Autonomy of Intellectual History," *Journal of the History of Ideas* 34 (1973) 499-516, esp. 516.

33. Michael Baxandall, *Painting and Experience in Fifteenth Century Italy* (Oxford 1972).

34. For a general orientation to this topic in the literature about the rise of modern science, I refer the reader to Ben-David (n. 24 above). I am aware of the controversy over the importance, or lack of it, of nautical science in this respect.

VII

The Sevillian Lodestone: Science and Circumstance

Among geographical discoveries of the New World, that of the Atlantic Ocean preceded that of the land. Continued exploration played a major role throughout the sixteenth century as the convoy routes from Spain to the Caribbean and Meso-american coastlines were established. The *Carrera de Indias* between Spain and the Indies depended heavily on the development of nautical science. The story of the Sevillian lodestone shows how pressures now well known to modern research, grew alongside modern science. A brief prelude introduces us to the subject, time, and place of the story. In the month of August 1269, Petrus Peregrinus summed up his observations concerning the magnetic properties of the lodestone in a famous letter to his friend Sigerus de Foucaucourt. His systematic discourse on magnetism and the properties of the lodestone was not improved upon until the publication of William Gilbert's *De Magnete*, published in 1600. Although the works of both Peregrinus and Gilbert have recently been subject to revised interpretations regarding their respective advances in science, my use of their names in this context is not invalidated.[1] In his book, Gilbert mentions Peregrinus as a worthy observer, and no one else was known among contemporaries to have improved usefully on those early "philosophical experiments" during the 331 intervening years. This long hiatus between systematically matching hypoteses to observations of the magnetic properties of the lodestone is particularly interesting in view of the intensive use of the compass throughout the years of reconnaissance and of exploration of the oceans. It is stranger still, considering the extensive litigation concerning a particular lodestone, its use and control, in the Spanish courts in Sevilla and Madrid, during the 1560s.[2] The case centered around one special activity, the feeding, i.e., remagnetising of ships'

---

[1] Petrus Peregrinus, *The letter of Petrus Peregrinus on the Magnet, A. D. 1269*, trans. Brother Arnold (New York, 1904), pp. xi, xvi.

[2] On the manufacture and history of the compass see W. D. Waters, *The Art of Navigation in England in Elizabethan and Stuart Times* (New Haven: Yale University Press, 1958), chapter 3; Park Benjamin, *The History of Electricity* (New York: John M. Wiley & Sons, 1898), chapters 7 and 8 give an account of the development from Peregrinus to Robert Norman's *The Newe Attractive*, of 1587. Luis de Albuquerque, *Contribucao das navegacoes do seculo XVI para o conhecimento do magentismo terrestre*, Centro de Estudos de Historia e de Cartografia Antiga Serie Separatas, NO. XLIV (Lisbon, 1970) discusses the progress of nautical science, stressing the action of the compass with respect to ascertaining longitude. As long as the cause for the "virtue" of the compass was sought in the stellar sky, a correlation of cause and effect of magnetism was impossible.

Terrae Incognitae 19, 1987, pp. 29–39. © Wayne State University Press, 1988.

compasses before each oceanic voyage, which was supervised by the Pilot Major's office of the Casa de la Contratación de las Indias or House of Trade in Sevilla.[3]

During the controversy over that lodestone, circumstances conspired to have it assessed for economic advantage of its monopolistic use, for legal rights of ownership, for political and social prestige accruing to the owner and user, and for the supernatural powers possibly inherent in its "virtue." Such approaches precluded experiment with the stone itself by "dispassionate" scientists, and public or open discussion or sharing of knowledge by instrument designers was not to be expected. The result, instead of an increase, was rather a diminution of knowledge. The story of Sancho Gutiérrez' lodestone is one of progress in science stifled by circumstance, and yet preparing the ground for it. To relate these circumstances requires narrative and digression. This, in turn, demands patience for a story however telescoped it may be, but it does not preclude a final attempt to substantiate the argument.

The leading character in the case was Sancho Gutiérrez who was attached to the Pilot Major's office of the Casa de la Contratación de las Indias since 1553 with the title of cosmographer in charge of the fabrication of charts and of instruments.[4] The subject of the story is a lodestone which is mentioned in the following passage from a report to the king about the state of cosmography at the Casa by the *catedrático del arte de navegar y de cosmografía,* who was then Hieronymo de Chaves:

> ... I inform your Majesty that the master instrument and chartmaker, Diego Gutiérrez, died in Sevilla, and that he left a lodestone with which the navigational compasses are manufactured, which stone is the best one known to exist in all of Christendom in our time.... and that among the heirs there is dissention concerning it so that the stone might be lost or stolen. I would advise your Majesty that it would be convenient to take the stone, and to pay the owners what is judged to be its value; and that it be put in the Casa de la Contratación of Sevilla for the use by all mariners. This would be a very great benefit which your Majesty would grant them because, for the lack of that lodestone, and because there is none other with which the compasses could be as well made, one would have to go to other kingdoms (to find them) which would cause notable damage and inconvenience... [5]

[3] José Pulido Rubio, *El Piloto Mayor* (Sevilla: Escuela de Estudios Hispano Americanos, enlarged edition 1950), pp. 313–32, has the only account of the subject of this paper which is based upon the documents of appeals from the archive of the *Consejo de Indias.* The first depositions are missing, and the bundles are in part unpaginated with documents and duplicates interfiled, and in no chronological order. See *Archivo General de Indias* (hereafter cited as AGI) Justicia 792, Lib. V. 2 Ramos. For rules of the *Casa* applicable to the supervision of instruments see Joaquín F. Pacheco, Francisco de Cardenas, and Luís Torres de Mendoza, eds. *Colección de documentos inéditos relativos al descubrimiento, conquista, y organizacion de las antiguas posesiones españoles de ultramar,* 25 vols.; 25: 288–91 "de los instrumentos" which has provision of 1564 and 1565.

[4] Pulido Rubio, *El Piloto Mayor,* pp. 982 and 90, note 42; Archivo General de Indias, Contratación 5784, fol. 65v. Madrid, May 8, 1553.

[5] José Toribio Medina, *Biblioteca Hispano Americana, 1494–1810,* Facs. ed. 2 vols. (Santiago de Chile, 1958–1962), 1: 305–6. This item is not dated, but the content suggests that it was part of the inquiry of 1563–65; ext in AGI Indiferente 2005, autografo, Jieronimo de Chaves (1554)

The most unusual occurrence in the prolonged dispute over this lodestone was witnessed by the citizens of Sevilla on May 21st of 1565, when the jail doors of the Casa de la Contratación de las Indias clanged shut behind Sancho Gutiérrez, one of the three royal cosmographers who held his title from King Philip II of Castile, León, etc.[6] Sancho Gutiérrez came to that place under arrest by the Casa's police officer for the following reason: The officer had been sent to take from Sancho Gutiérrez, by force if necessary, the lodestone which was used to remagnetize the compasses carried by the ships, then assembling in convoy for the annual voyage to the Indies.[7]

Sancho Gutiérrez remonstrated with the alguacil, refused to follow the judge's order, and insisted that by virtue of his office, and since the stone was his property, he had the exclusive right to service the compasses where and when he pleased. He declared that he was entitled to refuse this service and withhold certification of the instruments, which was required of every pilot before departure. He said he would be ready to bring his stone to the Casa if the alguacil were accompanied by an accredited secretary. Sancho Gutiérrez could hold the entire fleet in harbor, and he was doing so by keeping the stone in his pocket.[8]

The effect of this action was like touching the leaf of a mimosa tree which results in a chain reaction and the collapse of all leaves. Everyone came down on Sancho Gutiérrez because everyone stood to lose. Passengers required extra supplies, food would spoil because of longer storage, animals would need more forage, and cargos could be tampered with after manifests had been sealed as happened whenever chance permitted.[9] The result was loss to legitimate trade and traffic, and profit only to crime. Moreover the danger that sailors might desert was ever present in any harbor, and beyond such problems, there was always the progress of the season, and the worsening weather on both sides of the Atlantic, since even the traditional departure date was already later than optimum wind conditions allowed. Pilots and masters, sailors and passengers, shipowners, merchants and bankers, the officials of the Casa, and several judges, all were inconvenienced; some were injured, defrauded, robbed, and ruined. Such were the grievances of the people in front of the prison gate, and Sancho Gutiérrez, with a host of furious people in violent pursuit, had managed to get himself behind it.

---

[6] AGI Justicia 792, No. 5, Ro. 2, fol. XXXVIII.

[7] Huguette et Pierre Chaunu, *Séville et l'Atlantique (1504–1650)*, 8 vols. in 10 (Paris: SEVPEN, 1955–1959), 3: 38–42; The authors discuss the details of the troubled departure of that fleet, but no mention is made of the cosmographers, nor is the incident specifically mentioned in the official report to the king printed in *Colección de documentos de Fernández de Navarrete que posée el Museo Naval*, vol. XXI, fol. 466. AGI Justicia 792, No. 5, Ro. 1. In a petition of 13 March 1566, Sancho Gutiérrez requests compensation for having examined and licensed the instruments of the *armada and flota* of Pedro de las Roëlas.

[8] AGI Justicia 792, NO. 5, Ro. 1; Ro. 2, 1 December 1564. The story of the delayed departure of the fleet is described in the report cited above by Álvaro Bazán who mentions the state of the ships in need of caulking and painting as well as provisioning, but no special mention of trouble with the instruments. These may be included in the phrase: "no podran salir a 20 deste como lo escribi a V. M. *por no estar adelante el despacho dellas.* . . Navarrete, *Op. Cit.* vol. XXI, p. 466; see also AGI Justicia 792, Lib. V Ro. 2: "*. . .No se aceban las agujas a los pilotos que agora se aprestan para la primera flota.*"

[9] Chaunu, *Séville et l'Atlantique*, p. 38.

The concerns of all these people drew attention to issues removed from the cause: the unique magnetic properties of the lodestone. Just for good measure, one might add that Sancho Gutiérrez' aggravations were vastly increased by his new surroundings, the dank, humid, and stinking premises of the jail which offended the likes of he who had worked in the Casa de la Contratación for years.[10] The newest prisoner was roughly treated, but he was to stay for one day only, being released upon the promise that he would return with the stone to the Casa. Although he had to compromise his principles with regard to the stone Sancho Gutiérrez' determination to justify his claims resulted in his pressing formal charges against the officers of the Casa. These are based on old and varied grievances which characteristically divided the pilots, masters, and cosmographers into opposing parties.

The scene is always Sevilla, with an occasional injunction or decision emanating from the Council of the Indies, or the crown in Madrid. The Pilot Major's office was located in the Casa de la Contratación where the royal cosmographers were charged with supervision of the technical aspects of navigation of the Spanish traffic with the Indies.

Over the years there had developed a backlog of grievances among officials in the Pilot Major's office concerning various theoretical and practical aspects of what was justly called the art of navigation. The cosmographers had frequently sought judicial decisions regarding the manufacture, use, and supervision of instruments, as well as for their conflicts over the "two scale" map, which had been an attempt to deal with the effects of magnetic variation of the compass upon the design of marine charts.[11] In most disputes two families of cosmographers had been on opposite sides, the Gutiérrez' and the Chaves'. The decision to forbid the use of the two scale map had been a defeat for Diego Gutiérrez, father of three sons who followed his profession, Diego "el moço," Sancho, and Luys. Although Sancho had in fact favored the winning position of Alonso de Chaves in that case, the first appointment to the post of catedrático del arte de navegar y de cosmografía had gone to Hieronymo de Chaves, the rival aspirant, in 1553.[12] He was seven years younger than Sancho Gutiérrez, and was the only son of Alonso de Chaves, who held the title of Pilot Major during the fight over the lodestone. Sancho cited both father and son in his suit. A witness for Sancho declared that: "they [Sancho Gutiérrez and the Chaves] had not spoken for years", and "no word had passed between them"; another testified to "having seen [sic] no words of good intent pass from one to the other,"[13] which goes to show the decorum which those who favored Sancho Gutiérrez found it advisable to favor even when they volunteered to testify against the powerful, but esteemed, Hieronymo de Chaves, the catedrático and Alonso de Chaves, the Pilot Major.

---

[10] The jail was ordered built in 1532. There was mention of enlarging it in 1549. Later a complaint was registered in "advertencias de pilotos y maestres" AGI Patronato 259, Ro. 41; and again Indiferente General 739, fol. 328; Indiferente General 1088, Registro de Peticiones, 1584.

[11] Ursula Lamb, "Science by Litigation: A Cosmographic Feud," *Terrae Incognitae* 1 (1969): 40–58.

[12] Martín Fernández de Navarrete, *Biblioteca Marítima*, 2 vols. (Facs. reprint, New York: Burt Franklin, 1968), 2: 563–65 brings a biography of Gerónimo de Chaves.

[13] AGI Justicia 792, No. V, Ro. 1, fol. XLVIIIv.

The pilots and masters of the carrera ships were also immediately affected by the conflict. They complained about the lack of service on their instruments, and they testified that sometimes Sancho hid the stone and that they did not want to have to depend upon his good will nor be forced to go to his house for the remagnetizing of their compasses.[14] The pilots and masters, in their defense against Sancho Gutiérrez, who had sued them separately, were represented by four of their number, Juan Canelas, Alonso Pérez de Nizo, Diego de Lepe, and Marcos Falcón. They responded to the questionnaire of the advocates in the name of the rest. It must be mentioned that Sancho Gutiérrez had his own friends among the pilots, so that the opposition did not come from the *Universidad de Pilotos y Maestres*, nor from one of the *cofradias*, but only from an ad hoc party.[15] The bitter partisanship among cosmographers and pilots was a recurring and damaging reality of the naval establishment in Sevilla. It was due to the large element of insecurity regarding scientific explanation and prediction of so many new phenomena which were encountered on the voyages by the *pilotos de altura*. In his own behalf, Sancho expressed frustration and abuse toward the pilots of the opposing side "who know nothing either about using the compasses nor about examining them, being ignorant of principles and in practice . . . not one of them understands the technique, nor do they know how to examine instruments."[16]

Many merchants chose sides in the quarrel depending upon their relation with the Gutiérrez family as shipowners or business partners. Sancho had been involved in a protracted suit over the loss of one of the ships which he owned jointly with Jacomé Luys and Pedro Álvarez Ariscado, the *Nuestra Señora de la Concepción*.[17] She had been commanded, by the general of the returning convoy, to rescue a sinking treasure ship, the *San Marcos*, and to tow her into Cartagena, at the expense of her own cargo and with the loss of two weeks time. She missed the rendezvous in Havana, making port in Lisbon due to another storm. On her final leg home she was wrecked off Cascales with all hands, passengers, and cargo. Justified claims for the prize money, which had been earned for rescue of the treasure, were compounded with claims for

[14] Ibid., "Los pilotos y maestres sobre una piedra yman," Madrid, 2 June 1563. The compass consisted of a "box covered with glass and fitted with a removable wooden base in the upper center of which was fixed a brass pin or pivot for the needle or fly. . . . Before assembly the compass needle or wires were "fed" by being touched with "the face of the stone." Waters, *The Art of Navigation*, pp. 27-28.

[15] Luis Navarro García, "Pilotos, Maestres y Señores de Naos en la Carrera de las Indias," *Archivo Hispalense*, 2da epoca, 141–146 (1967): 241–295, 283ff, and 291.

[16] AGI Justicia 792, NO. V, Ro. 1, fol. XV: ". . . notoria cos es que ningún dellos entienden la teoría ni saben examinar los dichos ynstrumentos." Mistakes commonly found are listed by William Barlow in *The Navigator's Supply* (1597), cited by D. W. Waters, *The Art of Navigation*, p. 28: "The fly unequally divided; the wires of the fly imperfectly joined, eccentrically mounted, rusty, roughly cut, and, to level up the fly, daubed with wax; the capital set on the fly eccentrically, likewise the pin in the base on which it pivoted; the glass cover cracked or gnarled, ill-cut, or worse, set into the cover with an excess of resin; the gimbals so imperfectly made 'that you should offer a tinker discredit to compare his work with this'; the riveting of the gimbals done with iron; iron nails holding gimbals in position, and iron nails used in the making of the very binnacle." Sancho Gutiérrez' witnesses numbered 32 of whom only 23 could sign their names.

[17] AGI Justicia 765, No. 5, Año 1554, this comes in seven separate pieces.

replacement of the lost ship when the case came to court, and on appeal, reached the Council of the Indies. This suit, which is preserved in great detail, involved many aspects of maritime law as it defined the distribution of economic advantage and liability, and of social status and personal prestige, which played a major role in the proceedings. Since Jacomé Luys, who had sailed as *maestro*, was dead, it fell to Sancho Gutiérrez to fight his case as well, and in the end he carried it alone. Among the merchant community, however, Sancho also had friends as well as sworn enemies.[18]

There is no physical description of any member of the Gutiérrez family.[19] Diego had brought up his three sons in the business of instrument making and chart design from childhood. Diego, the oldest, worked in his father's house, as did Sancho. Luys had set himself up with a separate shop, bringing up his own children to help in the business. Diego the elder, in his testament deposited in 1552, left the famous lodestone which had come to him as a wedding gift, to Sancho. Diego el moço inherited his father's proprietary rights to the post of cosmographer in charge of instruments and charts at the Casa, and Sancho earned a regular income by servicing the instruments of the carrera de Indias, as well as selling instruments and charts on the open market. Luys, to all appearances, was left empty handed. Sancho stated that the will specified that he should inherit

> an Indian slave called Alonso, then ten years old. . . . a horse, saddled and bridled, a silver platter and a silver salt cellar, and *a lodestone with which they magnetize the compasses*, so that I could avail myself of it as did my father during his life.[20]

Diego the testator died in 1554, and the younger Diego followed him in his post at the Casa without incident. But a quarrel arose between Sancho and Luys over the use of the lodestone, which Luys claimed he was accustomed to use in the manufacture of his compasses. So Luys declared the will illegal, at least as interpreted by Sancho. Eventually the complaint went before the judges, but the brothers reached an agreement whereby Luys was to be allowed the use of the lodestone in his manufacture, and Sancho alone would be entitled to use it for the examination of instruments of the carrera. This, he claimed in his complaint of 1563, brought him 500 ducados per annum for licensing fees, a sum which was essential to "feed and sustain his person, his house and his family."[21]

---

[18] In the case of the lodestone Sancho Gutiérrez presented as a witness for himself a rich merchant, Álvarez Arriscado "que es notorio que vale mas que veinte mil ducados. . . ." details of his holdings in real estate etc. are then given. AGI Justicia 792, No. IV, Ro. 2, fol. XXXVII.

[19] There exists a picture of Hieronymo de Chaves giving his age as 22 years old (in 1545) engraved on the front page of his book *Tractado de la Sphera que compuso el doctor Ioannes Sacrobusto, con muchas addiciones;* Agora nuevamente traducido del latin por el bachiller Hieronimo de Chaves, el cual anadio muchas figuras, tablas y claras demostraciones juntamente con unas breves scholios necesarios a mayor illucidacion, ornato y perfection del dicho tractado. This is the longer title of the second edition of Sevilla, printed "en casa de Juan Leon," 1545.

[20] AGI Justicia 792, No. V, Ro. 1, fol. XXXVII.

[21] Ibid., fol. LVII, Dec. 1564. He had claimed earlier that the job brought him 400 ducados per annum. The inflation of prices explains some of the discrepancy.

The agreement between the brothers did not work, and their suit before the judges of the Casa in Sevilla is the quarrel alluded to by Hieronymo de Chaves, when he called the attention of the crown to its cause: the use of the lodestone, and its effect and the damage to the carrera de Indias.[22] In Sevilla, in the meantime, the pilots and masters had complained about Sancho to the judges on October 13, 1563, and Sancho went to Madrid before the Council of the Indies, posting bond in Sevilla and leaving a locum tenens with "another good stone."[23] The issues brought before the judges were the following: Sancho Gutiérrez accused Alonso de Chaves, the Pilot Major, of denying him access to the chest in which the cosmographic instruments of the Casa were kept. He stated that he was entitled to one of two keys of which one was to be given to the catedrático (Hieronymo de Chaves), and the other to the most recently appointed cosmographer of the Casa, namely himself. He accused the catedrático of denying him his right, and therefore the fees for examinations and certification (seller) of instruments and charts in his house.[24] To compel him to deposit the lodestone in the chest of the Casa to which he himself might not have access, at the whim of his enemies, was a situation which he could not tolerate. He also requested that his instruments not be examined by his enemies, naming Juan Canelas and Alonso Pérez. The pilots, on the other hand, complained about having to go to Sancho Gutiérrez' house for the examination. Chances of making work impossible for each other seemed unlimited, and the judges were spared none of the real nor imagined grievances in the ample record of depositions.

But the bruhaha in Sevilla was not viewed with equally gleeful partisanship in Madrid. From the distance of the court and Council of the Indies there emerged a different perspective. Sancho Gutiérrez was obviously taken seriously, but the council had other concerns than to address his personal grievances. Preceded by the usual questionnaires, by a clutter of *informes*, by testimonies requested and volunteered, and interspersed with marginal remarks, there appear the judicial decisions. The judges ruled so that the damage to the operation of the carrera should be kept to a minimum.

With respect to social prestige, justice had triumphed over status when the crown overruled the general of the fleet of 1552, Don Francisco de Mendoza, who could not even remember the incident of his promising the sizeable reward for salvage of the *San Marcos* to the maestre of the *Nuestra Señora de la Concepción*. Even so, Sancho Gutiérrez had been awarded the prize money.[25] It is characteristic of him, that he returned several times to appeal for total reimbursement for the later loss of the *nao* and all her cargo off the coast of Portugal. This was an accident long after the treasure ship had been safely towed into Cartagena harbor. But Sancho claimed that his own ship was damaged in the process, which it

---

[22] See note 5
[23] There is a note in a modern hand entered on fol. XIIv of AGI Justicia 792, No. V, Ro. 1, that no provision was found concerning the lodestone of Sancho Gutiérrez after 1554.
[24] Ordenanzas de la Casa, cap. 141, described in Ernesto Schaefer, *El Consejo Real y Supremo de las Indias*, 2 vols. (Sevilla: Centro de Estudios de Historia de América, 1935), 1: 91–93.
[25] AGI Justicia 765, No. 5, Sevilla, 1554; Contaduría 294, 7–7v. Cuenta del Tesorero Tello, 1562–1566.

undoubtedly was, and additionally, that the enforced delay of her return led to her loss. He found himself having to fight suspicion that Jacomé Luys deliberately made for a Portuguese harbor for illegal trade, and that he intentionally wrecked an "ancient ship," though it cost him his life. Sancho's claim for restitution of loss of the *Nuestra Señora de la Concepción*, in addition to the prize given him by the justices (who admitted his version of the complaint), was finally dismissed in 1566.

In the case against the Chaves's, Sancho Gutiérrez had to contend with another kind of prestige and power, that of his learned rival the catedrático Hieronymo de Chaves and of his friends in the Council of the Indies, and the reputation for wisdom and fairness of the aging Alonso, a personage much esteemed in Sevilla and in Madrid, as expert and "persona desapasionada."[26]

It is remarkable, therefore, that the decisions concerning the lodestone, almost uniformly supported Sancho Gutiérrez. As for the monopoly control over nautical instruments by either the catedrático or the cosmographer in charge of instruments and charts, the crown preferred to keep authority divided and to compel collaboration as defined in the statutes. Sancho was to be given the key to the "arca" or depository of cosmographical instruments and charts in the Casa.[27] In a separate decision, he also had restored to him the pay for his office, which had been suspended for sheer spite in Sevilla, during the time of his absence at court with the stone, because of his legal business. The judges of the Council found that he had adequately posted bond and delegated one of his sons as a caretaker with "a very good stone" which had come to him as part of the dowry of his wife. This was a vindication of his position. He was ordered to bring the stone to the Casa regularly on stated days, or when needed, in order to remagnetize the compasses of the fleet. This was the procedure he had followed before, according to his testimony, bringing his stone to the Casa on Monday and Friday afternoons, and on demand, when the convoy was being prepared. The order that he should participate in the examinations of pilots for licensing, which involved a fee denied him by some of his enemies, was reconfirmed, when he was finally named to the post he had coveted so long. Upon the resignation of Hieronymo de Chaves, he was named to succeed him as *catedrático del arte de navegar y de cosmografía* at the Casa de la Contratación in Sevilla in 1569.[28]

These were the results of the legal tangle at the Casa de la Contratación in Sevilla with respect to the cosmographer's quarrel over the lodestone. They are in fact marginal to the question of whether such circumstances would lead to a curiosity about the lodestone itself. There are only two passages of text which have a bearing on this in these documents. One concerns the trust of the sailors in the particular stone with which the compasses were remagnetized. "To deny these compasses to a ship would be like taking the eyes away from a man" so goes the testimony about compasses magnetized by Sancho's stone by one witness. This text implies the belief that all compasses should be serviced by the same

[26] Justicia 792, No. V, Ro. 1, fol. XXVIv.
[27] AGI Ibid., fol. XXVIIv.
[28] AGI Indiferente General, 2005, Madrid, 30 March 1569.

stone which should be the one "which is the best in the world" according to another witness.[29] Experience confirmed that the quality of stones, and the duration of magnetism which they transferred to the instruments varied. Of course, Sancho had insisted that only he knew how to use his stone properly, or he knew best, for the other party was ignorant. It is tempting to speculate whether the manner of the stroke, rather than passing the stone "to and fro" to rubbing it along the needle from the center by the respectively corresponding pole of the stone, might not have been used by the cosmographers, though not publicized.[30]

Sancho Gutiérrez himself had suggested an improvement for the construction of the ship's compass. He had submitted a model for a printed compass card to replace the need for handdrawn ones "made by everyone in his own house." He said they were frequently ill-made and mostly unreliable, causing the instruments to be hopelessly inaccurate. His suggestion was ordered to be referred to Hieronymo de Chaves for approval and license and a price of 300 maravedís was set giving him exclusive rights to sell the product.[31]

Ordinary sailors did believe in magic control of both stellar and magnetic phenomena, rather than in applied knowledge, and Sancho was the last to ignore the appeal of the argument of a secret he held, which required initiation or inheritance, rather than involving only knowledge open to anyone. It might be an accident that in the lawsuit he speaks of what he knows how to do and never of what he knows.

In a royal letter addressed to the Casa which approves the decisions of its judges, the situation is put most clearly. The king's letter says that "the compass which is the principal aid (matriz) of navigation although it is not understood just what are the reasons for it . . ."[32] (sin que se entiende) should be examined and sealed by the most impartial people who are also best qualified by their understanding as is, for instance Alonso de Chaves. Pilot Major, one of the most expert and wisest. The letter continues "and above all inform us about what has happened and what is happening."

What had in fact happened was that much mystery about the particular lodestone of the Gutiérrez had been lost during the pause in service when, it turned out, that other stones worked on the same principle and almost as well. It became obvious to all that the Gutiérrez were not possessors of secrets but only holders of a monopoly over an exceptionally powerful lodestone. The quarrel between the brothers had separated the matter of skill and of initiation from the properties of the stone. Its effectiveness was generally granted, but only the crown took the opportunity to consider the virtue of the lodestone "which is not understood."[33]

[29] AGI Justicia 792, No. 5, Ro. 1, fol. XIV, Juan Gomez Agrumedo.
[30] Waters, *The Art of Navigation*, p. 28 gives the construction of a compass by Martín Cortés (1551) translated by Richard Eden: "you shall rubbe the poynt of the iron as you wolde whette a knyfe: and so shall certen of those beards of the stone cleave and sticke fast to the iron." Ibid., p. 338 for a later method.
[31] AGI Indiferente General 1967, Lib. 16, fol. 270–270v; Waters, p. 217.
[32] ". . . que el aguja ques la matríz de toda la navegación sin que se entiende," AGI Justicia 792, No. V, Ro. 1, fol. XXVIv.
[33] Ibid., fol. XVIv.

But there was no hurry to action. The argument that the stone might be stolen or sold to a foreign power received no special consideration. There was too much competition for its use and ownership among Sevillians for anyone to be able to make a profit from the stone without identifying it, and so giving away its origin. Sancho himself seemed the least inclined toward giving it up. Yet there was a follow up to the story. In 1574, the stone was in fact stolen by the jailer of the Casa in conspiracy with his wife and a number of accomplices. A falling out among the thieves led to the stone being lost altogether, and the complaint about this, which Sancho Gutiérrez brought before the Council of the Indies, comes under the rubric of ordinary crime, of property stolen from his house, not of privilege and inheritance alienated from his person.[34]

The old idea that the social setting of science has nothing to contribute to the understanding of the structure of scientific ideas, therefore appears to be valid.[35] But "often we enter the unknown edifice of a new scientific discipline through a lesser gate."[36] There are common factors which the story of the lodestone shares with other developments in the Pilot Major's office in Sevilla during the life time of Sancho Gutiérrez, pointing in the direction of progress in science. The case of the lodestone substantially reinforced the stress on observation. It stressed the standard outcome to be expected from standard procedure, and it represents agreement on the need of systematic collation of data, cooperation of technicians, and coordination of procedures—the refreshing of compasses for each voyage—the consistent record of experience and, where applicable, of experiment. These issues were raised in reference to most of the work of the Iberian cosmographers in the sixteenth century. In the case of the lodestone, two phenomena are outstanding. Firstly, the challenge to magic, which was by no means new or unique, compelled the litigants to record all available evidence. This challenged old assumptions and contributed to speculation. Secondly, a new and more ample base of facts was assembled, which was necessary before precise concepts could be formulated, and new ideas could be accepted by the pilots and cosmographers.

It was left to a thinker at a distance from our case to react to this new reality. When William Gilbert wrote his *De Magnete*, empirical observations could be brought into focus. Taken together with the announcement of magnetic variation by Columbus, and the observation that the magnetic pole was distinct from the terrestrial pole by Martín Cortés, William Gilbert's work represents a new

[34] AGI Indiferente General 1956, Registro de Oficios, 2 September 1572–15 June 1576. Lib. I, fol 279; Salvador García Franco, *Historia del Arte y Ciencia de Navegar*, 2 vols. (Madrid: Instituto Histórica de Marina, 1947), 1: 37 confuses this theft with the earlier story of the missing stone, because the document by Hieronymo de Chaves is not dated. His reference is probably to the Ms. copy in the Académia de la Historia in Madrid (MS 095, fol. 73v) which belongs to the collection of Antonio de Herrera, later described as belonging to Antonio de León Pinelo. Navarrete also mentions the year 1575 for the theft.

[35] P.M. Rattani, "The Social Interpretation of Science" in *Science and Society*, ed. Peter Mathias (Cambridge University Press, 1972), pp. 1–32.

[36] Erwin Schrödinger, *What is Life? and other Scientific Essays* (New York: Doubleday Anchor, 1956), p. 236.

...is.[37] This became possible when postulating the whole earth as a magnet shown to agree with experience, and points to a convergence of evi-... book was hailed all over Europe because it fell on ground prepared by ...ce. What is meant by that phrase can be seen in the case of the ...destone.

...bert cites Martín Cortés several times in his book, probably based on the *Breve compendio y de la arte de navegar* (1551), in the Eden translation of 1561.

TRAC
TADODE
LA SPHERA.
QVE COMPVSO EL DOCTOR
IOANNES DE SACROBVSTO
con muchas additiones. Agora nue
uamente traduzido de Latin en len
gua Castellana por el Bachiller
HIERONYMO DE CHAVES:
el qual añidio muchas figuras
tablas, y claras demonstra
tiones : junctamente
con os breues
Scholios,
ce
ssarios á ma
yor illucidation, orna
to y perfectió ol dicho tractado.

Virtus sine aduersario marcescit.

CON PRIVILEGIO
IMPERIAL.:

Title page of *Tractado de la Sphera* ... (1545) by Hieronymo de Chaves
By courtesy of Museo Naval, Madrid.

VIII

The Teaching of Pilots, and the *Chronographía o Repertório de los Tiempos**

Pilots of the Iberian Discoveries found themselves beyond their accustomed range of geographical reference and under different stars. Interest in the oceanic discoveries began at the top of the social pyramid. In Spain, the Catholic kings, the Emperor Charles V and King Philip II, made the enterprise of the Indies their immediate concern. They had to deal with problems of global space which was tied to a new perception of time, as the future demanded long range planning of uncertain length over unknown distances.

Albert Einstein once defined science as "methodical thinking directed toward finding regulative connections between sensual experiences".[1] He is also quoted to have said: "It is not the task of science to explain the taste of the soup, but to identify the ingredients".

This culinary approach to knowledge had a precedent in a cosmography before Columbus, which goes to prove this. I refer to a folio written by Antoine La Salle (De La Salle) which he called *La Salade*. From the complete title of the first folio edition, it becomes clear that De La Salle was not concerned with either ingredients or taste, but rather with the whole dish. The title reads: "La Salade, nouvellement imprimée laquelle fait mention de tous les pays du monde et du pays de la Sybille, et aussi de la figure de la mer et de la terre et plusieurs belles remonstrances", a sample of the Imago Mundi at European courts, La Salade was entitled cosmography and published (Paris, Michele le Noir, 1521) 29 years after Columbus. The first inventory of the Atlantic discoveries was by Martín Fernández de Enciso: the *Suma de Cosmographía Universal de las Quatro Partes del Mundo, especialmente de las Indias, y es el primero que imprimió obra de geographia de ellas.*[2]

The navigators were indeed called upon to explain the new "ingredients" of the Einstein quote. There is a wealth of sixteenth-century texts which are increasingly the subject of study. The experts in charge of the overall collection and interpretation of the new data were the Pilots Major and the cosmographers, authors of texts, who also manufactured and experimented with instruments, drew charts, and were responsible for the astronomical data which were used for orientation at sea in the form of regiments of the sun and moon etc. Cosmographers make an awkward collective. They were a group only by virtue of their common interest, though in varied aspects of the Carrera de Indias, the Indies Trade

QVARTO

FVE IMPRESSO EN
LA MVY NOBLE Y LEAL CIV
DAD DE SEVILLA EN CASA DE
Juan de Leon, en el Año
de la Incarna
cion
de nue
ſtro Salua
dor d.1545. Y de
la creacion dl Mun
do ſegun los Hebreos.
Segun Paulo Oroſio
ſegun los primeros
padres dela ygſia.
Segũ el rey
don Al-
fonſo.
y
dela e-
dad del Au
tor dela preſente
Obra.

Años.

5497
6594

6744

8529

2-2

Virtus ſine aduerſario marceſcit.

Page of *Tractado de la Sphera* ... (1545), dating its publication
from the birth of Christ to the author's age at 22
By courtesy of Museo Naval, Madrid.

♦SPHERA DEL♠
MVNDO

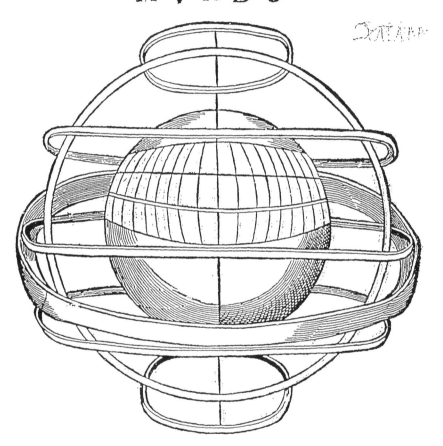

Schematic rendering of the celestial sphere
from *Tractado de la Sphera* (1545)
By courtesy of Museo Naval, Madrid.

Those employed by the Iberian powers in furtherance of their oceanic enterprises, the teachers of pilots, and mariners, were a diverse lot. A core of Sevillian residents mixed with Spaniards from other regions and men from other lands, they had no collective social identity. Cosmography, in the widest sense, concerned the terrestrial globe and the universe and everything that is around them, on them or in them, animate or inanimate. The cosmographer's teaching was orientated toward things, conditions, and events, as perceived by the senses which could be aided by instruments. It was as free of metaphysical speculation as the limits set by the definition of heresy allowed.

Problems defined: Alonso de Santa Cruz

Alonso de Santa Cruz is introduced as the teacher of the highest ranking student, the Emperor Charles V, the pilot of Empire, so to say, who commissioned Santa Cruz to give him private lessons about the sphere and cosmographic matters, to divert him when S.M. was laid up with bouts of gout in the later years of his rule. Santa Cruz left an extensive opus of manuscripts and maps, especially the *Islario general de todas las islas del mundo* which he produced between 1552 and 1554, and dedicated to the Emperor.[3] With additions, emendations and corrections, the book was recast in 1559 and submitted to Philip II.[4] The *Islario* is indeed among the most renowned cartographic compilations of the time in terms of comprehension and technique. Santa Cruz had been a member of the *junta* under the direction of Hernando Colón in Sevilla, to make a Padrón Real (master map) in 1528.[5] As *veedor* on Sebastian Cabot's expedition, 1526–1530, he had experience with the Atlantic route. In 1538 he was paid 30,000 maravedis salary to act as cosmographer of the Casa de la Contratación in Sevilla. That meant that he was to be available for advice on all navigational problems: exams of pilots and instruments, the making of charts, and the contribution of his experience on the transatlantic routes.

Santa Cruz made many maps of parts of Europe as well as the New World, and there is a debate about the extent that he experimentally anticipated Mercator. The major problem of determining the longitude of places moved him to compile of the Book of Longitude, *Libro de las Longitudines* (MS ca. 1555).[6] In it he presented the information which had been gathered for a *junta* presided over by the Marques de Mondéjar. Alonso de Santa Cruz dedicated his book on the longitude to King Philip II: "the most high and most powerful lord" during the latter's stay in Flanders. There the work was submitted to the local Dutch experts before returning it. It showed the interest of theoretical challenges of the oceanic world to cosmographers and *pilotos de altura*, based on the data (ingredients) which were brought in by each returning ship.

3

As for the book – deferring in all explanation and detail to the experts in this group – there emerge to the untutored eye some characteristics of the cosmographic enterprise. Santa Cruz begins by saying that there should be no worry about ascertaining latitude, a rather optimistic judgement. He proposes to divide all the material that he had learned and practiced into two parts: "In the first I shall put all the methods that have been used for finding the longitude", adding "those that I and others have invented ..." which can be used in the eastern as well as the western part of the world. In the second, Santa Cruz proposes to discuss the first book of Ptolemy's *Geography*.

The procedures for finding longitude to be discussed are twelve in number. No. 1: a prolix text describes the estimate of direction and distance by "astronomical means", that is the observation of the declination of the sun at noon of a twenty four hour day.[7] Citing ancient measurements he adopts the 17 1/2 leagues to the degree of longitude.

Next Santa Cruz mentions astrolabes, quadrants, quadrangles, squares, yards, and the Jacob's staff. He proceeds to measurement of longitude by triangulation including a calculation in prose, and having suffered through that, he gives the reasons why it does not work. The sphericity of the earth and water, he says, do not match the straight line calculations which should be made "more for an arch, than for a cord". The calculation of the square root also assumes the quantity of straight lines in a triangle whose whole surface is flat. He criticizes the reliance on eclipses because of the rarity of the events, and the inaccuracy of timing: "Pilots and mariners cannot understand the observations that are required for calculation of the said eclipse on account of their ignorance and being so lacking in the astrology that is needed".

A *junta* of pilots chaired by the Bishop of Lugo left Santa Cruz dissatisfied with the information about the amount of the variation of the compass. Asking the viceroy of New Spain concerning this, Mendoza said that according to his measure the needle northeasted a little less than two compass points which he found very confusing. In Lisbon, Santa Cruz had been told that there was no declination at all at the Cape of Good Hope, it northeasted a half a point at Zocotra and one and a half at Calicut, and a little less than two at Malacca. Don Juão de Castro the great surveyor of the Red Sea and Indian Ocean, himself gave Santa Cruz his records obliging him to not show the data to anyone in Portugal, but encouraging him to copy the material in order to preserve them.[8] This quest for a stable isogonic zero meridian – or line showing no magnetic variation – was a preoccupation of mariners, recognized in 1622 by Jean Bleau on his globe where he states: "it varies along the same meridian".[9]

Finding the longitude by means of clocks, divided into 24 hours presents problems of manufacture and use. Santa Cruz recommends the use of timing as such as the best so far suggested, but unworkable because of practical difficulties, the influence of weather on metal and wood, the drying out or sticking which results, the rusting of strings, the relaxing of guitar strings as they unwind. He concludes that: "therefore knowing the longitude by means of clocks, with the precision that is needed, will be a difficult thing". The rest of the procedures rely on astronomy. Among the fourteen illustrations the later ones pertain to cartographic projections.[10] In his discussion of the history of the compass, Santa Cruz begins with Homer. He himself uses the sixteenth century 32 winds or compass points which were common in his time. The compass in use by some pilots in Sevilla, had the needle set 1/2 point, i.e. 5 1/2 degrees east of north. Chaves was to complain that by its use the north star would be moved from its position.[11]

Alonso de Santa Cruz contributed many charts and finally his *Islario* to answer the question of how terrestrial space was aligned and related on the globe. The problems of Santa Cruz were concepts of substance: "science in diapers", as Don Ramón Carande called it.

The Pilot Major and the teaching of pilots

The anchor person for this discussion is Alonso de Chaves, resident of Sevilla over a long life span. He died in 1587, well over 90 years old. He does not seem to have ever been to sea. His manuscript (in part preserved in copy?) is entitled *Espejo de Navagantes*, also called *Quatri Partitu en Cosmographia práctica*.[12] There is no contemporary edition. The version available was brought out by the Museo Naval in Madrid in 1983. The manuscript of the Real Academia de la Historia is dated by recent commentators, 1538 (LaGuarda Trias); 1539 (Lamb); 1544 (Guedes); and lately by James E. Kelley, Jr. (1532).[13] There is general agreement that it was a text book in evolution compiled during Chaves' appointment as cosmographer and teacher of the pilots in Sevilla. The manuscript seems to be in various hands, and appears to be unfinished. One is probably looking at a book of lessons which in their geographical reference are based on the Padrón Real or master map and its fabrication. The input for this project reached the Pilot Major's office from various sources, which are inconsistently wrong more often, than would suggest a single author.

Chaves never lived in another town, though he visited Lisbon and the court in Valladolid. His activities are only partly caught in his biography as reconstructed through his appointments and the pay lists of the Casa de la Contratación.[14] He received his first official appointment to the staff of the Pilot Major in 1528 as *piloto/cosmographo/maestro de hacer cartas*. Don Alonso's work must have been known in the private sector well before Amerigo Vespucci was appointed first Pilot Major in 1508 and the licensing of pilots was formalized. The examinations were to be held before a tribunal of six cosmographers on salary at the Casa de la Contratación and six pilots, unpaid, who were entitled to one question each concerning a specific route.[15]

The story of the teaching and learning is recorded only in official pay lists, complaints about pay illegally levied, or else compensation left unpaid, in denunciations over the performance and illegal licensing for pay. Every aspect subject to dispute about performance of the job can be found in some document. Scientific matter hardly enters at all. The major controversy carried on over three years concerned the two-scale map, and the problem of variation of the compass. Instruments and charts were equally effected, and when the suit reached the Council of the Indies it remained without solution.[16] The other controversies over charts and instruments had to do with who was entitled to make them, how they were to be licensed, which ones were reliable, or why they were not, how they were to be sold, and so on. The merits and demerits of the Padrón Real were extensive. Again, this documentation is characterized by fights over the rights of the individual rather than any detail about the product. Certainly, during Cabot's absence, 1526–1530 a series of interim appointments did not contribute to the stabilization of the licensing procedure.

Alonso de Chaves was created Pilot Major on July 11, 1552; his son Gerónimo, at the age of 29, was named Catedrático de Cosmographía on December 4 of the same year. By the time of their appointment, Alonso de Chaves was a most respected senior official of the Casa, and author of the text mentioned. Gerónimo had published a commentary on Sacrobosco (1545), and was to issue a *Chronographía o Repertório de Los Tiempos* (1561) during his tenure of office. The examinations on cosmography, or rather the sphere, were subject to evolution, challenge, and reduction of the ambitious programs set by the first incumbent. Although there is no reflection in any of the cosmographic texts about mathematical training, except in conjunction with instruments, an order of 1586 did specify the study of the four rules of arithmetic, the rule of three, square and cube roots, and the tables of Peuerbach and of Alfonso X, the six books of Euclid, and spherical geometry as in Regiomontanus. Requirements for the examination were kept intact: experience of six years at sea and routes of the *carrera*, were followed by questions asked by the examiners. Votes were cast anonymously by white and black beans (*habas y altramuces*), collected by the Pilot Major.[17] A larger number of *habas* meant approval. Many irregularities are recorded. Candidates failed for being illiterate, and later on because they could not even sign their names. The required course on cosmography was reduced over time from one year to three months and finally, to two months which were to include holidays in order to facilitate attendance. Again the noise vastly exceeded the traces of substance.

The text of Chaves also points out that: "la marinería no se acostumbra porque los que los tratan no son tan doctos ni entienden la teórica ni la razón, ni proporción que la tiera tiene con el cielo, y la diferencia que hay entre los meridianos y paralelos ...". The four parts are treating:

1. all matter pertaining to the festivals, and to the instruments for navigation;
2. all aspects of cosmography and the practical art of navigation;
3. concerns the age of the moon and the natural movements of the ocean waters;
4. presents the itineraries (navigations) to all parts of the Indies.

Alonso de Chaves starts with the calculation of the Church calendar. This chapter consists of 20 pages of charts. The approach is entirely one of how to, and the why is considered sufficiently explained by reference to the when on the Julian calender. Our author opens his next chapter with another whole paragraph resuming, the foregoing, and stressing the importance of that material: "por que ninguno puede pretender ignorancia y quebrante los divinos preceptos por falta de avíso".

The chapter proper deals with all the instruments necessary for navigation. To this part there are nine subdivisions and as this is the substance of the course, I can't avoid lists:

1. explains the compass;
2. deals with the chart;
3. introduces the marine astrolabe;
4. concerns the quadrant;
5. treats the *báculo astronómico* or *ballestilla* (Jacob's staff), its manufacture and use;
6. discusses a sounding instrument sonda;
7. describes the nocturnal and the sand glass;
8. treats the altrimetric scale and its use; and
9. the geometry and geography for treating the measurement on the earth.

Any one of these chapters has its history in the development of the nautical sciences, which have been well presented in recent literature by the work of Commander David Waters, and of professors E.G.R. Taylor, Luis de Albuquerque, and José Maria López Piñero. This may be the place to inject the information that when I became interested in the subject, the texts now published by the Museo Naval were available only in part or not at all. I owe what I can do to the good will and generous help of many scholars in the Spanish archives and deposits over the years.

To resume, the chapter on the compass, Chaves names the 32 winds around the circle and the *fleur de lis* is on the top for north. In the chapter on the use of the compass, his instructions mention an otherwise omitted point, namely that the direction identified on the chart would require open water to conduct the ship, so Chaves recommends to seek "another wind" to indicate the course to be followed. A chart shows the outline of the oceans, he says, on a scale: "which no text could match in many words". In part nine one finds a straightforward listing of terrestrial measures since the Egyptians began to record distances.

The nine parts of the second book deal with astronomical phenomena, the movement of the sun through the zodiac on all the days of the year, and the true declination of the sun for a perpetual calender. The pilot is then instructed to calculate the degree of latitude by the altitude and declination of the sun. The following *figura* of the *horoscópio o reloj general diurno* or *instrumento horario* is left blank. There follow rules for finding latitude by measuring the altitude of the north star and its guards, and examples for knowing the time at night, including use of the *balestilla* or Jacob's staff. Last, the declination of some fixed stars of the first magnitude is treated.

A final paragraph deals with the natural signs by which the change of the weather can be known. This rather elaborate discourse shows how the *señales naturales de la mudança de los tiempos* are translated to account for oceanic phenomena. Chaves advises the pilots that such *señales* observed at sea, precede and anticipate the misfortunes (*los tales infortúnios*), which he warns the *pilotos de altura* will certainly run into during their long voyages. Alonso de Chaves tackles this task systematically, proceeding from the outer to the inner Ptolemaic universe: from the stars, via the sun the moon, clouds, fog/mist, rainbow, thunder, lightning, the behavior of birds, land animal and fishes, to signs of inanimate nature. His list shows the relatively slow adjustment to oceanic phenomena.

Number of observations

stars	18	
sun	34	fair, rain, storm, cold, dusk, dawn color
moon	25	fair, rain, storm, cold
clouds	19	wind, rain, storm, cloudy–calm
fog/mist	8	from all directions, calm
rainbow	10	when, what colors, double
thunder/lightning	8	both at the same time or separately
birds/fishes	27/17	long paragraphs on air, wind, rain, storm
land animals	2	frogs, cows, fleas before storm

Observations cont.

others	11	how they behave before rain and storm (no horses)
inanimate nature	35	bells, flowers, wells, smell, taste, rivers, rain drops
surface of the ocean	25	current flow, salinity, waves, temperature/ season, behavior of surface water, angle of wake, murmurs, light at sunrise etc.

(NB. Dreams of birds mean storms, the only reference to another state of being.)

Chaves adds in a note that some of the *señales* are common, others particular to a region, none hold for the whole world. Then he advises the pilots to think of all of these in relation to the phases of the moon and the seasons.

These detailed lists make a fascinating collection of observations of the *señales* which is impressively precise. Chaves says, for instance, that thunder and lightening are simultaneous events which appear to differ because of our quick eye and slower hearing. What is very general is the description of the actual weather. Thus rain is between fair weather and storm with no other expressions available. Identification by measurement of weather was left for much later times and into the future. If these lists go to show the slow elimination of inapplicable observations such as the behavior of frogs, fountains, and the tightening of ropes of church bells, the aim of the instruction is to assemble reliable and precise records of weather related phenomena. It stands in particular contrast to the contemporary popularity of books of prognostication such as Reyman's *Wetterbuch* of prognostic peasant lore which had 17 editions in 34 years,[18] or of the *Thunder Books*. Alonso de Chaves saw the consistent and cumulative records as useful for the transmission of knowledge, even though experience taught that repetition of weather conditions was confined to few regularities such as monsoons.

The third part of Chaves' text deals with the ship at sea. Another list of headings begins with the ship and its parts and the names for them. There are 39 names for ships, but only the type used in the Indies trade is to be discussed, the *naos* of ca. 200 tons. There follows an elaborate vocabulary of seaman's language in alphabetical order under separate headings, anticipating García de Palácio. Second, Chaves describes the crews and the pilot's duties to govern the ship in condensed detail. Next are listed.the provisions necessary for the voyages; and the arms required, i.e. guns and arms for hand to hand fighting. This is followed by an exhortation to all aboard to know and keep their station and stay by their office. Finally, Chaves speaks of disasters at sea and how to deal with them, including by first aid when a man is overboard, and after fishing him out of the sea. The fighting between two ships and how to prepare for it, and battle at sea between fleets round out the chapter.

This material is truly a mirror of the state of the Carrera de Indias during the time of Philip II. Again, the concentration on real experience is in evidence. For instance, in contrast to Pedro de Medina's dealing with a man overboard who instructs him to remember which day of the year it is, where the sun is, and to calculate where to direct himself, Chaves advises his sailor to shout and beat on the water to frighten any man eating fish.

The chapter on war and battle at sea is a feature of the Chaves text which has been largely neglected. There is a contemporary text the *Arte Da Guerra No Mar* by Padre Fernando Oliveira, published in Portugal in 1554,[19] which is addressed to the ruler of distant possessions, and therefore weighted differently with respect to reference as to who should be employed and how equipped. Chaves speaks to the members of the crew, not the king. He has advice concerning gunnery and its use. In case of a storm, Chaves points out that the worry of the captain of the enemy will equal that of the captain opposed, in order to preserve his ship. But if: "they say that the enemy will take the same thought and care as I, I answer that when both be equal in numbers and arms, then, in such case he who shall be more dexterous and have more spirit and fortitude he will conquer". He leaves the rest to those who are more knowledgable and better skilled, who often "have seen more than I can understand". He also advises the crew to settle any quarrels so that there will be no doubt as to who is the enemy when the fighting starts. These two last sections of part three are to quote Julian Corbett: "The earliest attempt to formulate a definite fighting formation and tactical system for sailing fleets".[20]

The text on war shows the dispersal of the practical sciences into disciplines such as physics and mechanics. During the sixteenth century and thereafter guns were made obsolete by better guns, and in 1633 an appointment was made in the Casa de la Contratación for a teaching post for artillery, fortifications, and squadrons. In contrast, weather observations led to new attitudes toward close observation, cumulative and consistent records over the long run, rather than to be considered immediately and sufficiently explanatory, reliably prognostic or reflecting supernatural origin.

The *Libro Quarto* subtitles: practical and modern cosmography called Mirror for the seaman or *Espejo de Navegantes*. This part is divided into twenty-five chapters, and each chapter is subdivided into sections which are numbered. Part four opens with an alphabetical listing of place names from the Bahamas to the Straits of Magellan, including all of the Central American coast and Brazil. Part four amounts to half of the book, pp. 251–422, and is in the form of a rutter.[21] In no part of the book are the difficulties of charting the world better recorded than in this outcome of repeated consultations of many pilots, occasionally forced to vote to resolve disagreement which was due in part to the fact that they still compiled their maps from magnetic compass, course data and dead reckoning, and not from latitude–longitude measurements. The magnetic variation led to much disagreement among pilots about the Padrón Real for being inconsistent, confusing and useless.[22] Suggestions for exploratory voyages to fix the positions of the Antilles (set 3 points too far north) fell on deaf ears. Such work would have entailed major coordinated surveying and was not welcome by many pilots. They had other problems, for instance, with the location of sandbanks and other hazards and with the description of the suitability of harbors for different types of ships at various seasons. Only the chart gives: "all the ports, bays, and senos (gulfs), rivers, promontories, and capes as well as the routes from one to the other ...".

There were twelve designations, names for ports collected for the Pacific side of Central America. All approaches to land needed to be probed by sounding, and described for size of the harbor, shelter from the prevailing wind, currents, cleanliness of the bottom, firmness or lack of it. In this way by general description, detailed derrotas, and noting special features, the *Espejo de Navegantes* is an *Islario* in prose, though not co-extensive in area. The texts on practices of navigation represent the accretion of ingredients for the development of nautical science.

Interest in that direction went quite a way beyond the cátedra and was resumed in the *Itinerario de navegacion de los mares y tierras occidentales* by Juan Escalante de Mendoza.[23] This text, also remaining in manuscript until 1985, reverted to the dialogue form of instruction by a pilot (in this case to a questioning traveller) used by Pedro de Medina. The author participated in the Indies trade with his own ship and he became Captain General of the Armada and Flota of New Spain. His manuscript is judged to be the most complete of the genre by its editors. It is written to explain as well as to give practical instruction. The manuscript reached the Council of the Indies, and because of the description of the make up and routes of the *carrera*, its author was never licensed to print it. It is much more a literary exercise than the Chaves text, though it treats of human interest such as seasickness, advising Chicken soup as a remedy, and mentions the case of the death of a mariner at sea without having completed his voyage. The question "does he get paid?" is answered by "yes, his wife and children are entitled to the pay for the part of the voyage he worked".

The collections of drawings of coasts and approaches to the harbors in the Indies, unique to this cosmographic text, was simply copied by a cleric – a one time member of the Consejo de Indias – Baltasar Vellerino de Villalobos. He printed the *Luz de Navegantes* under his own name in 1555.[24] This was published in facsimile in 1984.

At this stage of development one approaches an overall view of Philip II's extensive overseas holdings, after 1581 combining the Spanish and Portuguese ones. A unique booklet turned up in London some years ago which suggests the arguments shaping the debate over the choice of routes and the defense. Paul Hair of Liverpool made a careful edition of that text called *Instrucción que a Vuestra Majestad se da*: "that you may command that the Ocean Sea be fortified and defended against all enemy pirates, whether French or English, in all the Navigations of your Royal Crown within the Tropics, presented by D. Felipe de Albornoz, composed and set out by his Tutor in Mathematics, Licentiate Manoel de Andrada Castel Blanco, chaplain to your Majesty".[25] This is advice on global strategy offered to the King of Spain ca. 1590. The author was well aware of the important role of pilots, and he pleaded for their proper pay and privileges.

To sum up, instruction was available, practice had accumulated, and the official questions shifted from interest in nautical science to human problems, in particular the lack of examined pilots, the role of foreigners, and political and economic issues. All along the global space had become more familiar, the distant was accessible. It is no wonder that this growth in perspective on the globe would lead to a new look at the depth in time which had brought men to this stage.

Gerónimo de Chaves: *Chronographía o Repertório de los Tiempos*

The book is rather exhausting to read through, as it's organization requires the discussion of the same phenomenon in different contexts over again. The appended alphabetic index is a great help in consulting it. It was meant to be an ample reference to the phenomena of time as applied to the universe and man's world. Chaves searched for the "regulative connections" of the Einstein quote, and for correspondences in natures ways – one cannot yet say laws.

People most concerned with the measurement of time were the clerical hierarchy in charge of the calender, the merchant bankers, and the *pilotos de altura* on their voyages. The updating of the Julian calender which was ten days in arrear of the solar year by the sixteenth century led mathematicians to enquire how they got to now. This was also the direction for humanists interest in the classical past. The two major tasks were to find out the rational of the traditional dating systems, and to attempt to collate dates from whatever orientation, linear (Biblical) cyclical or prophetic, in order to establish a sequence and measure of duration to comprehend the record.

Gerónimo de Chaves met many of the leading cosmographers and pilots as a youth in his father's house, but he had many broader interests. He worked close to the considerable litererary and artistic communities then thriving in Sevilla. Francisco de Medina a famous painter, wrote that he studied cosmography with Gerónimo de Chaves who was "a man of great knowledge and good judgement" (*entonces muy estimado*).[26] Works cited by Chaves, who is described as an excellent mathematician, are his *Tratado de la Esphera, que compuso el doctor Ioannes de Sacrobosco* (1545), which he translated, corrected and annotated. His *Chronographia o Repertório de los Tiempos* appeared in 1561 and reached six editions. As he added material in successive editions, he cut back on some practical nautical matters refering the reader to his own Sacrobosco. A Scarobosco had become a genre of textbook on the sphere. Originally a translation of Ptolemy's *Almagest* and some additional Arabic work, it had been popular since the short though comprehensive treatise originated in lectures at the University in Paris in the mid-thirteenth century. Sacrobosco gave the structure of the Ptolemaic universe, and emendations and additions by any editor were expected. Looking at the colophon of the book, however, one sees a foreshadowing of the *Chronographia* (1561) namely in the dating of his work in some of the calendars which he treats. This feature is always credited to Joseph Justus Scaliger, "the father of chronology" then at Leiden, who published a work entitled *De emendatione temporum* in 1584, i.e. 23 years after Chaves. He followed a comparable procedure which was much admired but never mentioned in connection with the Chaves. What interested both, was chronography as a time scale of correspondences in the counting, not just of the Greek and Roman calenders, but of those of the Persians, Babylonians Egyptians, including Jews and Arabs, whose calenders hitherto had been treated separately. Chaves quite rightly regarded chronography as a science along with arithmetic, geometry, and music, and inspired by nautical science, he tried to connect the extant of life on the globe, the duration of societies, and of planetary motion and stellar phenomena.

The approach of Gerónimo's chronologies are a net to catch every conceivable measurable time in human experience. His prefatory note solicits advice from friendly readers if they were better informed, however he rebukes in advance "the frivolous and specious murmurings of the malevolent individuals whom I have answered in another place". There is something more implied in this device. Gerónimo de Chaves quit his teaching post in 1568 but remained active in his work. The frontispiece of the later editions of the *Repertório de los Tiempos* show a sick man. He died in 1574 at the age of 51, legend has it of syphylis, confirmed by medical opinion regarding the sad and rigid expression of the later portrait. His editions show this change over time. The preface to the *Sabio Lector* of the edition of 1586 ends with the motto *Virtus in infirmitate perficitur.*

The copy shown from the British Library is marked in handwriting "*está purgado en 22 de Septiembre, 1622*". The copy has blacked out lines only in the list of popes. There is a break in the sequence from the year 853 to the year 858. Within that time span on the Chaves list appears: "Juana, muger (female) who was in office for two years, 1 month, and 4 days". He adds: "and this is not put into the (official) catalogue which declares the Holy See vacant until 858" and continues: "at this time flourished Rabano Mauro, Archbishop of Maguntino", a piece of learned inference I have not checked out.

Comissioned by Philip II to make charts, he appears in accounts of pay for his work, which was well regarded in Europe. His maps of Andalusia and Florida were published in the *Grand Atlas* of Jean Bleau. His two world maps which gained renown have not been located.[28] The last revision (1584) – there is at least one later edition – of the *Chronographia* was seen through the press by Alonso de Chaves, his father, corrected for the Gregorian calendar, and with an extended list of cities of the world, situated by degrees of latitude and longitude. As for the ten lost days, when October 5 became October 15 in 1582. There is a note in the *sección contaduría* of the Casa that nobody was to be paid for the ten lost days.

The message of this text is that events do not determine chronology which exists apart. Except for religious reference, Chaves stays away from asking why, though elaborating on how the lunar joined to the solar calendar had caused complications to his day. So he does add what in American colloquial usage would be: how come? Not asking for origin so much as for precedent, in this case Egyptian, Greek and Roman.

Chaves' four parts sort out the content in the following way. In book 1, his time frame reaches from eternity, which has no time but accomodates immortal angels, through the creation, which gives way to *evo* or endless duration. Book 2 treats the four elements of earth, water, air and fire, and the heavens above. It discusses the zodiac and the meaning of the signs, also the order of the planets and their significance. Book 3 discusses the calendrical cycles especially of the Roman Church, the movable feasts, and Easter, also the lunar calendar and eclipses to the year 1600. The last book observes the critical days which are important in medicine, along with the use of the calender for prognostic purposes which is also called *astrologia rústica*. As for the weather, he mentions *serenidad*, i.e. fair weather, rains, winds storms, cold spells, adding earthquakes, plague and famine as the results of it to the roster of Alonso's *señales*. At the end he appends a catalogue of six pages listing 260 cities of Europe and of the "West Indies of the Ocean Sea" by latitude and longitude There follows an alphabetical index of the content of the volume, judged one of the most beautiful produced in Spain.

Starting with the division of time into days, natural and civil, he proceeds to break down the hours into *uncias* and *átomos*, and says that the natural day contains 24 hours, 4 quadrantes, 96 points, 900.06 *momentos*, 11,500 *uncias*, and 506,800.80 atoms. The atom of time may have been one of the notions sacrificed when the curriculum of pilot instructions was cut. From the day Chaves goes on to the month, the lunar month deriving its name, to the solar month and zodiac. He discusses the Roman calender, the practice of

Title page of a posthumous edition of the
Chronographia (1561) by Hieronymo de Chaves
By courtesy of Museo Naval, Madrid.

TRACTADO.

gares regadios, fobze montes y huertos, y fobze
los lugares amenos y deleytofos. De las pzouin
cias generalmēte tiene dominio fobze Efpaña, Dal
macia, Efclauonia, la tierra ò Marbona, Arabia fe
lir, la Detruria y parte de Lyguria. En particular
domina fobze Malta, Dierufalem, Buda, Auiñon
A ta. En Efpaña, fobze Jaen, Calahozra y Medi
na Celi.

ℭ Del figno de Capzicornio.
Titulo. rrriiij.

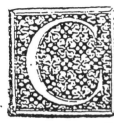 Apzicornio es el decimo figno en el
orden natural, figurado de los Poe
tas poz vna cabza, cuya cola era de
pefce. Significando que affi como
la Cabza es animal que fe enbiefta
y leuanta para comer las hojas de

Drawing of the Zodiac figure of Capricorn
from the *Chronographia* (1561)
By courtesy of Museo Naval, Madrid.

intercalation, and leap year. Next come descriptions of each month, how it got its name. Many references to sources of all kinds put together for each month are given in the margin: Marcobius, Aristotle, Pliny, Eusebius etc. Additional references appear in the text, including J. Stoefler a near contemporary humanist publishing in the 1530's.

Chaves measures civil days and months by lunar data and he follows this with a medical month with reference to Galen. The Venerable Bede, a frequent source, as he had been for Sacrobosco, is quoted for four seasons of the year. The signs of the zodiac are introduced with elaborate texts, and the corrsepondences to the planets with the ages of man are enumerated. There follows a table (1550–1600) which shows the entry of the sun into cardinal signs of the zodiac: Aries, Cancer, Libra, and Capricorn "*verificada al horizonte y meridiano de la muy noble y muy leal ciudad de Sevilla*". Eras, centuries, and ages of the past are succeeded by the ages of man. The ages since the creation – he starts with the year 5199 BC when Adam was created – is followed by the list of Ceasars and Emperors, from the year 48 BC.

It is in this counting that the rivalry of authors on chronography appears. Scaliger is disturbed by mistranslations when he meets them in his Greek, Hebrew, Aramaic and Latin sources, all of them printed in the original language. Chaves is worried about the fact that by his reckoning there was really no natural solar eclipse at the time of the crucificion as is mentioned in the New Testament (the sixth hour to the ninth hour, Mark 15,33). So it was a supernatural event. After another reckoning of Christian movable feasts, as in the *Quatri Partitu*, there follows the division of the world, adding the *Indias Occidentales* as the fourth part of the New World.

Throughout Chaves stressed the concern of the sailors along with some medical lore. A treatise on the moon is followed by a discussion of the planets, and the zodiac is likewise prefaced with a picture for each sign followed by the name, the order in which it is, and the traditions and qualities associated with it. The author ends with a table to memorize, and gives an example of how to find the zodiacal sign for each day of the year. The work is a rich mine of traditional lore. The chapters on lunar and solar eclipses fall within the contemporary discussion. Nine types of comets are described by color, shape and the impact on earth, nature and lives.

In the continuous medical reference as well as in the context of comets or the weather, one discovers another remarkable expansion, that of the perception of the five senses. This was indispensable to sailors whose observation called for the keenest awareness with all their senses in order to probe the many phenomena of the oceanic world, the importance of which for science was expressed in the first Einstein quote. All the books are shot through with reference to sensual perception, excluding the insults to them by life aboard ship. The humanist world extended the limits of the past to non-European sources. A step beyond them by Chaves is into the reality of the natural world. Tradition aside, he is willing to relate his chronology to all of the natural world.

Chaves also considered practical solutions to damaging experiences in the life of sailors of "altitude". For their observation of solar and also lunar eclipses he improvises an instrument to keep from hurting the eyes and to aid in accuracy of observation: "How one can see the solar eclypse very well without any insury to the organ of vision". Instead of looking through soot covered glass or through water he suggests the choice of two pieces of strong glass, one colored green and another the same or different color. A piece of paper should be cut to match the size of the glass, which he does not specifiy. In the center one should make a small peephole *"hagan en el medio del un agujero pequeño"* and put the paper between the glass which then should be glued together around the rim. This piece, now all in one, "hold before your eyes and direct both eyes to the sun and with the glass in front of you, you will be able to look at the sun through the hole without damage to your vision even though you be looking for a long period of time. In this way one can observe any eclipse even though it be very small, of the sun as well as of the moon".

Pedro de Medina and Escalante de Mendoza, using the dialogue format, contain some of the questions which might have been asked in the examinations. Alonso de Chaves wrote a book of answers taught in Sevilla. New information may still turn up in the proceedings of the pilot *juntas* before the Consejo de Indias and in advance of cartographic studies. What really went on in nautical science is a matter for reconstruction of results. The state of practice speaks from the record of the carrera.[30] The study of maps has put into doubt the extent to which learning was put to use. But on the coast of Andalucia, the smoky glass of observation was giving way through a peephole to a sharper image of the world and universe.

Endnotes

*This lecture was delivered on 3 April, 1993 at Imperial College, London, at a conference on "Iberia in the Golden Age: Mathematical Sciences and their Uses, 1500-1700", arranged by Professors J.V. Field and Eduardo Ortíz.

1. *Forum and Century* 84, *Forum* Series "Living Philosophies" 13, Simon Schuster, New York, 1931, pp. 193–4. The other remark often told by those who knew him.

2. Martín Fernández de Encisco, *Suma de Cosmographia*, 1519, retranslated and edited by E.G.R. Taylor from a sixteenth-century translation by Roger Barlow: *A Brief Summe of Geographie Universal*, Hakluyt Society Series 2/68, London, 1932.

16

3. Carriazzo, Juan de Mata, *"Estudio Preliminar"*. *Crónica de los Reyes Católicos* by *Alonso de Santa Cruz* 1, Publicaciones de la Escuela de Estudios Hispano Americanos de Sevilla 51, Sevilla, 1919, pp. 1–200.

4. Naudé, Françoise, *Reconaissance du Nouveau Monde et cosmographie de a la Renaissance*, Reichenberger, Kassel, 1992, chapter 22 on the *Islario*.

5. Pulido Rubio, José, *El Piloto Mayor de la Casa de la Contratación*, Escuela de Estudios Hispano Americanos, Sevilla, 1923; second enlarged edition, 1950, but documents of 1923 are not repeated in 1950.

6. Alonso de Santa Cruz, *Libro de las longitudines*, Y manera que hasta ahora se ha tenido en el arte de navegar, con sus demonstraciones y ejemplos, dirigido al Muy Alto y Muy Poderoso Señor Don Philippe II de este nombre Rey de España, Don Antonio Blazquez y Delgado Aguilero, Sevilla, 1921.

7. Bankston, J., *The Book of Longitudes* by *Alonso de Santa Cruz*, translated by J. Bankston, appendices, notes and a selected bibliography, available from: *Terrenate Research*, P.O. Box 5112, Bisbee, AZ, 1992.

8. Martín Fernández de Navarrete, *Disertación sobre la Historia de la Náutica y de las Ciencias Matemáticas que han contribuido a sus progresos entre los Españoles*, obre posthuma, La Real Academia de la Historia, Madrid, 1846, p. 182.

9. Washburn, Wilcomb E., "The Canary Islands and the question of the Prime Meridian: the search for precision in the measurement of the earth", *Coloquio de Historia Canario Americana, Coloquio Internacional de Historia Marítima* 4, Las Palmas, 1982, p. 876.

10. Thrower, Norman, "Projections of maps of fifteenth- and sixteenth-century European discoveries", paper delivered to the Conference of the History of Spanish Science, June 27, 1989, Madrid, *Mundialización de la ciencia y cultura nacional*, eds A. Lafuente, A. Elena and M.L. Ortega, Universidad Autónoma de Madrid, Doce Calles, 1993.

11. Lamb, Ursula, "Science by litigation: a cosmographic feud", *Terrae Incognitae* 1, Nico Israel, Amsterdam, 1969, pp. 47–57, especially p. 55.

12. Alonso de Chaves, *Espejo de Navegantes de Alonso de Chaves: Quatri Partitu*, eds P. Castaneda, M. Cuesta, P. Hernandez, Museo Naval Madrid, 1983, p. 35 n. 74 and p. 36 n. 75.

13. Kelley, James E., Jr, "The map of the Bahamas implied by Chaves' *derrotero*, What is its relevance to the first landfall question?", *Imago Mundi* 42, 1990, pp. 26–47; also "Puzzles the New World posed for European mapmakers", paper delivered at the World History Association, Philadelphia, PA, June 26, 1992.

14. Pulido Rubio, op.cit., 1950, pp. 607–39.

15. Op. cit, p. 139ff.

16. Ursula Lamb, op. cit, p. 55 n. 11.

17. Pulido Rubio, El Piloto Mayor, 1st edn, 1923, p. 37.

17

18. Bühler, K.F., "Sixteenth-century prognostications, part II", *Isis* 33/5/91; *Handbuch zur Geschichte der Naturwissenschaften*, sixteenth-century listing.

19. Padre Fernando Oliveira, *A Arte Da Guerra No Mar*, 1555, Ministerio de Marinha, Lisbon, 1969.

20. Corbett, Julian S., "Fighting instructions, 1530–1816", pamphlet reprint, Burt Franklin, 1967, pp. 3–13.

21. Kelly, James E., Jr., *Imago Mundi* 42, 1990, p. 11.

22. Lamb, Ursula, "The Spanish cosmographic juntas of the sixteenth century", *Terrae Incognitae* 6, Nico Israel, Amsterdam, 1974, pp. 51–65.

23. Juan de Escalante de Mendoza, Itinerario de Navegación de los Mares y Tierras Occidentales, 1575, ed. Museo Naval, Madrid, 1985.

24. Baltasar Vellerino de Villalobos, *Luz de Navegantes*, 1555, ed. Museo Naval, Madrid, 1985.

25. Manoel de Andrada Castel Blanco, *Instrucción* ... to defend your empire and the faith, advice offered to Philip, King of Spain and Portugal, ca. 1590. P.E.H. Hair, ed., Liverpool University Press, Liverpool, 1990.

26. Francisco Pacheco, *Libro de descripción de verdaderos retratos de Ilustres y Memorables Varones*, Sevilla, 1599, eds M. Pinero and R. Reyes, Sevilla, 1985, p. 154.

27. Pulido Rubio, op. cit., 1950, p. 70.

28. Leo Bagrow, *History of Cartography*, ed. R.H. Skelton, Harvard University Press, Cambridge, MA, 1951, p. 83 n. 1 and p. 237.

29. Archivo General de Indias, Contaduría, Cuentas del Tesorero Francisco Tello desde 1582–1584, Salarios pagados a los oficiales de la Casa de la Contratación, sig. 321.

30. Chaunu, Pierre et Huguette, *Séville et l'Atlantique, 1504-1650*, 8 vols, 10ème Librairie Armand Colin, Paris, 1955–59, compiles the annual traffic of the *carrera*: ships, owners, pilots, masters, crew, cargo, weather etc. They register the results of the training of Spain's mariners.

NAUTICAL SCIENTISTS AND THEIR CLIENTS IN IBERIA (1508-1624): SCIENCE FROM IMPERIAL PERSPECTIVE

When Europeans began to span the global world by regular sailing routes, there arose problems not known to earlier times. It was the task of the cosmographers to deal with the phenomena of the physical universe which confronted the people engaged in oceanic traffic of global scope. These included the problems of routes, of how to find them, how to keep to them, by what methods and means to equip and guide the ships, and how to train pilots and seamen. The work of the Iberian cosmographers was done under the auspices of the Pilot Major's offices in Sevilla and in Lisbon. From the point of view of the history of science during the age of reconnaissance, the results of the cosmographer's works are scattered among many disciplines, and are fragmented to such an extent, ranging from astronomy to zoology, that only specialists see any links between them. Yet the cosmographers lived in a world in which they had a clear identity, a world which was to them comprehensible and whole, though they worked within it toward limited and specific goals. What is needed, if scholars are to reconstitute their world, is a common reference, such as to their relationship with the clients on whose behalf they set about solving the problems which science developed on the basis of new information, its control, and its use.

From this point of view, the royal client was only one among a number who called on the special skills of the cosmographers. This paper, dealing with relations of three cosmographers to the Spanish crown, is the final one of a series and thus requires a brief resume of the earlier ones about other clients. It is the contention of these studies that nautical science was to an appreciable degree dependent upon the demands of clients, and that this imposed not only a certain restraint, but influenced the direction in which scientific inquiries could proceed. The effect of this referral led to scientific controversies being settled by such authority, or in a forum which suited the client, rather than the scientist.

As the earlier articles were determined, however, by the availability of sources and other extraneous factors, and the issue under review only developed after a fair amount of work on the Iberian cosmographers had been done.

I dealt with the quarrel between cosmographers of the *casa de la contratacion* over the advantages and disadvantages, or the virtue of accuracy over convenience, in the case of the two scale chart which reached the judges of the Council of the Indies on appeal from the court of the casa in Sevilla. This proved the inappropriateness of science by litigation. (1) Or to put it another way, doing justice to scientists is not the same as establishing truth in science. The *Junta* of Badajoz and Elvas, called by the kings of Portugal and Spain in 1524, to fix the line of demarcation between their claims in the Far East, showed the distortion of scientific truth in the service of diplomacy. (2) That information at the time would have been inadequate to a solution then, and later in 1566 and 1580, does not invalidate the contention that the difference of opinion had resulted from the primacy of political-diplomatic concerns. As a result there appeared to be significant scientific disagreement when there really was not. Or to make a point, scientific accuracy is not a diplomatic goal.

Another use of the junta seemed, at first glance, to be appropriate: the gathering of expert pilots and cosmographers to give testimony regarding the periodic correction of the *Padron* or Master Map of the casa de la contratacion. In case of conflict over the location of a place, the president of the junta took a vote, and the majority decision was entered on the charts. This compromise also proved an unreliable test of science by consultation. That is, majority vote is not concerned with truth but with consensus.

When the Spanish crown proposed to bestow a prize for the solution of the problem of determining longitude at sea in 1582, Spain's most learned scientists were compelled to act as judges in a competition. They complained bitterly over the waste of time spent as judges, and even more they disliked the distortion of scientific priorities which resulted from the misguided attempt to seek a solution to a yet insoluble problem by promoting science by competition. (3) From those papers emerged the story of scientific ideas being assessed by criteria drawn from other disciplines before a new set could be envolved especially adapted to cope with science.

Other studies showed the restrictions on scientific advance due to the social situation of the cosmographers who were a group only by elective affinity or devotion to their chosen work. That is, their knowledge and their skills did not come from one source, either the crafts, or the universities, nor did it depend on one client, such as the crown, the councils, or the merchants. Yet the cosmographers had to subject their work to assessment by the mechanisms which their clients used to judge the merits of their own concerns, or which were called for by circumstance.

Administrative decisions about monopolies of the manufacture of instruments and regulation of their use was discussed in the legal hassle over the

---

(1) Ursula Lamb, «Science by Litigation: A Cosmographic Feud», *Terrae Incognitae*, Vol. I, 1969, pp. 40-57.

(2) —— —, «The Spanish Juntas of the XVI Century», *Terrae Incognitae*, Vol. VI, 1974, pp. 51-65.

(3) —— —, «La nueva ciencia geografica; (una victima del sistema de concursos. Premios espanoles para la solucion de los problemas de la longitud», *Revista de Occidente*, Vol. XXXVII, n.º 110, pp. 162-183, Madrid, May 1972.

Sevillian lodestone. In that case attention was focussed upon rights and privileges, status and pay of the cosmographers, all to the disadvantage of scientific considerations. The nature and properties of the lodestone and its more efficient use were not even mentioned, making science completely subject to circumstance. (4) These studies pointed out the importance of purpose and funding for scientific work, especially by institutions. A closer look at the casa de la contratacion and the Council of the Indies then brought out the importance of social experience as a factor not to be neglected in an account of the history of science. (5) The study revealed the intimate association of the growing data base with conceptual progress, and the result when theoreticians ignored or were cut off from the stimulous and the control of new facts reaching the Pilot Major's office in Sevilla. The challenge to old assumptions which arrived with every ship which returning from reconnaissance was ignored in Sevilla and Madrid, even thought it carried indispensable information to help with the construction of an *imago mundi* more closely in accord with experienced reality. What is still missing from these accounts is a look at the royal client and the court. Social connections, professional status or money do not validate scientific claims.

Today's paper deals with the work of some cosmographers from the perspective of the Spanish empire «upon which the sun never set». Three men will be discussed, Juan Bautista Gesio, Diego Garcia de Palacios, and Hernando de los Rios Coronel. The first viewed cosmographic problems from the imperial base in Madrid, the second from the New World, and the third from the frontier of colonial enterprise in the Far East. This is neither the occasion nor is there time to do justice to the three individuals chosen, either biographically, or with an evaluation of their works. Only their response to the crown will be examined, in order to show how their science was helped or hindered by that relationship.

Of the three, Juan Bautista Gesio is the least noted in the literature because of the great variety of issues he treated over the fifteen years that he served the Spanish crown from 1565-1580, (6) and because he left no published

---

(4) —— ——, «The Sevillian lodestone: science and circumstance» to be published in *Terrae Incognitae*, Vol. XI, 1987, pp. 29-41.

(5) —— ——, «The Cosmographers of Sevilla: Nautical Science and Social Experience», *First Images of America* ed. Fredi Chiappelli, 2 vols., Berkeley, California, 1976, vol. 2, pp. 675-686.

(6) Gesio's time of service is variously indicated. He was paid as *fiscal* of the armada in Santander in 1557, El Escorial, MS. P I 20, cited in J. Zarco, *Catalogo de los mss castellanos de la Real Biblioteca de El Escorial*, 2 vols. Madrid, 1926, vol. 2, pp. 232-233. He writes that he served his Majesty for fourteen years «sono quator deci anni che sto en questa corte» on 15 Nov. 1571, in MS. El Escorial, MS. P I 20, fol. 34; and in his last plea, to have the sum of ten ducats paid him by the Council of the Indies transfered to his brother Pompeio he aludes to ten years service. These were the years when he was on the payroll of the Council of the Indies. See Archivo General de Indias, Sevilla (hereafter AGI) Patronato, 261, Ro. 2.

work. He was a Neapolitan with an intimate knowledge of the Western Mediterranean, both of the African and European coasts. By training he was a cosmographer and a mathematician, but his employment was that of a secret agent of Philip the Prudent. He was deeply involved in spying out the situation in Portugal during the last year of King Sebastian's life, when Philip II was preparing for his succession to the Portuguese throne, and Gesio was attached to the suit of the Spanish embassador D. Juan de Borja in Lisbon in 1569. (7)   When the ambassador was recalled in 1572, Gesio was ordered to accompany him to Madrid, and to bring along a large collection «dos baulas» of manuscripts, books, charts, and maps, which had been collected in Portugal. (8)   He was ordered to give his opinion concerning the merit of the material, what parts of it could serve the Council of the Indies, which papers should be kept secret, and what of the whole lot should be immediately deposited in the library of the Escorial.

The least exploited collections of manuscripts in Gesio's hand are in the British Museum and in the Escorial. (9).   They spell out his activity as a spy clearly and in fascinating detail.   They also contain his last attempts to be paid enough for his living at the court in Madrid, which he made by submitting to the king all kinds of unsolicited dissertations in the manner of the later *arbitristas*. (10)   These concern the organization of government, i.e., the distribution of authority, the morals of princes with reference to Naples, royal succession in general, and Spain's right to the Portuguese inheritance, the political situation in Europe, and news from around the globe as received in Lisbon by his friends and agents.   Whenever the occasion called for it Gesio gave scientific data concerning location, latitude and longitude of places, distances, and times.   He recommended a book written under the sponsorship of Viceroy Toledo (sic) about Peru, detailing its virtues by listing all the kinds of information about the nature, resources, flora, fauna, human society, language, social organization, religion etc. (11)   All this was in the spirit of

---

(7)   Gregorio Andres, O.S.A., «Juan Bautista Gesio, cosmografo de Felipe II y portador de documentos geograficos desde Lisboa para la Biblioteca de El Escorial en 1573». *Publicaciones de la Real Sociedade Geografica*, N.º 478, serie B, Madrid, 1976.   For documentation in the AGI see «Catalogo de los documentos relativos a las islas Filipinas existentes en el Archivo de Indias de Sevilla, precedido de una Historia General de Filipinas por el P. Pablo Pastells, S.J.; vol. 2, Barcelona, 1926.
Most of the documents are copied in Martin Fernandez de Navarrete, Coleccion, Museo Naval, vols. 14, 18, 20, 27, 28.
(8)   Ibid. p. 7, instruction to Lopez de Velasco.   British Museum, (hereafter BM) MS. Egerton 2047, fol. 325, letter to the president of the Council of the Indies to have Gesio give his opinion.
(9)   El Escorial, MS. L I 12; and BM, in vols. Add. 28.359 and 28.360.
(10)   BM, MS. Add. 28.359, fol. 1, has a letter to the King regarding the insufficiency of cyphers.   Gesio has no suggestions about improving them, but rather seeks personal audience with the king.
(11)   The text is published in M. Fraile Miguelez, *Catalogo de los codices espanoles de la Biblioteca del Escorial* (Relaciones Historicas), 2 vols.   Madrid, 1917, vol. 1, p. 84

the times when collection, description, and measurement were the means of integrating new knowledge with what was already known.

Gesio's mathematics is a matter of claim rather than demonstration. (12) He appears several times as consulting expert in cosmographic matters. The Consejo de Indias asked that he give his opinion regarding the *pareceres* of the junta of 1566 which had been called to fix the line of demarcation in the Far East, and he concluded that it had been drawn to the disadvantage of Spanish claims to the Moluccas. (13) Gesio judged a work on New Spain, which had been referred to him for appraisal, to be unreliable, and advised against publication. (14) His discourse on works concerning the straits of Magellan, and the fortification and settlement there, were accompanied by a *derrotero* which he had obtained in Portugal made by Andres de San Martin «que fue con Magellanes.» (15) Gesio also wrote a well known report about the coast, and the extent east-to-west of Brazil, or rather its fronting on Peru, in which he again stressed the interests of Spain as against the configuration then current in Portugal. (16) What he had to say on cartographic and cosmographic matters in these respects has entered modern discussions about them, so that what is of interest here is a residue of miscellaneous information which

---

carta autografa a Felipe II sobre la descripcion y geografia del Peru», Madrid, 16 Feb., 1576. The entire text is in Italian, but a *sobrecarta* has a marginal note by Velasco? «de la descripcion del Peru q hace don Martin Enriquez.» The text also by Jole Ruggieri, in *Bibliofilia*, anno XXXIII, disp. 5a-6a, pp. 258-259.

(12) Gesio was sent an Italian booklet about the calendar reform which had been forwarded from Rome to Madrid. He reported that there were enough of the best mathematicians in Spain to do the job as well. El Escorial, MS. L I 12, fol. 258, «borrador de carta anonima (sic) sobre la correcion del calendario». On the other hand, a petition to be given the job of mathematics tutor to prince «venceslao» also in Italian, is in a different hand. Fraile Miguelez speculates that it might be by Juan Bautista Antonelli.

(13) BM, MS. Add. 28.359, fol. 239, deals with the demarcation. Gesio considered himself an expert on that topic and complained about not having been consulted, for instance, BM, MS. Add. 28.341, fol. 148, 9 Aug. 1578; AGI, Patronato, 261, Ro. 2, 26 Feb. 1580. See also: Luis Mendonça de Albuquerque, «O Tratado de Tordesillas e as dificuldades técnicas da sua aplicação rigorosa», in *El Tratado de Tordesillas y su Proyeccion*, Segundas Jornadas Americanistas, Primer Coloquio Luso-Espanol de Historia de Ultramar. Ed. Demetrio Ramos, Seminario de Historia de America, Universidad de Valladolid, 2 vols. Valladolid, 1973, pp. 119-137; A. Teixeira da Mota, «Reflexos do Tratado de Tordesilhas na Cartografia do Seculo XVI», *Ibid.* pp. 137-149.

(14) Text in C. Fernandez Duro, *Disquisiciones Nauticas* 6 vols. Madrid, 1872-1881, vol. 6, «Los Ojos en el Cielo», pp. 308-316.

(15) Museo Naval, Madrid, Coleccion Navarrete, XX, fol. 114 et seq. includes *derrotero* of the strait by Andres de San Martin; also AGI Patronato 33, doc. 9, on fortification of the strait.

(16) AGI, Patronato, 29, Ro. 32, is very extensive. See also Leite Cordeiro, «Documentos quinhentistas espanhois referentes a capitania de Sao Vicente» *Revista do Instituto Historico de Sao Paolo*, vol. XLVI, p. 314 et seq.; Sergio Buarque de Holanda, *Visao do Paraiso*, São Paolo, 1969, p. 107. I owe these references and much encouragement to Prof. C. R. Boxer.

54

taken together with the rest, can lead to conclusions about the cosmographers of the Spanish court.

As a person, Gesio himself stays hidden. His education is a matter of conjecture. Italian was the language he used most comfortably though in a corrupt form. He was fluent, though equally shaky, in Portuguese, but his Spanish texts in final copy are in another hand, and *borradores* are always corrected for grammar and spelling. He did know the New World from travel, though to postulate extended and repeated visits, as does Picatoste, seems risky for lack of evidence. (17) There is no proof that he ever visited the Far East. His versatility concerning cartographic and political information, joined to a lack of specialization in any area, distinguishes him from other cosmographers only by the excessive degree caused by his varied employment. Gesio's relations with leading figures at court were also exceptional. He traveled in the train of Ambassador D. Juan de Borja in Lisbon He worked with Cristovao de Moura, the Portuguese adviser of king Philip whom he called D. Cristoforo de Mora. Antonio Perez cut orders for him, and his protector in Madrid was the cosmographer royal, Lopez de Velasco. (18)

Gesio's knowledge was most precise concerning Portugal. He forwarded ample information, including a pilot's report, on the approaches by sea from Setubal to Lisbon, and included a map in his own hand. (19) If his knowledge of the Caribbean, possibly also of the Brazilian coast can be defended as first hand, his praise of the book on Peru is entirely based on information which has been gathered for the Viceroy in Lima. His expert testimony on those regions and on the Far East was well founded on privileged information which he was able to obtain in Lisbon. Some of it was so sensitive that he would not give it to de Moura. (20)

The sources available to Gesio were many and reliable. His most famous informant was Luis Jorge de Barbuda, a Portuguese cartographer of rank, who furnished Gesio with precious information and with maps. (21) Barbuda

(17) Felipe Picatoste y Rodriguez, *Apuntes para una Biblioteca Cientifica Espanola del Siglo XVI*, Madrid, 1891, p. 129.

(18) BM, MS. ADD. 28.441, fol. 148-149, refers to «mio amico Juan Lopez de Velasquo.»

(19) Fraile Miguelez, *Op. Cit.*, indexes these papers in his catalogue of the MSS. of the Escorial in P I 20. There are 240 fols. A note concerning the sandbar in the harbor in Lisbon appears on fol. 79, and there is a double folio map of that harbor and the approach to it from Setubal.

(20) El Escorial, MS. P I 20, fol. 31v.

(21) Identification of Luis Jorge (various spellings) as Luis Jorge de Barbuda was made definite by Armando Cortesao, *Cartografia e cartografos portugueses dos séculos XV e XVI*, Lisbon, 1934, 2 vols., vol. 1, pp. 276-285. Since then, a letter dated 21 July 1579, has been published by Pedro Longas Bartibas from the Archivo del Instituto de Valencia de Don Juan, envio 44, doc. 159, entitled: «Carta del astrologo Juan Bautista Gesio al Rey Felipe II» in *Congresso do Mundo Portugues* vol. VI, 1940, pp. 169-172. An earlier letter asked for a commission to be given to Luis Jorge to «tracare alcun disegno de pro-

went over to Spain having been thoroughly compromised in Portugal, and Gesio recommended him to the King and to Lopez de Velasco, the royal cosmographer. «Luis Giorgio» now identified as de Barbuda rose to serve with the Pilot Major in a crucial revision of affairs at the casa de la contratacion, and the *cronista mayor* Lopez de Velasco undoubtedly drew on his information for his *Geografia General de las Indias*. It was a different situation with other members of the Council of the Indies. Even though Gesio worked with them, he did not trust them, and they did not favor him. He wanted very much to return to Lisbon and pleaded with the king for an audience, or for a new commission. (22)

Gesio's dedication to science would only come second to his other concerns. Cosmography was for him the indispensable factual base for empire, and his stock in trade to help the Spanish crown was information. But Spanish claims were paramount with him, and he may well have been a source for the anti-meridian drawn on the manuscript map of Lopez de Velasco, dated 1575, which goes through the tip of Malaya. His connections with Italian scientists were certainly close, though an anonymous report concerning a booklet about the Gregorian calendar reform, which had reached Madrid from Rome, may not be in his hand. The document states that there were as many and superior mathematicians available to the king in Spain as there were in Italy. (23)

The nearest proof we have of his interest in experiment was his scheme for a scientifically monitored transfer of spice plants from the spice islands to the New World. (24) This experiment was to be coordinated by the Council of the Indies. It was based on the assumption that all feasible climates and soils, elevations, and other natural conditions would be met within the latitudes and extent of the viceroyalties of Mexico and Peru. A successful transplant would terminate the conflict over possession of the spice islands. The king and council, however, were apt to assess any project first for profitability and feasibility, and it is impressive to read how Gesio tried to overcome those hurdles of parsimony and *Real Politik*. The insoluble problem was, that he had enemies in the Council of the Indies, and Lopez de Velasco was not heard to speak for him in this case. (25)

---

vincia». Gesio had been putting up his colleague in his own house for four months and, at the date of writing, did not know whether Barbuda had left the hospital clandestinely and without license; 12 Sept. 1574, El Escorial. MS. P I 20, fols. 58v-59.

(22) BM, MS. Add. 28.359, fols. 217r-218v; Gesio complains about having nothing to send to the king: «e desiderio convenire personalmente a far offerta de alcune cose e darle bona pasca...» in fact, he was ill by then.

(23) Frai Miguelez, *Op. Cit.*, vol. 2, p. 85.

(24) Ursula Lamb, «Dos Huellas científicas del tratado de Tordesillas», Primer Colloquio Luso-Espanol de Historia de Ultramar, *Segundas Jornadas de la Universidade de Valladolid*, 2 vols. Valladolid, 1973, vol. 1, pp. 185-193, based on AGI Patronato 48, Ro. 3, including transcription.

(25) «Io sto malsatisfatto e mal contento del consiglio d'India per molte cause...» BM, MS. Add. 28.341, fol. 148, 27 July 1579.

Juan Bautista Gesio, *mathematico y cosmographo de S. M.* died on September 14th 1580. His testament signed two days before in Madrid, is now in the Archivo General de Indias in Sevilla. It has greater significance than the enumeration of debts, and the state of poverty which it documents. Gesio left behind some working tools which entitle him to be counted among the «mathematical practitioners» or practicing scientists. The property listed consisted of a terrestrial copper globe, much used and not worth any money, likewise some books, equally used and valued at 50 reales. The instruments were a copper sphere, an astronomer's ring (anulo), a cuadrant (una red), and a clock shaped flat, also made of copper, two celestial spheres and one terrestrial globe of paper, much worn, «which instruments have been taxed and estimated at very low value, because they are almost all much used (ill treated), broken and damaged, and for that reason they have not yet been sold.» (26)

The state of penury reached to the New World as well. It was from Mexico that Diego Garcia de Palacio wrote that «matters in the Indies are so unfavourable that save for those (people) who serve in royal offices, or who are in trade, they are not living in the comfort which should befit yourself.» (27)   Don Diego had secured royal offices and had accumulated enough money and credit to offer to complete the conquest of the Philippines with his own funds in 1578. (28)   But at the time of his death, his widow sought «alguna merced» to sustain her life, because Diego Garcia had taken advantage of his offices to an extent which brought financial ruin when a *residencia* judge imposed the requisite fine. (29)

Garcia de Palacio came from a family of navigators in the city of Arce, and was the oldest of five sons all of whom were in the royal service. He followed a course of studies which would lead to a naval career. It is not known why he changed his mind to turn to the persuit of letters and the law, though he did not neglect his earlier interests. Garcia de Palacio served in the Consejo de Indias and in 1572, was named *fiscal* of the Audiencia of Guatemala. Within two months of that appointment he was promoted to *oidor* of the Audiencia, serving until 1579, when he assumed the office of *alcalde de crimen.* When Drake passed the strait of Magellan, and while he was raiding along the Pacific coast, Garcia de Palacio was charged to go in persuit of the English pirate. Under this «improvised general» as Fernandez

(26)   AGI, Patronato 261, Ro. 2, «Testamento otorgado por G.B. Gesio de S. M. Matematico que murio en Madrid 14 de sept. de 1580».   There is also a pay-list: «Relacion de lo que parece hacerse librado a Juan Bautista Gesio, Cosmografo», 27 June, 1580, *Ibid.*

(27)   Edmundo O'Gorman, «Nuevos datos sobre el Dr. Diego Garcia de Palacio, 1589,» *Boletin del Archivo General de la Nacion,* Mexico, vol. XVII, pp. 1-32.

(28)   «Carta al rey sobre la pacificacion y conquista de las islas Filipinas...» Museo Naval, Madrid, Coleccion Navarrete, vol. XVIII, fol. 59 et. seq.

(29)   AGI, Mexico 1, Ro. 40.   Consultas, 9 and 26 May 1596.   The final instruction reads: «Acerca de la merced que ha de haverse a la mujer e hijos del doctor Diego Garcia de Palacio, difunto oidor que fue de la Audiencia de Mejico».

Duro puts it, the task force failed to catch Drake. Garcia de Palacio, wrote a well known *carta al Rey* on 10 April 1579, about that venture, from the port of Realejo. (30) He is next heard of in Mexico when a doctorate of canon law from the *Real y Pontifica Universidad de Mexico* was bestowed on him in 1580, and he was named the 32nd rector of that institution from 10 December, 1581, to 10 December, 1582. He was also *consultor* of the *Holy Office*.

Don Diego was an exceptionally well informed colonial official. He was interested in many schemes. The plan to promote a rival crossing of the Central American Isthmus via Honduras, Puerto de Caballos on the Atlantic side, and the Bay of Fonseca on the Pacific, was one of them. (31) Suggesting himself as a candidate for the governorship of the Philippines was another. (32) He had his enemies. A royal *ejecutoria* (decree) of 1589, suspended him from his office of *oidor* for nine years, and sentenced him to pay a large sum of money because of abuse of his office of *juez visitador*, of acceptance of bribes, use of threats, mistreatment of Indians, and for favoring the youngest of his brothers by assigning him 26 *caballerias* of land, and water rights for a sugar mill. (33) He died in 1595 in Santander.

Among his papers are two books, the *Dialogos Militares* of 1583, (34) and his *Instruccion nauthica para el buen uso y regimiento de las naos y su traca y govierno conforme a la altura de Mexico* (1585). (35) According to Martin Fernandez de Navarrete, these works put him in the front rank of contemporary authors of nautical science, such as Sarmiento de Gamboa and Juan Escalante de Mendoza. They also put his name on the list of those men whose advice would be listened to by the Council of the Indies. If ulterior purpose guided his pen, the product was worth royal attention.

The *instruccion nauthica* is divided into four books. It begins with a chapter on the celestial and terrestrial spheres, their measure and number. There follows a description of the division of the globe by latitude and longitude, the position of the poles and of the equator. Next he gives a description of nautical instruments and their use: of the compass, the quadrant, the astrolabe, and the cross-staff, with instructions for calculating the hours of the day. The second part of the book is a dissertation on astronomy with tables and almanachs, followed by description of the movement of the sun,

---

(30) Juan Garcia Icazbalceta, *Bibliografia Mexicana del Siglo XVI*, Agustin Millares ed., Mexico, Fondo de Cultura Economica, 1954, p. 394.

(31) See note 28. The text continues: «... y las ventajas de hacerse la navegacion para ellas (las Filipinas) desde el puerto de Fonseca.»

(32) *Ibid.*

(33) The text of the *ejecutoria* in full is given by O'Gorman, *Loc. Cit.*

(34) Garcia Icazbalceta, *Op. Cit.* pp. 316-321, gives full bibliographical information and an abstract of the *Dialogos*.

(35) Facsimile edition Ediciones Cultura Hispanica, Madrid, 1944. Picatoste, *Op. Cit.*, p. 129; Navarrete in his *Dissertacion sobre la Historia de la Nautica*, Madrid, 1846, pp. 249-250 mentions that as late as 1621 Juan Gallo de Miranda published in Mexico an «imitation» of Garcia de Palacio's text.

58

the moon, conjunction of the planets, and the regularities of the tides. In the third book, the author writes about astrology (astrologia rustica) or stellar movement affecting the person. His next chapter which deals with ship construction is based upon experience and practice on the American Pacific coast and is therefore of major interest, as is the unusual and invaluable vocabulary of nautical terms in the appendix. (36) The final chapter brings the description of the «sufficient ship», or a ship fitted out for a voyage, and it discusses the personnel aboard.

His *instruccion nauthica* was highly respected in Europe as well as in New Spain and in Peru. The discussion of the sphere is no advancement over texts then in use, and it is written in the same tortuous style of the time and genre. His contribution consisted in his printing of tables based upon the Gregorian calendar, and in his reference of distances to Mexico City. His orientation toward the Far East which had a special appeal to pilots of the Pacific route, lies in his description, his practical experience, and can be seen in the advice which he made available to all who could read.

Garcia de Palacio made his living in the New World as an administrator, a businessman, and an entrepreneur, to stay with an alphabetical listing of his occupations, contrasted with his activities as a practitioner and teacher of cosmography. In the latter capacity he functioned as custodian of new knowledge, as observer of the oceanic environment, and as instructor in the art of war on land and sea.

The cosmographer whose career reached the farthest geographical distance from Madrid to be discussed to-day is Hernando de los Rios Coronel. His curiculum vita is made up of an even longer list of enterprises, commissions, and varieties of public services than were those of the two cosmographers just discussed. Nothing new has been found out about his origin and early days. (37) He entered the record as a soldier on his way to the Philippines in 1588. Upon arrival he joined several military expeditions and was promoted to Captain. He had risen to that rank when he accompanied the governor D. Luis Dasmarinas on his expedition to Luzon and Cambodia. Staying

---

(36) The *Instruccion Nauthica* was one of the books used by the Spanish Academy in its dictionary of authorities. It is more complete than the contemporary word lists by Andres de Poza. An English translation is being prepared by J. Bankston.

(37) Martin Fernandez de Navarrete, *Biblioteca Maritima*, vol. 1, pp. 636-647 contains a bio-bibliography of Rios Coronel. See also Antonio de Morga, *Sucesos de las Islas Filipinas*, Ed. W. E. Retana, Madrid, 1909, p. 431 brings a biographical sketch which is informative, especially about Rios Coronel in the Far East. A letter to Antonio de Morga of 3 December, 1598, says that because of a false projection of the papal line of demarcation, the Portuguese claim all of the Molucas, Siam, Cambodia, Cochinchina and China « e todo lo demas deste Archipielago» that is east of Malacca, which he finds unjust as some of these districts should be on the Spanish side; For the text see A. de Morga, *Sucesos* pp. 88-89. See also C. E. Boxer, *Fidalgos in the Far East*, The Hague, 1948, pp. 46-47; C. R. Boxer, *The Great Ship from the Amacon* Lisbon, 1959, pp. 61-62; Lawrence C. Wroth, «Early Cartography of the Pacific,» *Bibliographical Society of America*, Papers 38. N.º 2, New York. 1944, p. 159.

on in China in 1597, he prepared the first map of Luzon, the Isla Hermosa (Formosa, Taiwan), and parts of the coast of China. He stayed in the Orient for seventeen years during which time he became a secular priest. His knowledge of the Far East led him to correspond with the crown regarding royal policy, and it has been a prime source for historians since. In 1615 he returned to Spain, having been chosen «procurador», which meant that he was honored by the colonists of Manila to represent them before the King in Madrid. The time of his voyage from Manila to Puerto de la Navidad, in New Spain, from there to Acapulco and Mexico City (calculated at 23 33'), was well spent on fixing the positions of those places by astronomical as well as compass readings. He did the same in Vera Cruz and Havana, observed the variation of the compass in the Atlantic, and kept an exact reckoning of the time of his crossing to Cape Saint Vincent. (38) His work was well regarded and was esteemed for accuracy, and the useful comparison with earlier *derrotas,* especially by Urdaneta, of which he was well aware.

De los Rios Coronel was also an experimenter. He designed an «aparatus» of copper taking very little space, to convert salt water into sweet, which would be more efficient than the model then in use, thought to date from the voyage of Quiros. A petition to have it tested and licensed gives a summary description of the process of distillation. He asserted that his apparatus would use less firewood, and promised a slightly larger volume of converted water than had been obtained until then. (39) His experience on the Pacific and Atlantic made his observations very useful to the cosmographers of the Council of the Indies which was testing various «corrected» compasses, and other schemes, in the competition for solution of the problem of fixing longitude at sea. De los Rios Coronel became the head of the junta of pilots who were charged with the examination of the instruments submitted. The scientific advisers of the Council of the Indies wasted no time in employing this knowledgeable expert to test and to report the performance of some of the instruments during his return voyage in 1610 to the New World and the Far East. (40) While still in the Orient, de los Rios Coronel wrote to the king that he was preparing a book about the art of navigation, a work which has not been seen. He did submit an astrolabe of his own design which he presented to the Consejo de Indias as an improvement over the instruments then on the market. (41) Details of these works

(38) Biblioteca Nacional, Madrid, MS. 3176, fols. 110-117; Navarrete, *Op. Cit.* vol. 1, pp. 643-644. Museo Naval, Madrid, MS. 188, fols. 12, 63-73; Ms. 190, fol. 76, MS. 313, fol. 12v. There is no collection or edition of the extent «pareceres», «memoriales», and «cartas» by Hernando de los Rios.

(39) Martin Fernandez de Navarrete, *Obras,* Biblioteca de Autores Espanoles, 3 vols. Madrid, 1954, vol. 1, p. 70, has the report by the casa de la contratacion to the Council of the Indies concerning an experiment with the apparatus, performed twice on 25 May, 1610, to the satisfaction of the observers.

(40) Museo Naval, Madrid, Colleccion Navarrete, XVIII, fol. 316, doc. 58.

(41) The very rare booklet is entitled: *Memorial y Relacion para Su Magestad,* Madrid, 1621, ref. Morga, *Op. Cit.,* introduction of Retana, pp. 31-32.

have not yet been recovered. In 1618 he returned again to Spain, and in 1622 published his *Memorial y relacion de las Filipinas, de lo que conviene remediar, y de las riquezas que hay en ellas y en las islas del Maluco*, which is an entirely political document.

The choice of these three cosmographers was made because each provided in his work a special trait which contributed to the new way in which science approached natural phenomena. Gesio was remarkable for the comprehensiveness of his observations and the extent of his information about all of nature, sky and earth, and life and societies of the past and present. What ties him to his historic epoch is his purpose, to serve the Spanish king. He advanced science by asking how theory agreed with observation. His greatest limitation was secrecy which he could not abandon even in scientific matters.

Garcia de Palacio made progress in that respect by publishing his books on military and nautical topics. His question pointing toward future development of science was whether theory corresponded to practice, and he tried to make it do so, for his books are practical hand books. He also promoted public discourse by providing a precise vocabulary for common reference. Though his major purpose was self interest, and he depended totally on preferment by the crown, he advanced toward a concept of shared information which should characterize scientific work.

De los Rios Coronel was politically as involved as the others. An intellectual and a man of superior intelligence, stamina and rectitude, he was an experimenter of the new breed. The transition from experience to experiment is clearly seen in his work. Regarding natural phenomena he wanted to test, wherever possible, how cause relates to effect.

When the cosmographers were seen as scientists, it is interesting to note what qualities of character were expected of them. They were described as *perito, docto, experimentado, entendido,* and *desapasionado.* These attributes, when taken in conjunction, are not the terms most immediately appropriate for jurists, soldiers, or merchants. But they do spell out a certain relationship to the nature of the scientist's expertise.

It might be well, as this point, to emphasize that the social context of the work of the cosmographers does not address the problem of the nature of scientific knowledge. The closest to a workeable definition of science in the sense of these papers would be to say that science was made up of statements about the physical universe which showed a relational consistency, and allowed the possibility of repeatable experiment. The specific contributions to the various forms of integration of new knowledge is therefore a different and separate story.

The king as client of the cosmographers could draw on his widespread empire to find those who were known to be excellent at their work, and his network reached far. Gesio, a Neapolitan, through him Luis Jorge de Barbuda, had information from far-flung sources, while Garcia de Palacios and de los Rios Coronel, added personal acquaintance with distant regions, and first hand scientific experience. In the fifteen thirties, Emperor Charles V (Ist of Spain) was known to have listened to his cosmographer Alonso de Santa Cruz as a pastime for filling idle hours. And that is where the limitation of royal sponsorship can be seen. To the crown cosmography was either a means, an instrument to apply information to advantage, like diplomacy, or a diversion. Any deeper knowledge was either merely entertaining, or frivolous, or under the Habsburg Philips, possibly heretical. The science of the cosmographers, as sponsored by the kings and court, was limited in its very essence by being seen as a means, which in fact is science limited to technology.

The exception was the foundation of a mathematical academy by Philip II at his court in Madrid in 1582. In founding that institution, he was acting as a patron rather than a client. Putting the most knowledgeable scientists of his realm to work to create a corpus of translated classics, of updated treatises, and to charge them to undertake investigations and experiments, anticipated later foundations in Europe. (42) After the death of the great Portuguese cosmographer Labanha in 1624, the courtly audience of amateurs, and a king uninterested in science, withdrew their patronage, and even left the ranks of clients to be filled by government agencies when the need for some application of science arose. (43)

Scientific disagreements had been taken to the law by scientists, to the negotiating table by diplomats, and to arbitration by merchants. The cosmographers had been invited to the council table by the Council of the Indies for expert opinions to be made on political grounds, and gathered to vote in committee in the casa de la contratacion. The king made them judges in a competition, and found it useful to employ the cosmographers in the efforts to gain information, to control it and to use it. Once the crown settled for use of science alone, the cosmographers were deprived of their responsibility for vital new information, either by collection of data, by experiment and verification, or by assimilation to prior assumptions. Their interests were narrowed, and they lost the common ground achieved in the academy of mathematics by having science limited to use, and bereft of purpose. (44)

---

(42) Jose Fernandez Montana, *Felipe II el Prudente, Rey de España, Relacion con Ciencias y Sabios*, Madrid, 1912, pp. 354-359.

(43) The academy was the high point of support for scientific knowledge reached in Spain after Columbus. Beginning by being tolerated, science was being used and supported to be finally severely neglected when the established power became aware of the base for political and social dissent which its persuit might present. This experience was clearly identified only at a later date. *El Cientifico espanol ante su historia: la ciencia en Espana entre 1750-1850*. Santiago Garma, ed., Primer Congreso de la Sociedad Espanola de Historia de Las Ciencias. Diputacion Provincial, Madrid, 1980, has articles by different hands which in several instances furnish a sequel to this study.

(44) Robert Spaemann and Reinhardt Low, *Die Frage Wozu? Geschichte und Wiederentdeckung des Teleologischen Denkens*. Munich, 1981, is very suggestive, though the book addresses problems of contemporary sciences.

X

DOS HUELLAS CIENTIFICAS DEL TRATADO DE TORDESILLAS

EL PROYECTO DE 1558 SOBRE LAS ESPECIAS Y LA DEMARCACION POR LINEAS ASTRONOMICAS DE TIERRAS NO EXPLORADAS EN 1783-4

E L tratado de Tordesillas no constituye una excepción a la regla según la cual los acuerdos diplomáticos adquieren su plena dimensión histórica solamente cuando a sus causas, objetivos, negociación y texto se añade una reflexión acerca de los acontecimientos que se han desarrollado a causa de los mismos. Tordesillas fue un esfuerzo para prevenir las rivalidades de dos competidores, España y Portugal, por dominar el tráfico de especias. El tratado fue ocasionado por el desafío español a la pretensión de Portugal, en el sentido de obtener exclusividad en el comercio de esta codiciada fuente de riqueza, en momentos en que una ruta vía el Atlántico y el Oeste parecía practicable. El acuerdo de Tordesillas se basaba en el conocimiento de que las islas especieras existían al Este de las tierras alcanzadas hasta entonces por los portugueses, y en la certeza adicional de que estas mismas habrían de ser encontradas, si no por la ruta del Este, presumiblemente por la del Oeste. Sin embargo por donde hubieran de ser encontradas y por cual de las potencias ibéricas, era aún impredecible. Asimismo, también el hecho de que la fuente de las especias —Las Molucas— fuese la única, no era absolutamente seguro, de modo que otras islas que aún pudieran descubrirse en el océano, al oeste de las Antillas, bien pudieran rivalizar con las fabulosas islas de la tradición.

Tordesillas no solucionó la competencia empeñada sobre área geográfica alguna, sino que se limitó a confirmar las pautas establecidas por las bulas papales para los sucesivos descubrimientos. Estas proyectaron una línea longitudinal, derivada de regularidades observadas en el planisferio estelar sobre la superficie desconocida del globo terrestre, sobre *terrae et mari incognitae*.

Como si fuese producto de la casualidad, la ubicación de las Molucas, que hubieran eventualmente de encontrarse, estaba tan cerca de la línea divisoria, que se perdió de vista la naturaleza totalmente hipotética de ésta (1). Este hecho fué evidente al estancarse la Junta de Badajoz. En esa famosa reunión los cosmógrafos de ambas potencias no pudieron ponerse de acuerdo acerca de la ubicación exacta de la línea longitudinal. Como consecuencia, la línea meridiana no pudo establecerse de modo satisfactorio para ambas partes. De tal manera, Badajoz ha sido descrita como un fracaso del acuerdo científico.

De hecho si se hubiera de asumir que los científicos hubieran podido ponerse de acuerdo, de todos modos se hubieran producido negociaciones, puesto que el dominio del tráfico especiero hubiera sido disputado por el perdedor. Las instrucciones de Hernando Colón en Badajoz, explicaban el uso preciso de la información científica que se encontraba a su disposición, y los plazos de su publicación, a fin de apoyar las pretensiones españolas (2). Que la línea, pues, no había sido la solución del problema, sino tan sólo un tanteo, se puso de manifiesto en la venta de Zaragoza. Esta negociación suspendió la determinación científica de los derechos y solucionó el problema del tráfico de especias provisionalmente, hasta que se pudiera llegar a una revisión sobre la base de nuevos datos y la posibilidad de un acuerdo entre los científicos sobre la línea de demarcación.

El tratado de Tordesillas y la venta de Zaragoza dejaron pendiente dos cuestiones al problema de la división de los beneficios del comercio especiero: 1) la determinación científica de la línea, y 2) suplir de alguna manera la carencia de la especiería, por distintos medios de la habitual disputa por los territorios que las producían.

Mientras progresaban los experimentos científicos acerca de la línea longitudinal, aunque no mucho, los proyectos para resolver el problema pueden ser clasificados bajo dos epígrafes: el primero, encontrar una nueva fuente de especias, es decir, otras islas especieras, además de las Molucas orientales, dadas a conocer por los comerciantes árabes. El segundo, aclimatar las plantas especieras. Estos proyectos son parte de las consecuencias derivadas del Tratado de Tordesillas, tanto en la historia de España como en la de Portugal, y, lógicamente tratarán de ser llevados a la práctica.

---

(1) "Las Molucas son cinco islas, denominadas en el siglo XVI Bachian, Machian, Motir, Ternate y Tidor; están orientadas de Norte a Sur, y Bachian, un poco más al Sur, está sobre el Ecuador a 127 30' este de Greenwich. Si la demarcación de la línea en Brasil está aproximadamente a 47 30' Oeste de Greenwich, las Molucas están alrededor de 175 grados al Este de la demarcación de Brasil, y cinco grados dentro del hemisferio Portugués". Cita de Marcel Destombes, "The Chart of Magellan", en *Imago Mundi*, XII, 1955, p. 65, nota 1. Nuestro artículo se refiere a las Molucas, en modo general, como a las islas productoras de especies, incluyendo Ceilán y Luzón. Ver apéndice.

(2) "... y conforme a ello encamyneys los negocios por manera que parezca que de nuestra parte ro queda que hazer con el secreto y buena manera que de vosotros confío y de todo ello dareys parte al lic. de pisa mi secretario muy secretamente." A. G. I. Patronato, Leg. 48, Ramo 12, Badajoz, 7 de Mayo, 1524.

EL PROYECTO DE TRANSPLANTE DE ESPECIAS

E L propósito de esta aportación nuestra se encamina en la segunda dirección: pues sabemos de un intento de aclimatar las plantas especieras en los dominios españoles, que se encuentra en una carta escrita por Juan Bautista Gesio (3), cosmógrafo de Felipe II, y dirigida al mismo.

Gesio, ciertamente, pertenecía al círculo íntimo de Felipe II, como predecesor de Juan López de Velasco. Sus obras abarcan problemas que ocupan a los cosmógrafos españoles hacia fines de la decimosexta centuria, incluyendo la línea de demarcación en Brasil y en el lejano oriente. Sirvió a la corona desde su llegada a España, aproximadamente en 1557, y entre los años 1569 y 1573 estuvo en Lisboa como agente del rey de España, siendo llamado luego a la Corte. El 14 de Septiembre de 1580 murió en Madrid, y se conserva en el A. G. I. su testamento y papeles de familia (4).

Como científico de calidad que era, Gesio conocía los problemas planteados en torno a la fijación de la línea de Tordesillas, ante la dificultad de señalar las longitudes con exactitud. Por eso estaba seguro que habría de fracasar también la junta de cosmógrafos que nuevamente, en 1566, trataría de establecer la línea de demarcación sobre la base de los nuevos datos obtenidos (5). Convencido de que "no haviendo hasta hoy demostración por las apariencias del cielo", abandonó los esfuerzos para determinar la línea con este método y comenzó a preocuparse por otro medio para evitar la carencia y marginación de la especiería. Lo que hace notable la carta de Gesio, es su enfoque del problema. Hay varios pasajes significativos en este sentido.

Los dos argumentos de Gesio para la empresa no son nuevos pero fueron convincentes: su plan hubiera contribuido en forma sustancial a acortar la ruta de transporte, limitándola a la carrera de las Indias, y hubiera garantizado un envío seguro por tierra desde cualquier lugar del Nuevo Mundo donde pudieran encontrarse las plantaciones hasta un puerto de embarque, utilizando así una vía que discurriera totalmente a través de los dominios españoles. Que no se encontraba nada nuevo

---

(3) Gesio, nacido en Nápoles, vino a la corte de Madrid hacia 1557, apareciendo en 1567 como encargado del abastecimiento de la armada real en Santander. El está varios años en Lisboa al servicio de Felipe II, y fue llamado a Madrid en 1573, con orden de presentar y explicar sus libros y las cartas marítimas, recogidas en Portugal para la Biblioteca del Escorial. Véase Gregorio Andrés, O. S. A., "Juan Bautista Gesio, cosmógrafo de Felipe II y Portador de documentos geográficos desde Lisboa para la Biblioteca de El Escorial en 1573", Publicación de la Real Sociedad Geográfica, Serie B, Núm. 478, Madrid, 1967. Estas son las más recientes referencias sobre el material archivado, con excepción del material Portugués. El mejor sumario está en Armando CORTESAO: *Cartografía y Cartógrafos Portugueses del siglo XVI*. 2 vols., Lisboa, 1935, I, 276-282.

(4) Archivo General de las Indias, Leg. 261, Ramo 2.

(5) José PULIDO RUBIO: *El piloto mayor*, 2.ª ed. Sevilla, 1950, cap. IX, especialmente a partir de la pág. 436.

X

en tal proyecto, es algo que ya se indica en el párrafo inicial. Que el problema siguió siendo el mismo por muchos años, es también obvio. De tal modo, su nueva idea, radicalmente nueva en su detalle y en la vastedad de comprensión, consistía en sugerir una serie de experimentos supervisados a lo largo de todo el hemisferio occidental perteneciente a España, es decir, desde el Reino de Nueva España hasta el Reino del Perú. Gesio razona desde lo general hasta lo específico, de la estructura hasta el detalle. Esta fue la contribución del cosmógrafo a una solución de tipo botánico. Gesio se daba cuenta de que el hemisferio occidental cubría todas las latitudes, dentro de las cuales se sabía que se contenían todas las variedades de vida vegetal. Se podían encontrar en ellas las mayores alturas, todas las posibles variedades de clima (ubicación con respecto a rasgos geográficos que lo determinan), grados de humedad, y propiedades del suelo. Se podrían probar métodos de cultivo y, como buen cosmógrafo, Gesio menciona la influencia del sol, la luna y las estrellas, que podrían influir con su curso en el crecimiento de las plantas. Este experimento de trasplante hubiera sido de una dimensión gigantesca, abarcando todo el Nuevo Mundo en el cual hubiera sido probado. Gesio sugiere que solamente la Corona podría afrontar la coordinación de semejante empresa según lo requiere un experimento sistemático de trasplante. Pero sugirió confiar a empresarios individuales los diversos experimentos, otorgándoles los mismos privilegios que fueron dados a los conquistadores. Puesto que el periodo mínimo para una cosecha lucrativa de la pimienta negra es de dos a cinco años, fijaba un plazo semejante, solución que parece, ciertamente, satisfactoria.

La carta, pues, significa una orientación completamente nueva, basada en el conocimiento botánico contemporáneo, tal cual era desarrollado por los científicos en forma individual en lugares tales como Sevilla (el jardín de Monardes), Valladolid (las Moreras y la Huerta del Rey) o en Indias (experimentos de los virreyes), además de la información que llegaba a Europa desde el lejano oriente, vía Portugal (6).

Lo que es nuevo en la carta, es la puesta a prueba de hipótesis por medio de experimentos, en una empresa realmente gigante y coordinada. La virtud del esquema se apoya en la promesa de gloria para el rey en los anales de la historia, una gloria en la que los miembros del Consejo de Indias debían tomar parte, puesto que debían decidir en la materia, ya que se realizaría una hazaña extremadamente notable, que habría de tener largas consecuencias en el futuro, en el próximo milenio. Tan sólo el peligro de blasfemia parece que refrena al autor de sugerir que el transplante sería un acto de creación.

El documento, existente en Sevilla, carece de fecha y está escrito en italiano. Está depositado en el Archivo de Indias, donde fue exhibido en 1911, después de lo cual

---

(6) C. R. BOXER: "Two Pioneers of Tropical Medicine: García D'Orta and Nicolás Monardes", *The Hispanic and Luso Brazilian Councils*, London, 1963, hace una rápida referencia literaria de ambos en España y Portugal, además de lo específicamente médico. La especiería es tratada por el mismo autor en *The Dutch Seaborne Empire*, London, 1965, y *The Portuguese Seaborne Empire*, London, 1969, con algunas referencias a otros trabajos.

fue mal archivado, y encontrado por casualidad en enero último. Era conocido, y fue transcrito por Martín Fernández de Navarrete, en su Colección de Documentos del Museo Naval, en Madrid, (Tomo 18, folio 45-46), quien además lo cita en su *Biblioteca Marítima* como la primera obra en su lista de manuscritos de Gesio, posiblemente a causa de que se encuentra escrito en italiano (7).

El gran proyecto de Gesio no se realizó. Las razones por las cuales el experimento no fue intentado, fueron aquellas que, en general, afectaron a las empresas científicas en la España del siglo XVI, es decir, la ausencia de respuesta a vastas concepciones, las complicaciones militares y la falta de medios y de promotores individuales (8).

El conflicto acerca del comercio de especias no quedó limitado mucho tiempo a 'as potencias ibéricas. La idea de transplantar el clavo de olor y la nuez moscada, renació luego, y en el año 1744 los franceses lograron, por cierto, quebrar el monopolio holandés del clavo de olor, precisamente por esos medios, mientras la pimienta, también transferida al hemisferio occidental, no se convirtió en la mina de oro que había imaginado Gesio (9).

Sin embargo, la carta de Gesio al rey Felipe II refleja un importante elemento de la historia, frecuentemente ignorado a causa de la dificultad de fijar y registrar cronológicamente el proyecto. De hecho, los pensamientos de la gente de cualquier época presente son gobernados, tanto por lo que puede ocurrir, como por lo que ocurre. La grandeza, y los aspectos innovadores inherentes a la orientación sabiamente científica del esquema de Gesio, para superar los efectos del Tratado de Tordesillas, merecen ser registrados.

LAS LINEAS ASTRONOMICAS COMO PRECEDENTE

L AS causas del Tratado, o la distribución de la riqueza proveniente de la especiería por medio de demarcaciones longitudinales, fueron superadas con el tiempo por los hechos, como usualmente ocurre en tantos casos. Pero la invención intelectual del parcelamiento de la tierra por medio de líneas longitudinales y de latitud, tuvo una vida más prolongada en la historia de las ideas, tal como suele ocurrir con

---

(7) Los documentos, aun sin fecha, citan 1554-68 en Enciclopedias Españolas, Portuguesas y Brasileñas. Puede existir una traducción entre los papeles de Gesio en El Escorial que no he podido ver. El texto de la carta llamada Memorial no está publicado, según mi información, y se encuentra en el Archivo General de Indias, Patronato, Legajo 48, Ramo 3. Vid. nuestro *Apéndice*.

(8) Ursula LAMB: "Science by Litigation, a cosmographic Feud", *Terrae Incognitae,* I, 1969, 40-57. véase págs. 56-57. "La Nueva Ciencia Geográfica", *Revista de Occidente,* mayo, 1972, págs. 182-183, véase págs. 180-181.

(9) John HUTCHINSON and Ronald MELVILLE: *The Stry of Plants and Uses to Man.* London, 1948, págs. 208-209; Howard SCOTT GENTRY: "The Introduction of Black Pepper into America", *Economic Botany,* vol. IX, 1959, págs. 256-268.

muchos planes, perdurando sobre las circunstancias que les dieron origen. La línea de demarcación de las bulas papales fue útil para ordenar el universo, según las regularidades de las estrellas proyectadas sobre la tierra, abrazando el globo terráqueo íntegro de polo a polo, como sistema de abrir todo el mundo a la fe católica, mediante la asignación de diversas partes del mismo a las dos potencias activamente proselitistas. El uso de estas líneas para definir intereses seculares, políticos y económicos en el Tratado de Tordesillas fue, de hecho, un supuesto y se reveló como impracticable ya en Badajoz, aunque facilitó la expansión deseada.

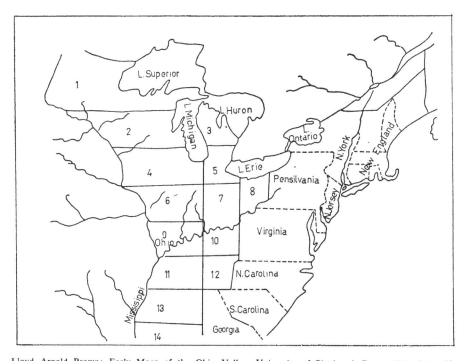

Lloyd Arnold Brown: Early Maps of the Ohio Valley, University of Pittsburgh Press, 1959. Plate 52.

Sin embargo, no entendida la fórmula como única "solución" posible para la época, —lo cual fue una gran idea para entonces—, la definición de coordenadas de latitud y longitud a fin de servir como fronteras, preocupó a las potencias ibéricas a lo largo de los siglos XVII y XVIII. Las líneas de longitud, que en rigor no podían ser medidas exactamente hasta la invención del reloj náutico, en el siglo XVIII, servían a los argumentos políticos y al juego del poder a causa de que eran convenientemente imprecisas. La mejor reflexión breve sobre este hecho, se encuentra en un reciente artículo del fallecido Garret Mattingly, titulado *¿Ninguna paz más allá de qué línea?* (10).

(10) GARRETT MATTINGLY: "No Peace beyond which Line?". *Transactions of the Royal Historical Society*, 5th Series, vol. 13, 1963, págs. 145-162.

El legado permanente de la división científica de la superficie terrestre, por imposición de un enrejado geométrico que se deriva de las bulas papales y del Tratado de Tordesillas, es el mapa de los Estados Unidos de América. Dejando de lado anteriores intentos, el gran esquema de Jefferson para trazar líneas de latitud desde los Estados del Atlántico netamente, hasta el Mississippi, que puede verse en el mapa de 1783-84 (11), constituye una predicción del actual mapa de los Estados Unidos. Durante el siglo XIX la vasta extensión de tierra que se encontraba hacia el Oeste de los Estados coloniales, en su mayor parte inexplorada por los europeos, fue dividida trazando una red de reservas de propiedad puramente conceptuales, en forma de un enrejado geométrico, formado por líneas de longitud y latitud, sin tomar en cuenta los detalles de la superficie del terreno. Este fue el resultado de un pensamiento que consideraba al globo terráqueo como una especie de naranja, dividida por líneas propuestas por primera vez por los científicos ocupados en asuntos náuticos del siglo XVI, pero dedicados ahora no a la búsqueda de rutas marítimas, sino al reparto político de zonas, contempladas por primera vez en el tratado de Tordesillas.

La época del Tratado puede llegar a su fin tan solo ahora. Durante el siglo XVI, los cosmógrafos se ocupaban de dividir el globo terráqueo y utilizaban como referencia el curso de los planetas y la posición de las estrellas. Luego procedían a igualar las virtudes de las mitades sugiriendo completas transferencias —es decir, trasplantes— de los recursos de una mitad a la otra. Tan solo hoy en día, nuestra referencia a las estrellas es más precisa, una vez más, gracias a que los astronautas han llegado a la luna. Ojalá entonces que su experiencia de haber visto el globo terráqueo como un todo, transmitida mediante satélites a la población de todo el planeta, pueda unir las mitades que deben su existencia al Tratado de Tordesillas.

(11) LLOYD ARNOLD BROWN: *Early Maps of the Ohio Valley*. Pittsburgh, 1959. Map by David Hartley, Plate 52. "A sketch of the new states proposed by Jefferson and others", 1783-84. Also. **págs.** 125-127.

MEMORIAL

Presentado al Rey por Juan Bautista Gesio sobre el trasplante de especieria y drogueria de las Islas y tierras orientales a los reynos de Nueva España y Perú y de ellos a los de Castilla. (Copia de Martín Fernández de Navarrete: *Colección,* Museo Naval, XVIII, fols. 45-46 v.)

S. C. R. M. Molt' anni gia sono ch'io vasallo non solo obligato al servicio et bene-ticio de la corona Reale ma particularmente affectionatissimo alla M. V. hó discorso et pensato como le potrebbe fare alcun importante et signalato servicio, et mentre gli altri ne habbiamo retrovato uno, el quale concede molto in grandezza utile et honore ho lasciato de avisarlo fin aqueste hora per alcuni respeti tra i quali è stato a ció ché con la lungezza del tempo hauesse con piú maturo discorso ben esaminate et escriuellate difficultá o facilitá del negocio, le spese con l'interesse o giornamento que no potrebbono uenire et quanto piú no andato discorrendo et considerando la qualitá del negocio tanto piú l hó retrovato in quantitá et qualitá importantissimo utilissimo et necessario et si fin al d'oggi non se ha posto in esecutione, credo hauerse causato o che non sia stato avisato, ne avertito o che non sia stato ben considerato il suo fine, et i debbiti mezzi o che alcuna apparenta difficultá l'habbia desaminato, il que essendo stato molto ben considerato et discorso da me retrovo questo negocio molto piú facile et molto piú utile che non appare. Questo negocio e V. S. M. l'impresa di fare transpiantare e transportare le specierie et drogherie dell'Isole et Reoni orientali, ne i regni del Perú et Nova Epagna, *la qual empresa retrovo esser una de le piú sustantiali piú utile et gloriose che convengono alla corona Reale* et esser un atto tanto heroico che alla M. V. apportera una gloria et immortal fama et a i suoi sussesori et Regni richezze inestimabili et abenche appareche nel principio debbia daro piú tasto spese che giovamente, considerato il fine dara molto piú utile, et la gloria et fama sará de la M. V. et il giovamento de suoi posteri et successori: Justa impresa tanto piú la laudo et approbo, quanto piú vedo che niuno Re ne Principe christiano ne Moro la possa fare solo la M. V. perche oltre de la potentia ha, tiene i luoghi atti a cio cossi per la pruductione et nutrimento de dette specierie como per la perpetuita et conservatione. Et conviene che queste specierie et drogherie s'habbiano a conservare et perpetuitare ne i luochi et reggioni meno sugette alla alternationi et revolutioni de i tempi, et alle invasioni esterne d'exerciti d inimici, questi son: i Regni del Perú et Nova Spagna, i quali Dio et la natura provi-denno fossen tanto lontani da altre Provintie et Regni del globo terrestre separando li colmezzo de duoi tanto grandissimi Arcipelaghi da tutte le parti che temeno poco a nulla l'invasione d'eserciti d'inimici esterni solo son sogetti a pericoli intrinsechi alli quali, et di quanti modi possono essere et como s'habbia a remediare et levar via ogni sospetto et como s'habbia a remediare et levar via ogni sospeto et como s'habbia a fare l'augmento de i stati facultá reali et beni de i populi, et de la fe, et como s'habbia de introduse la politica et religione estirpando dal tuto l'idolatria con prestezza et facilitá, et in tutte le cose fanse quel processo in cinquanta anni, che si possa fare in cinque cento o mille anne, (a ben che il de d'hoggi siano ben retti, et governati da questi signori del suo conseglio) daro una nova traeza et ordine

*conforme alla filosofia morale, dandome a dito (??) et luoco a cio la M. V. hora
tornando alle specierie et drogherie, le quali haueran a dare un tesoro et richezza
inestimabile,* dica che colmezzo de la filosofia naturale et de l'astrologia si possono
traspiantare et multiplicare per che considerando nosi è siti et qualità de la terra
donde nascono, si è secca o humida, arenosa o petrosa, piana o montuosa, appan-
tanata o rigata de fiumi, terra tenacie o leue negra o rossa, minerale o senza, le
parti del mondo con i colori et altri qualità che con il mezzo de detta filosofia se retro-
vanno et con il mezzo ancora de l'Astrologia considerando gli anguli conche i loro siti
recebeno gli raggi et influentie del sole et de la Lune et de qual altri corpi celesti
*et plantandonosi ne i louchi et siti che tengano somigliana con i proprij et naturall
siti, donde nascono che siano del mesmo clima et sotto pasti a medemi paralleli et
che ricevano i simili anguli senza dubbio non solo si nutriranno et multiplicheranno
ma diventeranno piú eccellenti et di maggior virtu et perfetione como gia manifesta-
mente si vede in molt altre alberi han spiantati d'una reggioni in un altera dove
non ni erano simile a l'altra del che si potrebbono assignare infiniti esempli de modo
che con l'industria et diligentia de transportale et con l'arte et sapere di transpiartarle
questo tal negocio verrà a tanta perfectione che sarà una mina de oro multiplicativa
di dover mai mancari da donde la corona reale et suoi regni s'arriecheranno et saran
liberi de andare no le atrovare in altri Regni et Provincie lontane con molti interesse
et perili et per ciò potendonose trovare in una regione tutti que i beni che indiffe-
rentemente se retrovano in diverse parti del mondo pare piú costo opera divina che
industria humana le specierie et drogherie che si possono transpiantari son questo:
Pepe, cannalla, garofani, zensiforo, noce, moscata, et mace, ligno aloe sandali, cano-
fora, belruilani, mirra et incenso, riobarbaro, et altri piante et non le doviamo confidare
et dimenticar monede questa impresa con dire che nell' Ysole de Thuroni et altri
Ysole di quell Oriente subdite alla Mta. V. le siano alcune specierie como pepe et
cannella perche quell' Isole como stanno tanto lontane et nel mezzo de tanti Regni
di Mori non siamo sicuri del perpetuo possesso di quelle, et de piú la canella che
se retiova nell' Ysola de Luzone et en Celebes non è così bona et perfetta como
quella de l'Isola di Zeilan, perche quell' Isole non recebeno la virtu de i raggi de
gli corpi celesti con quelli anguli che gli receve l'Isola de Zeilan et perciò teneno
meno perfettione. Questo e l'aviso ho voluto dare alla Mta. V. il quale s'io non me
inganno per esser tanto importantissimo exorto a doverse fare et quanto all industria
como et di quanti medi si possano transportare et quanto appartiene alla sciencia
de la transplantatione mi offero servire in ciò alla M. V. et quando fosse dissuaduta
de ciò o per alcune difficultà o espese* dico che conviene che questa impresa se
dia a altre suoi subditi cassi como se danno de l'altre conquiste *et credo si retrove-
ranno molti che piglino questo assunto con alcuni pochi ayuti de la M. V. et con
che possano eligere i siti et longhi in qualunque parte dell'Indie et con l'altri pre-
minencie convengono a tal impresa.—Di V. C. R. M.—Humilde et devotissimo creato.—
(firmado).*

X

ABSTRACT

Two Traces of the Treaty of Tordesillas:
Avoiding the Effects and Using the Method

The Treaty of Tordesillas of 1494 required Portugal and Spain to continue their exploration in opposite directions from a longitudinal line dividing the Atlantic. It did not lead to a consensus regarding the Spice Islands, with respect to their position east or west of the line of Tordesillas when it was extended to the Pacific. On three occasions the differences between Spain and Portugal over the right to the Moluccas left the parties uncertain. Plans to ascertain the line by joint exploration were never followed up. The dispute over longitude outlasted the last meeting at Zaragossa in 1529, when the emperor provisionally sold his claim to the Portuguese. A renewed attempt in 1566 to establish the longitude in the Pacific scientifically by a naval expedition was again aborted, and it is probable that the scheme for transplanting of the spice plants, found in a letter by Juan Bautista Gesio, was a consequence of that scientific fiasco.

Juan Bautista Gesio was a royal cosmographer at the court of Philip II, whose advice was often sought by the Council of the Indies. The letter about the spices is in the form of *Memorial*, submitted to the crown for consideration. The suggestion to the king is for a schematic experiment of transplantation of the spice plants all along the western hemisphere, including the Caribbean, across suitable latitudes. Varying elevations and climatic conditions and soils were also considered. The experiment would have royal sponsorship, and be undertaken by private capital in return for ample rewards upon successful completion within two to five years, which the pepper plant would need to produce a salable crop. Transplantation would eliminate the dangers of transport outside of Spanish control, and it would result in a major source of royal income. The mix of technical (scientific) considerations and political aspects of such an experiment are in the tradition of the Treaty of Tordesillas.

An imitation of the method of Tordesillas was the use of a graticule of longitudes and latitudes cast over unexplored regions for delimiting political claims. In 1873/4, the casting of a grid of global coordinates over unexplored regions was applied on a land map by Thomas Jefferson. He divided the territory between the extant thirteen American colonies and the Mississippi river into fourteen rectangles of a size that seemed practical for future colonies. Without taking into account the geographical features of the land, and the existence of native settlements, the wholly theoretical map of claims cast over unexplored regions, is a direct descendant of the Alexandrine bulls which had established a longitude to sort out geographical claims confirmed by the Treaty of Tordesillas.

XI

Ursula Lamb, Gary Miller (Tucson, Arizona)

PUERTO DE CABALLOS, HONDURAS:
AN ABANDONED CHOICE

A most intriguing problem of early Latin American history is the selection of terminal ports for the interoceanic route across the isthmus of Central America. Much is known about the history of existing ports and about some which were abandoned, such as Nombre de Dios and Natá. This paper deals with a port which had a double existence: the actual Puerto de Caballos on the Honduran coast, which was a landfall for the central isthmus (the regions variously identified, in a time prior to the final establishment of jurisdictions, as Honduras-Higueras, Guatemala-Comayagua and Nicaragua),[1] and the other Puerto de Caballos, a great port-city of fantasy in a sea of paper, of political imagination, economic ambition, and geographic myth. This was a port designed to supersede Nombre de Dios as the terminal of the Atlantic fleets, to draw the combined wealth of the Far East — the Manila Galleon — and Peruvian silver fleets via the Bay of Fonseca on the Pacific side and the land route through Guatemala. Such a superport never developed. While Puerto de Caballos played its role as terminal for the Honduras ships, the theoretical superport-city took shape in the imagination of its promoters and made up the substance of many a legal brief, filling many a secretary's copy file.

The history of the actual port and the rise and decline of its traffic is charted in the magisterial work of H. and P. Chaunu, *Séville et L'Atlantique*,[2] which also uses some of the papers to be discussed. Anyone who wishes to know that history can do no better than consult its pages.

We came across the bulk of the documentation in another context in the Section "Patronato" of the *Archivo de Indias*.[3] What is remarkable about Puerto

---

[1] See map of the "Audiencia de Guatimala" taken from vol. 1 of A n t o n i o d e H e r-r e r a' s Historia General de los hechos de los castellanos en las islas y tierra firme del mar oceano. Madrid, Academia de la Historia, 1934. original Madrid 1601-1615.

[2] H. and P. C h a u n u, Seville et l'Atlantique, 1504-1650. Paris, 1955-58, 8 vols. in 11 parts; vol. 8 part 1, Pierre Chaunu, Structure Geographique, 870-883 discusses the basic documentation and economic aspects of the story.

[3] Archivo General de Indias, Patronato, Leg. 259. Ramo 24, Number 1: Expediente sobre mudar la navegacion que se hacia del Peru por Nombre de Dios por Puerto Caballos en Honduras seguido en la Contratacion de Sevilla. . .; Number 2: Capitulacion y registros que hicieron las provincias de Guatemala y Honduras con Juan García de Hermosilla sobre la dicha mudanza de la navegacion del Peru; Number 3: Traslado de la anterior capitulacion. Somewhat abridged copies of this material are in the *Coleccion de documentos de Fernandez de Navarrete que posee el Museo Naval,* which has been printed in reduced facsimile of the MSS by Kraus Thompson, Organization, Nedlen Liechtenstein, 1971, vol. XXI, docs. 53, 54, 55, 58. This material will be referred to as *Coleccion Navarrete.* Another brief abstract in English (MS.) is in the Bancroft Library in Berkeley, Cal. Made by E. Squier from the

de Caballos, is the repeated assessment for over half a century of the arguments concerning where and why to build a great port-city. These documents are not metahistory or trivial play with probabilities; they are not a *tratadista*'s way to prove himself busy on behalf of his patron; rather they tell the history of realistic assessment and of critical dispositions regarding the transisthmian route over a long time span.

The story of Puerto de Caballos is certainly not *histoire événementiel*. Nothing ever happened. The comparatively insignificant place was not subject to important change except occasional raids or climatic mishaps. Demographers, economists, and institutional historians all might ignore the great paper-port that never was. Yet Puerto de Caballos shows the role played by navigator-entrepreneurs, by *letrados*, councillors, and judges in making the map of Spanish America which is usually assigned to soldiers and settlers.[4] When Lawrence Stone writes in a recent article called "History and the Social Sciences in the 20th Century" that "maybe the time has come for historians to reassert the importance of the concrete, the particular, and the circumstantial, as well as the general theoretical model and the procedural insight,"[5] the case of Puerto de Caballos seems to fit the suggestion. It documents in detail how choice is subject to the process of decision and to chance.

One outstanding feature of the controversy over Puerto de Caballos as a Pacific terminal for the great fleets is that the case was presented by one individual, Juan García de Hermosilla. He bore much of the cost from 1556-1588 in promoting a change of traffic pattern affecting the whole imperial design, and he saw his case through to it's presentation before the Consejo de Indias and the court itself.[6] All of this was done with the consent and co-operation of the governmental agencies, the Audiencia in Guatemala, the Casa de la Contratación in Sevilla, the Consejo de Indias, and crown officials. Juan García's eventual aim, was to enter a *capitulación* with the Crown (to be defined in great detail), for the construction and operation of the new route. It is obvious from this that many people were involved, and our interest was to discover the responsibilities of the individuals and to ascertain what set the limits to their activities.

A first stage of our work was, therefore, a kind of prosopography — also Mr. Stone's term — in this case people grouped together in favor or against the new terminal for the isthmian route, as well as listed by their profession or function as mariners, merchants, settlers, and as officials on either side of the Atlantic.

Archivo Nacional de Mexico. He translated the title to read: "Memorial presented by Juan García de Hermosilla native of Chillon del Rey in Valladolid in the year 1556, in favor of changing the navigation and route of the fleets of Spain, from Nombre de Dios and Panama to the ports of Honduras, showing the injuries and inconveniences which have been suffered in the voyage from the kingdom of Spain to the Provinces of Peru by way of the ports of Nombre de Dios and Panama and the advantage and conveniences which would result from making it by way of the Port of Caballos and that of Fonseca on the South Sea." Supporting *memoriales* by the *cabildo* of Santiago are dated: Dec. 22, 1599; May 17, 1561 and Jan. 26, 1562. The *interrogatorios* by royal cedula are dated 1570-76.

[4] A. C a t i l l e r o. Políticas de Poblamiento en Castilla del Oro y Veragua en los Orígenes de la Colonización. Panamá, Ed. Universitaria, 1972, p. 96, 97, discusses the geostrategic importance of the towns of the isthmus, also the lack of social history.

[5] L. S t o n e. History and the Social Sciences. — The Future of History. ed. Charles F. Delzell, Vanderbilt University Press, 1977, Chapter 1.

[6] Archivo de Indias, Patronato, 259, Ramo 24, Num. 1, this considers the entire coastline from Cartagena to Vera Cruz and Florida and the adjacent road network.

Next, we considered the role of procedure in our case. While we found that the Crown derived a great variety of information from the testimonies required for processing of the *memoriales, pareceres, informes* and *interrogatorios*, the entrepreneurs who funded most of these activities did not benefit from any commentary by the authorities. Beyond the formal record which only licensed the next step in the proceedings, they must have had to rely entirely on the goodwill of the secretary of the Casa and Council. Official delays were such that the initial arguments for the change were overtaken by events and the applications were unable to reflect the change of political priorities because of the rigid structure of the question and answer format. The fixed text of the questionnaires, each of which was answered over a span of two years or more, did not allow for any flexibility or reflection of current problems, such as the vast increase in silver shipment from Peru, and the growing threat of piracy and its spread to the Pacific, etc. Action at the local level was hampered by ignorance of imperial designs, which increasingly sacrificed exploration or change for security of access to known resources. The Crown, on the other hand, prejudiced its understanding of the larger issue, a redesign of the entire traffic and reassessment of the role of Honduras vs. Panama, by marking only those passages which quoted exact price reductions for the transport (as from twelve to eight pesos per mule load or per person), or a variety of specific suggestions, such as a price range for the contracting parties. These concrete figures were entirely hypothetical and did not deserve as much attention as the supporting information and the overall design.

An advantage of using the papers on Puerto de Caballos for history, despite their hypothetical nature is the immediacy of language to the purpose required by the format of the *interrogatorio*. For instance, the clause: "I know and I have seen" vs. "I know and I have heard it said" is a very important check to numbers mentioned. Quite often the agreement on specific numbers is the result rather of trust by the witnesses in what one had said, than of true knowledge. Too often this element of trust in a man instead of knowledge of fact has been neglected in the use of such material. Woodrow Borah, himself a most acute collector and interpreter of quantitative data for early colonial Hispanic American history, has recently warned that the language of quantitative statements must be closely watched.[7]

The quantitative data in the papers concern distances and time needed for transport to cover them. In this case genuine information is easily sorted out from hearsay. As for the description of the area one can say that the potential for mining and plantations is poorly represented except by the officials who recommend it in glowing though general terms. Mining is mentioned, but never identified with any locality, for instance, and sugar mills appear a very few times. The marine interests, concerning the problems of ports and of the route, are in contrast specifically dealt with, and the papers do report on productivity in support of the fleets. Native manpower almost escapes any concrete assessment, except that "multitudes" are claimed to exist and the interrogation of the members of three religious orders, Dominicans, Augustinians, and Mercedarians, is requested, because "they have walked all over those kingdoms." However, there is no testimony by any of them, either on numbers of natives or on the nature of the route.

Information from the papers also makes possible the reconstruction of the historic landscape of Honduras-Guatemala-Nicaragua and of Panama,

[7] W. W. B o r a h. Latin American History. — In: The Future of History, ed. Charles F. Delzell, p. 163.

which fills in our scanty knowledge of the country between the earliest settlement and the *Relaciones Geográficas* of Lopez de Velasco in 1570.[8] Since the papers were assembled to serve a partisan cause, however, they do not represent a complete picture of conditions as they were. No mention is made of cacao, for instance, which by all accounts was one of the major resources of the area, but which had no direct impact on the traffic of the Carrera de las Indias. The only information given was that which would be useful in recommending the sites for new ports and land adjacent to the new routes and useful in support of them. Unlike the accounts of the *Relaciones,* the statements in our papers are precise regarding available pasture, livestock, and grain production.[9] All accounts were rendered under oath by people who could be relied upon to help in the construction of the ports and in the operation of the transisthmian route.

A consideration suggested by the papers is that of the development of the map in the consciousness of the people in the Indies and in Spain. Generally speaking, American cartography shows the following development: while more and more names appear on the shore lines, only few of the landfalls are starting points for charted tracks inland and connect with native population centers.[10] While American native cultures had their centers of gravity inland, the earliest footholds of Spain were a spider web from coastal points to Santo Domingo or other points in the Antilles.[11] The cartographic story illustrates

---

[8] R. C. C h a m b e r l a i n. Plan del siglo XVI para abrir un camino de Puerto Ca - ballos a la Bahia de Fonseca en sustitución de la ruta de Panama. — Anales de la Sociedad de Geografia e Historia, Mexico, March 1946; C. L. J o h a n n e s s e n, Savannahs of Interior Honduras. Ibero-Americana, 46 University of Cal. Press, Berkeley, Cal., 1963, discuss the description of the Honduran landscape by J u a n Lopez de Velasco (Geografia y descripcion universal de las Indias, recopiladas desde el ano 1571-1574. Madrid, 1894), and the man-made changes to the landscape which have had wide-ranging effects. The descriptions of our documents are supported by modern historical geography. Physical features are well described, though the wet and dry seasons, rainfall, and temperatures, are not presented in any consistent manner. See also: W. D a v i d s o n. Historical Geography of the Bay Islands. Honduras: Anglo-Hispanic Conflict in the Western Caribbean. Birmingham, Alabama, Southern University Press, 1974.

[9] See summary Appendix 1; data note 3, number 3.

[10] Narrative and Critical History of America, J. W i n s o r ed., by a corps of eminent historical scholars and specialists. 8 vols. Boston, Houghton Mifflin, Co. 1886, vol 2, many maps. The *Derrotero* of the first Padrón Real by Alonso de Chaves, Cosmographer Major of the Casa de la Contratación, (1536) gives exact distances and directions for the Honduran Coast. Puerto de Caballos is mentioned in the table of contents, though curiously missi g from the coastal stopping points in the body of the text. MS in the Biblioteca of the Académia Real de la Historia, Madrid. MS 9-14-1 2791. Baltasar Vellerino de Villalobos, *Luz de Navegantes*, MS Museo Naval, undated signatura: 5864, has a profile of Puerto de Caballos; this quarto size manuscript of texts and charts has been said to illustrate J u a n Escalante de Mendoza's unpublished *Itinerario de navegaciòn de los mares y tierras occidentales.* Printed unedited from an imperfect copy by C. F e r n a n d e z D u r o. Disquisiciones Náuticas, 6 vols, Madrid, 1875-80, vol. 5, p. 412-513. Escalante de Mendoza was also the author of a *Relación al Rey,* undated, in support of Juan García de Hermosilla, as well as witness in Sevilla, testifying on behalf of the Puerto de Caballos route, Archivo General de Indias, Patronato, Ramo 45, Num. 2.

[11] Attention should be called to the recent discussion and analysis of "Trends and Issues in Latin American Urban Research, 1965-1970." by R. M. M o r s e. Two Parts, Latin American Research Review, vol. VI, numbers 1 and 2. Spring and Summer 1971. Number 1, discusses "Colonial Towns." It is a wide-ranging analysis of precedents, origins, and development, which brings order to a burgeoning field. P. 5 discusses the port-city which is not created by a hinterland but, in order to support Spanish penetration, inland. See also J. E. H a r d o y, C. A r a n o v i c h. Urban Scales and Functions in Span ish America Toward the Year 1600: First Conclusions. — Latin American Research Review, Vol. V, no. 3, Fall, 1970, p. 69 discusses the towns of the Audiencia de Guatemala.

here, as in other instances in Latin America, the dual problem of coping with accelerated growth of information which reached Spain, while guarding against the disappearance of knowledge represented by experience of the navigators, soldiers and entrepreneurs, among whom the death rate led to frightful attrition. The increase in actual geographical knowledge of the region is distinct from the demand made upon the latter, which resulted in maps drawn to prove a point of view and which makes the use of texts indispensable for the history of cartography.

There are, for instance, amazingly accurate early maps and rutters (derrotas),but, as the isthmus attracted foreign interlopers, a policy of official tontrol of information led to ludicrous cartographic distortions.[12] The large Peninsula of Yucatan becomes an island shrinking in size and Lake Nicaragua a vast inland sea of fantastic outline and orientation. Later literature that points only to the tremendous "ignorance" of the authorities often neglects the reason for this.[13] American cartography was drawn according to plans for action concerning the lands. What is remarkable is not the slanted information, but the fact that it was monitored so well and the truth, *opinion desapasionada*, was so often solicited.

Attention must be drawn to three factors which had some influence on the development of the shaping the Atlantic trade routes. One, the Spanish international situation in 1556 favored a stock-taking of colonial development. This was a year of transition when the Emperor Charles V abdicated in favor of his son. Toward the end of the Emperor's regime he had entertained serious thoughts concerning basic changes. On the other hand, the need for immediate income led to a sacrifice of possible long-term gains to short-term certainties. This is proven by the marginal remark *ojo* (noted and seen), where the specific price reductions which Hermosilla promised appear in the text.

On the local level one must keep in mind the state of flux of political allegiances.[14] Honduras was annexed to the *gobierno* of Guatemala and ruled by a deputy governor from 1539-1554. In judicial affairs Honduras was first subordinate to the Audiencia of Santo Domingo, then (1528-1534) to Mexico, then for a second time to Santo Domingo (1534-1544). In 1545 the new Audiencia of *Los Confines* (Guatemala) established residence at Gracias a Dios. This body appointed an *Alcalde Mayor* to govern the province, while in the meantime governors had been sent out from Spain or New Spain for Honduras since 1522. In 1549 the Audiencia moved to Santiago de Guatemala; and Honduras had had its own bishopric since 1545. At the time of Juan García de Hermosilla's petition there was no reason to consider these allegiances and the status of the region fixed or immutable.

A third point is a most intriguing fact exemplified by the case of Puerto de Caballos that Latin American cities had often an existence in law prior to a

---

[12] Maiollo in Winsor, (see note 10) Fig. 14, p. 219, shows Yucatan an island lying north of a marvelous "Streito Cubitoso." There are several later maps of Yucatan island.
[13] C. H. H a r i n g. Trade and Navigation between Spain and the Indies. Cambridge, Harvard University Press, p. 184: "The bundle of memorials preserved in Seville is only another monument to the Spaniards' gross ignorance of the geography of these regions". H. H. B a n c r o f t. W o r k s, 39 vols., San Francisco, 1882-90, Central America, 2 vols., vol 2, p. 397-399.
[14] P. G e r h a r d. Colonial New Spain, 1519-1786: Notes on the evolution of Minor Political Jurisdictions; XV, Yucatan, XVI Guatemala, XVIII Soconusco, XIX Honduras, XX Nicaragua, XXI Costa Rica, XXI San Salvador. — Handbook of Middle American Indians. Giude to Ethno-Historical Sources, H. F. Cline, ed., Part One, Austin. University of Texas Press, 1972; F. M u r o - R o m e r o. Las Presidencias Gobernaciones en Indias, Siglo XVI. Sevilla, Escuela de Estudios Hispano-Americanos, 1975, p. 15-24.

real one, or distinct from an actual one.[15] In many instances founding a city was a cooperative venture in which the legal corporation, the *cabildo, regidores,* and officials, had rights and functions not necessarily tied to a specific town site, but rather to any one to be chosen. This is not the "stake in the ground" approach of other colonial empires, but presumes a stake somewhere, and surroundings to the limits of jurisdiction, often bordering on land of a neighbouring grantee. That is, limits were drawn against rival settlers' claims before firm location on the map. Many cities and ports changed site frequently as is well known in the case of Buenos Aires and of Vera Cruz for example. This elasticity of Spanish occupation, which cast a legal network of boundaries over unknown sites, holds for cities, as well as whole areas, such as the Moluccas. It is, of course, well-known, but by neglecting to mention it in this context in which it has been completely ignored, one loses a dimension of urban history and tradition which became acute as Spain went outside the Ptolemaic map. The legal existence could, for instance, contribute to the survival of a town beyond its economic or strategic usefulness, though the attempt to advance Puerto de Caballos into the front rank of port-cities, the existence of its *cabildo,* did not help.[16]

Chronologically speaking, earlier plans for making Puerto de Caballos a major traffic center to replace Nombre de Dios had been put forward in the 1530s.[17] They were initiated or had the support of Governor Alvarado, the founder of Puerto de Caballos in 1524, of Governors Montejo and Cereceda, and of the bishop of Honduras, Pedraza. Their intent was to develop Honduras-Guatemala into the major economic and political center of Central America. In other words, they looked to the ports from the inside outward, from the hinterland, which was their power base to the outside.

Our major sources deal with a different development proper to this conference, with interests which are directed from the sea to the shore, and with the primary problem of the best route to and from Spain. To make Puerto de Caballos the site of the terminal of the silver fleets and access route from Peru, via the Bay of Fonseca, and to the Pacific and the Philippines, was the intent of the *memoriales* submitted by Juan Garcia de Hermosilla. This mariner-merchant, experienced in many parts of the Empire as soldier, navigator, and shipowner, presented two extensive *memoriales* detailing his plan, the reasons for it, and the feasibility of it in 1556.[18] He drew support first of all from fellow navigator-entrepreneurs, such as Juan de Escalante, and from the cosmographic establishment of the Casa de la Contratación in separate *pareceres,* dated 1556 to 1558. These papers reached the Consejo de Indias and the Crown and resulted in a *cedula* which empowered Juan García to request the proclamation of *interrogatorios* or public inquiries in Sevilla, as well as in

---

[15] D. R a m o s. La Doble Fundación de Ciudades y las Huestes. — Revista de Indias, Ano 32, Num. 127, Jan.-Dec. 1972, p. 107-139.

[16] Puerto de Caballos is said to have had 20 houses in 1570. It had only two people answering the town crier, a mulatto and a negro. The negro, a slave, volunteered to contract the use of one *barco* and he was duly supported by three witnesses. The other man would not register his ship. The town crier had the secretary register the fact that "many people heard him." He was under obligation to read the proclamation twice. He himself was a mulatto. A governor of Cartagena testifying in behalf of a change of the Atlantic terminal to Cartagena said in Puerto de Caballos there lived only "negros and some mulattos." Colección Navarrete, XXII, p. 640.

[17] R. C. C h a m b e r l a i n. Op. cit.

[18] See note 3, introduction to Number 1.

Honduras-Guatemala.[19] The seventy witnesses who answered the *interrogatorio* of twenty-five questions by 1560 were unanimous concerning the deplorable state of Nombre de Dios and the perils of the route to Panama. They agreed on the bad conditions of the harbor, the dirty bottom, limited searoom, lack of shelter, venomous insects, the *broma*, or ship worm, lack of food, danger of attack by foreigners and by runaway slaves (the *cimarrones*), sickening of mules, high prices of housing, lack of high ground nearby for recovery from the voyage or for a healthy stay for women who could not bear children in Nombre de Dios, etc. In comparison, the testimony concerning the alternate ports lacks specifics and diverges in aims. The sailors and cosmographers mostly agreed on Puerto de Caballos or Truxillo farther to the West on the Honduran coast. While Truxillo had more inhabitants, Puerto de Caballos had been the preferred port in the early years. Its protection by two off-shore islands and an inner harbor commended it to navigators and theorists. But its population preferred, when no ships were in harbor, to live in the higher altitude of San Pedro, a town nearby. As for Fonseca Bay, there is very little useful testimony except by one experienced South Sea pilot, but even he gives no particulars concerning the actual site of a prospective port in the large bay. His recommendation of the bay for careening and repair of ships, though of considerable value, is not taken up by other witnesses, nor built upon sufficiently. It became obvious from the vague information concerning the ports that the inner route rather than the oceanic terminals were going to be the decisive element in any decision about choosing a different Atlantic port.

That this was the crux of the matter became evident in the next step of the proceedings, the collection of testimony by residents along the proposed routes authorized in 1570 and taken between 1572 and 1576. Sixty-four people obliged themselves under oath to supply 4500 mules, ranging in number from thirty-two hundred (mostly fifty and one hundred), and ships (only one with an exceptional two in Truxillo) with cattle, pigs, grains, bread, ships biscuit, cheeses and, in one case, honey.[20] Fruits had been mentioned in the *memoriales*, but they are not specified in the *interrogatorios*. The document licenses public testimony of seven towns in the Audiencia of Guatemala, but there are additional reports from other *pueblos*.[21] This suggests that the Nicaragua route was under consideration as well, as it had been in the Consejo de Indias all along, and that a better terminal on the Pacific, far inside the limits of New Spain, was also being sought. The stress, however, was definitely on alternatives to Nombre de Dios-Panama, and on the petition for a monopoly over the route, wherever choice would dictate it to be constructed. Puerto de Caballos became increasingly the term for a dream and not a place.

In 1576 García de Hermosilla got as far as he could go, through the Casa de la Contratación to the Consejo de Indias and to the Crown itself. He had the full support of the Judges of the Casa in Sevilla, who sent him on to the Consejo, and it is known that he lobbied for years at court.

---

[19] Archivo General de Indias. Patronato, Leg. 259, Ramo 24, nums. 1-3, brings the bulk of the documentation. A summary listing made by Pedro Coco Calderón in 1587 mentions some pieces which are now missing. On the other hand, there are some papers in other sections. The three numbers mentioned include duplicates. They appear in part bound backwards in chronological sequence, that is with later material preceeding earlier testimonies. There are two short quantitative summaries, one of comparative distances and one of the census of the towns for the support of the new route. These are discussed by C h a u n u, op. cit.

[20] Archivo General de Indias, Patronato, 259, Ramo 24, num. 2.

[21] Ibidem. León and Panama, have witnesses testify. Other cities appear in testimony.

Meanwhile, other voices urged leaving Nombre de Dios. Felipe de Avi-
ñon had the support of three distinguished officials, Dr. Gómez de Santillán
(past *Oidor* of Mexico), Dr. Manuel Barros de San Millá, (ex-*Oidor* of the Audiencia of Guatemala, who had risen in rank since then), and Antonio Gonzalez,
president of the Audiencia of Guatemala, (1568-1572). They cosigned Avi-
ñon's *parecer* which is very strong on intent and very weak on detail.[22] Diego
García de Palacios, who was touring the province of Guatemala as *visitador*,
had his eyes on the Philippine trade. He praised the Bay of Fonseca as an excellent harbor and was concerned with a chance to lure the Pacific trade from
Panama to a new site.[23]

As the years passed without action, a final assembly of all the documents
was made by Pedro Coco Calderón in 1587. He enumerated all the papers which
had accumulated in the case through the various stages of petitions and *informes* over thirty-one-years, starting with García de Hermosilla's memoriales and ending in his own endorsement of the case.[24] He wrote an additional
note in support, addressed to Padre Mariano of the Consejo, recommending a
change in the Pacific terminal for the Philippine trade in behalf of the Far
Eastern Missions.[25]

With respect to the final decision made in Spain, the importance of time
passing or of the case outliving the cause is notable. The reasonableness and
feasibility of the proposal of 1556 could no longer be supported by the original arguments in 1581. Death had taken its toll from among the partisans
of the cause, and time had overtaken the effective lifespan of bribes. Another
notable feature is the tenacity of vested interests, which began when the initial crossing, aiming for Peru, started from Panama. Also, what is familiar,
even if uncomfortable and of doubtful merit, has the edge over the new. In
this case the risk would have been the Crown's, while the doubtful gain would
have had to be shared. The moment for a change of the Panama route had passed and with it the hope for a great Honduran port.

On September 11th, 1581, the decision with respect to García de Hermosilla's proposition to be in charge of the construction and operation of an alternative transisthmian crossing for the silver fleets was shelved. His long
suit at court was ended and his presence there declared unwelcome. The royal
cedula reads:

> Aviendo visto por los senores del consejo real de las yndias en onze de sept. de 1581 el
> negocio que tracta Juan Garcia de Hermosilla sobre que pide se mude la navegacion
> que agora se haze por nombre de Dios y panama por honduras y puerto caballos de la
> provincia de guathimala para las provincias del peru parece alos dhos senores que no
> conviene que se haga movedad nynguna en ello y *se este como se esta* Y quel dho Juan
> Garcia de Hermosilla se vaya y no se detenga mas en esta corte por esta pretension.

Or to put it as brutally as it must have felt: "We will stay as we are" and
"go home."[26]

---

[22] Colección Navarrete, vol. XXXIII, doc. 81. In the MS the name appears as ANINON,
it may well be AVINON, as it appears in the catalogue made by the Almirante Julio Guillén and in Bancroft. The MS is undated. Navarrete assigns the year 1610 to it, but internal
evidence suggests that it is datable before 1589, Squire gives 1565.
[23] Colección Navarrete, vol. XVIII, doc. 14. Carta del doctor Palacio escrita al Rey
desde la Ciudad de Guatemala, March 8, 1578.
[24] Colección Navarrete, vol. XXII, doc. 117. Parecer que dio Pedro Coco Calderón,
March 20, 1587.
[25] Ibidem, f. 656-657.
[26] Archivo General de Indias, Patronato, 529. Ramo 24, num. 3,

The turn away from Puerto de Caballos had come with the problem of foreign attack and "el Draque," the appearance of Drake. On February 15, 1586 Baptista Antonelli was named the King's engineer and commissioned to look after fortifications in the Caribbean. He went on to Cartagena and up from there to Nombre de Dios. His alternative for that silted estuary and pestilential site "subject to all the plagues of Egypt" was a slight shift along the Coast to Porto Bello, which could be joined by a short route to the old transisthmian crossing.[27] In 1589 Antonelli also made a survey of Puerto de Caballos and the Bay of Fonseca. By this time he was working in behalf of developing the inland region of Guatemala and, possibly, an improved stopping point for the Pacific trade. The Peruvian treasure fleet could no longer be weaned away from Panama. The Plan for Puerto de Caballos as a rival to Nombre de Dios on the Atlantic was dead.[28]

Yet how lively a role had it played in the minds of so many people: Puerto de Caballos as a safe port for the sailor, a splendid market for the merchant, a prize for the politician and royal functionary, a refuge from attack, a gambling venture, and a real site, placid in its setting on the Caribbean shore. Puerto de Caballos had served a purpose: it had offered an alternative and the chance of change, it provided a reference point, it required periodic assessment of affairs, of the *derrotas* of the Caribbean and of the transisthmian route. It was a challenge to enterprise and called for the king's engineer's consideration: Puerto de Caballos that never was, except on paper.

Some of the documents have served traditional historians, and they have also been used to emphasize features not visible, except by modern method, in search of trends of the *longue durée*, or for demographic developments, or for the minutae of microhistory.[29]

Our attempt has been to read the documents for their intent and their result: to offer an alternative, to document a choice. The time spent on the case of Puerto de Caballos by the Crown, councillors, protagonists, witnesses, functionaries, settlers, and even slaves is testimony to a slice of colonial life usually neglected. This case comprised the entire official life of García de Hermosilla, and it occupied as well a sizable part of the population of Guatemala. By extrapolation, one can say that the colonial population spent substantial amounts of time in such pursuits of alternative choices.

As for the procedure, one may observe a typical mismatch in the relation of near means to distant ends. Information about what is and what has happened does not suffice to suggest what could be and what should happen. As to the allocation of initiative and responsibilities in political decisions, the papers of García de Hermosilla show the manner, and the strength and weaknesses of the Spanish system. In colonial Latin America the *memoriales* and *pareceres* of individuals, often found in judicial proceedings, are rich sources for such inquiries. The Spanish government relied heavily on adversary procedure or debate to handle what in other countries would be administrative business. The argumentative nature of such documents reflects the feel-

---

[27] Colección Navarrete, vol. XXII, fol. 68v.

[28] Archivo General de Indias. Indiferente General, 1090, fol 20v. With his grand plan in shambles, Hermosilla petitioned in 1588 to be allowed to take passengers on his own ship to Lima via Puerto Caballos and the Bay of Fonseca. The license has not been found.

[29] One further topic which could be explored on the basis of these papers is the relation of information to decision-making. A recent summary of theoretical literature which might guide such a study of the material is I. L. J a n i s, L. M a n n. A Psychological Analysis of Conflict. Choice and Commitment. New York Free Press, 1977.

ing of the people about many issues, the more so the farther removed from fact. Petitions are a much neglected source for the dynamics of colonial history.

The various stages of the case also show what helped and what hindered developments of the Atlantic routes. The earliest proponents for Puerto de Caballos were navigator-entrepreneurs and cosmographers. Then the pilots of the Atlantic and Pacific fleets and some residents along the shore added their testimony. Finally prospective partners in the monopoly of construction and operation of the new ports and routes under a royal *capitulación* were heard. This shift was in some sense counterproductive, as the greater focus on the route weakened the emphasis on the goal of a new design for the entire region and traffic pattern in the Caribbean.[30]

Our point is that the decision, which becomes part of the linear sequence of events constructed in later times, looking backwards is not an accurate reflection of life at any one time in the past. Each time when choices are before us, many are abandoned and only one will be that decision, while the nature and consideration of abandoned choices make up the very texture of history. Puerto Caballos was a spectacularly long-lived example of such an abandoned choice.

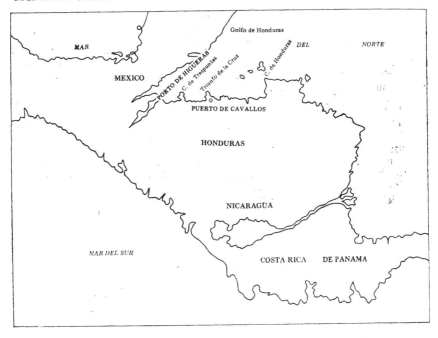

Fig. 1. Based on Antonio de Herrera. Historia General (ca 1570)

---

[30] Juan Escalante de Mendoza's *Itinerario* is a link between the case of Juan Garcia de Hermosilla and the renewed attempts to establish alternative isthmian crossings in 1605, 1610 and 1611.

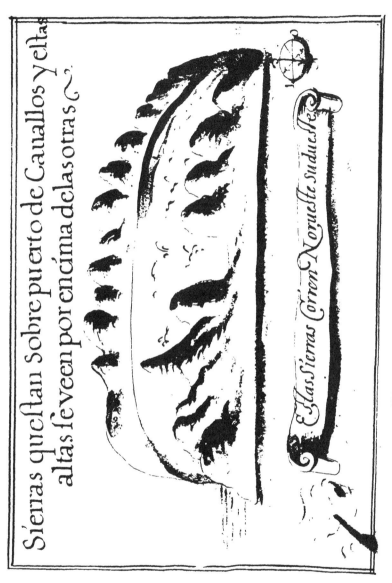

Sierras questan sobre puerto de Cauallos y estas altas se veen por encima de las otras

Ellas Sierras Corren Norueste sudueste

'Sierras questan sobre puerto de caballos ...'
from *Luz de Navegantes* by Vellerino de Villalobos
By courtesy of Museo Naval, Madrid.

'Nombre de Dios'
from *Luz de Navegantes* by Vellerino de Villalobos
By courtesy of Museo Naval, Madrid.

XII

The Silver Masters: a Link in the Spanish Silver Chain

> Some went down to the sea in ships,
> doing business on the great waters
> Psalm CVII

The silver chain which bound the Spanish Indies to Seville during the colonial period was made up of well-defined links. The silver masters were in charge of one of them, the transport of treasure from the port of departure in the New World to the recipient in Spain. Legislation concerning the silver master's office has been seen for the period 1592 - 1655 (1), but their activities ranged beyond those dates. The earliest provision defines and regulates an existing office and the last one only revokes procedures. Although the silver masters were part of the personnel of the Carrera de Indias for well over 150 years, they are relegated to footnotes or mere paragraphs in our histories of the Indies trade for two reasons: they did not affect the amount of treasure in any substantial way (except in case of fraud), and they had nothing to do with the management of the ship as did other masters who were called maestres de nao and maestres de raciones. Veitia Linage quite clearly states that the maestre de plata should properly have been called depositario, tesorero or receptor (2).

Although the amount of treasure and the safe passage of the fleet did not depend on the silver master, the fortunes of hundreds of people did, including the royal treasurer, and that is the reason for this study. Firstly, the records of the office, and of the men who held it, should be rescued from the context of naval legislation where they are forgotten. (3) Secondly, beyond the structure of the office and personnel, attention should be called to the role of the silver masters as middlemen, and to the reflection on Spanish society and its values which is found in the relevant documentation.

The history of their office parallels in precise detail the grande ligne of the financial history of the Empire. Amounts of treasure in the care of the silver masters, intensity of the traffic, and regulation of the office and officers, articulate in manageable quantity the policies of the Spanish Crown. The pathology of the office, i. e., its abuse and malfunction, reveals by its impacts the role played by money from the Indies when the owners could and did seek redress in cases of loss. This is a chapter of social history which equates money and treasury by methods other than assaying, conversion into currency and purchasing power, with the meaning it had in the lives of many people who wanted it for celebration of masses (4), for a dowry (5), for covering a debt (6) - whether commercial or of honor (gambling) - , or for whatever multiple purposes surface in the papers.

The Catálogo de las Consultas del Consejo de Indias in the Archivo General de Indias, prepared by Antonia Heredia Herrera drew my attention to this subject of the silver masters. (7) The proximate appearance of a catalogue of the Sección 12: Papeles de Cadix, 1543 - 1711, especially the ramo of Averfa from the same archive, and under the exemplary vigilance of the same editor, suggests the following possibilities for research on the link in the silver traffic which can be made at this stage:

I. Who were the silver masters?

II. What was their office?

III. The conduct of their office.

IV. New sources and expected contributions.

The silver masters were men of substance "siempre   personas muy honradas y de calidad y credito." (8) The responsibility for the transport of treasure from American ports to the recipients in Spain, who were either private owners or crown agents, had originally been assumed by captains or more often by masters who frequently owned their vessels. The conflict about provisions concerning the handling of treasure, the manner and timing of registration and valuation in the Indies (9), the requirement for the masters to stay in Seville at the Casa and remain available until the last shipment had been claimed, and other provisions put them in conflict with the Fiscal at the Casa.

The task of the silver master was well defined by the cedula of June 5th, 1598 which made reference to 1592 and the accustomed way of procedure. The maestre de plata was put in exclusive charge of all treasure (bullion, coin, etc.). His duties were the provision of equipment and labor for the packing of treasure, supervision of the loading in the Indies (10), transshipment where necessary (sometimes three or four times because of the shallow draught in Nombre de Dios and in San Lucar), unloading in Seville, transport to the Casa de la Contratación, which involved cartage, and delivery to private owners.

The silver masters, when first regulated, were appointed by the general of the fleets. The change in the cédula of 1598 was to transfer the right of nomination to the

judges and president of the Casa. The year is, of course, one which reflects the raid
on Cadiz of 1597, and the general revision of affairs of the Casa and of the handling of
the treasure in the Indies. In the book entitled: La organización financiera de las Indias
(siglo XVI), by Ismael Sánchez Bella, the parallelism of financial rearrangements of
the cajas in the Indies and its consequences parallel measures concerning the silver
masters quite well. (11)

The remuneration for the office was set, to begin with, at 1 % of treasure in the
care of the silver master. Almost throughout the seventeenth century the rates were set
at 1 % for coin, 3/4 % for bullion from New Spain, one peso de ocho for every 100 pesos
de minas of Peruvian bullion, 1/4 % of all royal treasure from New Spain and 90 maravedis for every bar of 50 marcs weight for the royal treasure from Peru. (12)

This compensation amounted to a goodly sum as the traffic increased. But due to
growing volume the silver masters became responsible for the wages of a secretary of
accounts, for two guards aboard, and for two guards per cart of transport overland in
the Indies and in Spain. As though this were not enough responsibility, the Universidad de
Mareantes requested in 1600 that the maestres de plata, along with the other masters,
be required to pass the Pilot Major's examination in navigation, since in case of death
or incapacity of the pilot, the silver masters should be able to sail the ship. (13)

To insure the safe delivery of the treasure the maestres de plata were required
to post a substantial bond of 25.000 ducats, (a sum which remained constant over most
of the seventeenth century) as against the 10.000 ducats required from the maestres
de nao. These fianças were to be registered in the Casa, and since the silver masters
frequently had to borrow money to put up the bond, the taking of depositions in the Casa
of all pledges on behalf of the silver masters (originally limited to four but later extended
to more people) was a lengthy process. (14) This aggravated the problems of the departing
fleets and led to corruption and irregularities, often with the connivance of the judges of
the Casa, whose first concern was for the fleets which could not tolerate delay. (15)

A memorial submitted by the pilots and masters sums up their views of the silver
master's office circumscribing its function by grievances and requests. In its fourteenth
and final clause this memorial states that in order to promote the growth of the traffic
'' rich and honored people should be prevailed upon to orient their children toward such
a calling'' (... que para la navegación de las Indias vaya en crecimiento y las personas
ricas honradas orienten a sus hijos hacia ella). (16)

Correspondence dealing with grievances a out how the treasure and freight should be handled characterizes this early phase of the developing trade. The scandal caused by the default on 340.000 ducats of private treasure by Lope Díaz de Armendariz, who could not be seized, was a factor in the transfer of the right of nomination for the post of silver master to the Consejo de Indias in 1615. (17) At this juncture the recommendation of the Universidad de Mareantes commending "rich and honored people" to be charged with the treasure was taken too literally by the Crown. The office was made salable, to be cried at auction and the honored and rich whose bid succeeded were the Conde-Duque de Olivares and the Marqués de Aguilar who had been granted "ciertas cantidades según la calidad de los maestrages para las mercedes que sobre ellos hize el senor Rey D. Felipe IV." (18) It is possible that the request by the Universidad de Mareantes that the maestres de plata be required to take the Pilot Major's examination, was submitted in hopes that its members would stand a better chance in competition for the office.

Especially heavy losses of treasure in 1654 and 1655 once more affected many people. Domingo Ipenarrieta, maestre de plata in the flota of Panamá under general D. Martín Carlos de Mencos, and of two maestres in 1655 (Francisco Galvano and José de Reina in the flota of Nueva España under general D. Juan de Urbina (19) led to legal suits and, eventually caused the abolition of the system of selling the silver master's office at auction. Nomination to the office was once more transferred, this time to the Consejo de Cámara. (20)

What can be seen from this sketch is that the history of the silvermaster's office developed pari-passu with the regulations concerning the royal hacienda. When high profits were consistently anticipated, more direct control over the transport was enforced by the Crown. In the process the elevation of status over function of the office stressed the importance of rights and privileges to an extent which undercut the professionalism in its conduct. Exactly when an office ceases to gain by the "riches and honor" of its holder is not easy to decide, but the divorce of the official from the office always spells a decline, leading to aggressiveness in the holder (demand for higher profits from the sale of the office which becomes unsalable), and to recession insofar as all innovation in the job ceases and competence is reduced. This experience is quite frequent in the Indies administration as in the Habsbourg Empire generally, and the silver master's case lends precision of detail to the story so well presented by John Parry in his Sale of Public Office in the Spanish Indies under the Habsburgs (21), and interpreted by John Phelan in his article " Authority and Flexibility in the Spanish Imperial Bureaucracy." (22) The " disorderly appetites" of absolutist government, so called by the Duc de Rohan, are discussed by Albert Hirschmann. (23)

The record of fianças and of autos entre partes have not been examined with reference to the wealth of data for the social aspects of economic history because of the overwhelming mass of documentation. The fianças of the silver masters can be used as tracers to record what goods were given as bond and at what equivalent monetary value. They tell what guarantees were acceptable, and by implication, they reflect on the capacity of people of varied status to put up such bonds. What did it take to get started as a middleman in the business "on the great waters"? Family guarantees, partnerships and the support of sponsors all represent a web of dependencies within which people moved. (24) Fianças show how they made good their word and how they thought security could be assured, not to say treasure insured, for the fianças of the silver masters are one aspect of the familiar and complicated story of marine insurance.

The autos entre partes, when they do not clearly relate to criminal fraud, which is mostly the case, were the result of mishaps or misunderstandings. Whatever their origin, they are informative about prices. A random sampling from the catalogues of the Archivo de Indias shows the values of miscellaneous goods, skins (25), anil (26), Chinese beds and rosaries (27), of bullion in various categories and of gold (28). There are inventories of properties left by people who died on the voyages which are quite detailed. (29) (If the bienes de difuntos are an almost unmanagable source, these samples can be used with profit). Two claims, one by a Frenchman and another by a Fleming, show the particular situation of foreigners in Seville . (30) Next, the purposes for which these monies were intended and which have already been mentioned, also appear in the autos entre partes. They show the impact of treasure from the Indies which is among the most elusive and useful aspects for an understanding of Spanish society. All of this , it must be stressed, concerns money before it enters the market. What role was it to play, what planned expenditure would move a judge to support a claim, what use of money would most condemn a debtor ? To know how such arguments have changed - where they have - would be a great help toward empathy with the society one tries to understand.

The contribution which a thorough study of the silver masters, based upon the fianças and autos entre partes can make to financial history can easily be shown. For social history there is one other aspect which comes to mind worthy of exploration. That is to consider the role of the silver masters as middlemen. Spanish silver, from mine to market, went through the hands of several such people: the owners of mules or llamas, of carts and pataches, and, there were on an ascending ladder of professionalism and entrepreneurship, the assayers and the silver merchants. The silver masters differ from them in so far as they also represent a state of mind, the search for security. As a link in the chain of Spanish silver, they represent a safety catch.

As such they elude altogether the grand designs of Max Weber's (31) and Robert Merton's bureaucracies (32), they escape Roland Mousnier's "Societies of Order" (33), and their role in statistical and serial accounts, or of economic history (Chaunu, Hamilton and Haring) is quite properly very minor. (34) Alfred Hirschmann's turn to non - economic texts for a look at the rise of capitalism is on a new track which promises to break through accustomed thought patterns. (35) It might now be suggested that the silver masters as middlemen join other such transient aggregations not only for description or analysis of them as a neglected group, but as convenient tracers of real as well as of perceived needs. The often illogical manner of filling such a need, is shown here when the concern with the safety at sea of the entire Atlantic traffic, of goods and men, becomes a preoccupation with profit from the sale of an office for two courtiers. A further study of the men who "went to do business on the great waters" that link in the Spanish silver chain, the maestres de plata, would secure our knowledge and broaden our reference concerning the values by which their society lived.

NOTES

1. Joseph Veitia Linage, Norte de la Contratación de las Indias Occidentales, Buenos Aires, Comisión Argentina de Fomento Inter-americano, 1945 Lib. II, Cap. XI

2. Veitia Linage, Op. Cit., p. 601

3. Ismael Sanchez Bella, La Organización Financiera de las Indias, Sevilla, Escuela de Estudios Hispano Americanos, 1968 p. 108 note 128, says they are not in the strict sense officials of the royal hacienda and he omits them in his book.

4. Archivo General de Indias (A.G.I.) Contratación 498 Autos Fiscales, part IV, No. 1 (1606)

5. A.G.I., Contratación 282, Autos entre Partes No. 5, (1608)

6. A.G.I., Contratación 740, Autos entre Partes No. 15, (1595)

7. Archivo General de Indias: Catálogo de las Consultas del Consejo de Indias, ed. Antonia Heredia Herrera, 2 vols. Madrid, Direccion General de Archivos y Bibliotecas, 1972

8. Veitia Linage, Op. Cit., p. 601

9. Sánchez Bella, Op. Cit., Cap. IV, pp. 238 - 247; A.G.I. , Catálogo de las Consultas, v. I, 3197, 1596; 3180, 1597; 3205, 1597

10. Veitia Linage, loc. Cit., law of 1605; Mendel Peterson, The Funnel of Gold, Boston Little Brown, 1975 p. 363 for stowage of treasure

11. Sánchez Bella, Op. Cit., growth of hacienda, p. 55; contadurias mayores, 1596, 1598, p. 64; cajas reales pp. 53, 77, 78, 90, 99

12. Veitia Linage, Op. Cit., Clarence H. Haring, Trade and Navigation between Spain and the Indies in the Time of the Habsburgs, Cambridge, Harvard University Press, 1918

13. A.G.I. Indiferente General 1953, Lib. V, 31 May 1599 - 14 May 1607 fol. 28 - 28v; also José Pulido Rubio, El Piloto Mayor de la Casa de la Contratación de Sevilla, Sevilla. Escuela de Estudios Hispano-Americanos, 2 ed. 1950, cap. VIII, p. 201

14. Veitia Linage, Op. Cit., p. 604

15. A.G.I. Contratación 751, No 2, (1601); Pulido Rubio, Loc. Cit.

16. A.G.I. Indiferente General 2002, Cartas escritas por los oficiales de Sevilla, Año 1562, fols. 143v - 135v

17. A.G.I. Contratación 793, No. 14, (1615) "El Prior"......"

18. Veitia Linage, Loc. Cit., John H. Parry, The Sale of Public Office in the Spanish

Indies under the Habsburgs, Berkeley, University of California Press, 1953, p. 60 on auction, p. 54 on Olivares and Cámara

19. A.G.I. Contratación 957, Escribania, año de 1655, "La sentencia de Ipenarrieta..."; Escuela de Historia Hispano Americana 1935, vol I 344 - 345

20. Veitia Linage, Op.Cit., p. 603

21. Parry, Op.Cit.

22. John L. Phelan, Authority and Flexibility in the Spanish Imperial Bureaucracy Administrative Science Quarterly, vol. 5, pp. 47 - 65, June 1960

23. Albert O. Hirschmann, The Passions and the Interests, Political Arguments for Capitalism before its Triumph, Princeton, Princeton University Press, 1977

24. Ruth Pike, Enterprise and Adventure. The Genoese in Seville and the Opening of the New World. Ithaca, Cornell University Press, 1966, treats that society.

25. A.G.I. Contratación 735, No. 2, Autos entre partes, (1593) ; Alonso Perez de Fonseca..."

26. A.G.I. Contratación 750, No. 21, Autos entre Partes, (1600), Francisco de Torres.. treats of "quatro fardos de anil"

27. A.G.I. Contratación 792 No. 12, Autos entre Partes, (1615), "Francisco de Aguayo..."

28. A.G.I. Contratación 646 Autos Fiscales 1614 - 1619, No. 2, contra los maestres de plata siguientes y sufriadores sobre ciertas cantidades de plata que dejaron de entregar; 2 ramos Contratación 735 No. 4 Autos entre Partes, (1593), "El monasterio de San Gerónimo de Espeja con Bernardino Salerno, maestre de plata, sobre entrega de una partida de plata. Ibid. No. 6, Juan de Chaves; There are at least ten more cases identifiable now from the Torres Lanzas catalogue but any listing of them would not serve beyond illustrations.

29. A.G.I. Contratación, 498, Autos Fiscales, part IV, No. 1, (1606) "Sanetorum Bingochea.... con testamento en la mar', Autos sobre sus bienes.

30. A.G.I. Contratación 278, part 3, No. 3, (1607), "Pedro Vazquez, Maestre de Plata y difunto.....inventario y almoneda de sus bienes".

31. A.G.I. Contratación 770, no. 3 (1608): "Henrique Serval mercader flamenco", and No. 7 " Jacques La Maire..."

32. Max Weber, Wirtschaft und Gesellschaft 3rd. ed., Tuebingen 1947, vol. III, "Bureaukratie."

33. Robert K. Merton et al. eds. Reader in Bureaucracy, Glencoe, Free Press, 1952, especially chapter VI

101

34. Roland Mousnier, <u>Social Hierarchies, 1450 to the Present</u>, New York, Schocken Books, 1973

35. Pierre et Huguette Chaunu, <u>Séville et l'Atlantique,</u> 8 vols, Paris, A. Colin, 1955; Earl J. Hamilton, <u>American Treasure and the Price Revolution in Spain 1501 - 1650,</u> Cambridge, Mass., Harvard University Press, 1934; Haring, <u>Op. Cit.</u>

36. Hirschmann, <u>Op. Cit.</u>

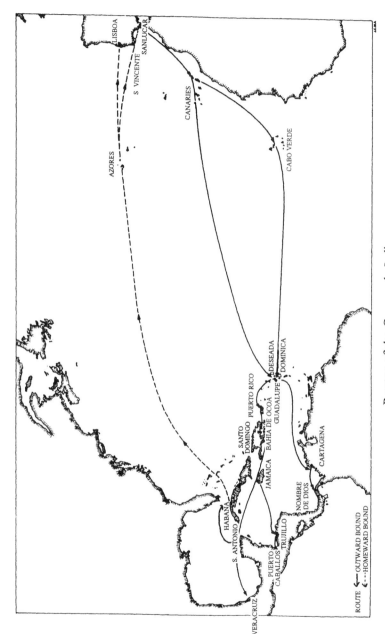

Routes of the Carrera de Indias
from *Luz de Navegantes* by Vellerino de Villalobos
By courtesy of Museo Naval, Madrid.

XIII

Advice to the King:
I. The Route to the Indies;
II. The South Atlantic*

Advice to the king: the route to the Indies

How the Carrera de Indias was organized, changed, and functioned was shown in the eight magisterial volumes by Pierre and Huguette Chaunu in *Séville et l'Atlantique*.[1] That work was followed by several more distinguished inquiries into the subject, particularly by Kenneth Andrews in *The Spanish Caribbean: Trade and Plunder, 1530–1630*,[2] and Paul E. Hoffman who published *The Spanish Crown and the Defense of the Caribbean, 1535–1585*.[3] This paper cannot claim to add any new knowledge about how the Indies fleets operated in the economic and political arena. It is interesting that basic sources for the story how the ships moved still remain in manuscript, lack modern editions and are difficult to access. The *Quatri Partitu en Cosmografía* by Alonso de Chaves was discussed in 1969.

Another major work known to scholars, which remains in several manuscripts without a modern edition is the *Itinerario de la Navegación de las mares y tierras occidentales* (1575) by Juan de Escalante de Mendoza.[4] This was accessible to me only to the extent that I could copy from it on the premises of the Museo Naval where it was to be prepared for publication. A third work by a cleric cosmographer, Manoel de Andrada Castel Blanco, was called to my attention, *Instrucción* "... que a V. Magestad se da para mandar fortificar el mar Oceano, y defenderse de todos los contrarios Piratas, ansi Franceses, como Ingleses, en todas las navegaciones de su Real Corona dentro de los Trópicos. Ofrécela Don Felipe de Albornoz. Compuesta y ordenada por su maestro en la Mathemática, El Licenciado Manoel de Andrada Castel Blanco, Capellán de Vuestra Magestad". This is a unique printed copy in the Dr Williams Library, London.

These are books of instructions and advice about the composition and the manner of operation of the Carrera de Indias in the North and South Atlantic. I decided that from them one could get a pretty complete picture of the problems of the traffic and of the people dealing with the Spanish fleets, their operation and routing. Moreover the fate of such works identified the various interests in the operation of the *carrera* from the king through the Council of

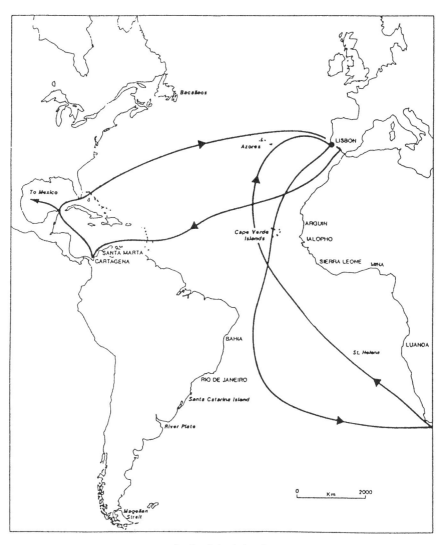

Andrada's Atlantic
By courtesy of P.E.H. Hair.

Taking the height of a star with a Jacob's staff (*ballestilla*)
from *Itinerario de Navegación* by Juan de Escalante de Mendoza
By courtesy of Museo Naval, Madrid.

the Indies and the Casa de la Contratación (House of Trade) in Sevilla, to the student pilot. Alternatively, in reverse order, it showed that access to the crown was sought on the part of experts from various callings, for instance astronomers at the universities, instrument makers, and cartographers, who wanted to help with their advice.

A *Memorial* of the Consejo de Indias to the king, of July 14, 1582, signed by Antonio de Rojas, discusses the license to print Escalantes' *Itinerario de la navegación de los mares y tierras occidentales*. The response was an order to keep one copy guarded or secret, presumably in Sevilla, and to forward a second one: "where I can deposit it as I find advisable; and (also) to consider what compensation he (Escalante) might be assigned, where to send it, in what manner, and let me know about it".[5] There is no record of payment which was to be drawn on the receipts, *receptorio*, of Mexico and the book was never licensed for printing.

Concerning the fate of the manuscript, the documents tell us that the reason for denying the right to publication (October 5, 1593)[6] was in order to avoid some inconveniences and that parts of the manuscript were circulating in copies. An order of November 17, 1593 called for them to be collected and brought to the Consejo.[7] This was in response to a petition by the son of Juan de Escalante who described to the Council this state of the Indies in a *Representación al Rey*, which survives not in an original but in a copy by Navarrete. It conveniently summarizes the larger work in straight forward prose showing just how sensitive the context must have appeared in Madrid. Proof of the copying is the almost plagiary of the illustrations of the piece, with often identical texts from Escalante, but with a few changes of spelling or identity of place, presumably drawn from a trumped up list of "sources", but judged to be copies. This, I am told, will be demonstrated in the forthcoming publication of Baltasar Vellerino de Villalobos' work *Luz de Navegantes*.[8] The manuscript, slated for publication, is in the library of the University of Salamanca. It demonstrates one case of borrowing from a superb guide to the routes and harbors of the Carrera.

Juan de Escalante de Mendoza prefaces his work with a short autobiography. He came from a noble family and was of legitimate birth.[9] He quickly advanced to the rank of *maestre*. One of his uncles was Captain Alvaro de Colombres, a veteran of the Indies trade, and Juan married Doña Juana Salgado, the daughter of Alejo Salgado Correa, a judge of the Casa de la Contratación. He trained aboard his uncle's ships from a very young age, on the route to Honduras/Guatemala, acquainting himself with those regions. So he was put in command of his own ship, and advanced in public affairs to become 24, *veinte y cuatro*, which is roughly equivalent to a member of the city council of Sevilla. His name appeared twice in the list of candidates to be named captain-general of the fleet, on May 26, 1593 and again on February 26,

3

1594.[10] It was the very accuracy of the picture, the detail, the intimate acquaintance with the strong and the weak points of the Carrera de Indias which made an impression. A provision dated August 18, 1582 states that it would be proper to award Captain Juan de Escalante de Mendoza for his book one payment of fifty ducats for expenses drawn from the account, *receptoria*, of Mexico.[11] His connections not withstanding, he only advanced to Captain General of the Armada y Flota de la Nueva España, in 1595. He died in Nombre de Dios, that pestilential harbor, before the return trip in 1596. On February 18, 1597, his widow was forgiven debts he owed the Avería, customs, which is the only financial accommodation with the heirs on record.[12]

The *Representación al Rey* is directly addressed to the crown, condensing the message of the larger text, in a demonstration of its pertinence and usefulness. Its motivation was the circumstance that publication of the larger work had been denied the author because it would have meant publishing an authoritative comprehensive picture of the organization of the Atlantic fleets. It is a summary in straight forward text. The dates for departure and return of the ships, are shown to depend on knowledge of the wind and current systems explored by the Spanish and earlier Portuguese voyagers in the Atlantic. The supplies and security measures taken to lead and guard the fleets are discussed in detail. The manning and arming, the command structure, the supplies, where taken aboard, astronomical, cosmographic, and cartographic theories and practices are discussed, and the dangers and advantages of various organizations in transit, communication at night etc., are clearly described and explained.

A brief look at the introductory pages of the *Itinerario* can demonstrate the contention that the book would have given away too much information. The text of Escalante is cast in the popular dialogue form adopted, for instance, by Pedro de Medina for his *Arte de Navegar*. Escalante chose this format of discourse to present his subject in order to personalize instruction which, he says, dates from "Greek and Roman" times . A questioner watching a ship in Sevilla inquires about the possibility of booking a passage to San Lucar, the harbor down river, because he wants to join the Indies fleet. He is referred to a pilot to whom he explains his plan to write a book about the Indies voyages coming and going as run by the Spanish fleets. The pilot dressed in blue – which is proper for the sea – accepts his questioner, who introduces himself as "Tristán", as passengers. So the dialogue is between Tristán and the pilot. There follows a point by point discussion of the preparation of the fleet, the use of different sizes of ships, their construction, rigging and anchors used on the Indies route. A comparison with ships of other countries follows. The artillery carried, the reasons for caliber and positioning, and the assembly of the fleet at San Lucar, distant one mile from the start, are described. A discussion of the chain of command and work of the mariners follows.

4

Some incidents of prior voyages relate the work of famous captains general, D. Alvaro de Bazán and D. Bernardino de Mendoza among them. The complications of departure by a fleet which had to clear the barrier sand-bank at the mouth of the Guadalquivir was elaborate and precise. The point made is that knowledge of the organization as presented in such order and with such precision, with information made clear, and procedures explained, would most likely have led to copy and use of the manuscripts in Sevilla as alleged by Escalante and his heir. The extant manuscripts are discussed by Cesareo Fernández Duro in his *Disquisiones Nauticas*.[13] A future edition of the manuscript by the Museo Naval will bring clarity to the state of the sources.

Advice to the king: the South Atlantic

This uniquely printed pamphlet was first discussed at a meeting in 1982 in hopes of provoking interested scholars to help with the editing and publication of this valuable tract. The edition, eventually published by Paul Hair, is entitled *To Defend Your Empire And The Faith*.[14] An indispensable introduction and chronology precede the facsimile reprint. My short notes show the early state of work on the manuscript and the problems encountered. They serve to introduce the document, and in their vagueness and state of incompleteness they advise that consultation of the printed edition is indispensable for any scholarly reference.

My purpose is to introduce a printed pamphlet of the late sixteenth century which concerns the ports and sea lanes of the South Atlantic, and the security of shipping on the high seas. Charles Boxer called my attention to this piece two years ago, in a conversation about my work with the Spanish cosmographers. It was described to me as full of cosmographic references: latitudes, shooting the sun, etc. I had no time to copy it once I looked it up in London, nor were there facilities for copying, or even a typewriter to borrow. So I took what notes I could and put it on the back burner. When I returned to London last spring, I found a copy machine on the premises and the curator obliged me with making the copy himself.

The provenance of the piece goes back to 1727 when it appeared in a printed catalogue of books made for a testamentary bequest of a collection in the year 1711. This date makes acquisition years earlier likely, and the validity of the testament and subsequent unbroken record, are the guarantee of it being genuine. The pamphlet could have reached England in any number of ways when the subject of Spanish sea-power was acute in England, or it might, by 1711, merely have attracted the attention of a clerical collector. This is more likely as the pamphlet is an anti-Lutheran tract and the testator was the English clergyman, Dr Williams. The pamphlet is of octavo size, bound and in good

5

condition. It has 46 pages of text, and some as yet undeciphered notes in a seventeenth-century hand in Portuguese on the empty back pages. The spelling is not consistent, as is to be expected.

The booklet has no printing date, nor any reference at the beginning or end to indicate place and date of printing. Internal evidence suggests a date between 1590 and 1598, the latter date the death of Philip II, who is the "your Majesty" addressed throughout. This I deduce, not from the mention by name, but rather by association with "your father the Emperor", "your uncle the Señor King D. Sebastian", and "your sainted grandfather Don Manoel". I have not been able to identify as yet the person to whom the tract is dedicated, D. Felipe Albornoz. For the career of the author, Manoel de Andrada Castel Blanco, and the origin and effect of the text, I have to rely – as of now – entirely upon internal evidence. No other copy of the pamphlet has been found in London, Paris, Germany (Munich and Wolfenbuettel), Portugal or Spain (Museo Naval and Biblioteca Nacional in Madrid) so far, nor have I found mention of the author.

The style of the piece is typical of late sixteenth century expository prose which dispenses with punctuation or uses it erratically. Loose clauses follow one another over pages at a time, strung together rather indiscriminately with "and" or "which". The "and" might mean but, however, moreover, or besides, and the "which" can relate to any subject in any prior paragraph that seems to make sense. I have had to make some major revisions as I went along translating. Verbs which are scarce can be interpreted in contradictory ways. Selling can mean buying or trading, and "returning" does not necessarily relate to any definite point of origin. The troubles of rendering the text in English are various, and several careful readings do not allow me to claim that I have a valid translation. What I have is a workable one.

The author states that he is a self-taught cosmographer. His text tends, by and large, to support what is known of Portuguese practice and problems with the colonial traffic in the South Atlantic of the 1580s, when Spain and Portugal were joined in personal union of crowns. With respect to theoretical cosmography, the contributions of the text are negligible, except for a first hand account of the state of geographical knowledge concerning the position of places (with respect to latitudes only) and experience with the wind and current system of the ocean.

The piece is one of special pleading for a course of action to be taken by the crown, and so comes under the rubric of "arbitrista" literature which is characteristic of the later Habsburg period. It is a sample of information from private sources routed through personal contact to the responsible agency or person in charge of the matter addressed, in hopes that it might reach the crown most probably through one of the councils. Such advice was offered frequently "for the sake of my conscience" by public spirited men, as in this case, or by those in search of recognition of their service. If it reached someone who thought it useful, there might result a request to present the material more formally, as seems to have been the case with Andrada's presentation. He says in a later passage that he gives this information as: "I have been commanded to do". It is this feature which gives me hope to find another trace of the matter elsewhere. It would then fit the pattern of texts by other cosmographers, such as Escalante de Mendoza on the Carrera de Indias (see part I of this essay), Juan Bautista Gesio and Rios Coronel concerning the Pacific.

The title spells out how Spanish shipping in the tropical regions can be protected against all enemy pirates, French as well as English, and rendered defensible. This plan is offered by D. Felipe de Albornoz, composed and put in order by his master of mathematics, licentiate Manoel de Andrada Castel Blanco, *capellán* of your Majesty the King.

In continuation the text is like a table of contents: discourse of this entire instruction which treats the importance of navigation and proceeding against the Lutherans. This discourse treats the fortifications of the kingdom of Jalofos, its people and resources; Sierra Leone, its site and resources; San Salvador and Brazil, its estuary and barrier; San Sebastian and Rio de Janeiro, captured by the French; and the island of Saint Helena on the route to the East Indies. These references show the Spanish concern with shipping around the globe after the union of crowns in 1580, and the author's preoccupation with the South Atlantic.

The author's acquaintance with the conditions of colonial traffic and problems of pioneer government was extensive. He says he served his Majesty nine years in Brazil, and later five years in Guinea. In the latter place (Sierra Leone) and an earlier posting to the La Plata in 1572, with Juan Ortíz de Zárate, on the occasion of his abortive attempt at settlement, Andrada was commissioned as vicar general accompanying the *adelantado*. He knew the Azores well, and had been driven thence to Bahia by a raid in 1560, while his ship was unable to rescue the San Pablo in Sierra Leone. Its Captain Ruy de Melo set out again in the month of October and because of the conditions of the season they: "fell into such errors, that upon finally rounding the Cape of Good Hope, we missed the island of San Laurencio (Madagascar) and passed by India until we reached Sumatra".[15] Andrada found himself one of only thirteen survivors of a voyage which had counted 840 men at the start. He touched bases at Mombasa on the way back, after two years in the East, which enabled him to throw in some advice concerning the importance of fortifying Socortara (Zocotra) to guard the India route from depredations by heretics out of the Red Sea. He mentions having sailed in "high-boarded ships", i.e. caravels with Jorge de Lima and Jorge Tubara in the Terceiras, Pedro Meléndez, Juan Ortíz, Estacio de Sáa, Cristóbal de Barros, Antonio Vello

7

Tinoco (patrolling around Saint Helena) and Pedro Leitão among others, and in galleys with Fernández Alvarez, Bernabé de Sosa, and Pedro López de Sequeiras.

Although I have as yet been unable to sort out the exact sequence of these adventures from the text, enough references check out to confirm the author's contacts. To get that extraordinary curriculum vitae straightened out, one must keep in mind the crucial date of 1580, fix "the year your Majesty was in Portugal" (Philip II was there two and a half years after the surrender of Lisbon), and try to identify "these parts" in which Andrada worked for thirty-one years to establish his expertise. Those are just some of the problems, but they are a challenge of interest beyond the one life.

The mid-eighties to early nineties were decisive years for redefinition of naval defense. The book by Paul Hoffman, cited above, on the defense of the Caribbean ends with 1585 as a convenient date for the completion of a comparatively stable traffic pattern for the *Carrera de Indias*. The union of crowns in 1580, caused a shift of problems more noticeable in the South Atlantic, India, and the Far East where the enemies of Spain now took on Portugal in open war. Meantime Philip II was aging, and the recent biography of him by Geoffrey Parker entitles a chapter on the years 1589–1598 as leading "toward the grave". Philip never recovered from a fever in 1595. He once wrote to his secretary in response to an inquiry that he would answer if he were to wake up in the morning. Under such conditions one would look for an echo to Andrada's text in the papers of some Council member, rather than in royal correspondence. In earlier times, the king's interest might indeed have been aroused by the account of so knowledgeable a party as Andrada. The *capellán* knew the peoples of the areas he discusses at first hand as well as the specific sites he suggests for fortification.

Starting with his chapter on Jalofo he uses the work to mean either the Grand Jalofo (who is like a Grand Duke called Gudumel, that is Gudumel is the title, not the name, since Cadamosto met a Gudumel), or he refers to the territory between the Senegal and Cape Verde, extending toward the northeast along the trade route to Timbuctu or Tumbucutum, which was largely controlled by the tribe of Jalofos. He describes the Great Ialofo as powerful and civilized enough to deserve a diplomatic mission with gifts of some value, suggesting some jewel and horses harness. The capital of the tribe is Bezeguiche (modern Dakar, though probably not the identical site), also called Ialofo, and located opposite the Cape Verde Islands. This place should be fortified. Though the chief and some so-called courtiers are Moslem and keep the prayers, the rest of the population is heathen and: "would be easily converted if the gospel were preached to them". Andrada mentions the savage tribes of Sierra Leone (among the Bujafras) who live by the Rio Grande (the Geba River) as not worthy diplomatic courtesies, but who would make good

Christians and reliable allies if given arms by the Iberians rather than by the English.

On the American shores Andrada mentions the Pitiguaros, Tupinambas and Tamoyes around Rio who are given arms by the Lutherans and the Carijos of the La Plata. He warns of the danger of Lutherans living among them, and the threat they pose to the province of Charcas and Peru via the La Plata and ascending river systems. He documents the ease of communication by land to the West by telling of his meeting with an Araucanian chief in company of the Carijos of the La Plata while on the island of Santa Catalina. He mentions that he preached in the native tongue (singular) in Brazil as well as in Latin which, he said, served the additional purpose of keeping his skills sharpened.

Among the intellectual skills which Andrada cultivated were mathematics and cosmography. He claimed to be self-educated in the theory but practised in his many voyages in the art of navigation. His text bears him out with respect to the former which concerns knowledge of the sphere and the globe. In this department he declares himself prepared to explain the basic tenets to anyone any time he were asked to do so. He considered knowledge of the globe essential and requested that it be taught to all sailors.

A brief sample of his explanation of the various motions of the sea and atmosphere under the twelve signs and the seven planets etc. makes it clear that the pilots and sailors may have been spared a good bit of confusion. When he discusses the need for practical experience of tides and winds, of currents, monsoons and calms, the importance of local information, and consideration of seasonal variations at sea, he speaks from bitterly won experience, repeatedly and accurately.

The body of his text consists of arguments for the fortification of coastal points and islands to offer safe ports of call for the trade ships, to control pirates at close range and to prevent interlopers from entering the coasts. The text partakes of the ebb and flow of the sea, with shifting winds of reference to places away from the issue at hand, with miscellaneous information of natural phenomena, economic and strategic considerations, and the whole stretched over an imperial frame of reference, shot through the threads of chronology and colored by clusters of mostly disastrous events. Concerning the fortresses he more or less consistently presents four points: the reasons for the choice with respect to the role on the route or adjacent colony; the site, manpower and materials for construction; the financing of each project; the problems of maintenance and the manpower for the convoys which he suggests replace individual licenses for the Atlantic and Eastern sailings.

He describes the accessibility of the harbors, the available sea room, he does not mention the nature of the bottom, the shelter from storms, and the control over the entry. In Bahia only reconstruction would be required for the security of that superb harbor, and San Sebastian on the Rio de Enero offered

9

advantageous sites for gun emplacements. Likewise Cape San Antonio would only require reconstruction of a neglected fort, as would Filipina, the settlement in Pernambuco (João Pessoa). This is a suggestion added after the plan for the booklet had been written. There are no earlier references to those northern places now presented in only summary form. This gives some clue to the modification of arguments over time, with an interest in the Spanish Main developed after 1580.

In Jalofos there is a barrier island which could be easily fortified and manned. Sierra Leone would offer at least two choices at river mouths, (Tagarin or Mitombo). From such a strong point, the raids upon Arguim and the whole Guinea coast could be controlled. Santa Catalina Island would protect the La Plata and even the entry to the Strait of Magellan, and Saint Helena would be a most desirable watering and supply station, and a safe shelter on the Far Eastern run since: "everything grows there that grows in Spain". Materials, mostly wood for repair of the ships are available at all his sites and manpower comes under two headings: natives, especially in Africa; and men under some criminal indictment, among them sailors of whom there are many who would welcome pardons and be willing to purchase citizenship.

For the La Plata area and Saint Helena, Andrada suggests the founding of *encomiendas* for knights who are landless, especially of the Order of Malta. They would bring soldiers and make themselves respected by colonial rivals. For maintenance he suggests that a religious order be established at Sagres (apparently in Portugal and not in Africa) where knights, soldiers and mariners would be trained to earn their living by arms. The religious members of Iberian orders should be encouraged to go out to preach the gospel instead of living on their incomes at home.

Suggestions for paying for the fortresses consist of the warning implied by the recital of the many losses and the exhortation to consider that if you do not believe in the cost of construction, the cost of losses far exceeds them. Also the taxpaying future of a thriving citizenry is anticipated. Andrada breaks a lance for the pilots and sailors. He advises that their training be improved and their status enhanced. As for pilots they should be ranked as they are in England and France. After all, their calling is ancient and honorable as proven by the fact that among pilots are counted Solomon, Ptolemy, Charles V, Don Manoel, Don Juan de Austria, Alonso de Albuquerque, Don Vasco da Gama, Marco Antonio, Andrea Doria, el Marqués de Santa Cruz, and Pedro Meléndez. He then suggests that those who profess to know navigation be knowledgeable about: "the mechanics, the building of ships and *baxeles* (small craft), that they should know how to protect themselves at sea and on land, that they should know artillery and be *polvoristas* (know how to service guns)". This is indeed quite a tall order and such skills should command greater recognition.

As for sailors, they should not only be better qualified but better paid. Andrada says that by Don Sebastian, they had been given one ducat per box they carried to be paid by the India House in Lisbon which they no longer receive. In addition they were made to pay a tax by the Jesuits, called Theotinos, for the building of the Church of San Roque. This tax was still being collected long after the church was finished. So: "there are now no men to be found who want to go to sea", and ships are getting lost. Sailors deserve to be better paid and trained.

Hard facts in the document are the descriptions of sites and the latitude observations given. Many incidental bits are of interest, part rumor and part fact. The resources of Africa include unicorns (possibly the African Onyx or Rhinos) and the news about the Mandinga tribe mentions that it was ruled by the wife of the chief. The distance from Guinea is not mentioned and the breadth of Africa does not lead to speculation. The word for pepper from Sierra Leone which I have not found in the literature is "matibilia".

To end on a note of incidental interest, and staying as close to the actual wording of the text as a sample of the flavor of the piece, I shall close with the passages concerning Drake. Andrada was well acquainted with him. "With the help of mathematics Francis Drake became such a perfect mariner and corsair, that in the year 1576–77, when I served your Majesty in the Cape Verde Islands, we drove him and his ships away from the shore, and with nine galleon the (English) went robbing and destroying Spanish shipping in the entire sea, down to the Straits of Magellan which he crossed, and then raided in the South Sea, stealing great quantities of gold and leaving the ships of the ocean sea of the south in disarray and without artillery. That was the first voyage he made after he turned himself into a pirate. In this year he took with him much artillery and many noblemen with the intention to fortify the remote provinces. This he did not do, however, having changed his mind after he saw the ships laden with gold. He returned via the same strait heading north, having dared to sail into the second hemisphere, motivated by greed, and laughing at Jean Ribaud, the famous corsair, who had fortified himself in Florida which is on the coast of Mexico, a sterile and swampy land, because he was defeated there by the good captain Pedro Meléndez, general of your Majesty's galleons of the Carrera de Indias, who destroyed him in the year 1569."

Further on in the pamphlet he writes: "Pedro Bayão went to England where the queen made him a general. He instructed Francis Drake, who is an infernal being, as has been seen. I do not know whether I have the courage to tell what I saw after Guinea was taken (where I served as provisor and vicar general for King Don Sebastian) which was the great pirate taking the sun then hidden behind clouds and overcast, when he used the astrolabe in mid-day and one of his Jacobs-staffs which I had in my study for a long time (graduada doctrina) and without any doubt he admitted frankly to not having studied Ptolemy because all the latitudes of East to South are a matter for the mariner's astrolabe which I also had, and he shot the sun according to the rule of East to West, four hours after mid-day, which is the greatest achievement of that art which nature provides in order to tell the sailor in subtle and delicate ways what is well worth knowing for entire world". It's a simple procedure, an involved text!

This goes to show that this paper is really a glimpse into the workshop. My excuse for presenting it is that I hope to get help on various aspects from the experts. I have so far been reduced to the use of my own library since Arizona's collection does not have the specialized literature on seaborn empires. I have relied heavily on Teixeira da Mota's thorough work called *Do Mar Alem Mar* (1972). This study of early cartography of Guinea has kept me from attempting to identify the site of Jalofos, the rivers of Sierra Leone etc., while helping me to get my bearings in general and not to make hasty assumptions. This also holds for Max Justo Guedes' *Historia Naval Brasileira* (1975). Both works end before the time of Andrada's pamphlet. For the La Plata I hope to use Julio Guillen's *Monumenta Chartographica Indiana* (1942) which I have not been able to check out for this study. I must therefore plead your indulgence for the unavoidable vagueness and limited interpretation I have presented. In addition, the edition of the pamphlet by P.E.H. Hair, an expert on the Cape Verde Islands and African west coast must be consulted for an asessment of the *capellán*'s information.

Endnotes

* These papers were read in 1967 and 1981 respectively at the meeting of the Society for the History of Discoveries, University of Michigan, Ann Arbor and the University of Georgia, Atlanta, Georgia. See notes: 5 and 15. They have since been published.

1. Chaunu, Pierre and Huguette, *Séville et l'Atlantique, 1504–1650*, 8 vols, 10th Librairie Armand Colin, Paris, 1955–59.

2. Andrews, Kenneth, *The Spanish Caribbean: Trade and Plunder, 1530–1630*, Yale University Press, New Haven, 1978.

3. Hoffman, Paul E., *The Spanish Crown and the Defense of the Caribbean, 1534–1585*, Louisiana State University Press, Baton Rouge and London, 1980.

4. Juan Escalante de Mendoza, *Itinerario de la Navegación de los mares y tierras occidentales*, p. 626, published under the same title, with Commentary by Roberto Barreiro Meiro, Museo Naval Madrid, 1985, copies exist in the Museo Naval and the Archivo General de Indias and possibly in private hands.

12

5. *Documentos Inéditos de Ultramar: Indice General de los Papeles del Consejo de Indias* 5, XVIII, October 5, 1593, ed. Antonia Herrera Heredia, 2 vols, Dirección General de Archivos Bibliotecas, 1972.

6. Ibid., vol. 5, XVII, p. 228.

7. Op. cit., vol. 2, V, p. 161.

8. Baltasar Vellerino de Villalobos, *Luz de Navegantes* donde se halaran las derrotas y senas de las partes maritimas de las Indias, Islas y Tierra firme del mar océano.

9. Martín Fernández de Navarrete, *Biblioteca Marítima*, 2 vols, 1851, Burt Franklin, New York, 1946, vol. 2, pp. 222–6.

10. *Catálogo de las Consultas del Consejo de Indias*, 2 vols, Dirección General de Archivos y Bibliotecas, Madrid, 1972, vol. 2, pp. 2103, 2190.

11. Archivo General de Indias, Indiferente General, Leg. 740, Ramo 85.

12. Ibid., AGI no. 3093.

13. Fernández Duro, Cesareo, *Disquisionces Náuticas*, vol. V, "a la Mar Madera".

14. Manoel de Andrada Castel Blanco, *To Defend Your Empire and The Faith*, Advice on a global strategy offered in 1590 to Philip, King of Spain and Portugal, translated from Spanish and edited by P.E.H. Hair, with an account of Spanish material in Dr William's Library, London, by A.M. García, Department of History, Liverpool University Press, 1990.

15. This story, later worked out by Paul Hair, looked very suspicious from the start.

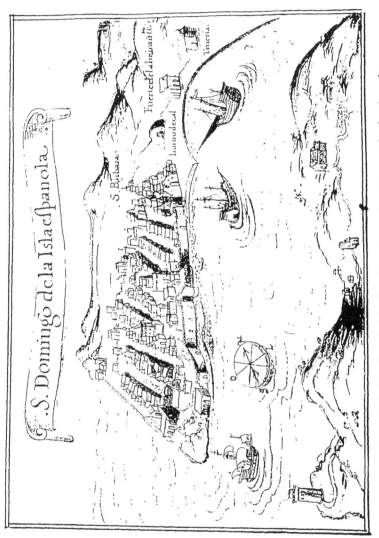

'S. Domingo de la Isla Española', the oldest Spanish settlement in the Americas from *Luz de Navegantes* by Vellerino de Villalobos

By courtesy of Museo Naval, Madrid.

XIII

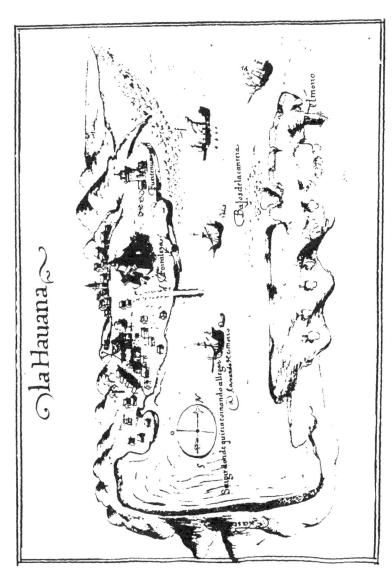

'La Havana', harbor where all Caribbean fleets gathered for home
from *Luz de Navegantes* by Vellerino de Villalobos
By courtesy of Museo Naval, Madrid.

Argos and Polyphemus: eyes on the New World five hundred years ago and now*

The purpose of this essay is to examine the impact on old notions by new experience of time and space in the age of geographic discoveries and to compare it with our galactic era. Context and circumstance have been so altered over the five hundred years since Columbus, that comparable reference from the age of discoveries to ours are to problems, not effects. Charles Lamb, the essayist wrote in a letter to Thomas Manning on January 2, 1806, that: "Nothing puzzles me more than time and space; and yet nothing troubles me less because I never think about them". Both the understanding of the period of discoveries and settlement and of our day would be ill served if no one thought about these challenges then and now.

In our day the experience of time is changing, in one direction shrinking to nano-seconds, and in the other to cosmic expansion. Measures related to human life, generations, eras, periods, give way to calendar and clock. In space, our presence in the most distant areas via television and remote sensing, and the simultanity of access to events anywhere on the globe result in our fictional ubiquity. Our notions of distance and duration are challenged now as they were 500 years ago.

For the Spaniards arriving in America, the sense of sight, "eyes on the New World", has been chosen because it is the prime receptor of information that is necessary for consciousness, that is, for knowing, and doing, directed by intelligence, instead of reacting by instinct alone, as other senses cause one to do to varying degrees.

The myths of Polyphemus and Argos of classic legend recommend themselves for use as Polyphemus was the brute giant chief of the one-eyed Cyclopes in Greek legend and Argos had a hundred eyes all over his body. They acquired an iconography which appeared on the explorer's maps of the sixteenth century: the world seen by one eye or by many.

Then

The Greek myth of Polyphemus and Argos concerns awareness, the step from seeing to knowing. It resumes to register, in a state of wakeful consciousness, all of the world round, keeping the closest watch for unpredictable circumstance. Everyone within reach of some effect of Spain's "Enterprise of the Indies" needed to adjust his sight, broaden his horizon, sharpen his vision, and stay alert. Government which never sleeps, the monoculus Polyphemus, directed the many eyes of Argos on the far frontiers to see, or rather caused them to look. The Spanish crown sent out into the New World requests for reports on what was seen by the many eyes of the explorers, conquerors, administrators, merchants, and clerics. Like a marksman, sharpening his sight by closing one eye to hit the target, so the Spanish king insisted that he be the preeminent destination of all information about everything. His vision was collective of all the visible stimuli of the New World, pulled together as in a satellite dish. Through multiple agents and agencies in the New World, the hundred eyes of Argos, the crown received the widest possible range of information from Santiago in the south to Santa Fe in the north. The king also had at his disposal a diplomatic network supplying the facts concerning his interests in the Old World. From the top of this mountain of information, the metropolis sent messages with directions to the proper agents, on how to deal with specific matters within their competence. From the earliest records speaks the king's voice, demanding again and again, in instructions to the Council of the Indies and agents that they: "inform Us of what has happened and what is happening ... so We can provide ...".

Here and there

This situation, the need for information as reflected in the above, presented the major challenge faced for the first time at such a degree of magnitude: the oceanic distance of a large new land and alien people to which Europeans had to respond. There were no known intermediaries as in former conquests. Although the desert like the ocean was a challenge to travel and transport, oceans differed in kind from any preceding experience. The deserts, geographically similar barriers, were linked to Europe in stages by caravan routes leading to markets. The early Portuguese maritime empire coasting along Africa and beyond was an extension of this. Though camels were called ships of the desert, time, duration, place, and circumstance of European links across deserts were radically different from transoceanic contacts. From the Azores west to the north and south, the hydrographic environment was unknown, and the destination was not a market, but a huge terrestrial space which, together with the life upon it, came under the purview of Europeans. This was an expansion of responsibility and opportunities without precedent.

Our documentation confirms that fact. The first reports are mainly by eyewitnesses about what happened. The discoverers and explorers recorded action. In contrast, pure description of what was what is more often than not, based on false assumptions; many of them almost ludicrously inaccurate. Leonardo Olschki's seminal essay on "What Columbus Saw on Landing in the West Indies" has been followed by extensive commentaries.[1] A case recently discussed by Richard Eaton in "The Calicut Columbus Sought"[2] bears exactly on the point is. It took nearly a century (1492–1571) before a systematic questionnaire was drawn up by the Council of the Indies, which inquired about what is rather than what was happening. This was the exhaustive questionnaire which made up the *Relaciones Geográficas*, sent out by the Council of the Indies, to be answered and forwarded from America to Spain. It examines the Indies more or less like a European country, its resources, including human labor, and how tradition might promote or hinder exploitation and conversion. Up to that time, most documentation of America, consisted of suggestions, or requests, about what was done or what to do, on the basis of the information collected and interpreted in Madrid. There is a similar time table for Brazil.

Proceeding from Polyphemus to Argos, from the vision of the one-eyed metropolis to that of the observers seeing with many eyes, one crosses the Atlantic to the Western hemisphere with the participants in the conquest and settlement. For them, this is the transition from looking, or directed sight, to seeing, or mental perceptions of the entire visible spectrum. Yet, there was a dearth of description.[3] The perception of Europeans in America did not lead to description of what was actually seen, but was conditioned primarily by expectations and intent. The papers we have serve a limited purpose.[4] Documents of record were apt to be local, such as registers of birth and death and other rites of passage. Customs and tax records, business papers and litigation were based on specific situations. The famous service records of *méritos y servicios* were curricula vitae submitted for licenses, promotions, honors and so on. They reflected only the local base at each stage.

Another factor limiting perception was the function of any document. It could be a letter, a deposition, an instruction or command, an enumeration or register, and so on.[5] The direction in which it was sent, also constituted a major distinction. It divides the bulk of our documentation into the two types of vision by Polyphemus and Argos. Lest the reference falters, one must follow through to realize that in the New World, the one eye of government was established in the commands, conferred on viceroys, governors, civic and military authorities, and the clerical hierarchy. Although they were recipients of information from many sources, they were beholden to execute the wishes reaching them from one source, the metropolis, which were built on information received there. Special enabling legislation was required to assume local initiative. This was then presented as the will of the king. How it succeeded was told to Madrid in response to the intent which had been formulated there.

Argos, the many-eyed, an entity only in imagination, is represented by all the recent arrivals in the New World. Their collective vision in histories or as presented by historians, is an artificial construct on the basis of useful categories: the judges of all the *audiencias*, the bishops, the town authorities, and then the sailors, the soldiers, the merchants, the natives, the women and children. A slight twist of the historical kaleidoscope will regroup these collectives so that each individual will be differently positioned, as a family member, plaintiff or defendant or witness in court proceedings, as a petitioner or recipient of privilege, as resident of a specific town, or as participant in an expedition, as Catholic or heretic. In any one of those capacities he was aware of his immediate surroundings, and alert some of the time to the imperial context, but mostly he was otherwise preoccupied, as some of the family correspondence has shown. In addition one must remember that the *grupos de conquistadores* came with the varied traditions of their *patria* which has been defined as the house, the street, the village or other place of origin.[6] Although their interest was in forging a company of like-minded entrepreneurs who needed to count on mutual support, they were spread over such wide areas so quickly that their loyalty in America was soon local as well.

And what was it that the one and the many eyes needed to be aware of, needed to know? In the first instance, the difference between them was the proximity in time, space, and circumstance, to the point where action or response was required. When a ship lands, the question is of course: where are we? But the immediate answer required is to the question: what do we do now? The crown needed information as to what had been done and what was being done, in order to command what should be done next. Furthermore, in the case of the Indies enterprise, and because of the remove from events, the government had to give reasons, and to state the expected consequences. The argument that: "We say to do such and such because it is in our power", was not useful to guide future action in the Indies. The one eye must be watchful for on-going events. Reports from the scene, so to say, on the other hand, must report on what was done, justify the action taken, and suggest, or request direction from the monocular Polyphemus in Spain, whose ever wakeful eye was cast over the whole of the empire. The colonists had to concentrate their waking minds on the task at hand, while implementation of the more distant vision as well as of wishes and dreams had to be suspended. They could not consider the future at the same rate, nor with the same breadth of vision, as did the sleepless crown, nor connect it over the large canvas of imperial expansion.

To know and to believe

An even greater distance separates the participants in the Enterprise of the Indies on either side of the Atlantic with respect to what was considered known, and what was believed. In Spain there was total dependence on reports, and that meant reliance on reporters. The credibility of the source of information was basic to the acceptance of it. Any report was subject to check and argument. Even so, what emerged as credible in Spain often differed substantially from reality. In the first instance, proximity to the event or issue was crucial to veracity. Then, experience counted as against a report by an amateur, as in the description of coastlines, the lay of the land, the nature of the inhabitants, the actions of individuals and the disposition of the natives. Experience was the determining factor in accepting reports as true. Next, the degree of learnedness of the observer – is he a licenciado? – was often important. And that was only a step toward the greater credibility associated with persons of higher rank, who were usually considered less biased.

Added to the distance from Spain, one must construct the path for conveying information across the Atlantic. The lines of communication were themselves subject to static, so to say. That is, information was filtered through various agencies or agents, each deciding what to put in, what to stress, and what to omit. One must consider that the distant Spanish overview was subject to considerable noise down the line, a matter of distortion on the way to Spain and of diffusion in the colonies. In sum, the colonial focus was a clear but limited view, while the distant Spanish overview was wide, but fuzzy at the edges.

This however, is not the proper vocabulary to identify the difficulties discussed here. Perception in America and conceptualization remote from the place of the experience is not a problem of "information" as used by information theorists. There was no common vocabulary to cover the news from the exotic New World. Describing only what one party could see was the difficulty. Description proceeded by assimilating phenomena to the nearest known category, animal, vegetable, etc. Perception was one thing, conceptualization was another. Early illustrations such as in Oviedo helped the texts and made description more accurate. But the behavior of men and animals depends upon perception at the point of action. Friendly or hostile behavior required a whole set of mutually agreed upon perceptions on first encounter, circumscribed by intent and context.

Not only did things happen during the travel time of information, response, and action, but development over decades in the Indies created its own self reference as it were. The discussion above reflects the possibilities of a growing sense for local priorities, rather than pulling together of images of America. This occurred because of the diversity of development and specialization in the Western hemisphere. Each of the five vice-royalties from its inception had different elements of cohesion, internally, and of connections with Spain and Portugal. Moreover one must add to these the problems of the *gobiernos*, the maritime communities, and the Carrera de Indias, the Indies trade.

A further element to be considered is the unwillingness to see what one does not wish to know. This is a psychological verity, generally granted, and experienced by most people and many governments. There is a poem from a different time and place, which has the title and refrain: "The king does not know." ... "You know and I know of the misery of the poor, the preference of status over merit, the unequal treatment by the law etc., but the king does not know." Willingness to see is essential for the conversion of information into a useful base for action.

Such were the main reasons taken in sum for the different realities as perceived in the New World and received in the Old. While the cause of government action was determined by the vision of how to direct and affect the course of events in the desired direction, the implementation of commands was two-faced. One sought to obey the order as received, and the other was to achieve the effect desired as interpreted by the agent. This problem was well understood and formulated in the phrase: "received and obeyed", which might involve a considerable adjustment, to use a mild word, in the execution of the command. The absolute necessity of trustworthy agents was obvious. Their competence, however, had to be exposed to confrontation with the realities of the local situation. Although this did not differ from European experience, where any commander in a battle would be responsible for suiting action to intent, the unprecedented expansion of dimension in space and time made this problem less tractable on the imperial canvas.

The problems of time and space are inextricably joined. There was a great difference in proximity to action, and therefore a lack of understanding of what a report had sought to imply when seen in a different context. Cause and effect differed greatly as seen from Europe and America. For instance, the cause, a pirate's threat to Santiago and the Chilean coastline, was seen as a unique and separate event by the local population, ranking first in their concerns. The view from Madrid, considering the effect, led to an immediate response which ordered the protection of the Peruvian silver fleet and dispatch of a naval force from Realejo to intercept the raider in the Pacific, to protect Panama. The protection of the Straits of Magellan (Sarmiento de Gamboa) and plans for settlement of Southern Chile were slower in coming.[8] Geographic growth was a prime reason for different perceptions of cause and effect between the metropolis and the American possessions.

A world record of the discoveries would show the impetus to the break- up of the medieval œcumene, to be sure well under way on its own account, and reinforced by the religious and dynastic wars, shifting the power balance in Europe. World wide, the redistribution of wealth which developed with the influx of American silver and Oriental trade, which fractured the Old World, also ran fissures through accustomed patterns remote from the site of the mines in America. The impact of Peruvian silver in China via the Manila galleon trade is not without a trace. Various networks of trade, or of religious communities in the Far East and South East Asia, the American empires of the Aztecs and Incas, and the Central American web of markets were all affected by incursions from outside. Like the impact of a Tsunami wave, which travels far around the earth, large phenomena of global readjustment affected the peoples all over the earth upon the discovery of America and the circumnavigation of the globe.

To sleep and to dream

While compatible vision was thus diminished by the course of history, a local reaction to new information on both sides of the ocean was a growing familiarity with the respective scenes and roles. It no longer necessitated great imagination to adjust to the narrowing perceptions in Spain. They were undifferentiated, and other than those in the Western hemisphere. Increasingly, the power struggles of the Spanish crown in Europe meant that America was to pay more and to cost less. On the other hand, The Enterprise of England, the Armada, was not a first order of public awareness in Mexico City, let alone Bogotá. Likewise the threat to Spanish power on the frontiers of New Spain and Chile was up against penury in Spain. Then there came the time when institutions of law and order were in place, with agents following a cursus honorum in a settled bureaucracy, when the machinery of *residencia* or performance review for officials was intact, that the oceanic distance was taken for granted. No longer perceived as a challenge, it became merely a matter of delay. Familiarity had stretched mañana from the borders of Spain to the Indies. Additional time and distance needed to get response to information from the Indies, and vice versa, was simply put in the local context. "If death were to come from Spain, I would be immortal," as one viceroy put it.

Thus administration became standardized and was not adjusted to changing conditions. Attempts to inculcate new information slowed in the arthritic channels of an imperial bureaucracy. Both sides were overtaken by sleep, the famous siesta colonial. And the dreams arrived soon thereafter. For the Spanish king the sweet dream was the arrival on schedule of an ever richer silver fleet, and the nightmare was fear of attack upon it. If innovation in the management of the Carrera was slow, a curiously similar approach steadied the enterprise of the pirates for some time. Not much was moving over the maritime chart of the *histoire événementielle*. But, as in sleep, an alteration of position aroused the consciousness of confinement by the blanket of indifference. A literature grew up in the late seventeenth to the mid-eighteenth centuries which concerned itself no longer with what was, but what ought to be and what could be. The awakening was to be to the dawn of the Bourbon reforms on one side of the Atlantic, and of the *independistas* on the other, both leading to death blows of empire.

The transoceanic distance, the enormous range of hemispheric space and length of time to be in touch, contributed to the discovery of local loyalties and new identities based roughly on the Spanish administrative maps of the American colonies. History went the way to separation and independence of the separate colonies. The purpose of the foregoing construction of Spanish trans-oceanic history is an attempt to point to the causes for historical divisions in contrast to the geographic achievement of the wholeness and accessibility of the terrestrial globe. In the light of the comparable galactic challenge by expanded time and distance currently explored by science, and a shrinkage of the earth resulting from technology, what comparable impacts are becoming visible? Can the continued splintering be overcome? Where is the difference of vision discernable in our time?

Then and now

To compare the sudden challenge of new facts posed by the geographical discoveries to men of the Renaissance with that of space in our time, it is helpful to realize the rarity of such episodes. Francisco López de Gómara, official chronicler of the Indies, said in his *Historia de las Indias* (1552) that not since the birth of Christ had the world seen such change. Notions of time and space were profoundly affected. Christianity was to define and populate the space of heaven after the ascent of Jesus, to construct the heavenly hierarchy, and define the space of Hell, so that Dante could report on a visit there. The notion of time joined eternity to the reckoning of earthly days beyond death counted in purgatory. Our basic challenge today is to assure alertness to the experience of the expansion of space into outer galactic regions, and of time to the expanded scale of archaeo-anthropology and geology, the big bang of physics, and the exploration of time and space of the inner realm of the mind and psyche. Today's reservoir of imaginative references – as against the classic myth of Polyphemus and Argos – might be to the fairy tale or to science fiction. The modern fairy tale was the romantic reaction to the industrial revolution, and science fiction deals with the imagined possibilities of galactic neighbors. Both include drastic manipulations of space, time, and vision.

In contrast to the global expansion of the geographic discoveries, our age, looking into and from stellar space, compresses the world into so dense a habitat that the challenge to life is faced jointly by mankind around the globe for the sake of survival. Geographic distance has changed in character as perceived by the mind. The easy and frequent displacement of many people whether voluntary or not, mostly by massive transport, changes the relation to the local scene over much of the world. But the notion of knowing, by being elsewhere, of perceiving new things, and of behaving differently in adjustment to surroundings, is remote from the challenge met by the explorers of the sixteenth century. To see is no longer a matter of how far the eye can reach, but what the mind registers. Compared with the separation over oceanic distance, the sense of being elsewhere is also made possible by means of television. Ubiquity characterizes the "news every half hour". One can see into the farthest corner of the globe and universe by remote sensing. But we are no closer to people half around the globe than to Martians, and the effect is one of alienation.

Political, economic and demographic impacts of our extended geographic space are not comparable to Renaissance conditions. Simultanity of contact wipes out the parallels to the colonial experience. Primitive and advanced cultures exist side by side, simultaneously occupying space on the globe. The forced displacement of people over distance as formerly accomplished by slavery, has given way to migrations as a means of control. Being bound to a region on the other hand is now the experience of citizens of a less developed country, or members of a big city street gang who are confined to a few blocks of "territory". The problem of our time is no longer expansion in terrestrial space, that is over distance but mobility. The relative freedom of mobility over the known geographic space is today the decisive gulf between references of vision of space and over time.

The one and the many

The necessity of dealing with alien peoples in distant regions during the sixteenth century was characterized by the concept of encounter around the globe, so envisioned by the organizers of the quincentenary of the discovery of America and ongoing studies of like time spans with reference to later developments. In fact, this challenge now, has to be strengthened by foreseeing the need to meet one another. In our time, there are two aspects of vision: first, respect for the value of the vision of one, or "as I see it", in any particular context and circumstance; and second, a weighing of the opinion of many. Simultanity in time of various frames of reference and the sharing of space in multicultural settings demand a reconciliation of these visions. The one-eyed cyclops and the multivisioned Argos are dead since the demise of transoceanic empires. Two-eyed mortals face each other across the negotiating tables around the world in search of answers. This was clearly formulated by Clémenceau: "l'affaire d'un seul est l'affair de tous".

We share one aspect of orientation with the discoverers. The diverging references, on either side of the ocean, frequently led to the selection of a course of action based on the record of the past. This meant a turn back to experience which increasingly became the blueprint for action. As it was difficult to keep alert with respect to the various projections of intention, actions turned into the grooves of the familiar. Today this phenomenon of approaching contradictory visions by turning back is observable, for instance, in politics.

About sleep and dream, one can ask the question: how much information can be absorbed by individuals or any collective over how much time and space before the restraints on understanding, the need to adjust to accustomed order, interferes with the flexibility of imagination, with an approximation to what is real and what is new. This is an acute problem in "official" science, and in the fine arts. The requirement to translate into lay terms – by definition unfitting – a radically new phenomenon, in order to obtain public support, abridges progress.

Proof and trust

In the age of Reconnaissance, there was an important shift from belief as knowledge, to proof and trust in ours. Religious belief, i.e. faith, depended on baptism or conversion to the knowledge within, expression of which is worship. This religious knowledge, anchored in the Bible – for Christians – did not easily accommodate the flood of new data from without, and resulted in the attempt to establish knowledge of the global world by proof. As tested by the Renaissance art of the sixteenth century, the senses were not entirely reliable. The art of the Renaissance pioneered *trompe l'oeil* effects with great subtlety. Statues on a flat surface to resemble free standing sculpture, deception of the eye by perspectives, etc. were used to good effect. As against that, the new breed of experts attempted to establish knowledge by proof in experiment.

Leonardo da Vinci formulated this fact in a paragraph on "mechanical and non-mechanical science". Elaborating on the confusion of the meaning of knowledge, *szienze*, he states: "that real kinds of knowledge (*szienze*) are those perceived by experience through the senses, where silence is imposed on the tongues of would-be disputants, which does not nourish its investigators on dreams, but rather proceeds from first truths and known principles successively, and by continuous steps which really follow right to the end, as in fundamental mathematics ...".[9] An example, not too frequently quoted, shows Galileo's attempt to convince doubters of "The Natation of bodies upon, and submersion in, the Water". He tried to convince people who looked without bias at pieces of paper floating in a basin of water, and of a stone falling in. At a time of heavy ships losses this kind of argument was of great interest.[10]

The great difference therefore, between the Renaissance and our time, is the rise of science since the Renaissance, and the development of its methods and concepts. The role of pilots, our guides across the oceans are now taken over by scientists, our guides with respect to our globe and cosmos. This casts the whole of our world and universe for two-eyed mortals in different terms from those of a pre-scientific age. Today visual perception, as well as that by other senses, prefers two approaches to knowledge. One is to arrive at an uncontested proof by demonstration, as pioneered in Renaissance science. In matters that cannot be proven – leaving aside the Popperian discussion – a shift can be observed, from metaphysical knowledge reserved for belief, to trust. This is specifically focused on phenomena and not on principle, and it is not based on conversion. The basis of trust lies in the honesty of experiment, the veracity regarding procedure and statement, the backing of experience, and an openness to new occurrences. Trust is the very backbone of the "peer review" system in science and the humanities; indispensable in human transactions. The prime requirement is common procedure and shared reference. The submission of sense experience to reason leads to cognition by the whole mind when it is engaged in finding expression for newly perceived knowledge.

People have become accustomed to unambiguous statements of new knowledge from the scientists while the social scientists are relied upon to identify and define problems and ways to deal with them. But reality increasingly lies somewhere in between, with hard science having to consider uncertain or incomplete information and varied projections, suggesting "if then" choices, as in most cases concerning the environment. Meantime, social science has evolved precise figures for the outcome of various scenarios by predictive modeling or sample surveys.

Configuration and cooperation

It is easy to see that the two claims to knowledge by religion and science will not leave everyone satisfied. For many people too much experience is left without explanation, open to use or abuse, as the ways of God are inscrutable, and progress of science is characterized by the increasing awareness of ignorance. A recent book entitled *The Encyclopedia of Ignorance* opens its editorial preface thus: "Compared to the pond of knowledge, our ignorance remains atlantic".[11] Still, we are left with a large reservoir of experience of "knowing" in our lives beyond religion and science. It exists undeniably, and it antedates the historic record, blending into the evolution of all life and survival of species on the globe. It is built upon a glut of unprocessed information, diffused by uncontrolled media. Only an examination of experience over long stretches of time, and around the globe, which is shared with other lives in nature can make such knowledge useful. It was characterized in a speech by Jacob Bronowski when he said: "we know more than we can tell". Such knowledge is future orientated toward a common goal.[12] Men, joined in the enterprise for survival, may operate, as computer idiom has it, in configuration on separate tracks, but in parallel process.

Lest this reference sounds spurious, the relevance and usefulness of concepts developed in one context to another to which they have never been applied before is successfully demonstrated by Albert O. Hirschman, an economist with a Latin American orientation. His very titles suggest the juncture of hitherto totally separate concepts, for example *Exit, Voice and Loyalty*.[13]

The experiences to be considered here, in view of the common need for survival are those of cooperation and conservation. There exists an unexplored historic reservoir for increasing knowledge in such a direction as is known to be needed to promote survival. The point would be to explore cooperation for what, not against whom. In this context it is interesting to note the creation of a new chair, the Arnholt Professorship in International Cooperation and Development, at the New School for Social Research, New York.

A now accepted method of how to approximate reality in history, was introduced by the school of the *Annales* in Paris. If one were to look from a distance, as Bloch and Braudel taught historians to do, hitherto separate phenomena become visible and comparable. But the *longue durée* over which to search for new identities on a larger scale, was still a Eurocentric test tube approach. William H. McNeill in "Mythhistory" took the profession to farther global and chronological extensions, as did Bernard Bailyn in a recent assessment of the Turner thesis.[14] Looking at the state of history now, the proliferation of styles of approach to the past leads to an impression of chaos. As for subjects treated, the "General" heading in the American Historical Review lumps together an extraordinary variety of subjects. This hardly conceals the fragmentation of the discipline. A myriad of specialist journals are supported by a proliferation of groups, who are often unaware of each other. Though the computer is changing that scenario fast, reference being ever quicker and easier, the machine is blind. The clutter must as yet be sorted but by minds. But the promise is there for a safety net of certified data, available to inquiry from anywhere, leaving the mind more freedom to range across human concerns.

Over the centuries after the age of Reconnaissance, knowledge of the terraqueous globe expanded, and people increasingly relied, for practical use, on regularities in nature – for example in navigation they employed the order of the stellar universe. In history, and then the social sciences, reasonable prediction was expected to improve when built upon an ever more comprehensive and exact data base. No longer confined to power and politics, they became the *sciences de l'homme*. These must now be correlated with the history of man's relation to nature in order to arrive at an understanding of demands by all life and life giving elements upon of the global environment. There is a residue of experience of living in harmony with nature which is accessible to examination of the past, and in some remote areas of aborigines in some parts of the world. One must presume a larger identity of life beyond the individual, which leads to the noticeable awakening of assessment of benefit to harm across the whole spectrum of environmental concerns.

Writers on social science have stressed measurement, have been alert to succession as well as simultanity or discontinuity of developments, and have certainly designed methods of approach to what they investigated. Results have been classified, and predictions of what came to pass have been derived from new evidence, or evidence differently employed. And so, historians are closer

13

to the mind set of science than used to be acknowledged. The arrival of the interdisciplinary approach of the cognitive sciences, based on the unity of mind, is an indicator of new directions. However, multiplicity of themes or methods in historical work should not be a cause for concern, but a proof of alertness, and a stimulant to seek company in the common enterprise of building a comprehensible past. It is inviting to speculate that many ingredients, at least of the earlier changes, were not "new" but only more massive than experienced before. They fit into a "conjuncture" of circumstance which led to a change of course in human history. The discovery of America, in this sequence, is not as significant as the voyage of Magellan/ElCano, which confirmed the hypotheses of the terraqueous globe, and the presence of man in habitable space.

It must be remembered that the Greeks had designed a giant globe, and that the idea of the globular shape of the earth was not new. The finding of America and its inhabitants were the unexpected by-product of a straight line of thought and speculation from Classic times.[15]

From Spain we inherited the terraqueous globe. From the moon we must assure the survival of life upon it. Abstaining from prophesies, historians, as custodians of the past, should direct their vision in the probing spirit of finding out, to ascertain what becomes visible in the dawn of cognition. Otherwise the fate of Argos and Polyphemus might await us.

Endnotes

*This lecture was one of a series to celebrate the Qunicentennial of the first Columbian voyage, arranged by Professor Norman Thrower at the University of California at Los Angeles, Aug 8, 1991.

1. Olschki, Leonardo, "What Columbus saw on landing in the West Indies", Proceedings of the American Philosophical Society 84, Philadelphia, 1941, pp. 633–59; Bernard Cohen, "What Columbus 'saw' in 1492", *Mundalización de la ciencia y cultura nacional*, Actas del Congreso Internacional Ciencia, descubrimiento y mundo colonial, eds A. Lafuente, A. Elena and M.L. Ortega, Universidad Autónoma de Madrid, Madrid, 1993, pp. 53–66.

2. Eaton, Richard, "The Calicut Columbus sought", *Primary Sources and Original Works*, Haworth Press, New York, 1995.

3. Chroniclers like Enciso, Vespucci, and Oviedo, for instance, represent a phase of transition from reports which exlusively dictated by intention (Columbus, Cortés) to description and representations.

4. Díaz, José Joaquín Real, *Estudio Diplomático del Documento Indiano*, Sevilla, 1970.

5. Lockhart, James and Otte Enrique, *Letters and People of the Spanish Indies in the Sixteenth Century*, Cambridge Latin American Studies 22, Cambridge University Press, 1976.

6. Góngora, Mario, *Los Grupos de Conquistadores en Tierra Firme.*

14

Fisionomía Histórica Social de un Tipo de Conquista, Centro de Historia Social, Universidad de Chile, Santiago de Chile, 1962.

7. Hoffman von Fallersleben, August Heinrich, "Der König weiss es nicht", *Unpolitische Lieder (1839)*, Georg Olms Verlag, Hildersheim–New York, 1976, p. 22.

8. Herrera, Antonia Heredia, *Catálogo de Consultas del Consejo de Indias*, 2 vols, Dirección General de Archivos y Bibliotecas, Madrid, 1972, vol. 1, p. 298 n. 818 (1580).

9. Leonardo da Vinci, *Trattato della Pittura*, ed. Angelo Borselli, 1914, codex vaticano Urbinate, 1270, cap. 29. I am obliged to Gordon Griffith for this reference.

10. Galileus Galilei, *A discourse presented to the most serene Don Cosimo II, Great Duke of Tuscany, concerning the natation of bodies and submersion in the water*, translated into English from the second Italian edition by Thomas Salisbury, London, 1663, Stillman Drake, University of Illinois Press, Urbana, 1960. Acurrent discussion about the meaning of experiment in the sixteenth and seventeenth centuries is of great interest, but peripheral to this paper.

11. Ronald Duncan and Miranda Weston Smith, eds, *The Encyclopedia of Ignorance: Everything you always wanted to know about the Unknown*, Pergamon Press, 1977. The book ranges from biology to physics and the authors are authorities in their fields.

12. Gosden, Christopher, *Social Being and Time*, Blackwell, Oxford, 1994, p. 188.

13. Hirschman, Albert O., *Exit, Voice, and Loyalty*, Harvard University Press, Cambridge, MA, 1970.

14. McNeill, William H., "Mythistory: or Truth, Myth, History and Historians", Presidential address to the American Historical Association, *American Historical Review*, Philadelphia, 1986, pp. 1–11; Bernard Bailyn, "The Old World and the New", The John Carter Brown Library, Providence, RI, 1992.

15. Gandía, Enrique de, *Nueva Historia del Descubrimiento de América*, Serie V Centenario del Descubrimiento de América, Universidad del Museo Social Argentino, Buenos Aires, 1989. This book ranges from discussion of the classics today's scholarship.

XV

MARTIN FERNANDEZ DE NAVARRETE CLEARS THE DECK: THE SPANISH HYDROGRAPHIC OFFICE, (1809-24)

I

The Navarrete manuscript called «Apuntes para continuar la notícia histórica de la Dirección Hidrografica de Madrid desde el ano 1809, en que se publicarán sus dos tomos de *Memorias, hasta 1824»* (1), is a valuable addition to published information about the history of the Spanish hydrographic service. Apart from occasional mention there is no history of the Spanish *Dirección Hidrográfica* or *Depósito,* as it was also called, or for that matter of the Portuguese institution, comparable to Vice Admiral Sir Archibald Day's comprehensive account of the British Admiralty Hydrographic Service, 1795-1919 (2).

With the foundation of the *Dirección Hidrográfica* (1797) in Madrid, Spain joined the great maritime powers in their transit from the enlightenment to the age of institutionalized science. Informal and dispersed initiatives

---

(1) Colección Navarrete at Ábalos. This is the archive of Martín Fernandez de Navarrete, kept in the house in which he lived for many years before his death. It is currently in custody of D. Francisco Fernandez de Navarrete, Marqués de Legarda.

The «Apuntes» give a title to a folder of the archive section 56 as recorded in an *Inventario* which was published by Admiral Julio Guillén (late director of the Museo Naval in Madrid) in 1944. I would like to express my thanks to the Marqués de Legarda for his gracious permission to use the material. There is also a scrap of paper in the hand of Navarrete dated March 21st, 1824, containing a title which reads in translation: «Works published by the Dirección Hidrográfica and constructed in London, Madrid and Cadiz, from 1809-to date, as at that time the establishment was divided between the two latter cities due to political circumstances.» There is no further text. The title may have been an alternative to the eventual «Apuntes».

(2) Vice Admiral Sir Archibald Day, *The Admiralty Hydrographic Service, 1795-1919.* London, H.M.S.O. 1967: For Spain see Cesareo Fernandez Duro, *Disquisiciones Náuticas,* IV, «Los ojos en el cielo», 332-343; and his *Armada Española desde la unión de los Reinos de Castilla y de León.* 9 vols. Madrid, 1895-1903, vol. VIII, 431-432, «Ciencia y Literatura» 1788-1808, and vol. IX, 385-387; José María Martinez Hidalgo, «El grabado cartográfico en España», *Revista General de la Marina,* vol. 130, April 1946. For Portugal see A. Teixeira da Mota, «Some notes on the organization of the hydrographical services in Portugal, until the beginning of the nineteenth century», *Sixth International Conference of Historical Cartography,* Greenwich, Sept. 1975, 11 pp. multigraph.

Research supported by the National Science Foundation.

in the nautical Sciences were to be henceforth coordinated and directed from a center. As Spain also found herself in possession of documents which covered a long tradition of maritime exploration a *Depósito de Hidrográfia* became part of an institution soon standing at the forefront of the international enterprise in that field (3).

The *Apuntes* of Navarrete, as their full title above implies, were meant to continue the historical record of that *Direccion Hidrográfica* from 1809-1824. A first essay, called *Idea General del discurso y de las memorias publicadas por la dirección hidrográfica sobre los fundamentos que ha tenido la construcción de las cartas de marear que ha dado a luz desde 1797*, describing the years from its founding to 1809, also written by Navarrete, had been published in Madrid in 1810. The occasion for the *Apuntes* was the need to clear the deck for Navarrete's directorship of the institution to which he was appointed in 1823. The *Apuntes* therefore continue the record from the founding of the Spanish office. There is no sequel in a similar format which covers those years of Navarrete's directorship to 1844. To continue the convenient summary of the *Idea General* and the *Apuntes* one would have to consult the annual reports to the secretary of the admiralty and the many draughts of requests and other official correspondence preserved in the Museo Naval in Madrid.

Spain's tradition of support for nautical science was next to Portugal's the oldest institutionalized effort under royal protection in the West. While the training of pilots and the making of charts and instruments took place in several port cities, the discovery of America had resulted in the concentration of oceanic exploration and the organization of supporting nautical sciences in Sevilla (4). The progress of various disciplines during the age of exploration had reached a peak slightly past the middle of the 1550's and declined in visibility after that, to reach a near vanishing point in the literature after 1624. Current efforts to redress this total absence of nautical science and other sciences in seventeenth-century and early eighteenth-century Spanish literature are now under way. But the fact remains, that public and official concern experienced a dramatic revival in the late eighteenth century. Martín Fernandez de Navarrete played a major role in support of a Hydrographic Office which was founded as *Depósito*, and established in 1797 as *Dirección Hidrográfica*. Both nomenclatures characterize the enterprise which was

---

(3) The French hydrographic office operated since 1720, the British office opened in 1795 as successor to the activities of the East India company and the Danes established an office in 1784. Newton's prediction that «The land would send mathematicians to sea» on a regular basis, as quoted in A. Day, *Op. cit.*, p. 19, note 1, had arrived, and the British «Put their hand to the continued charting of the seas» under the first director. Ibid.

(4) Ursula Lamb, «Cosmographers of Seville: Nautical Science and Social Experiences» in *First Images of America*, ed. Fredi Chiappelli, University of California Press, 1976, pp. 675-686; José Pulido Rubio, *El Piloto Mayor de la Casa de la Contratación en Sevilla*, 2nd. augmented ed. 1950.

to give direction to the nautical sciences and to develop a deposit and curatorship for all works on nautical science from the past and present. It also was to support new research and to supervise the production and sale of charts, sailing directions, almanacs, and other relevant information. In contrast to the sixteenth century Pilot Major, the director of the new center was not in charge of the making of instruments nor directly involved in the teaching of pilots.

The record of the *Idea General* and *Apuntes* goes to show that from the time of its inception, the activities of the *Dirección Hidrográfica* were on a par with those of France and Britain both as regards the diversity of enterprise in nautical science and the quality of results (5).

There existed an impressive variety of documents of the age of discovery, which could be consulted with profit. Moreover, the geographical extent of Spain's empire had left an unsurpassed wealth of information, although of very inconsistent density and quality, reflecting the history of widespread geographic reconnaissance.

The first three directors of the *Dirección Hidrográfica,* José de Espinoza Tello, Felipe Bauzá and Martín Fernández de Navarrete were all trained in the Spanish navy and rose through its ranks. Navarrete was commissioned to assemble the records of Spanish naval history and sciences in 1789 as a young man of 24, for his splendid academic record and because he had practical experience at sea, both in war and peace (6). His published accounts of the work of the hydrographic establishment are therefore technically reliable ant yet lend an historical dimension to what would otherwise be a mere catalogue of publications.

Such circumstances of immediate bearing upon the work of the Hydrographic Office must be set against the history of the years 1797-1824. While the text of Navarrete's two discourses do justice to the former, they relate rather sparingly to the latter. These were indeed turbulous years. While Spain was under successive regimes, including French occupation, 1808-14,

---

(5) Luís María de Salazar, «Discurso sobre los progresos y estado actual de la hidrografía en Espana», in *Memorias,* 2 vols.. Dirección Hidrográfica, Madrid, 1809. There is a final section of charts, maps and views published by that date.

In 1808 there were 80.000 charts, plans and views, and other publications by the hydrographic service in stock, among them 300 plates, estimated at 300.000 reales. The Library contained 6-70000 volumes. A vast copying program, which covered all provincial archives and the major private collections, to serve as basis for a Spanish maritime history was under way since 1789 under the auspices of Vargas Ponce. In that program Navarrete played a major role. C. Fernandes Duro, *Disquisiciones,* IV, p. 334-335. The British Hydrographic Office registered in 1850 — the first recorded year — 32.000 chart-printings (all purposes). Day, *Op. cit.,* tabulated statistics. 1795-1920, p. 348.

(6) Carlos Seco Serrano, ed. *Obras de D. Martin Fernandez de Navarrete,* Biblioteca de Autores Espanoles, vols. LXXV-LXXVII, Madrid, 1954, see pp. XVII «El Merlin de los Papeles» and pp. xxxiv-xxxv; Also Dalmiro de la Válgoma, *El Marino D. Martin Fernandez de Navarrete, su linaje e blasón,* Burgos, 1944.

Europe was living through the Napoleonic upheaval, and it is astounding that so much scientific work was carried on (7). A tribute is due to the hydrographers for the tremendous stamina and devotion to their calling during those heroic years of a new scientific age.

Partly because of this devotion and the individual achievements in adversity of the first three directors of the *Dirección*, the office which they served has been neglected by historians in preference to attention focussed on their particular work and fate. The short discourses by Navarrete can serve as an assessment of the impressive achievement by a scientific institution whose existence furnished the scientists with reference beyond their politically bankrupt homeland, their individually broken careers, their exile, cheerless lives, and their lonely work.

The Spanish *Dirección Hidrográfica* had been in the planning stage half a century before it came into being. Beginning with the instructions to D. Jorge Juan y Santacilia by the Marqués de Ensenada in October 1748 (which resulted in the famous «noticias secretas») the systematic collection and recording of logs, coastal surveys, and other scientific information, and the correction of charts was once more required as under the orders of the old Pilot Major's Office (8). The code written for the Armada in 1748 contains the rudiments of provisions for a hydrografic office which by 1792 grew into a major plan spelling out its functions and requirements. As presented to the ministry it contained the following suggestions:

1. A library of printed books and manuscripts
2. A hydrographic collection (charts)
3. A section of experimental physics
4. A cabinet of chemistry and laboratory
5. A workshop in mechanics
6. A collection of ship models and machines used at sea
7. A natural history collection including of woods
8. A workshop for nautical instruments (9).

The building to house all this was estimated at a very high sum and was delayed, but the collection of books and manuscripts got under way. In 1788 surveys had been ordered of Cuba and of the straits of Magellan with many scientific experiments which were required of the captains, and response to the above suggestions for a hydrographic office were not lacking support

---

(7) For the background of nautical history the best reference is still C. Fernandez Duro, *La Armada Española*, vols. VIII and IX used in reprint by the Museo Naval, Madrid 1973; and for political history Raymond Carr, *Spain, 1808-1939*, Oxford, 1966, chapter II, 3; chapter IV incl.

(8) Luís María de Salazar, «Discurso» p. 39. From 1837-48 a «tribunal» or «consejo» del Almirantazgo existed which was abolished in the reorganization of ministerial government in 1748 and the Spanish navy received a new code. Salazar, *Op. cit.*, p. 37, note 1.

(9) C. Fernandez Duro, *Disquisiciones*, IV, pp. 318-319.

by successive chiefs of the Spanish navy, but the time was not yet as far as financial support from the government was concerned (10).

The *Depósito* and eventual Hydrographic Office had its beginning when the problem was not only how to fund it, but how not to lose a considerable investment. This was the collection of drawings for the Atlas of Spain's coastlines and adjacent islands which had been very badly engraved so that the charts for sale negated the entire opus of Tofino's famous survey of 1783-87. Thus the custodial function of a *Depósito* (1787) preceeded the addition of a *Dirección Hidrográfica* established in 1797 (11). (The Tofino charts, newly engraved, were to be in use by the British navy as late as 1823).

In 1809 the *Dirección* published an account (Memorias) of its work over the first dozen years of its existence which opened with an essay by Luís María de Salazar, Intendant General of the Armada at that time. He wrote about the progress and the actual state of hydrography in Spain, including a survey of the cartographic work (12).

Navarrete included long passages from that article in his summary account already mentioned, the *IDEA GENERAL DEL DISCURSO Y DE LAS MEMORIAS...* The full title of this essay of 37 printed pages describes what the *Memorias* contained namely the circumstantial accounts for the gathering of cartographic data upon which the Spanish charts were based. There are three large essays in addition to the piece by Salazar (13). They contain many tables of latitude — and longitude — calculation, based on astronomical observations made aboard survey ships. There are logs, (derrotas), and land based observations. All the data are identified as to source, that is as to who gathered them, where, when, and under what circumstances. Miscellaneous information includes ethnographic data, much description of natural phenomena, measures of the speed with which sound travels over land, and barometric records gathered during the track across the Andes between Valparaiso and Buenos Aires by Espinoza and Bauzá of the Malaspina expedition.

Navarrete's *Idea General* is a résumé of these essays, stressing the year by year production of charts by the Hydrographic Office (14). The *Apuntes,* which remain in manuscript, were intended to serve a different purpose. They were meant to outline a future set of memorias, thus preceding the detailed accounting. Yet the format is similar to the *Idea General,* so that we have in fact a chronology of the maps and a record of work published by the Spanish *Dirección Hidrográfica* from 1797-1824 by the same hand.

---

(10) Salazar, *Op. cit.,* pp. 52-53.

(11) Salazar, *Op. cit.,* pp. 49-50; C. Fernandez Duro, *Disquisiciones,* IV, p. 333.

(12) See note 5.

(13) See Appendix. The first essay is Navarrete's «Idea General» which also appears to have circulated as a separate publication.

(14) A summary list without indication of the year the work was done or published appears in Salazar. Note 5, Appendix II.

34

This list, in contrast to the volumes of *Memorias,* gives only a very occasional clue to the circumstances under which the work was carried on. In 1809 Felipe Bauzá, veteran cartographer of the Malaspina expedition, and employed in the Hydrographic Office, was commissioned to set up the *Dirección* in Cadiz (15). Fleeing via Sevilla to Cadiz, ahead of the French invasion, with all he could manage to move of the holdings and assets of the *Dirección Hidrográfica,* he risked his own life. This institutional move was made at the cost of much loss by fraud and robbery along the way. Meantime, José Espinoza Tello, the director, had been relieved of his post in Madrid, but was reinstated by the Junta in Sevilla which functioned as an interim government. On November 6th, 1809 he was commissioned to proceed to England, where he was to work as hydrographer for the office in London. He was to undertake specifically the construction of a map of the Viceroyalty of New Spain. For this enterprise he had been promised the use of Alexander von Humboldt's map of the province of Guadalajara through the good offices of the viceroy Francisco Javier Venegas. Whether the map was ever made was not known to Navarrete, who proceeded to list the maps printed in 1810, 11, and 12. These included some historical routes of Spanish discoveries which interested him for his work on Spanish voyages of exploration. Espinoza befriended his British colleagues in London who in turn invited him into their workrooms, and let him examine their almanacs, instruments, and maps. Early in the year 1815 he was called by the Spanish Secretary of the Admiralty to resume his former posts, among them the directorship of the Hydrographic Office now moved into splendid quarters in the calle Alcalá. Espinoza resigned all but the directorship. He did not serve long, however, since he died suddenly on September 6, 1815.

His successor as second director, was Felipe Bauzá who supervised the preparation and engraving of many charts, views, and plans. Bauzá himself was especially interested in the American coastlines, and was planning an atlas of the gulf of Mexico and the Caribbean. In that endeavour he had the cooperation of Cosmé Churrura for the Antilles, of Joaquín Francisco Fidalgo for the Spanish Main, and of Bernardo de Osta for Vera Cruz (16). He also saw to the touching up and correction of plates which the *Dirección* had in stock. His aim for this work was foreshadowed in a speech of 1807 published by the Bavarian Academy of Sciences in 1814 which pointed out the lacunae in American cartography (17).

---

(15) I spell Espinoza and Bauzá with z as they signed themselves in their letters to Navarrete.

(16) For all the foregoing see the Apuntes appended.

(17) D. Philipp Bauzá, «Ueber den gegenwaertigen Zustand der Geographie von Sued-Amerika» uebersetzt durch Wilhelm Friedrich Freiherr von Karvinsky, *Koeniglich Bayerische Akademie der Wissenschaften Mathematische Klasse,* Muenchen, July 20, 1814, pp. 89-124; C. Fernandez Duro, *Armada Española,* vol. VIII, p. 442, lists a Spanish version read before the Spanish Academy of History in 1807.

One activity of these years not mentioned by Navarrete in the *Apuntes* was the experiment with lithographic reproduction of maps and charts. Spanish experts were sent to Paris and to Munich to study the process at the source. An atelier was set up, fully equipped with presses and other necessary equipment, but nothing came of the venture for the *Dirección Hidrográfica*. Politics once more intervened (18).

Bauzá was a Mallorcan, and his fellow citizens elected him as a most distinguished scientist, career naval person and popular figure, to the Cortes of Cadiz. With the collapse of that body and the restoration, a sentence of death was passed on Bauzá for having cast an anti-royal vote. He had to escape via Gibraltar to London where he took up residence in 1823 (19).

The vacant headship of the *Dirección Hidrográfica* went to Martín Fernandez de Navarrete on Oct. 13, 1823. He was by then a very prominent man of letters, a career naval officer, member of three Spanish academies, several foreign scientific societies, and a non-political person. The story is told that when his name was suggested to the monarch, he said brusquely: «Navarrete, but he is liberal», but on second thought he added: «but he is liberal as we all should be...» (20). Navarrete having stayed out of politics in the name of service to the nation, and not without cost to his health and spirits, showed what the king implied when he accepted the post only as «interino» i.e. *locum tenens* for the absent Bauzá (21). The *Apuntes* summarize the work of the Hydrographic Office to Navarrete's assumption of the interim directorship in 1823.

The lists of charts in the *Idea General* and *Apuntes,* and that of plans and profiles from the *Memoriales* show the rise of output by the office in the earliest time and the slow down due to politics and the French occupation later. The definitive listing of charts must await a check-out of surviving items, especially those made abroad for the Spanish office. A comparison of the routes of survey ships, now available for Britain in Admiral Day's book and for Spain in C. Fernandez Duro's *Armada Española* (which lacks, however, precise information concerning the exact derrotas as well as of scientific personnel), would certainly substantiate the international cooperation in the field of marine surveys despite the state of war (22). This is not a new fact but

---

(18)   Ursula Lamb, «Early Spanish plans for lithographic reproduction of maps: a fruitful failure», paper read before the *Society for the History of Discoveries,* Charleston, 1976.

(19)   Juan Llabrés Bernal, *Breve noticia de la labor científica del capitán de navío D. Felipe Bauzá,* Ed. Gualp, Palma de Mallorca, 1934. This booklet gives a complete biography of Bauzá.

(20)   Serrano y Sanz, *Op. Cit.,* Introducción, p. XXXIII.

(21)   In 1827 the chances for an amnesty for Bauzá vanished and Navarrete accepted the permanent directorship (proprietario) in view of the imminent raids upon the institution's assets and functions by other branches of the admiralty. Museo Naval, MS 2404, also MS. 1768 gives proprietory office dates 2 August 1828 — 8 October 1844.

(22)   Colección Navarrete, Ábalos, correspondence of Bauzá. He mentions being informed especially by Parry of new survey data; also the cooperation of Baron v. Humboldt, Mr. Oltmann and Baron v. Zach in astronomical questions is repeatedly indicated.

XV

one which is worth special stress in our time, and which should be followed up as the history of nautical science emancipates itself from reference to the national origins of scientists as a selective principle. English contributions to the charting of American coastlines, especially along the Pacific, and Spanish activities in the Mediterranean may not be suspected by nonspecialists. As the motives of the respective powers were political, these surveys are not generally referred to because the expected political moves were not made (23).

The liberality in sharing information is mentioned in the *Apuntes* and discretion in the use of captured documents from the survey ship of the Frenchman D'Entrecasteaux. Dalrymple, head of the British Hydrographic service at the time, is quoted holding those charts «as a secret and sacred deposit». He said that the originals were sent back to France and copies kept in Britain to prevent accident on the passage to France but had never been communicated. He added that «... in such voyages of discovery the public faith has been mutual and even Bonaparte has given orders in triplicate for captain Flinders' release» (24). Domestic politics, on the other hand, brought the Spanish navy into dire straits, forcing the abandonment not only of plans, but increasingly of extent enterprises as one reads in C. Fernandez Duro's last two volumes on the Armada.

Not all international progress in science was peacefully achieved. The tale of French attempts to get hold of the Spanish maps of the *Depósito*, and the suspicion voiced by Bauzá in his correspondence about Russian pilfering of the Malaspina papers remain to be cheched out. There is no apparent reason to assume that «Kreuzenstern», the explorer of the Pacific in 1803-6, was a beneficiary of Spanish information. But Bauzá's speculations on the subject, their tone of mistrust and assumption of conspiracy, are interesting in the context (25).

Our information suffices to say that the contrast between the cartographic enterprise in marine charts in England and Spain was very sharply drawn. In Spain the initiative came from professional navy men who needed royal support, or government support for their every enterprise. Once this was forthcoming, the centralized operation made possible rapid and coordinated progress. In England private enterprise in both surveying and map printing made for lively competition and stimulated innovation. England had a flourishing chart market and many skilled engravers and printers, as well as a wide clientele, since maps and charts were popular items. There is a list of the

---

(23) C. Fernandez Duro, *Armada Española,* vol. VIII, pp. 438-439, mentions the designs of Godoy for the annexation of Morocco and the mission of D. Domingo Badia y Leblich, a versatile scientist, envoy to the emperor Muley Soliman, with instructions for costal surveys to be made.

(24) A. Day, *Op. Cit.,* p. 19.

(25) Colección Navarrete, letter by Bauzá, Gibraltar, 1813. Reference to the news of the publication of Adam J. von Krusenstern's *Voyage around the World in the years, 1803, 1804, 1805 and 1806.* London, 1813. The Russian ambassador was Taticheff, called «persona sagaz» by C. Fernandez Duro, *Armada Española,* IX, p. 135.

works by José Cardano, exiled cartographer from the Spanish *Depósito*, who made his living in England. He enumerates many maps of battle positions during the Napoleonic wars, and of European political and regional maps which he put up for sale to the general public (26).

Apart from the maps and other published works listed, the *Apuntes* contain reference to the office order approved in 1817. There is a separate manuscript in the hand of Navarrete which summarizes those regulations as based upon conditions then prevailing (27). They probably reflect an earlier state of affairs as it had evolved from the beginning, with some minor modifications. On January 10, 1817, Navarrete says, the *Dirección* employed a director and an executive officer (Oficial de Detall) or chief clerk, which is the title of his counterpart in the British Office. He had to have the rank of captain in the navy. All four cartographers employed by the office had to be career pilots, and had to have experience at sea. There was a librarian--editor, a custodian of properties, mainly of scientific instruments, and a guardian of stores who doubled as assistant to the executive officer. There were three secretaries whose duty it was to copy under the supervision of the chief clark, including historical documents which Navarrete himself kept collecting for the *Depósito*. There were furthermore a doorman, and a printer and his helpers.

The rules for work in the office were minutely described. Silence was to be kept in the work-room, talk was to be restricted to the work in hand, which was to go from eight o'clock on summer mornings and nine in the winter, to two in the afternoon. Permission to leave the room had to be requested from the executive officer. Salaries for the personnel were «somewhat higher than to scale», probably with reference to naval ratings, so that extra qualifications and demands could be made on them.

This office order seems to have been in advance of the organization in other countries since inquiries regarding it came from St. Petersburgh and London (28). The Russian inquiry about the personnel and rules of the office also requested information concerning the state of the Spanish navy (number and types of ships) and the nature (scientific design) and location of navigation lights. The English inquiry was reported to Navarrete by Bauzá upon his arrival in London in 1824 (29). The English Office, he wrote, employed ten persons. It had been set up in 1795 but was not exclusively staffed by naval personnel. Only recently were charts published at government expense and freely sold to the public. English regulations of the Hydrographic Office are dated November 18th, 1825 (30).

---

(26) Museo Naval, MS 1433.

(27) Colección Navarrete, *Ábalos* sección 56.

(28) *Ibid.*

(29) Colección Navarrete, *Ábalos,* letters of Bauzá.

(30) A. Day, *Op. cit.,* p. 35.

The required training for the cartographers calls for special mention. Firstly, the aspirants had to be Spanish citizens, of sufficiently good health and character and under thirty years of age on the day of their employment. A Candidate had to satisfy requirements in seven different fields:

1. He had to be capable in linear drawing and lettering, to be able to draw a coastline by eye or from surveys, and to project a profile a given point.

2. In arithmetic he was to be familiar with the decimal system, and with marine measurements used in Old Castile and in England. He was to be able to convert one kind into the other, and he was required to know the «rule of three» (31). Other requirements covered 3. Algebra, 4. Geometry, 5. Topography, 6. Cosmography and 7. Navigation.

Conspicuously missing from the account by Navarrete are engravers. The reason for this is that there were none but supernumerary craftsmen in Navarrete's time. He repeatedly begged Bauzá in London to find a good engraver to come to Spain for at least a long enough period to train two young Spaniards. The shortage of skilled men in that line of work who would want to join a naval office rather than to work for private printers was very great. Even in England the Hydrographic Office employed two French engravers (32).

The *Apuntes* also refer to the work done by the astronomical observatory of San Fernando on the isles of León in Cadiz. The almanacs and the solar and lunar tables published by that institution were issued under the authority of the Hydrographic Office in Madrid. By 1830, Navarrete reported the work up to date, the almanac for 1831 being available for sale. Liaison between the two institutions was close, since the textbook and examinations in astronomy for the navy were written by the scientists of the San Fernando Observatory.

Navarrete never did write a second set of *Memorias*. His attempts to revive the issue of lithographic reproduction of charts, resulted eventually in the alienation of the cartographic service from the *Dirección*. What was left of the *Depósito* was finally integrated with the library and collection of the Observatory of San Fernando. A catalogue of its holdings, recently published, looks impressive until one realizes how much has been lost and scattered (33).

Navarrete's *Idea General* and *Apuntes* list the works accomplished by a vital institution. The men who founded it, ran it, and worked for it, deve-

---

(31) D. W. Waters, *The Art of Navigation in England in Elizabethan and Early Stuart Times*, Yale University Press, New Haven, 1958, p. 346.

(32) A. Day, *Op. Cit.,* p. 32.

(33) Instituto y Observatorio de Marina, San Fernando, Cádiz, *Catálogo*, Biblioteca, 1974, covers the XVth to XVIIIth century and is chronologically arranged by date of publication. The earliest instructions for this institution relating to H. M. service at sea are dated 1772. Item 1062, the first volume of «observaciones astronómicas hechas en el Real observatorio de la Isla de León correspondientes a la clase de longitudes terrestres» is dated December 1798 and annual vols. followed. Item 1076.

loped a fierce loyalty to it which speaks from their correspondence. Beyond the typical account of other hydrographic offices, planned under the same influences of practical need and enlightened vision, the service played a role of substitute home base in a period of exile of Spanish intellectuals, whether internal (Navarrete) or external (Bauzá). The Hydrographic Office belongs to that network of official organizations which followed the tradition of the old scientific academies and the «invisible Colleges». It reflects the gradual specialization and the professionalization of scientific enterprise of the age.

II

Apuntes para continuar la noticia historica de la Dirección hidrográfica de Madrid desde el ano de 1809, en que se publicaron sus 2 tomos de Memorias, hasta 1824. (por Martín Fernández de Navarrete).

Al anunciar la publicacion de las memorias en la Gaceta de Madrid en Marzo de 1810 se dio un extracto tan puntual de su contenido que se estimo conveniente imprimirlo por separado como se hizo en el mismo año en la Imprenta Real con este titulo: IDEA GENERAL DEL DISCURSO Y DE LAS MEMORIAS PUBLICADAS POR LA DIRECCIÓN HIDROGRAFICA SOBRE LOS FUNDAMENTOS QUE HA TENIDO PARA LA CONSTRUCTION DE LAS CARTAS DE MAREAR QUE HA DADO A LUZ DESDE 1797. Madrid en la Imprenta Real Año de 1810. un cuaderno en 8º.

Dividida entonces la nación, desde el cautivario del Rey N. S. y asamblea de Bayona, habia salido de Madrid por Cadiz D. Felipe Bausá (2º director del Depósito) en Mayo de 1809; y en Set^ee lo verificó D. Josef de Espinosa, su primer director, dejando al Ministro de Mar e D. Josef de Mazarredo un estado muy detallado de todas las obras y fondos del establicimiento que apenas en 12 años dejaba en gran pie de prosperidad: después de haber intentado aunque en vano, trasladar a Cadiz todos los efectos de planchas, cartas, libros etc.: pero mucho se llevo para establecer allí otro Deposito. Llegado Espinosa a Sevilla y reintegrado en todos sus empleos por la Junta Central y habiendo acreditado con prueba documental la/
más relevante conducta y puro patriotismo, fué comisionado (en 16 de Novre de 1809) para pasar a Inglaterra a procurar restabelecer el depositó hidrografico que entonces se consideraba perdido para nuestra navegación, estando los franceses apoderados de Madrid. Entre otras comisiones importantes que tuvo en Inglaterra e informes que desempeño por encargo del gobierno procuró formar en Londres el Mapa geográfico del Reino de Mejico por lo cual solicitó algunas noticias del Virrey D. Francisco Javier de Venegas q. le contestó haberse dado todos los auxilios para ello el Barón de Humboldt, y que se estaba levantado un plano de la provincia de Guadalajara sobre el terreno y que se le remitiría. Ignoro que Espinosa llevase a efecto esta empresa. Aplicado especialmente a la hidrografia trazo e hizo gravar en Londres a sus expensas y bajo su inspección dos cartas, una del oceano atlan-

tico setentrional y otra del meridional, el año 1810; y poco después otra carta del mar de las Antillas y costas de Tierrafirme. En 1811 trazo e hizo grabar en Londres una carta del seno Mejicano y Golfo de Honduras y otra de las costas de España, Islas Canarias y Mar Mediterraneo. En 1812 dirigio, e hizo grabar alli mismo, una carta de la parte interior del Mediterraneo hasta Constantinopla, otra de las Islas Baleares, y otra en 6 hojas para las navegaciones a la India oriental por el mar del sur, donde señalo las derrotas y descubrimientos de los/ antiguos navegantes españoles Villalobos, Mendaña, Quiros, y otros. Estas cartas son dignas de todo aprecio por su exactitud, claridad y bella ejecución. Entre tanto Espinosa se procuró en Londres el trato y la amistad de los mejores y mas acreditados Geógrafos, visito en talleres, examino sus obras y cuidó de la impresión y formación de los Almanakes náuticos permaneciendo allí hasta principios de 1815 en que se le llamo para secretario del Almirantazgo y ocupar en el su anterior plaça; pero vino (trayendo muchas y útiles obras para el Depósito) y renunció a todos sus destinos a excepción de la dirección del mismo Depósito hidrográfico que quiso conservar por su afición a esta clase de conocimientos y trabajos.

Entretanto se formaron y publicaron en Cadiz bajo la dirección de D. Felipe Bausá en 1813 una carta del Océano Atlantico Setentrional, y otra del Mejicano y Golfo de Honduras; surtiendo también a nuestras Americas de las cartas y obras que necesitaban para su navegación habiendose establecido el Depósito de Cadíz bajo la protección del Gobierno en la casa llamada de *la Camorra* que entonces pertenecía a represalias.

Los empleados que quedaron en Madrid protegidos del ministro y General Mazarredo concluyeron muchas obras que tenían emperadas y las fueron publicando sucesivamente. En 1809 se publicó en 2 hojas una carta del Archipielago de Filipinas, y otra del Oceano Indio tambien en 2 hojas. En 1811, una de lo interior de la America meridional o/ camino que conduce de Valparaiso a Buenos Aires conforme a las observaciones que en este viaje habian hecho Espinosa y Bausá: Un plano del fondeadero de Callao de Lima; una carta de los canales de San Martín y de la Anguila en las Antillas. En 1812 se dió a luz una carta muy corregida del rio de la Plata y en 1810 se publicó el derrotero de las islas Antillas, de las costas de Tierrafirme y de las del seno Mejicano de que se dio un extracto o noticia muy circunstanciada en la Gaceta de Madrid no. 233 del Martes 21 de Agosto de aquel año.

Así el Depósito dividido en tres partes o secciones por las circunstancias de la guerra interior de la Peninsula, trabajó y adelantó sus obras con gran utilidad. Arrojados los franceses de España, vuelto el Gobierno a su centro, y restituido el Rey N. S. desde su cautiverio a su trono, se reunieron también en Madrid los individuos y trabajos del Depósito, y bajo la Dirección de D. Josef de Espinosa esperaba recoger los frutos de su estudio y observación en Inglaterra; pero en 6 de Setëë de 1815 falleció casi repentinamente este ilustre General a los 53 1/2 años de edad: de cuya muerte y servicios se dió noticia al publico en la Gaceta de Madrid de Marzo de 1816. Para succederle en la dirección nombró entonces el Rey a D. Felipe Bausá capn de navio y 2º director que era del mismo establecimiento. Oficial muy benemérito e intelligente, que como Espinosa habia acompanado a Tofiño y a Malaspina en sus expediciones hidrográficas./

Aprovechando los trabajos de Dr. Cosmé Churruca en las Antillas, de D. Joaquín Francisco Fidalgo en Costa Firme, y de D. Bernardo de Osta en Vera Cruz se trazaron y publicaron succesivamente las siguientes cartas: en 1816 el plano del puerto de Vera Cruz: Carta de la Isla Margarita y sus canales; carta del Estrecho de San Bernardino: las dos las hojas de la carta que comprende las costas de Tierrafirme. — en 1817 las hojas 3ª y 4ª de la costa de Tierrafirme; y una carta de la costa de Darién del Norte con las Islas Mulatas. — En 1819 el plano de los canales de la Isla de Flores y Banco Ingles; y otro de la Isla de Stª Maria en la costa de Chile. — En 1821, carta de la costa meridional y parte de la setentrional de la Isla de Cuba: carta de la costa setentrional del mar Negro.. — En 1822 carta desde el Golfo Dulce en Costa Rica hasta San Blas en la Nueva Galicia. — En 1823 carta que comprende las costas de la Peninsula de España o num. 1º del Mediterraneo. — en 1824: la carta n.º 2 que comprende las costas de Italia, mar Adriatico etc. — Además se han publicado desde 1809 hasta hoy, 76 planos del Portulano de America, y 71 planos del Portulano de España comprendida la costa de Portugal/

obras muy importantes y desempenadas con suma perfección. También se han retocado muchas láminas ya cansadas haciendo en las cartas y planos importantes correciones y mejoras según los adelantamientos que cada dia se hacen en la hidrografía: se han impreso los Alamanakes náuticos de los años respectivos hasta el de 1827 y se esta imprimiendo el de 1828: y en 1822 se ha hecho 2ª edicion del derrotero de las Antillas con muchas adiciones útiles y un discurso sobre las corrientes en el Océano Atlantico que ahora estan traduciendo los Ingleses (según noticias recientes de Bausá) al mismo tiempo que están copiando nuestras cartas de costa firme para el uso de su navegación y tráfico mercantíl.

En 1816 debí la confianca al Ministerio de que formar un reglamento o Institución para el régimen del Depósito hidrográfico y luego que la concluí, se examinó por orden del Rey N. S. y se sirvió aprobarla en 10 de Enero de 1817, imprimiendose con este titulo *Instrucción aprobada por el Rey N. Sr. para el gobierno facultativo y económico de la Dirección o Depósito de hidrografía.* — De Ornm. superior. — Madrid en la Imprenta Real, año de 1817. — Esta Instrucción para la que se tuvieron presentes las observaciones hechas por los directores anteriores y las judiciosas practicas que habían establecido, es la que rige en la actualidad.

Los sucesos de Marzo de 1820 y sus consequencias no/ pudieron dejar de influir en este establecimiento. Comisionose por el Gobierno a Dº Felipe Bausá para trazar una carta exacta geográfica de España y hacer la nueva división de sus provincias en lo que trabajo mucho y con gran inteligencia: fué después nombrado Diputado en Cortes por Mallorca, y como tal siguió al Gobierno a Sevilla y Cadiz desde la primavera de 1823; y luego en Octubre se trasladó a Gibraltar y de allí a Londres. El Gobierno a su salida de Madrid llevó consigo los caudales del Depósito (10.000 duros): en Bilbao y en otras partes desaparecieron los encargados de los Depósitos particulares de las cartas y obras puestas para su venta en los principales puertos: la falta de comunicaciones tenia paralizados los trabajos e intereses del Depósito, los consulados nada pagaron de sus respectivas consignaciones desde 1820 y así luego que el Rey N. Sr. salió de Cadiz en Octubre de 1823 se sirvio nombrarme director interino *por convenir que el Depósito hidrografico de esta corte no subsista por más tiempo sin tener un gefe ideoneo y caracterizado que entienda en todo lo cientifico y economico de este importante establicimiento segun los fines de su institución.* — Desde luego se empezó por dar trabajo a los empleados, habilitar a otros, arreglar la administración de/ sus fondos y consignaciones, reclamando y resucitando sus antiguos derechos y créditos, y tratando de liquidar y dejar corrientes los muchos que tiene a su favor. Se concluyó y publicó la carta del golfo de Californias o mar de Cortés, se dió principio a trazar las cartas de las costas orientales de los Estados Unidos de la America setentrional, y yá está concluido y grabandose la Nº 1º que comprende desde el rio de S. Juan en la Florida hasta Nueva--Yorck. Se continua con el Nº 2º hasta cerca de Terranova con los planos de los principales puertos de esta costa y sus Derroteros. Se concluyó y está grabandose la carta nº 3º del Mediterraneo que comprende el Archipielago hasta Constatinopla; y concluydo el plano importante de la via de Guayaquil, está ya en poder delos grabadores; y se han escrito los Derroteros de estos mares.

Se ha concluido una carta muy rectificada de nuestras costas de Catalunya: se trabaja en otra de las costas del Brazil y en rectificar y mejorar las del mar del sur desde cabo de Hornos. Hasta Panamá con los Derroteros correspondientes. — Ha sido menester restabelecer o entablar de nuevo las correspondencias estrangeras para entrar al nivel de los conociminetos hidrograficos que cada dia se adelantan por los Ingleses, Rusos y otras naciones maritimas. — Se han recuperados colecciones importantes de manuscritos de nuestros antiguas viages y descubrimientos que yendo a Cadiz habian sido interceptados en su transito; y se procura recoger y reunir cuanto se ha extraviado en tan fatales revoluciones. Finalmente se trabaja con zelo por conservar al Depósito hidrográfico el honor y gloria de que hasta ahora se ha hecho digno.

APPENDIX

*IDEA GENERAL DEL DISCURSO Y DE LAS MEMORIAS PUBLICADAS POR
LA DIRECCIÓN HIDROGRÁFICA SOBRE LOS FUNDAMENTOS QUE HA
TENIDO PARA LA CONSTRUCCIÓN DE LAS CARTAS DE MAREAR, QUE
HA DADO A LUZ DESDE 1797.* MADRID EN LA IMPRENTA REAL ANO
DE 1810.

II

Memoria primera.   Observaciones practicadas en las costas de Espana y Africa,
y en las del mar Mediterraneo, islas Canarias y de los Azores, con un apendice donde se
da razon de otros trabajos dirigidos a perfeccionar la geografia interior del reino, por D. Josef
de Espinosa y Tello, primer director, que ha sido, de la Direccion hidrografica.

pp. 24-27

III.

Memoria segunda.   Observaciones practicadas en las costas del continente de América
y sus islas desde Montevideo, por el cabo de Hornos, hasta los 60° de latitud setentrional,
con un apendice que contiene varias observaciones astronomicas y fisicas hechas en un
viage por el interior de la America meridional, y de las executadas en ambos hemisferios
con un pendulo invariable, por el mismo autor.   pp. 27-30

IV.

Memoria tercera.   Observaciones practicadas en las islas Marianas y Filipinas, en
la nueva Holanda, y en el archipielago de los Amigos: con un apéndice que contiene varias
noticias utiles a la hidrografia de los mares orientales, por el mismo autor.

pp. 30-33

V.

Memoria quarta.   Observaciones astronomicas practicadas en Puerto-Rico, la Guaira,
Cartagena de Indias, la Havana y Veracruz, para la exacta colocación de estos lugares;
y noticia de los trabajos hidrográficos ya executados en las islas de Barlovento y Antillas,
en las costas de Tierra-firme y en el seno Mexicano, por el mismo autor.

pp. 33-37

APPENDIX II

[Note 5]

Cartas.

1797-1809

Carta esferica del globo terraqueo, en que se hallan trazadas las derrotas de los mas celebres navegantes modernos: en punto menor. — Carta general del Oceano atlantico u occidental, desde 52º de latitud Norte hasta el Equador: marca mayor. — Idem del Oceano meridional desde el Equador hasta 60º de latitud, y desde el cabo de Hornos hasta el canal de Mozambique. — Carta esferica del golfo de Gascuna y canales de la Mancha y Bristol. — Idem de las costas de la peninsula de Espana, las de Francia e Italia hasta el cabo Venere, y la correspondiente de Africa en esta parte del Mediterraneo, con las islas y escollos que comprehende esta extension de mar. — Idem de las costas de Italia, las del golfo Adriatico desde el cabo Venere hasta las islas Sapiencie en la Morea, y las correspondientes de Africa, parte de las islas de Corcega y Cerdena, con las demas que comprehende este mar. — Idem de la parte interior del Mediterraneo y del Archipielago de Grecia, con los golfos y canales hasta Constantinopla y el mar Negro, y con los planos de puerto Mandri en la Grecia, y de San Nicolás en la puerto Mandri en la Grecia, y de San Nicolás en la parte N.O. de la isla de Zea. — Idem particular del Archipielago de Grecia para facilitar su navegación Archipielago de Grecia para facilitar su navegación desde los canales de Cerigo, Candia y Rodas, hast la isla Ipsera. — Idem del paso de los Dardanelos, del mar de Marmara, y del canal que conduce al mar Negro, con el plano de la ciudad de Constantinopla y canal del mar Negro o Bosforo de Tracia. — Idem particular del mar Negro con los planos del estrecho de Jenikala, y la confluencia y embocadura de los rios Bog y Dniepali. — Idem de las islas Antillas con parte de la costa firme hasta Cumaná. — Idem de las islas Caribes de Sotavento. — Idem de una parte de las islas Antillas, las de Puerto-Rico, Santo Domingo, Jamayca y Cuba, con los bancos y canales adyacentes. — Idem que comprehende desde el rio Guaurabo hasta Boca Grande en la parte meridional de la isla de Cuba. — Idem del mar de las Antillas y de las costas de Tierrafirme desde la isla de Trinidad hasta el golfo de Honduras, con los planos de los fondeaderos de Cumana y Truxillo. — Idem que comprehende los desemboques al norte de la isla de Santo Domingo, y la parte oriental del canal vicio de Bahama. — Idem de una parte del canal viejo de Bahama y placeres adyacentes, desde punta de Maternillos hasta la de Icacos. — Nueva carta del canal de Bahama, que comprehende tambien los de Providencia y Santaren, con los baxos, islas y sondas al E. y al O. de la peninsula de la Florida. — Carta que comprehende las costas del Seno mexicano. — Idem particular de las costas septentrionales del propio seno, que comprehende las de la Florida occidental, las margenes de la Luisiana, y toda la ribera que sigue por la bahia de San Bernardo y el rio bravo del N. hasta la laguna madre. — Idem de la parte S. del mismo seno, que comprehende las costas de Yucatan y sonda de Campeche, las de Tabasco, Veracruz, y nuevo reyno de Santander — Idem del rio de la Plata, con la sonda y las principales vistas de los puntos de recalada, y con los planos de los puertos de Maldonado y Montevideo. — Idem de las costas de la America meridional, desde el paralelo de 36º 30' de la latitud Sur hasta el cabo de Hornos. — Idem de las costas del reyno de Chile, comprehendidas entre los paralelos de 38 y 22º de latitud Sur, con las islas de Juan Fernandez y de San Felix. — Idem de una parte de la costa del Peru, desde el paralelo de 7º hasta 21º 45' Sur. — Idem de la costa occidental de America desde 7º de latitud Sur, hasta 9º de latitud N. — Idem de los reconocimientos hechos en 1792 para examinar la entrada de Juan de Fuca, y la internacion de sus canales navegables: dos hojas — Carta general del Archipielago de Filipinas, levantada en 1792 y 93 por los Comandantes y Oficiales de las corbetas de S.M. Descubierta y Atrevida durante la campana que hicieron con este objecto, enriquecida de nuevos reconocimientos que han practicado despues otros Oficiales de la Armada. — Carta esferica de la bahia de Manila con los planos de los puertos de Mariveles, Cavite y San Jacinto. — Idem del Archipielago de Babao. — Carta geografica en quatro hojas de la provincia de Quito y de sus adyacentes, hecha sobre las observaciones astronomicas y geograficas de los Academicos reales de las ciencias de Paris, y de los Senores Don Jorge Juan y Don Antonio de Ulloa.

Planos

Plano geometrico del puerto, capital de la isla de Puerto Rico. — Idem del puerto y ciudad de la Havana. — Idem del puerto de Veracruz en la costa occidental del Seno mexicano. — Idem del puerto Cabello, y de los de la Guayra y Barcelona en la costa Firme. — Idem de los puertos de Santa Elena y de Melo en la costa Patagonica. — Idem del puerto de San Carlos en la isla de Chiloe en la America meridional. — Idem de los puertos de Valdivia y de la rada de San Juan Bautista en la isla de Juan Fernandez en la propia America. — Idem de los puertos de Sorsogon y Palapa en las islas de Luzon y Samar.

Vistas.

Vista de la ciudad de Lima. — Idem de la de Santiago de Chile. — Idem de la de Buenos Ayres. — Seis vistas en pliego de marca de diferentes parages de America y Asia, fondeaderos y otras curiosidades.

Ademas se estan abiendo varios planos de America, que con los ya grabados llegaran al numero de ciento, grabados llegarán al numero de ciento, sin contar los que hay de las costas de España y sus islas en el Oceano y Mediterraneo para formar los portulanos que haran juego con los respectivos derroteros de los distintos mares de Europa e Indias. Para mayor comodidad se dividirá por quadernos el portulano de America en esta forma: Primero, de las islas Antillas. Segundo, de las costas de Tierrafirme, Florida y Seno mexicano. Tercero, de la isla de Cuba, y quarto de la Jamayca y Santo Domingo. Tales son los frutos que ha rendido el establecimiento hidrográfico de Madrid en solo el espacio de doce anos, y aún en circunstancias no las mas favorables para el fomento de sus empresas. A ellas se debe por decontado el que ya ningún navegante español use de cartas extrangeras en donde pueda valerse de las nuestras, y que de este modo se haya desterrado el vergónozoso trafico que hacian con nosotros como si fuesemos incapaces de fabricar los mapas de nuestras propias costas, ni de navegar en ellas sin ageno auxilio.

XVI

THE EVA G. R. TAYLOR LECTURE

The Eva G. R. Taylor lectures were founded in 1959 to mark the occasion of the late Professor Taylor's eightieth birthday and are presented each year by a distinguished scholar in the branches of knowledge to which she made such notable contributions. They are arranged in turn by the Societies which sponsored the original appeal which, besides this Institute, include the Royal Geographical Society, the Society for Nautical Research, the British Association for the Advancement of Science, and so on.

Professor Lamb's lecture was presented at an Institute meeting held at the Royal Geographical Society on 4 March with the President in the Chair. Ursula Lamb is Professor of History in the University of Arizona. She is US representative for the International Reunion for Nautical Science and Hydrography.

The London Years of Felipe Bauzá: Spanish Hydrographer in Exile, 1823-34

I am very pleased to be with you on this occasion which gathers annually the friends and admirers of Professor Eva G. R. Taylor to honour her memory. My presence here reflects the globe-circling impact her work continues to have, as more and more people from many disciplines rely on her varied contributions. As for the distance of the echo to her work, I qualify, coming from close to half way around the globe, or from Long. 110° 58′ 08″ west of Greenwich. I have elected to talk about Felipe Bauzá who, on an autumn day of 1823, presented himself to the Royal Geographical Society here in London, some way north and east from his birthplace, Palma de Mallorca, and his port of departure, Gibraltar. For he was one of the Spanish liberals with a price on his head under orders of that treacherous puppet of the Holy Alliance, Ferdinand VII.

Felipe Bauzá's first official contact with England had been the sight of a warship, *Terpsichore*, and the sound of her guns. Bauzá was aboard *Mahonesa* when, on 13 October 1796, at half-past nine in the morning the ships' guns came within range, and the fight began. By a quarter to twelve it was all over, and *Mahonesa* ingloriously hoisted the flag of surrender.[1] Lieutenant Bauzá, left unhurt, became a prisoner of the British for eight months, until May 1797. After his release he was no longer permitted active service and was posted to the Hydrographic Office in Madrid. The next martial conflict of 1810 found Bauzá in Cadiz, fighting by the side of the British against the French invaders of Spain. He accepted a British commission (though not the pay) equivalent to the rank of a *capitán de fragata*, and he was charged with the supervision and direction of British engineers on the island of León (now the town of San Fernando) where there was an observatory attached to the Spanish Hydrographic Office.[2] Upon the lifting of the siege, and the expulsion of the French 'rey intruso', Bauzá received permission to return to Madrid. He went back with all the charts and papers which he had saved from the French, and in 1815, upon the death of the first director of the *Depósito Hidrográfico*, Don Vicente Espinoza y Tello, he succeeded to the directorship of the Spanish Hydrographic Office.[3]

Bauzá fully shared the continued disruption of life and work which was the lot of Spaniards during the subsequent years of regency and civil strife, until in 1823 Ferdinand VII, the restored reactionary king, dismissed the Cortes, exiled the liberals, and put a price on the head of those whose votes had displeased him. Bauzá, having been a liberal member of the Cortes from his home district of Mallorca, was among them. He joined the refugees who crowded the dockside of Gibraltar in the fall of 1823. Prior to leaving, he was able to execute a will before the British Consul in Gibraltar which left all his possessions to his wife, since he had spent her entire *dot* and much of his own estate upon his work.[4]

Bauzá wrote the first letter of the collection on which this paper is based, on 6 November 1823, probably from Gibraltar or in transit.[5] The recipient was to be Don Martín Fernández de Navarrete, a distinguished naval person and a renowned scholar, who had volunteered to act as locum tenens or interim director of the Hydrographic Office during Bauzá's absence, in the apparent anticipation by both men that Bauzá would soon reassume his post. Bauzá remarked that

> there is no help in this situation, some are caught for cause and some without, and it remains to be seen where it will (all) stop. In the meantime it is necessary that I leave and go to London where you know you can command me privately and as director. I shall advise you about everything useful for the Hydrographic Office (*el establecimiento*) as well as for the Navy generally, since my being a member of the Royal Society may offer me the means to acquire news to write to you from there.[6]

He then referred to a good friend and intermediary, one Gutiérrez, the first of successive links necessary to communication between the exile and his country.

Although cut off from his family, Bauzá was able to take with him his sketches, charts and plans, and many of his books and papers. When he arrived in London he settled in Somers Town, a borough preferred by Spanish refugees with limited funds. The affluent members of the emigration lived on the other side of the New Road (Euston Road) in more prosperous surroundings.[7]

Bauzá kept his promise of sending letters to Navarrete to 17 January 1834, just before his planned return under the amnesty of the new Queen. This never came to pass. Felipe Bauzá died in his rented house, number 48 on Johnson Street in Somers Town, of a massive brain haemorrhage on 3 March 1834, at the age of seventy[8]. Except during a short stay in Paris of about three months in 1826, and a probable much shorter visit in 1828, his dateline is London. There are 61 letters on 145 closely written folios, distributed over ten years. No answers by Navarrete or other correspondents are included in the collection.

Don Felipe Bauzá was sixty years old when he arrived in Somers Town. His naval career had been a steady rise from the age of 15, reflecting the appreciation of his talents and accomplishments by his superiors. His change from active service aboard ships to a post with the Hydrographic Office was more one of place than of activity, since the work he was doing had for some time been astronomical observation and the compiling of charts. At twenty-one years of age he had joined surveying parties working on the famous Maritime Atlas of Spain,[9] prepared by Valdés and Tofiño, and subsequently he was chosen to take charge of all the maps and plans to be made on the famous exploring voyage 'around the world' under Alessandro Malaspina. He was assigned to the *Descubierta*, sailing from Cadiz on 30 July 1789, which returned five years and four months later, on 2 December 1794. He and his scientific companion Espinoza y Tello were in ill health on the return voyage, and were advised to travel the overland route from Valparaiso to Buenos Aires, in order to avoid the rigours of rounding Cape Horn. Bauzá took many sights, fixing points en route, he recorded experiments with a pendulum, he made barometric readings as he crossed the Andes and, among other such observations, he compiled data on the propagation of sound over land. The scientific readings made on this trip contributed substantially to Bauzá's fame.[10]

The tragedy of the enterprise was that publication of all data was prohibited because of a court intrigue by the Queen's favourite Manoel Godoy against Malaspina.[11] Still, enough information from way-stations in America reached the scholarly world to bring a series of honours to Bauzá. In 1805 he was chosen for his literary achievement to be a member of the Royal Society of 'Friends of the Country (Amigos del País) of Madrid'; in 1807 he was made supernumerario of the Royal Academy of History. He was elected to membership in the Royal Bavarian Academy of Sciences (section of Physics) on 3 February 1816. In the same year, the Russian Tsar Alexander I bestowed upon him the Order of Saint Wladimir, fourth class[12]. Bauzá was chosen to be a corresponding member of the Academy of Science in Turin (1821), and on 1 April 1819 he was elected, after the required fourteen readings, to be a foreign member of the Royal Society of London. On this occasion he was introduced with the following words:

> Late pupil and assistant of Tofiño in all his surveys, director of charts and plans in the voyage of discovery of Malaspina, author of charts and memoirs between Chile and Buenos Aires, compiler of ancient voyages of the Spaniards in the Pacific from original manuscripts now in course of publication, and superintendent of the hydrographical bureau in Madrid.[13]

The eminence of his position was noticed already in Gibraltar. Admiral Fleming, a personal friend of Bauzá and the son of the First Lord of the Admiralty, Melville, used his influence on behalf of him, or so Bauzá speculated in his report of the offer to him of transport to London for him and all his effects aboard an English man of war (brigantine). Bauzá was also known to Lord Holland, that generous supporter of Spanish refugees. He was received by Lady Holland during her stay in Spain, and she reported with approval his exploits in saving the Malaspina papers from M. Laborde, the French agent and author.[14]

Despite the modesty of his lodgings in London, a man of Bauzá's stature was soon sought out by colleagues. At sixty years of age, he was a gentleman of agreeable presence, conversant with English, personally modest, though proud of the tradition and culture of his country. He was quite aware of this special status as he writes that he had acquired a multitude of contacts with people 'who received me with the customary formality of this place'. But he was surprised that they also took a personal interest in him and 'they heap distinctions upon me which they extend to few foreigners'.[15] So they made him a member of the newly founded Athenaeum 'of which most members are Lords (Lores), among them Canning. It is true (he continues) that none of this means anything but the appreciation and recognition of my country and of the corps which I have served'.

As a member of the Royal Society, Bauzá received an invitation to the house of 'el señor Davis (sic), considered the first chemist in Europe, and president of the Royal Society', so he wrote to Navarrete, and he proceeded to report upon experiments with zinc and corrosion of copper sheathing by seawater, suggesting that these experiments be repeated by the Hydrographic Office in Madrid.[16]

On 26 February 1823 Captain W. E. Parry, who had just been appointed Hydrographer of the Navy, succeeding Captain Thomas Hurd, introduced the distinguished Spaniard officially to the Fellowship of the Royal Society. Bauzá was surprised at the youth of Captain Parry and was charmed by him. He reported with pleasure on the formal seating of himself at his place, and was even happier with the offer of free access to the library. He soon joined the weekly evening sessions at 8 p.m. of the astronomers which were normally attended by around thirty people.[17] Although Captain Parry was just about to leave upon his third voyage to the Arctic, Bauzá had time for the exchange of information and could give him useful reports on Spanish experience in the South Pacific. His friendship with Parry held fast, despite the harmful effect of the Hydrographer's absences upon the London Office. This meant a decline of official attention to the Hydrographic Office and of funding of surveying activity at the time when Secretary Croker, as First Secretary of the Admiralty, could implement his budget restrictions.[18] Among the stalwarts of the office, John Walker, cartographer and engraver, his sons, and Lieutenant A. B. Becher kept working, and Bauzá befriended especially the former, whose house was within hailing distance of his own, and he reports seeing him almost daily at dusk when daylight no longer sufficed for their 'geographic' work.[19]

Bauzá's acquaintance among surveyors was extensive and close. Captains P. P. King, Purdy, Beechey and Franklin generously gave information and often sought it.[20] But two major figures stand out, the Scottish maritime scientist of the Royal Society, Basil Hall, and the distinguished surveyor of the Mediterranean, W. H. Smyth. Hall introduced himself with a letter by Lord Holland and Bauzá was delighted and impressed as he got to know him better.[21] One may assume that they kept in touch since their common interests touched on many points. Bauzá reported visiting his house and working with Hall's figures concerning the Pacific coastline of the Americas in 1826. With Captain Smyth's appearance, an element of true affinity enters the correspondence, which was reflected in the intellectual collaboration of the two hydrographers. Smyth must have been an extraordinary character, able to find the right word or gesture as evidenced in his correspondence with Beaufort.[22] He extended an invitation to Bauzá to stay for a few days in his house in Bedford, but he did so in the name of his wife, a courteous gesture to a man deprived of his family life. Bauzá was full of admiration for the work he saw on this first of many visits, and he was overwhelmed by the generosity and openness of this colleague who gave him permission to copy anything he wished, and offered him a completely free hand to do with the data what he wanted.[23]

Bauzá had been a very young apprentice hydrographer when Tofiño compiled his survey of the Spanish coasts.[24] But it had been a pioneer enterprise and the Spanish achievement was fully appreciated by W. H. Smyth. More will be heard of that. It is very sad, therefore, to see that friendship clouded at the end of our record. Bauzá reports on a visit to Bedford, made upon the request of Captain Beaufort, to check Smyth's chart of the Straits of Gibraltar and to consult with him concerning the shoal at Tarifa which was not yet entered on Smyth's chart because of differences over his survey. Bauzá's information concerning its location was based on a more recent survey and it was impeccable.[25] Yet Smyth, not having entered it, was unwilling to admit to error and retired into a cool politeness. He became distant and formal, says Bauzá, and Beaufort's attempt to assume responsibility for relying on the more recent survey and having sent Bauzá to get Smyth to amend his chart, does nothing to justify the assumption that this estrangement was a passing cloud.[26]

The only person who comes off badly in the correspondence is Sir John Barrow, Second Permanent Secretary of the Admiralty under Croker. Bauzá did not meet with the accustomed urbanity when he called upon him. Barrow showed him the office (Depósito) but did not ask him where he lived, while other colleagues (socios) invited him to their houses. Bauzá expressed his disappointment with the man

> who is not frank and not at all forthcoming. He is eager for glory and full of envy, while the rest of the people are open with me, giving me all I ask for, as do Captain Smyth and Captain King; and with the return of Captain Parry, we shall make progress in establishing a correspondence between the Madrid Office and this one which the man who should further it is not doing... Mr Barrow is a man who neither understands nor cares for it (the Hydrographic Office). The man in charge is the First Hydrographer, and he is the one who makes and engraves the charts.[27]

Bauzá was invited to go to the Greenwich Royal Observatory as a member of the examining board of the Royal Society the day of the annual visit. There he met England's foremost astronomer, Sir John Herschel, who invited him to come to his house to see his telescope.[28] The invitation was gladly accepted and Bauzá describes the trip into the country around Windsor with pleasure. His news about the visit was of particular interest to the Spanish astronomer Sánchez Cerquero and the hydrographer Baleato. Sánchez Cerquero came to England himself in 1829 and spent some weeks in Greenwich, having been introduced by Bauzá. They were also both invited to Captain Smyth's house where they spent ten days, searching and copying to their heart's desire in the rich store of that hospitable study. After additional time spent in London, Sánchez Cerquero returned to San Fernando with a new transit instrument designed by the British artist Thomas Jones, who eventually helped install it there. Clocks and barometers also were sent to Spain at various dates, as were engraving tools and copper plates, both new and engraved. With respect to equipment and manpower the advantage was with England which had a surplus of skilled technicians, many freelance engravers, printers, and designers and, except for Jones, whose interminable delays Bauzá blamed in part to his fears of not being paid, the manufacture and care of instruments was reliable, and the production of charts prompt and good.

Not so was the performance of the Hydrographic Office before Beaufort. Here the advantage lay with Spain's early royal monopoly and the sponsorship of survey work and scientific publishing. Since 1795 the Spanish *Depósito Hidrográfico* had ample premises, trained naval personnel at all levels, and a respectable record of publication. Almanacs were printed annually and had been kept up to date, and the number and variety of charts available through the office, though not comparable to the free enterprise system of public sales in England, was in advance of those carried by the British Navy.[29] The English office appeared to Bauzá in disproportion to the size of her navy and to the wealth of the country. Information from foreign sources was completely missing.[30] On the other hand, data brought in by British captains to the Admiralty was given back to them and they were free to negotiate with a private firm to print and sell their charts.

> The captain gets two to four £. for this which he can pocket, so the government is served and the captain satisfied, and if you say this is at the expense of the government, I can answer that in this way many people are trained and as a half dozen corvettes are steadily in service, this amounts to a well educated work force. There is also an entirely separate group of such as Captain Purdy and Captain Hosburg, (sic) who are self-trained geographers, collecting data and publishing on their own, or selling their work to the Hydrographic Office.[31]

It was Purdy who requested Spanish data on the Antilles from Bauzá, while Becher, a member of the service, expressed an interest in translating the Memorias of the Spanish office which apparently became an officially aborted project.[32]

In a letter of 26 July 1824 Bauzá described the London hydrographic establishment as follows:

> It is much less rich than ours, but is on the way to catch up very soon. Opened in 1796, it employs ten people, six during the day, who are draftsmen as well as compilers of charts, and two are engravers as well, who engraved the charts of Espinoza. Their wages are not very high, about 100 to 150 £. The chief is Captain Parry, and during his absence it is the secretary of the Admiralty who is not a naval career man. This office has only very recently begun to publish charts financed by the government and the admiralty and sold to the public. They have warships for making surveys but they also buy a lot of small private craft for survey work, wherever and whenever available, and at the cheapest price. With that you have an account of the entire establishment.

On 1 August 1828, there is another account which compares the problems of how to find and pay engravers as it was in London and Madrid. There were none to be found in Madrid. Bauzá preferred non-military men for that office:

> Here the office really consists of the Hydrographer (John Walker) and his two sons who draw and engrave charts as well as print them. This accounts for the small output, and the purchasing from private geographers of charts which are given to the fleet. During the absence of Parry the premier geographer who is also an engraver looks after everything from nine to four.[33]

The situation in the Hydrographic Office changed drastically when the Office of Lord High Admiral was bestowed on his Royal Highness the Duke of Clarence. He had a look at the 'mean accommodation' mentioned by

Bauzá, and noted the shortage of skilled draftsmen. His changes included the increase of manpower and the expansion of programmes, which led to immediate growth, since skilled engravers and designers were plentiful, and demand for charts was expanding pari passu with Britain's trade and patrol of the seas. As an example, on 25 May 1827, in connection with new surveys, Bauzá wrote about points fixed on the route from Calcutta to China by a schooner called *Dhaulle*, which had surveyed a shoal at 9° 35′ N., 112° 22′ E., at a distance of 42 miles from a shoal called West London. This shows the wide flung network of interest, the multiple sources of information, and the concern to get the most accurate charts for the navy.

Bauzá thought that under the regime of the Duke of Clarence a mutually beneficial relationship between London and Madrid might be forged. He suggested to Navarrete that a collection of the best charts, except for the Mediterranean, but including the Straits of Magellan, and the chart based on the data from *Sútil* and *Mexicana* taken on the survey voyage of Espinoza along the Pacific shores of America should be sent, addressed to the Duke of Clarence

> who is presently the head of the navy, and this material should be accompanied by a letter for this Office. Advise me so I can verify this.[34]

It is at this stage that the operation in London should be compared to the Madrid establishment in 1823, when it was at its best with respect to staffing, accommodation and enterprise. If Spain did not have so many surveys, she had the advantage of large backlogs of rutters and observations of the turn of the century, along with a successful publishing enterprise, and even a spirit of innovation, as shown in experiments with lithographic printing of charts.[35]

When Bauzá arrived in London, it was not surprising that Captain Hall asked him for the Spanish Office orders which also described the training of its staff. Inquiries about the Depósito had come from as far as St Petersburg, where Captain I. F. Kruzenshtern had been impressed by diplomatic reports on the excellence of the organization.[36] But after the departure of Bauzá, the activities of the Spanish hydrographic office were stalled under mere custodianship, though Navarrete, as interim director, did his best, since he had in fact originated some of the programmes himself. We read about the demand for the volumes of voyages collected and published by him, and there were continued requests for Spanish survey data from before 1823. The only current items of interest were the almanacs compiled by the observatory in San Fernando.

For a while, the activities of the Madrid office had enough momentum to proceed in anticipation of the director's return. In the view of Navarrete, Bauzá's stay in London was only the continuation of the official Spanish mission established by Espinoza during the French occupation of Madrid. At that time Navarrete listed three stations for the Spanish hydrographic office, Madrid, Cadiz – i.e. the observatory of San

Fernando on the island of León recently equipped by Bauzá with his own instruments – and London.[37] By the summer of 1827, all efforts to arrange for Bauzá's return came to grief. His exile, converted into a leave of absence, and which he had thought might last a summer better spent in France, was to become permanent residence in England as a private person and a bona fide refugee.[38]

Under the circumstances, the appointment of Navarrete as his permanent successor (holding the office 'de propriedad') was fortunate, because he was anxious to continue the fruitful collaboration with Bauzá in London, albeit this now had to be in a private capacity. The support of the navy continued to decline in Spain, and the Hydrographic Office came ever nearer to dissolution. For Bauzá these were to be the lean years of financial straits. He turned his hand to drawing charts as well to compiling them,[39] and he may have given lessons in Spanish, since learning that language was all the rage among educated Englishmen, he wrote, and requested that a simple grammar be sent to him. He spent many evenings at the *tertulia* of his friend, turned book dealer, Don Vicente Salvá, and as he was a connoisseur of rare books, and in touch with Obadiah Rich and the likes of him, he may have done some dealing. There is a lot of book talk in the letters, concerned with his own library in Spain on which he drew from time to time despite the difficulties of shipping, as well as with the steady enrichment of the collection of the *Depósito Hidrográfico* by English works.[40]

In London, the resignation of the Duke of Clarence threw a passing shadow over the Hydrographic Office, and helped provoke the resignation of Captain Parry.[41] Happier news for Bauzá was the appointment to the post of Hydrographer of Captain Beaufort, who immediately assured him of his continued interest in the Spaniard's hydrographic work, and in the liaison with Madrid and San Fernando. Bauzá reported on Beaufort in a letter of 22 May 1829, as author of the charts of *Caramania* (*sic*) and 'who is held to be knowledgable and the right man for the job'. By August of that same year, he wrote that Navarrete should pursue direct correspondence with Captain Beaufort:

> The actual director is an excellent individual (*sujeto*) with a special dedication to hydrography and with whom I have a very special friendship (ever) since he questioned me extensively on the position of Rio de Janeiro which he says drives him crazy because of the difference of 10' of long. between the data of the French and those of Captain King and Lieutenant Foster, the one who left with 32 chronometers which all had been checked out at the observatory here.

He continues:

> I must laugh with him about the idea that they now have to fix every point on the globe with many chronometers, coming and going; it is not a bad idea, but it will not bring the exact result which they seek; Astronomical observation of some points with the spaces between them timed by chronometers coming and going, I believe to have an advantage over chronometric measurement by

itself. Well, we do have our little differences (*disputillos*) but he is so frank with me and gives me anything I ask for from the Hydrographic Office, that I can finish with the help of others, to gather very valuable data for the *Memorias* which I continue.

In March 1830 Bauzá reported that Beaufort

always a good friend, gives me some work to do (*me ocupa en algunas cosas*) and I owe him special consideration as now they expect the expedition of Captain King, who has finished his reconnaissance of the East and West coasts of Patagonia, to Valparaiso in the West, and from Cape Horn to Buenos Aires in the East.

A part of this had been Bauzá's route on the way West with Malaspina and the collaboration with Captain King in comparing and collating position data was a close one.[42] Besides taking an interest in Bauzá's astronomical and cartographic work, Beaufort made a request which delighted the Spaniard. He asked for views of Madrid and its monuments and especially of the Hydrographic Office which was then housed in the palace formerly of the Knights of Malta. These views were eventually received to appear in a series of publications of the Society for the Diffusion of Useful Knowledge, or DUK, destined for the general public and heavily supported by Beaufort.[43] It was also Beaufort who invited Bauzá to join the recently founded Royal Geographical Society, and to write for the new *Nautical Magazine* which he initiated[44]. Navarrete was persuaded to become an early subscriber, and Bauzá alerted Madrid to the successive numbers as they appeared. He himself contributed an introductory essay to number one and other material later on. During the Beaufort years, the exchange of Madrid's *Memorias* and the *Transactions* of the Royal Society, and a lively correspondence between the nautical observatories, is reflected in Bauzá's letters. Madrid acquired a copy of Captain Smyth's great Mediterranean survey. Whether this was of the supersize chart which Bauzá admired in Bedford is not certain.[45]

The last major commission we hear of came from Beaufort, and concerned the instructions to Captain Fitzroy for the voyage of the *Beagle*. On 27 September 1831 Bauzá reported with considerable levity how Captain Beaufort had asked him to give instructions regarding the planned survey of Patagonia, the east and south of Tierra del Fuego, and the search for a port on the east coast of the Malvinas (Falkland Islands) as well as other parts, and that he had been rather pressing. Bauzá went to see Beaufort and said he enjoyed the joke, but after all, the Captain's own nationals could furnish him with much more knowledge and information than he. To this Beaufort answered that neither he nor the Admiralty were laughing at Bauzá, certainly not he, and that he would appreciate it if Bauzá would tell them what Captain Fitzroy should seek out, and what positions to fix in his survey. Upon that reaction says Bauzá, 'I did get to work and did what was asked of me.'[46] On 4 September 1832, Bauzá reported that a chart of Captain King had already appeared and that Captain Fitzroy would fill in the whole archipelago of Tierra del Fuego, and 'as soon as they will have completed those charts, the latter would be forwarded to Madrid'. Captain Fitzroy mentioned Bauzá in his account and expressed his respect for the Spanish work.[47]

When Bauzá arrived in England, the liaison of her hydrographers with France was nearly non-existent. The link established across the Channel by Bauzá was through Alexander von Humboldt. His work about America, which was published in France, was the connection with the Spanish cosmographer. Humboldt emerges very recognizably from this correspondence. His multiple interests, his humanity and practical help, his high scientific standards, and the vast reach of his interests, all become evident. Bauzá first reported to Navarrete on 28 April 1824 that Humboldt had written to ask for several geographic positions, and had offered to get a passport for Bauzá to visit Paris where, he wrote: 'geography is not much favoured'. By November he had not been able to do so, but in May of the following year a permit was forthcoming, and on 2 August 1826 Bauzá wrote his first letter from Paris to Navarrete. He reported that 'el barón' was 'un sujeto activo e incansable' (indefatigable) 'and I owe him a thousand attentions'. Humboldt took Bauzá everywhere and, said his guest,

> I have never seen anyone who gets so much consideration . . . I have never had personal contact with him before, and I am very glad now to have seen that he is a man of understanding (un hombre que lo entiende) . . . He is not the charlatan into which some people try to make him.

Whoever those people were, Bauzá and history have decided against them.

Of all Humboldt's interests the one which resulted in true collaboration was astronomical work on the American charts. This developed in an uninterrupted correspondence between the two scholars and Jabbo Oltmanns,[48] the astronomer who worked for Humboldt in Paris. Bauzá and Oltmanns never met, nor did the Spaniard ever get to know the other continental astronomer of note with whom he was in constant touch, the Baron Franz Xaver von Zach at the Seeberg observatory.[49] Bauzá was a contributor to the published correspondence of Zach, and he registered his regret at the termination of the publication on 5 May 1827, as well as expressing regret at the death in a cholera epidemic of this most active and useful scientific correspondent.[50]

Bauzá's Parisian stay, planned for two months, lasted from 19 July to early October 1826. Resentment of the French could be assumed on the part of a Spanish exile, though when it took the form of specific criticism it has some interest. 'The French do not document their (geographical) positions as to when and how arrived at', he complained. He particularly criticized Depons who gave the estuary of the Orinoco four branches, and located Caracas on the shore. 'He never visited those regions', said Bauzá. How mortified would he himself have been, had he known that in his statement in a speech cataloguing the mistakes of others, he would be proven wrong. He said that the Orinoco originated in Lake Parima. He had never been there either, and the Parima legend haunted geographers as late as 1847, being nearly as persistent as El Dorado.[51]

Paris, though exciting, and cheaper, full of life day and night, unlike London where the light fades so early and the morning's work begins late (*la gente no madrugan*) did not suit him for a permanent stay as long as his wife and daughters could not join him.[52] He preferred his study with the bay window in Somers Town and the English steadfastness to the Gallic sparkle, especially as Humboldt had promised to visit. There is no noteworthy news of a scientific nature in the letters from Paris.

As Humboldt took Bauzá around Paris, Bauzá was soon to return the favour in London. When Humboldt visited there, from mid-April to early May 1827, though he stayed with Thomas Young, Bauzá reported that Humboldt could not possibly have complied with the hundreds of requests for his presence. 'So he came to see me every day especially at first for two or three hours at least.' This is a remarkable record for a two-week stay. A highlight of shared tourism was the visit to the Thames tunnel then under construction and already lit by gas, the marvel of Europe. On 25 May 1827 Bauzá had to report on the failure of that enterprise due to siltage of sand into the tunnel which could not be stopped.[53]

At a further remove from London, one meets with the Russian director of the new Hydrographic Office, I. F. Kruzenshtern. He had been in touch with Spain through diplomatic channels and it appears by notes in his work that Espinoza gave him a chart when they met in London.[54] One might not gather that from the reference in the letters. The first mention is an inquiry about a rumour to the effect that the Russians had announced the publication of Malaspina's voyages in Russian.[55] This would have been a severe blow to Bauzá who was denied publication in his own language. The story is a bit involved but it has two salient points. There was in fact a Russian publication based on a Malaspina manuscript[56] and the two volumes of records which Bauzá had saved from the French had not been taken for or by the Russians. Unhappiness and misunderstanding, rumour, politics, diplomacy and envy, all play their role in this story.[57] The exposure to suspected malevolence caused only by a lack of discretion and ignorance is an affliction of refugees. Bauzá had his fair share of it.

In the opposite geographical direction from Russia, Bauzá's letters reflect the interest of Latin Americans in the Spanish survey work. Charts and other Spanish materials were made freely available, though the idea was not for the Americans to publish them without acknowledgment, which apparently they did. French publishers were not far behind with pirate editions of Spanish works, nor were the English. While Barry published the *Noticias Secretas* of Juan and Ulloa, Obadiah Rich secured a copy of the manuscript of Sahagún on Aztec Antiquities which had not been published in Spain but which was revered by its scholars.[58] A lively interchange of information regarding such matters took place in the house of Salvá, also in Somers Town, which included notable figures from Latin America, such as Andrés Bello, and entrepreneurs such as Ackermann, the first publisher of Spanish literature in England produced for the Latin American market.[59] From short digressions in his letters concerning these matters, Bauzá unfailingly returns to latitudes and longitudes. He says that his fate would be to die among them as others' is to die among bullets.[60]

This remark is amply substantiated by the correspondence, which contains a wealth of position fixes, of comparative lists of geographic points, of calculations and observations. The major work reflected in Bauzá's early correspondence is the collection of charts on the *Seno Mexicano*, the Gulf of Mexico, which included all of Cuba, and a good stretch of the Central American coast. From earlier times, and later because of British political, strategic, and commercial interests, Bauzá also worked on a chart of the northern coast of South America. The letters reflect a growing refinement and precision of measurement by improved techniques and by repetition. They demonstrate how in this laborious and tedious process the better drove out the good. Bauzá's talent was doubly appreciated because of his practical experience.

The major problem arising from his position between cartographic traditions and scientific conventions (as between French and English measures and Spanish and English choices of the prime meridian) was to cope with endless re-calculations.[61] On the 1 April 1827, Bauzá submitted a list of about 350 geographical positions, covering the whole of South America, including the Malvinas and the Straits of Magellan, and ranging north to Mount Elias in Alaska, including some Pacific islands on the way. Bauzá quotes among his authorities Bustamante, Bauzá, Malaspina, Galiano and Valdés, Martínez, Hall, Humboldt, Haywood, de Mayne, Ferrer, and Duperrey. The methods used by each observer are given as, for instance, the transit of Mercury or of Venus, an eclipse of the Sun or the Moon, occultation of a star, eclipse of the moons of Jupiter, passage of the Moon across the meridian, etc. Similar care was required for listing various methods by which shore points and sight lines were put on the chart, for instance checking on whether measures of angle were compatible with the length of the sides of the triangle given. There is a little sketch in one letter pointing out such a mistake. In these matters Oltmanns was a close collaborator, but he lacked the experience as well as the information which Bauzá had concerning the conditions under which some positions had been fixed, whether by sextant, station pointers and triangulation or by theodolite alone, and whether by repeated astronomical fixes or a single observation, and by how reliable an observer. Another problem was the reduction of a myriad of depth soundings from the surveys to useful patterns for navigators on the charts (fathom lines or contours were not yet common). The letters also mention the difficult decisions concerning the language to be used on the charts, about whether a chart should be lettered in Spanish or in English, the latter to increase sales.[62] The remarkable contribution of Bauzá was that to exact observation and reliable calculation he added a constant awareness of all the facts surrounding the survey activities. This kept him from fruitless bickering over seconds of degrees, and calculations of illusory precision in latitudes where observations simply could not be confirmed, as by sailing craft around Cape Horn.

The standard of his drafting was up to that of his compilations, though he admitted that he only went into that work in order to give employment to a cousin of his, José de Cardano, a lithographic printer of maps and charts, like himself stranded in London.[63] Cardano eventually submitted a map of the Pyrenees to the Spanish authorities which Bauzá endorsed, though it must have caused him some regret. He had himself compiled a more accurate survey with his own assistants, paid by his own funds, as part of the major commission of his life before his exile, to make an atlas of all of Spain.[64] This commission he was to begin with a map of the Pyrenees in 1808, to continue in expanded format in 1818, and Bauzá never gave up hope to return to it. He always regarded work on the map of Spain as the highlight of his scientific career. He was never allowed to publish his own map of the Pyrenees because of the war with the French, and the rest of his mission was of course aborted.

Bauzá's charts, of which many individual examples survive, some in the works published by the Hydrographic Office after his death, several in foreign works such as Kruzenshtern's atlas, many in the collection of the British Museum and other places, show a distinctive Spanish style, developed by the end of the eighteenth century.[65] It is possible that Humboldt might have spoken to him about his interest in 'Pasigraphie', the device of a standard symbolic language for geological maps.[66] Another subject which they probably shared was the nature and location of ocean currents, since Humboldt had expressly planned his visit to discuss the problem with James Rennell.[67] Beaufort, who because of his long tenure as Hydrographer of the Navy was able to create the uniform style and high standard of the English Admiralty chart, and considering his collaboration with Bauzá, might have been influenced by him. If this be idle speculation, one might ask whether the spread of scientific progress need be reserved to the printed word.

Bauzá is an example of the role of knowledge contained in a human being, transmitted, as one can read in the letters, over a period of years, to his colleagues in London. Yet his name does not appear in any index of any English work I have consulted, though he might be mentioned in the text. In Spain he could only be officially mentioned after his death, and only three short sketches of his life were written, two by his immediate successors, Navarrete and Fernández Duro.[68] On the hundredth anniversary of his death, a compatriot of his from Mallorca, Juan Llabrés Bernal, compiled a curriculum vitae and a list of works by

Bauzá, which together with the Navarrete correspondence certainly rank him among the mathematical practitioners whom Professor Taylor introduced to the history of science. Despite his status as a foreigner, Bauzá's work impinged on much that was done in England in marine cartography. Although he was prevented from publishing his major works and from continuing his great projects, especially the Spanish atlas, his experience and knowledge were as alive among English hydrographers as any printed book could have rendered them.

This leads me to justify the presentation of the Bauzá letters to this audience. The record of the cartographic enterprise of England is enriched by many details. The state of marine cartography is intimately portrayed. The roster of mathematical practitioners, English and Spanish, enriches a chapter on the history of scientists, technical experts, and theorists, which Professor Taylor did so much to pioneer. In these letters can be seen the scientific community in action. I would plead for publication of the letters in their original language on the basis of the usefulness which an ample index would represent for many disciplines, and for the pleasure of an introduction to a respected former member of this company.

But my attention was not called to Bauzá because he was a mathematical practitioner. Rather my study of Spain's sixteenth-century cosmographers had reached a stage where I needed to look for a reference point outside the immediate subject in order to gain some perspective. This was necessary because the interdisciplinary and multifaceted cosmographic enterprise makes for almost unmanageable scattering of possible connections in the history of science. For the purpose of the larger study I look at three subjects, extrapolating from whatever small base on which I find myself, as in this case a mere 10 years of one lifetime – a rather claustrophobic topic by itself.

The subjects are the history of science, the history of scientists, the society and developments of the scientific fraternity. So I reduced the problem addressed by the cosmographers to one of the questions asked by the classic orators, to the 'where' from among the where, who, what, when and how. This would provide a focus in the history of science whenever the question reached the foreground of scientific interest and public curiosity. It did so during the ages of the Iberian discoveries and of *Tudor Geography*.[69] It did so again between the 1780s and the 1820s when all over Europe hydrographic offices were organized. In our day, space exploration and oceanography unite the efforts of many scientific disciplines in trying to find the answer, and public interest is aroused.

The unusual aspect of this sequence is that it is not affected by the seventeenth-century scientific revolution to the extent noted in the other sciences. The decisive change of the world picture was pre-Copernican and pre-Newtonian. It was the expansion of the Ptolemaic universe following the discovery of the great oceans, and the spread of information caused by the invention of printing. The later advances in astronomy, mathematics and physics did result in more reliable calendars or regimens, and the mathematical practitioners made more exact measurements and also improved methods of surveying and charting. By the early nineteenth century the growth of new techniques and collections of data suggested an inventory of knowledge then available about man's orientation in the physical universe. Alexander von Humboldt's *Kosmos* served that function well. The next step in this sequence is the recent one of the astronauts upon the Moon: 'a giant step' which led to a notable resurgence of popular attention to the question of man's place.

I look at these later periods, Bauzá's time and ours, from the perspective of a cosmographer. In this I follow Professor Taylor who reconstructed a chronology for mathematical practitioners beyond the time in which that term was current. The abandonment of a word in the course of linguistic evolution does not necessarily end the existence of what it connotes. This becomes quite evident in a comparison of the questionnaires drafted by Spain's cosmographers in 1571 with the instructions to Captain Fitzroy for the *Beagle*. These show in which direction cosmographers looked to ascertain the orientation of man in the physical universe. The questions for Captain Fitzroy are better organized and show an advance in sophistication, but they are closer to the Spanish *relaciones geográficas* than today's scientific probes.[70] It was with the concept of evolution, which resulted in part from the voyage of the *Beagle*, that a new world picture began to take shape. Today research is stretched to the limits of outer and inner space, crowding the barrier of our capacity to collect evidence and to infer hypotheses. In our time, ideas of where we are from a cosmographic point of view (i.e. descriptive, historical-evolutionary and explanatory), are most readily seen, not in the multiplicity of specialized probes, the information we want to get, but in the message which we beam into the cosmos about the Earth, mankind, our species, societies and selves, in anticipation of other life, environments and circumstances.

Felipe Bauzá was as much a cosmographer as a mathematical practitioner. Despite the discontinuity of the scientific record of cosmography, the recurrent need to fix our position in the natural world with respect to ever-widening horizons needs both practitioners and theorists as it did from early times. The social positions of people engaged in pursuing such questions were those of individual cosmographers during Elizabethan times. In Bauzá's epoch much of the work was attached to an institution, the Hydrographic Office. To Bauzá the *Depósito* was the prime anchor. In all his letters, as far as his work is concerned, his immediate loyalty was to an institution. So it was with Captain Beaufort. Today's main hold on scientists seems to be exerted by the task in hand. The project ranks before the specialty, the discipline and the institution. This sequence from cosmographer to hydrographer to project member belongs to the history of the men of science.

The study of Felipe Bauzá reduces such speculations to a concrete case. Nothing that has been said violates his words or the spirit of his letters. One further topic which can only be mentioned suggests itself for consideration. It is the construction of international networks of elective affinities among scientists, despite political conflict, especially by those deprived of familial ties. (These networks were a sequel to the 'invisible Colleges' and precursors of Helsinki.) The term elective affinities, derived from a Swedish publication on chemical bonds in 1755, via Goethe's book *Die Wahlverwandtschaften*, has since been used by sociologists and the historians of ideas. To Bauzá's fellow hydrographer, Captain Smyth, we owe a gesture which clearly points out the existence of such an elective affinity, reflected in a collegiate tribute. It will serve as well to highlight the most permanent trace of Bauzá's London years.

On 22 September 1826 Bauzá wrote that Captain Smyth had informed him that, in recognition of the Spanish achievement in astronomy and hydrography, he had named the individual features of a cluster of volcanic rocks on Spain's Mediterranean shores called collectively 'Las Columbretes' after Bauzá himself and his associates, the other Spanish hydrographers.[71] The names entered by Captain Smyth are still carried on today's charts. They appear on a Spanish version of the Smyth chart of 1833 as well as on the current one.[72] Bauzá writes:

> The main port is called Tofiño and the other islands are Malaspina, Galeano, Churruca, Cerquero, Ferrer, Luyando, Fidalgo, López, You and I [i.e. Navarrete and Bauzá].

A description of the formation appears in the British Mediterranean Pilot 1963. 'El Bauzá' is described as 72 feet (21·95 m) high, pyramidal in shape, separated from the north-eastern side of La Ferrera by a narrow and foul channel. I shall not indulge in hunting for symbols. The gesture is what counts.

The research for this paper was supported by the National Science Foundation.

REFERENCES AND NOTES

[1] Martín Fernández de Navarrete, *Colección de Opúsculos*, vol. II (Madrid, 1848), pp. 109–114, 'Felipe Bauzá' ; Juan Llabrés Bernal, *Breve noticia de la labor científica del capitán de návio Don Felipe Bauzá y de sus papeles sobre America 1764–1834* (Palma de Mallorca, 1934), pp. 8–9.

[2] 10 Aug. 1810, Cadiz: 'D. Eusebio de Bardaji y Azara comunica al Secretario Del Despacho de Marina que el Consejo de Regencia concede permiso al Teniente Coronel D. Felipe Bauzá para que puede asistir y dirigir a los oficiales de ingenieros británicos en la isla de León...', Museo Naval Madrid, MS 2111 Miscellanea, doc. 41, fol. 128.

[3] Museo Naval Madrid, MS 1190, fol. 35, Hoja de servicio.

[4] Museo Naval Madrid, MS 1821, Testamento, Gibraltar, 22 Oct., 1823. He was married to Doña Teresa Ravera, native of Madrid, and there were three children, Felipe aged 21, and two minor daughters, Ana and Amalia. A discussion of family news reflecting political conditions is not within the scope of this paper.

[5] Collection of Navarrete papers at Ábalos in custody of D. Francisco Fernández de Navarrete, Marqués de Legarda, who has generously given permission to use the *legajo* containing the letters by Felipe Bauzá, and some papers concerning the Depósito Hidrográfico.

336

[6] 11 June 1823 (N.B., a date without further reference refers to a letter).

[7] Vicente Llorens Castillo, *Liberales y Románticos. Una emigración española en Inglaterra* (*1823–1834*), 36 ff.: Un Barrio español en Londres; Claire Gobbi, 'The Spanish Quarter of Somers Town: An Immigrant Community, 1820–1830', *Camden History Review* (1978) VI, 6–9.

[8] Museo Naval Madrid, MS 1820, fol. 1, 'Partido de defunción...', Death certificate and register of burial at the Catholic chapel, Moorfields, in the Parish of St Stephen, Coleman St, in the City of London, vault 6, 8 March 1834. Among a number of papers received by Bauzá there is one addressed to No. 48 Union Street in Somers Town, 8 July 1823 (British Library, MSS Add. 17,649, fol. 170). The street still exists, and among a row of houses are some facing north with an ample bay window. The current numbering, however, does not coincide with one of them. Bauzá only mentions that he did not live alone, and was in cramped quarters as far as storing his papers was concerned. In the papers accompanying the copy of the death certificate, made in Gibraltar, the street name is given as Johnson St, now Cranleigh St, also in Somers Town. I have been unable to ascertain date and circumstances of the change.

[9] Martín Fernández de Navarrete, *Biblioteca Marítima*, 2 vols (Madrid, 1851). For full bibliographical detail, II, 776–777. This atlas covered both the Mediterranean and Atlantic coasts. A second revised edition was published by the Hydrographic Office in Madrid in 1832. There were separate editions of parts of the atlas made in Paris and Copenhagen. The atlas was a standard reference work for the coastlines covered until well into the 1820s. For Bauzá's part and promotion see Museo Naval Madrid, MS 2141, doc. 19, fol. 62, 14 Feb. 1789.

[10] Llabrés Bernal, *op. cit.* 17, cites the *Memorias* published by the Hydrographic Office in 2 volumes, with various appendices. Vol. I, pp. 169–182, brings an article entitled 'Observaciones de la velocidad del sonido, de latitud, longitud y variación, hechas en Santiago de Chile por el teniente de navio don José de Espinoza y el alférez de navio don Felipe Bauzá en 1794.' For the Malaspina voyage see *ibid.* pp. 17–19.

[11] Marcos Jiménez de Espada, 'Una causa de estado', *Revista Contemporánea*, 28 Feb. and 15 March 1881, year VII, vol. XXXII.

[12] Llabrés Bernal, *op. cit.* pp. 43–47.

[13] For final admittance see Royal Society, Certificates, 1801–1819; 1 April, 1819. The certificate is signed: Melville, Vassal Holland, Wm. Marsden, Wm. Lambert, Wm. Barrows. It reads as follows: [Felipe Bauzá,] 'assistant of Tofiño, later Malaspina, author of a chart and memoir between Chile and Buenos Aires; compiler of ancient voyages of the Spaniards in the Pacific from original MSS now in the course of publication; and super-intendent of the Hydrographic Depot at Madrid, a gentleman well skilled in astronomy and hydrography, being desirous of becoming a fellow of the Royal Society of London. We whose names are hereunto subscribed do, from our personal knowledge, from his works, and scientific reputation, recommend him as highly deserving that honour and as likely to become an useful and valuable member on the foreign list. Read fourteen times.'

[14] *The Spanish Journal of Elizabeth Lady Holland*, ed. The Earl of Ilchester (London, 1910), pp. 359–360.

[15] 18 Nov. 1824.

[16] 11 March 1824.

[17] 28 Jan. 1824; 17 Jan. 1825; for Library, 11 March 1824.

[18] G. S. Ritchie, *The Admiralty Chart: British Naval Hydrography in the Nineteenth Century* (London, 1967), p. 159.

[19] 8 Aug. 1825.

[20] Captains Roberts and Willoughby are also mentioned as discussing their work with Bauzá, 20 Nov. 1824.

[21] 29 May 1824.

[22] Beaufort papers, Huntington Library, San Marino, California, letter by W. H. Smyth to Francis Beaufort, 18 Dec. 1833.

23 28 April 1824, Bauzá calls him 'un hombre sumamente prolixo y exacto...'; also on 6 Jan. 1825 he comments with enthusiasm on the map of Sicily; 11 Jan. 1831 on a visit for copying.

24 Navarrete, *Biblioteca Marítima*, II, 776–777.

25 Bauzá himself had surveyed the area in 1814, letter of 21 July 1829. Admiral Fleming's chart had the entry from the Spanish surveyor Luyando. Later survey data were available from Captain Purdy and more recent Spanish surveys. Beaufort had sent out a survey party as well (*ibid*). A drawing of the shoal of Tarifa appears in the letter of 13 Aug. 1831.

26 The 'desengaño' of Smyth, 12 Oct. 1832.

27 26 April 1824; 28 March 1824; 28 April 1824. Sir John Barrow, Bart, *An Autobiographical Memoir,* London, 1847, does not mention Bauzá. It suggests the contrast in the temperaments of the two men.

28 15 June 1825; he was delighted with the countryside near the house about twenty miles from Windsor.

29 31 July 1829. The holdings of various libraries of the Spanish publications are substantial. Collation would only be useful and it would be necessary if one were to check out any individual item. Ursula Lamb, 'Martín Fernández de Navarrete Clears the Deck: the Spanish Hydrographic Office, 1795–1823', appendix II, 'Apuntes', in Centro de Estudos de Cartografia Antiga, Sepcrata C XXXI, Coimbra, 1980.

30 9 April 1828: 'Only one person knows Spanish...'

31 11 March 1824.

32 He also mentions that there is no tradition of printing data equivalent to those in the Spanish *Memorias,* a lack partially made good later by the appearance of the *Nautical Magazine* in 1831, and subsequently to the regular publication of *Notices to Mariners* (1833).

33 1 Aug. 1828; Bauzá recommended two refugee children, eighteen years old, one trained by Cardano and very skilled. They were apparently rejected.

34 25 May 1827; on the Espinoza voyage see: *A Spanish Voyage to Vancouver and the North West Coast of America being the narrative of the voyage made in the year 1792 by the schooners Sútil and Mexicana to explore the Strait of Fuca.* Translated with an introduction by Cecil Jane (London, 1930), these had been published by the Madrid Depósito in 1802. See also Museo Naval Madrid, MS 2406.

35 Colección Navarrete, Ábalos, Noticias históricas de la Dirección Hidrográfica. Ursula Lamb, 'Early Spanish Plans for Lithographic Production of Maps: a fruitful failure', paper presented at the annual meeting of the Society for the History of Discoveries, Charleston, S.C., 1 Oct. 1972.

36 Colección Navarrete, Ábalos, *ibid.* 37. Ursula Lamb, *op. cit.,* Navarrete's 'Apuntes'.

37 Ursula Lamb, *ibid.*

38 On 26 August 1826 the death sentence on Bauzá was confirmed and any chance for a resumption of office was ended. Navarrete was confirmed as proprietary holder of the directorship of the Spanish Hydrographic Office (Llabrés Bernal, *op. cit.* p. 10); On 25 August Bauzá congratulated Navarrete on succeeding to the office: 'No puede Ud. figurarse cuanto he celebrado que la propiedad de ese Depósito haya recaido en Ud...'

39 15 Sept. 1827.

40 Lloréns Castillo, *op. cit.,* especially chapter v. The book is a publication of the *Nueva Revista de Filología* and it covers literary interests extensively.

41 G. S. Ritchie, *op. cit.* pp. 160–161.

42 Ministry of Defence, Royal Navy, Hydrographic Department Archive at Taunton, Somerset, has among the papers by Bauzá lists of positions which were used by British surveyors Captain P. P. King and Commander Henry Foster of HMS *Chanticleer,* though there is no mention of Bauzá in the published account. I owe this and other information concerning Bauzá's papers at Taunton to the kind help of Lieutenant-Commander A. C. F. David and I would like to express my thanks for his personal attention to my inquiries.

43 Alfred Friendly, *Beaufort of the Admiralty, the life of Sir Francis Beaufort 1774–1857* (London, 1977), chapter 24: 'Hydrographer: The Right Man'.

[44] 12 Nov. 1829; Bauzá was received as member on 14 Oct. 1831. He published in the *Transactions* 'The Tables of Heights of various Points of Spain, alphabetically arranged', vol. II (1832), pp. 269–273; Bauzá also contributed to the first number of the *Nautical Magazine*. Thanks for this and other items are due to Dr David V. Proctor, Head of printed books and MSS department of the National Maritime Museum, Greenwich.

[45] In March 1830 and March 1832, Beaufort sent Bauzá three charts to compare with Spanish data of the Mediterranean (Cadiz) to San Lucar (no days given) on the Smyth chart, 14 June 1830.

[46] 11 Jan. 1831; Lieutenant-Commander David sent me the translation of letter No. B 914 from the archive in Taunton. Don Felipe Bauzá writes to Captain Beaufort regarding the proposed voyage of Captain Fitzroy. It has mainly position fixes and is about one-and-a-half pages of single-spaced text. There are also many lists of comparative position fixes submitted by Bauzá in the Archive.

[47] 28 May 1824; Robert Fitzroy, *Narrative of the Surveying Voyages of H.M. Ships Adventure and Beagle*, 3 vols. (London, 1839); vol. II, p. 24 contains the 'Memorandum' with the instructions for the voyage of the *Beagle* sent to Plymouth Harbour. There are various mentions of Spanish charts, of their insufficiency, of the fact that there are none other, and on p. 31 the text reads: 'At the Gulf of Peñas the last survey terminated. Of the Peninsula de Tres Montes, and of the islands between that and Chiloe, a Spanish manuscript has been procured from Don Felipe Bauzá, which may greatly abridge the examination of that interval.'

[48] The entry for 1 Jan. 1827 mentions that the exchange got under way on the suggestion of Humboldt. A sample of their correspondence was published in the German periodical *Hertha* (Berlin), vol. XII (1828), entitled 'Hydrographie und Geographie von Amerika. Auszuege aus Briefen des Spanischen Schiffskapitaens Don Felipe Bauzá an den Freiherrn Alexander von Humboldt und Professor Oltmanns.' The first letter is dated London, 12 Feb. 1827. He cites Malaspina, Brown, and Hall, as well as Humboldt. The frontispiece of the issue is a portrait of Captain W. E. Parry, R.N.

[49] 6 June 1827; Franz Xaver Baron von Zach (4 June 1754–2 Sept. 1832), editor of *Allgemeine Geographische Ephemeriden*, 26 vols. from 1798. My reference is to vol. 13 of *Correspondance astronomique, géologique, hydrographique et statistique*, 14 vols. (1818–1826), for a contribution by Bauzá, but from the mention in the letters one would expect more. The publication is rare, and since it was irregular in appearance it is seldom complete.

[50] Zach's death from cholera is recorded on 12 Oct. 1832. Cholera in London is mentioned as it 'rises and abates with the change in the weather.'

[51] 30 Aug. 1825; Edward J. Goodman, 'The Search for the Mythical Lake Parima', *Terrae Incognitae*, VII (1975), pp. 23–31. The article by Bauzá is entitled 'Discurso sobre el estado de la geografia de la América Meridional' and was translated by Wilhelm Friedrich Freyherr von Karvinsky: 'Ueber den Zustand der Geographie von Sued-Amerika' for the Bayerische Akademie der Wissenschaften, *Denkschriften* (Munich), VIII, 81–124.

[52] From London, 2 Oct. 1826. On 4 Sept. 1828 Bauzá mentions an application for a passport to France.

[53] 25 May 1827; the visit to the tunnel took place on 26 April, in the company of the architect Marc Isambard Brunel.

[54] Ivan Fedorovich Kruzenshtern (1770–1846) (the spelling is so varied in the letters and even in modern transcriptions that I stay by the currently accepted version). In 1827 he issued his *Atlas de l'Océan Pacifique*. St Petersburg, engraved by S. Froloff, elephant folio. On the title page of the Atlas it says that an accompanying volume is the 'Recueil de mémoires hydrographiques, pour servir d'analyse et d'explication à l'atlas de l'océan Pacifique', par le Commodore de Krusenstern, Saint Petersbourg, de l'Imprimerie du Département de l'Instruction Publique, 1824. In vol. I, pp. 293–295 appear words of high praise for Espinoza's *Memorias sobre las observaciones astronomicas etc....* (Madrid, 1809), cited above. The text intended to present the work of the Spanish hydrographers is a very good summary of the significance attributed to it by a foreign colleague. Bauzá is mentioned as preparing a third volume of *Memorias* of which he speaks in his letters but

which were never published. A part of the *Memoria* may well be documents at Taunton, Miscellaneous papers, Data Book, No. 125, dated London, 1 April 1828, which concerns positions on the West coast of Mexico and the Gulf of Honduras.

[55] 24 Sept. 1824; repeated inquiry 18 Nov. 1824.

[56] An article by Kruzenshtern had actually appeared in the Memoirs of the Russian State Admiralty Department (1815), part III. Professor Raymond H. Fisher of the University of California at Los Angeles found the item and transcribed the Russian title as follows: 'Information about the Spanish expedition undertaken for discovery in the years 1791, 1792 and 1793 under the command of Captain Malespina (*sic*)'. We have not been able to obtain a copy thus far.

[57] 11 Nov. 1824. Bauzá reports that Kruzenshtern is said to have announced a publication of the Malaspina voyages in two volumes. This must have been a rumour built upon the favourable mention of Spanish work cited above. On 4 Oct. 1825 Bauzá, who had only checked the American coast of the Atlas – which is in Russian – doubts that there is any improvement over the Spanish data and those of 'Hall, Brown, Byron, Roberts, Ferguson, Bremmer, Duprey, Lartigue, Maclean, Hunter etc., etc. and other Spaniards'. The controversy over the quality of the Russian atlas can be followed in the introduction to his voyages by the English translator who says the lack of plates is no loss, and an article in the *North American Review*, no. LVI (July, 1827), pp. 1–32, which pronounces in his favour. Kruzenshtern did name a cluster of islands in the Pacific (Marquesas Islands) after Washington rather than any specific 'discoverer'.

[58] 19 Oct. 1826. Bauzá says that there is a copy in the Real Académia, and that there may also be one in the Depósito. Rich (American book dealer) whom Bauzá calls a friend, should be advised in this and other matters, so that he would be helped 'without hurting us' and he pleads for information about the state of these affairs. On 4 Oct. 1827 he mentions French pirating of Spanish editions.

[59] The references are miscellaneous but of interest to non-literary historians. They shed light on the epoch when public collections of museums, academies, and learned societies entered the literary market to rival royal collections and private bidding. Yet on 18 July 1826 Bauzá records a depression when no one will buy books. There were many bankruptcies which were getting public attention. For Ackermann see Pedro Grasses, *La primera editorial inglesa para Hispano América* (Caracas, 1955).

[60] 16 Nov. 1824.

[61] Carta Esférica que comprehende las costas del Seno Mexicano, Construida de Órden del Rey en el Depósito Hidrográfico de Marina...Ano de 1799. This is no. 21 in the *Atlas Marítimo*. There are various editions; one says: corregida en 1805...F. Bauzá la delineó. It was this chart which he kept under continual revision. It showed Florida Peninsula and the Gulf Coast. An interesting discussion of this work is in the catalogue of the Lowery Collection, *A descriptive list of Maps of the Spanish Possessions*, by Phillip L. Phillips (Washington. G. P. O. 1912).

[62] Hydrographic Dept. Archives, Miscellaneous papers, vol. 49, pp. 29–44 and 206–207. The letters have many pages of comparative position fixes and there are many more in the Museo Naval in Madrid, dispersed in various MSS. The major collection of Bauzá's papers in the British Library Manuscript collection contains a wide variety of subject matter. The holdings are primarily identified in one purchase made on 2 Dec. 1848, Add. 17556–17676. The collation of those holdings from various lists, Gayangos, Fernández Duro, and the BM catalogue does not appear to be of any use except when one wants to track down one specific item. On 7 Aug. 1827 he writes 'I have constructed a chart of the *Seno Mexicano* from 70° to 90° 30' of longitude East from Cadiz and Latitude 18° to 31°, matching the degrees to the chart of 1799 printed at the time of Lángara. It is heavily corrected and I am finishing an analysis of the data which I have used for the construction. I decided to make that chart to that measurement, because the old one was very much appreciated, and was of a good size for navigation...I have it engraved, although not yet lettered, and I am consulting you as to whether it would be possible that the Depósito would buy it from me. In that case, you might take the one of 1799 for the lettering and I

340

would give you a rebate'. He then mentions that he could not afford to make a gift of the chart to Madrid. Bauzá did not want to send the unlettered version for fear someone else would use it, and he implies that he needed to be paid for his work (20 Nov. 1827). Hydrographic Dept. Archives, Geographic Positions, Q 12, Minute Book No. 1, (2), 289, Captain Beaufort directs Mr Barrow to pay the sum of Lb100 for charts of the West coast of North America. Bauzá reports selling two charts and handing over ten more.

[63] José de Cardano, nephew of Bauzá, made a naval career in the Hydrographic Office as delineador (draughtsman-cartographer). He was sent to Munich to learn the lithographic process with Senefelder, and went from there to Holland, and on to London, where he settled with his family. Bauzá thought him somewhat mad and suffered from his importunities. 'Hay locos en el mundo dignos de compasion...' (4 Nov. 1832).

[64] Archivo Histórico de Simancas, Catálogo XVI, p. 400; Mapa geográfica de los Pirineos que pretende publicar don José Cardano e intervencion de Don Felipe Bauzá. He describes his full commission in: Museo Naval Madrid, MS 1436, fol. 14: 'Memoria de la comision nombrada para formar un proyecto de division del territorio de la Peninsula, por D. Felipe Bauzá'. 18 March 1821, Madrid.

[65] 6 Jan. 1834; Bauzá reports that he is packing his papers and that he has 1230 maps and plans for the hydrography and geography of Spain alone. The British Museum Catalogue of Printed Maps and Charts, vol. II (1964), lists nine charts by Bauzá posthumously published by the Admiralty, the last in 1876. I have also been informed of extensive holdings in the Library of Congress by Dr John A. Wolter, Chief of the Geography and Map Division, Dr John Hebert, Acting Chief, Hispanic Division and Mr Robert S. Martin, Director of the Library of the University of Texas at Arlington, to all of whom I express my thanks.

[66] Alexander von Humboldt, *Mexico Atlas*, ed. Hanno Beck and Wilhelm Bonacker (Stuttgart, 1969), elephant folio. Introduction p. 12, 'Pasiegraphie' (= allgemein-verstaendliche Schriftzeichensprache).

[67] Margaret Deacon, *Scientists and the Sea, 1650–1900, a study of marine science* (Academic Press, London, 1971), pp. VII and 220–223; the Hydrographic Department Archives possess a booklet in Spanish and English translation sent by Bauzá which concerns icebergs sighted off the Cape of Good Hope (Miscellaneous Papers, vol. 81, pp. 335–340). Rennell is mentioned Oct. 1833; Bauzá was doubtful concerning his work, probably with reference to a north Atlantic current.

[68] Note 1, and Cesareo Fernández Duro, *Disquisiciones Náuticas* IV, 'Los Ojos en el cielo' (Madrid, 1881), pp. 319, 333, 336, 343 ff. Llabrés Bernal, *op. cit.*; in the *Memoirs of the Royal Astronomical Society*, vol. VIII (London, 1835), pp. 288–289 appears the following text: 'Signor Don Felipe Bauzá was among the foremost of those officers, whose hydrographic talents reflect such credit on the Spanish navy. He made his escape to England in company of Admiral Valdés...but even in exile his industry did not forsake him as was evinced by his reconstructing the maps and charts of South America, and the compilation of a luminous memoir of the data on which they were founded. He expired at an advanced age in Somers Town...[he is] remembered for several important papers especially that by D. José Feirer on the longitude of Havannah inserted in our memoirs.' The London *Times* carried an obituary with less detail on 11 March 1834, 3b.

[69] E. G. R. Taylor, *Tudor Geography, 1485–1583* (London, 1930).

[70] Ursula Lamb, 'Cosmographers of Seville, Nautical Science and Social Experience' in *First Images of America*, Fredi Chiappelli ed. (Los Angeles, 1978), vol. 2, pp. 675–686, note 21.

[71] 27 Sept. 1831, Bauzá reports on a visit to the house of Captain Smyth who showed him the chart of the Columbretes and asked him to supply some biographical data about his colleagues to be published with the new list of names. These were of the various people concerned with the Spanish survey of Tofiño, or other Spanish Mediterranean surveys which Smyth had consulted for his charts.

[72] The Museo Naval in Madrid sent me a blow-up of the Columbretes from the chart of 1833. I am obliged to the staff of that institution for their continued help and advice.

XVII

EARLY SPANISH PLANS FOR LITHOGRAPHIC
REPRODUCTION OF MAPS: A FRUITFUL FAILURE

This essay is a tribute to the wide ranging interests of Luís de Albuquerque, and an exploration of a by-way in the record.

The revival of nautical enterprise in science and technology was one aspect of Spain's Bourbon reforms in the eighteenth century. Alexander Malaspina's mission of oceanic reconnaissance in the western Pacific (1789--1794) was engaged in many branches of the sciences which were later associated with the Hydrographic Office, or *Dirección de Hidrografía* founded in 1797. The impressive work accomplished by the Malaspina expedition remained unpublished, and was scattered because of court intrigues against him. Subsequently, the events of war and revolution, which spread from France all over Europe, led to the occupation of Madrid under Napoleon. The experiments with lithographic techniques of printing were contemporary to these upheavals and were affected in two ways: negatively by the lack of stability, funds, and authority, in the Hydrographic Office, and positively by the increased contact among intellectuals and other refugees due to exile from their base. Thus, while steady activities, and experiments were ever harder to conduct in an orderly fashion, news of them travelled by word of mouth and correspondence among the European capitals and other places which exiles passed, or where they gathered.

The process of lithographic reproduction of printing reached these centers from Munich, where Alois Senefelder had established a lithographic press and made experiments with the process. This invention combined knowledge of the nature of inks (chemistry), the properties of stones (geology), the use of presses, and techniques of the transfer of images (technology), that were part of the industrial revolution coinciding with the events of the time. In other words, a closer look at a single activity, the lithographic enterprise of the Spanish hydrographic office, is anchored deep in the fabric of circumstance surrounding it. Although no maps or charts were produced under that program, it had one unforeseen result which has lost the association with its peculiar origin, namely the pioneering lithographs by Francisco Goya. This fact alone makes the enterprise to be described a «fruitful failure».

The lithographic activities came to my notice because of a contradiction. In his essay on the «Lithography of Maps, 1796-1850», W. W. Ristow states that, «From 1817 on lithography flourished in France ...» He continues that «Lithographic presses, reportedly, were also operating in 1820 in Austria, Belgium, Italy, the Netherlands, Spain, and Russia. There is meager record, however of any cartographic items they may have produced in this period.» (1) The manuscript collection of the Museo Naval (Madrid), in apparent contradiction, contains a note to the effect that a French general made use of the Spanish lithographic press to reproduce orders and official documents in 1818, and that the *Dirección de Hidrografía,* in charge of charts and maps, operated a lithographic workshop in Madrid from 1806. A batch of papers which came into my hands from a different source promised to cast light on the lithographic enterprise of the hydrographic office which was officially in charge of charts and maps (2).

The documentation is very scanty and can be quickly accounted for. First, there are the bills of account. These show the expenses of the Dirección de Hidrografía for work on the premises assigned to the lithographic workshop. The monies paid to carpenters, glaziers, masons, ironmongers, and painters appear on a bill headed: «for repair of the house where the lithography has been established on Hortaleza Street Num. 4. (3) A royal order of March 1819 confirms the establishment of a lithographic workshop under the supervision of the Depósito de Hidrografía. (4) This appears to be a license for the unit operating since 1806, and the reason for the post facto date has something to do with the monopoly of the process granted to the atelier which will be mentioned again.

Next there is a request of the year 1815 for papers of three sizes, for stones, and for various inks suitable for maps and charts: «para el uso de la lithografía y para cartas de hidrografía.» (5) A detailed inventory lists

---

(1) Walter W. Ristow, «Cartography and Maps, 1796-1850,» in *Five Centuries of Map Printing,* David Woodáard, ed., Univ. of Chicago Press, 1975, Chapter IV, p. 92.

(2) *Inventario de los papeles pertenencientes al Exmo Dr. D. Martín Fernández de Navarrete,* existentes en Abalos, en el Archivo del Marqués de Legarda, Madrid, 1944. These are the private papers of D. Martín Fernández de Navarrete in possession and custody of D. Francisco Fernandez de Navarrete Marqués de Legarda. I thank him for permission to consult the *legajo* containing the papers of the Hidrographic Office. Most important for this essay was a set of notes headed: «Apuntes para continuar la noticia historica de la Dirección Hidrográfica de Madrid, desde el ano de 1809» — en que se publicaron sus dos tomos de Memorias hasta 1924.

(3) Museo Naval, Madrid, MS. 1394, p. 7, «Desembolsos hechos por el Depósito Hidrográfico en el arreglo de la casa calle de Hortaleza Num. 4».

(4) *Ibid.* p. 5; María Luísa Martín Meras, «Fondos Cartograficos del Museu Naval de Madrid». *Revista de Historia Naval* Ano VI, num. 20, 1988, pp. 107-112, p. 107.

(5) *Ibid.* p. 13, «Precios y Tamaños del papel con cola y sin ella para la Litografía y para cartas hidrográficas.»

equipment of the workshop, its presses, machine parts, stones (their quality and state of preparation, i.e., polish), inks, and ink barrels.

To the record of place and equipment can be added the names of people employed in the workshop. In 1802, three skilled cartographers, two brothers with the naval rating of pilotin (second pilot) Felipe and José Maria Cardano and Don Tomas Gonzales, were sent to Paris to study the reproduction of maps by lithographic printing. The Cardanos are mentioned in the *Inventario* of the papers of D. Martín Fernández de Navarrete published by Julio Guillén. (6) The brothers appear to have returned in 1806 while for Don Tomas Gonzalez there is no date. In 1808 Felipe was, in Paris again, and being an ardent royalist, he decided to stay on, and did not return to Madrid until the usurper of the Spanish throne, Joseph Bonaparte, had left Spain in 1814. The first director of the Direccion Hidrografica, D. Jose de Espinosa, was meantime visiting England and establishing a liaison with London. He had Spaniards working there on commission from Madrid, so that Navarrete names as the three cartographic centers under supervision of the Direccion Hidrografica: Madrid, Cadiz, and London. (7) Don José de Espinosa had returned in 1810 with many plans for maps to be made in Madrid on the basis of new data he obtained in London, for that city was at the forefront of cartographic enterprise both with respect to new data available and the private enterprise of its skilled cartographers.

Upon the death of its first director (September 6, 1815), the appointment went to D. Felipe Bauzá, uncle of the Cardonas. He had been cartographer abroad the «Atrevido» of the Malaspina expedition and was a higly cultivated man holding the rank of captain in the navy. Beginning to rebuild the Madrid archive and to increase the cartographic activity of the Deposito, he called back such documents as had been shipped from Madrid to Cadiz or other deposits ahead of the French in 1808. Felipe Bauza supported the lithographic atelier, and the shopping list for papers suitable for charts and stones from Bavaria, for machine parts and presses, appear to have originated under his administration. The cartographic activity of the Dirección de Hidrografía is truly admirable considering the political confusion of the country (8).

In 1810, the Depósito was relocated in new quarters in the Calle de Alcala and received a set of office orders and rules of procedure; it employed

---

(6) *Ibid.* 1384, p. 2, *Inventario*, «Apuntes ...» contains a page: «Obras publicadas por la Direccion de Hidrografia y construidas en Londres y Madrid y Cadiz desde el año 1809 hasta la actualidad mediante a que en aquella fecha se subdivido este establiciemiento en las dos ultimas ciudades por las circunstancias politicas. Appears dated March 24, 1824.»

(7) For the Cardanos and the Hydrographic Office see Juan Carrete Parrondo, «Los Grabadores Felipe y José Maria Cardano, iniciadores del arte de litografico», *GOYA*, 157, July, August 1980, pp. 16-23.

(8) Navarrete, Abalos, «Apuntes».

three cartographers. The lithographic workshop at the Calle de Hortaleza is not mentioned in the rules, but it was in charge of one of them, Jose Maria Cardano, and lithography was very much discussed. Felipe Cardano rose quickly after reappointment to his post in the Direccion Hidrografica. In 1814, he was made royal engraver (Grabador de Cámara), and on February 5, 1815, he was elected «Académico de Merito» of the Royal Academy of Fine Arts (de San Fernando). The record of the many commissions for maps which he was given is dated October of 1815.

His brother José Maria was meantime head of the lithographic workshop and the extensive shopping list mentioned above stems from that busy period. There is a letter of August 8, 1817, by D. Rafael Santibanez, which speaks of the receipt of a book by the distinguished French engraver, Charles Philibert the Comte de Lasteyrie (9), mainly based on the work of Senefelder. On the 19th of February of 1817, Jose Cardano went to Munich via Paris, to study the advances made in the technique which had originated in the Bavarian capital. There were then new presses operating, and multicolor printing was in an experimental stage. In 1822, José Cardano went on to Holland to study paper making for lithographic printing when learning of the latest political upheaval in his homeland: the abrogation of the constitutional regime in Spain. He decided to go to England to see how things would turn out.

Meantime, his brother Felipe acted as head of the lithographic establishment, now renamed Deposito Hidrografico (10). But Don Felipe was not a well man. He suffered a heart attack that left him in the deplorable condition recorded by Fernandez de Navarrete in his papers. Don Felipe petitioned to be granted leave with pay to go to Malaga for four months to regain his health, but he died on April 15, 1823 (11).

Felipe Bauzá, the director of the Hidrografic Office, had also risen in the esteem of his contemporaries and had been chosen deputy in Parliament of Cadiz in May 1809. When this honorable body was declared traitorous by the invading French, he had to leave the country. Bauza sent many charts and maps with the government to Sevilla and others went to Cadiz. Bauza himself fled to London via Gibraltar in 1823.

There is another issue of interest raised in the Museo Naval papers that concerns the monopoly granted to the lithographic office. Martinez Hidalgo affirms that the lithographic establishment of the Deposito held a complete monopoly for lithographic printing in all of Spain for two years from 1819 to 1821 (12). The earliest record I have seen is one that excludes

---

(9) Museo Naval, MS. 2181, pp. 194, 196.
(10) Museo Naval, MS. 1394, p. 2.
(11) *Loc. Cit.*
(12) José Maria Martinez Hidalgo, «El Grabado Cartográfico en Espana», *Revista General de Marina,* Madrid, May, 1946, p. 690.

from this the printing of music and of texts. Apparently, private business was encouraged to patronize the establishment in the Calle Hortaleza. Stones were for rent, presses could be leased, and inks purchased. There appear to have been a number of protests against the monopoly, registered by private printers, especially from Cataluna, i.e., Barcelona, but the whole story is not yet clear. When D. Martín Fernández de Navarrete succeeded Bauzá the Dirección de Hidrografía, he accepted the job only as temporary replacement (interino) during Bauza's absence. One can be sure that the cartographic production of the Hidrografic Office as well as the atelier in the Calle Hortaleza were of first concern to him. Since he was also a member of the Academy of Fine Arts, as had been Felipe Cardano, he sponsored the study of the lithographic technique in Paris by a well-known painter, Jose de Madrazo. It appears that this artist worked out of the lithographic establishment as well, though apparently on private commissions (13). Anyway, the royal monopoly for Fine Arts and cartography remained on the books until the industry was officially opened on January 25, 1830, to all «individuals who in this land in any town (pueblo) of the monarchy ddiecate themselves to that branch of industry.» (14)   There are also jurisdictional disputes settled by cedula concerning the interagency control between the printing office of the Ministerio de la Guerra and the Deposito outside the scope of this paper.

In fact the document concerning the monopoly supports the records available in Don Martín Fernández de Navarrete's papers which is the one that put a halt to my search for maps and charts printed in the lithographic workshop (15). It is headed:

«Observations concerning the fulfillment of the rules which are laid down in the royal order of March, 1819, with respect to the Lithographic Establishment.»   A copy of the «rules» has not been found, so that one has to reconstruct them from the answers to the questionnaire.

Article 1.   Executed with respect to the Lithographic Establishment and with reference to the exclusive privilege in Madrid. (This I interpret to mean the establishment of the facility and its monopoly.)

2.   Completed in all its parts: instruction given on printing and the polishing of stones (the preparation of presses, etc. — illegible in copy —) and how to make prints.

3.   This article has not been implemented because no work was ever done for the Depósito. What was done was for private parties.

---

(13)   Navarrete, Abalos, Letters from Madrazo; Museo Naal, MS 1394, pp. 16.
(14)   Museo Naval, MS. 1433, «Ministerio de Fomento General», p. 169.
(15)   Navarrete, Abalos; Museo Naval, MS. 1433.

4. This is believed to have been obeyed because monthly expenses for lithography appear in the documentation of D. Felipe Bauzá.
5. The matter of giving instruction to two apprentices has not arisen.
6. The press has been installed and it exists and it is of the description given, but there is no one to run it (no hay ayudante).
7. Obeyed. The printer's and his assistant's posts have been refunded by combining them, and the employee draws 8 reales per diem.
8. Complied with. There is a portero (concierge). But since there have been hardly any works for sale, he has been added to the list of employees of the Depósito.
9. There has been no opportunity to sell stones or stencils and the stones have been very scarce.
11. Completed, and this has cost the Depósito already nearly 1200 (reales).
12. Account books have never been laid out or kept by the Lithographic Establishment.
13. There is no record in this office that Cardano has written anything mentioning secrets of specific instructions concerning the art of lithography.

To this are appended two pages of translation into Spanish from Senefelder's introduction.

There is a more elaborate clean copy which adds the following elaborations: To article one: this question is answered by common knowledge concerning the existence of the Lithographic Establishment at this Court. The absence of its director D. José Cardano on commission in Holland and England, to study paper manufacturing for lithographic prints, has paralyzed operations. There is no information about whether another institution of this sort exists in Spain.

To article two is added that Cardano left behind him people to whom he had taught skills, the polishing of stones, the preparation of inks and chemical pencils, and other such technical matters: «so that they can work in his absence, although their work should be improved. It is hoped that the return of the director will re-animate the establishment and further its progress.»

Article 8 has the following supplementary remarks: that the portero is a retired sergeant to whom have been assigned three per cent of the value of lithographic prints sold from the Establishment, but there have hardly been any sales since the material printed there has been sold out of the Calle de Alcalá (Depósito). As the portero has no coal to heat his premises during the winter, he has been assigned 4 maravedis a day because of his limited income.

Article 9 has the additional information that there are not sufficient stones for the works under consideration. What happens is that stones are rented to private parties who pay rent for the time that the designs remain on them. Pencils and inks can be bought by the public when they ask for them. Article 14 adds that the Establishment has a copy of Senefelder's book on the premises, and that the work in the Establishment is governed by its rules.

This document implies the attempt to recall José Cardano and it shows how progress of the Atelier had come to a halt. In fact, the cartographic work was eventually taken away not only from the Lithographic Establishment but from the Navy altogether. This is implied in a final document, which is a scrap of paper with the writing of Navarrete, headed: «Establicimiento de lithografía, gravoso al Depósito y mandado enanejoar» i.e., «the lithographic establishment. How it is burdensome to the Depósito and to be detached.» (16) It goes on to say that despite the fact that the «machines were installed at great expense, not even proofs had been run which were good enough to serve any common purpose» (i.e. the Depósito could neither use them nor sell them) and at that line the page is torn. Martinez Hidalgo infers from a letter of 1836 that map making was again contracted out or commissioned as before 1796. The lithographic shop disappears from the records of the Depósito though royal sponsorship for fine arts printing contined. The official production of maps throughout this period was by engraving (17).

To this story of Spanish failure with lithographic map printing I would like to add three footnotes. The organization of the Deposito, its workshops, and the contact of its directors with people abroad, led to inquiries by England and from St. Petersburg concerning its organization and activity. According to Navarrete, the British asked to be sent the office rules, personnel lists, and organization records, (18) and an inquiry from St. Petersburg exists in a two-page questionnaire. Navarrete says that the English followed through with a similar organization, while the Russian inquiry concerned as well latest data available such as ephemerides, catalogs of the works in the Deposito, the latest posting of «faroles» and a general account of the

---

(16) Navarrete, Abalos; Museo Naval, MS 1394, p. 1.

(17) Biblioteca Nacional, Sección de Cartografía has the famous copper plate of the «Mapa de los Reynos de Espana y Portugal», of 1821, by Felipe Cardano. Sección Cartográfia, Núm. Rê185. See also Navarrete, Abalos, Apuntes.

(18) Navarrete, Abalos, letter by Bauzá, London, Nov. 16, 1824, says that the English Deposit was established in 1796 with ten persons, not all naval personnel. Only recently were charts officially published at government cost and freely sold to the public. He also says that «they think of adopting many rules' (piensan adoptar muchar reglas de el-nuestro reglamento —». These rules are printed in the *Complilación Legislativo de la Armada,* Edic. Oficial, Ministerio de Marina, Madrid, 1907, Vol. II, p. 775, «Delineadores constructores de cartas: R. O. 10 DBRE (Dec.) 1817.

state of the navy (una guia del estado de marina). (19)   So, in the midst of
war and revolution, the Spanish administative organization and the results
of work under its auspices were known to and sought out by others.   In
the English case, private enterprise was ahead of the Spanish one in many
instances, but the British Navy as well as cartographers could conveniently
profit from the model of the institution in Spain, and for St. Petersburg specific
information was of utmost value.

A second note of interest concerns José Cardano, who earned his living
as cartographer in London after 1823.   There is a list of maps that he made
elsewhere, but that would be out of place here.   What I did find in the Biblioteca Nacional was a lithographic copy of an engraved map by him — also
available in Madrid — which shows the region of San Lucar de Barrameda.
On the lithograph there appears an insert marked: Villa de Rota and a space
has been left on the upper right with the following legend: «Proyecto para
construir un camino de hierro según se expresa en la memoria que acom-
pana desde Xerez de la Frontera al Puerto de Sta. Maria desde Rota y desde
Rota a S. Lucar de Barrameda.   Presentado a S. D. Marcelino Calero y
Portocarrero, entitled» Plano de las inmediaciones de Cadiz.   W. Day Lithographer, 17 Gate St. Thomas (20).

The point to which I wish to call attention is the coarseness of the lithographic copy, a feature of the technique at the time when compared with
engraving which I find mentioned by Navarrete as one reason for his dissa-
tisfaction with the process. (21)   It is also worth noting that the new technique
matched the new purpose.   The lithographic copy was probably an invitation to investors because Cardano, in one of his letters to Bauzá speaks
about the free capital funds available in England. (22)

Ristow remarks in his essay on «Lithography and Maps...,» that the
technique «was early viewed as a potential medium for reproductions of
unique or rare paintings, portraits and maps.» (23)   An early use in this

(19)   Navarrete, Abalos, questionnaire and answers.

(20)   Biblioteca Nacional, Sección de Cartografía, MS. M12 v: «Inmediaciones de
Cadiz.»   This matches the printed Map listed as of «San Lucar de Barrameda, Conyl, de
Medyna, Xerez y Campyna» dedicated to «Sr. D. Henrique Wellesley», Plenipotentiary
of SM «inmediato al Gobierno de Espana en nombre de SMC Fernando VII por su atento
servidor J.S.M.B. Jose Cardano.» 52:33 cm in size.

(21)   *Art and Cartography: Six Historical Essays.* ed. David Woodward, University
of Chicago Press, 1988, has a concise discussion of the advantages of the two techniques in
the essay by Ulla Ehrensvaerd, «Color in Cartography: A Historical Survey», pp. 140, 141.

(22)   José Cardano was quite unsuccessful as a businessman, causing his uncle Felipe
Bauza, exiled in London, many concerns.   Ursula Lamb, «The London Years of Felipe
Bauza: Spanish Hydrographer in Exile, 1823-1834».   The Eva. G. R. Taylor Lecture,
The Journal of Navigation», Vol. 14, No. 3, Sept. 1981, pp. 319-340.   Note 63.

(23)   Ristow, *op. cit.* pp. 97, 98.   João de Castro's *Roteiro em que se contem a viagem
que fizeram os Portugueses no anno de 1541, partindo da nobre cidade de Goa atee Soez ...
Paris,* 1833.

sense was made by the Portuguese historian and cartographic expert, Manoel Francisco de Barros, Second Viscount de Santarém, he recorded the Portuguese discoveries from the xth century in three editions of historic maps 1840-41, 1842 and 1849 (24).

It is the application in art, however, which constitutes the most permanent contribution of the aborted experiment with lithographic technique in the Hydrographic Office in Madrid. This was the introduction of the renowned painter, engraver, and lithographer to be, Francisco Goya, to its lithographic workshop, while it was still developing. José Cardano was his teacher, and there are three lithographs among the early works in this medium by Goya marked «Madrid.» In 1823, Goya joined the Spanish exiles who fled to France, and he embarked on a career in the newest artistic medium of his time, as lithographer, when he was past seventy years of age. He retired to Bordeaux, but not before a short stay in Paris, where fellow exile, José Cardano, once more became his guide. This time he introduced him to the French lithographers of the capital, thus rendering a great service to Spanish art. The Spanish Hydrographic Office and its failed enterprise of lithographic mapping, sufficed to inspire one of the artistic monuments of the technique, the work of the last years of Francisco Goya (25).

---

(24) Of particular interest because of the studies of Castro's work in view of twentieth century interest in science by Luís de Albuquerque of Coimbra and Lisbon. A new facsimile *Atlas de Satarém* based on the last edition of 1849 with explanatory texts by Helen Wallis and A. H. Sijmons, appeared at R. Miller, Amsterdam, 1985. measure: 73 × 53 cm.

(25) Jaques Fouque, *Goya y Burdeos 1824-1828*. trs. In French, Spanish (Ramos Villanueva Etchevarria) and English. Ediciones Oroel, Zaragoza, 1982. Especially on Cardano pp. 558-559. Affirms that Goya pulled proofs in the atelier of the Hydrographic Office under the tutelage of José Cardano.

POST SCRIPTUM

With regard to recent literature about the subjects treated, I have included references in the endnotes of the three unpublished papers. A particularly rapid and significant development of the study of marine archaeology has been registered in recent years and a most pertinent book of late summarizes some of the results in exemplary fashion: Roger C. Smith in *Vanguard of Empire: Ships of Exploration in the Age of Columbus* (Oxford University Press, 1993). The author manages to put the study of under water wrecks into historical context with the industry of ship construction and repair, including discussions of the supplies needed, the work force, and their expertise. This is an addition to the other growing field of study in maritime communities, which is also increasing in attention. An article by Pedro García-Barreno of the Royal Academy of Science of Spain: 'The Madrid Academy of Philip II' (whose origins are sketched in my article VI) gives the institution the thorough examination it deserves. Starting at the beginning, it carries the story through the Jesuit phase forward to the present day. The documentation is exhaustive and it brings to light many Spanish texts. It is to be published with the papers collected by J.V. Field and Eduardo Ortíz of Imperial College, London, on the occasion of the Colloquium entitled: *Iberia in the Golden Age: Mathematical Sciences and their Uses, 1500–1700*. Victor Navarro Brotóns, in an analysis of 'La actividad astronómica en la España del siglo XVI perspectivas historiográficas', *Arbor* CXLII, 558–560 (1992), pp. 185–216.

Considering the problem of being up-to-date, I realize that my papers throw minor sidelights on some major issues of the history of science, its problems and results, as it is now written. For a congress held in Madrid in 1991 to discuss *Science, Discovery and the Colonial World*, Professor Navarro Brotóns took over the panel which I had originally been asked to set up for the meeting. When I fell ill and could not proceed, he organized the discussion around the theme I had initiated. In the absence also of Luís de Albuquerque, who was originally scheduled to talk, Professor Navarro was able to persuade two Spanish colleagues to join the panel to make up the following program: Bernard Cohen, 'What Columbus "SAW" in 1492'; Victor Navarro Brotóns, 'Cartografía y cosmografía en la época del descubrimiento'; Helen Wallis, 'Cartography in the Age of Discovery'; Norman J.W. Thrower, 'Projections of maps in fifteenth- and sixteenth-century European discoveries'; Mariano Esteban Piñeiro, 'La Academia de Matemáticas de Felipe II y la enmienda de los instrumentos de marear'; and Nicolás García Tápia, 'Los inginieros y la cosmografía en España en los siglos XVI y XVII'.

This large gathering of scholars resulted in a volume of 750 pages of proceedings: *Mundalización de la ciencia y cultura nacional*, A. Lafuente, A. Elena and M.L. Ortega (eds) (Universidad Autónoma, Doce Calles, Madrid, 1993). Relevant to my subjects were papers in the first section *Perspectiva del Nuevo Mundo*. The discussion was to illustrate the importance of the experience with transoceanic enterprise which enlarged the need to deal with vastly increased measure of distance and of duration. Today's measured and quantitative perception and description of nature and the world developed only gradually. Formerly numbers had inherent qualities of good or bad, they were tied to events, or based on traditional lore. A universal system of measure based on numbers became necessary with action over distance and effect over time. This does not change the customary association of increasing precision of measurement with Renaissance science, but it stresses a major cause for the change, the oceanic experience. The issue is not that it happened, but how it happened. This has led me to a consideration of what happened, that is, to examine the entry of the oceans into the consciousness of humanity, and the chronology of perceptions of the sea. A preparatory exercise is article XIV, showing how a wholly land-based orientation developed which conceals the problems and opportunities of the oceanic world in its own terms, that might be usefully examined.

Appendix of General Information

Table of pilots major, professors and cosmographers serving at the Casa de la Contratación, 1508–1613

Name	Appointed	Further information	Died
Pilots major			
Amerigo Vespucci	Mar. 22 1508		Feb. 22 1512
Juan de Solís	Mar. 25 1512		1516
Sebastian Cabot	Feb. 05 1518	left for England 1548	1588
Alonso de Chaves	Jul. 11 1552	served from Oct. 1 1552	Aug. 28 1587
Rodrigo Zamorano	Apr. 13 1586	resigned Nov. 12 1596	
reappointed	Apr. 14 1598		Jun. 24 1620
Andrés García de Céspedes	May 15 1596	resigned	
Professors of cosmography			
Gierónymo de Chaves	Dec. 04 1552	resigned 1568	
Sancho Gutierrez	May 25 1569	resigned Mar. 3 1574	Aug. 13 1580
Diego Ruíz	Mar. 11 1573	served from Mar. 3 1574	
Rodrigo Zamorano (Pilot Major)	Nov. 20 1575	retired Feb. 23 1613	

Other cosmographers

Diogo Ribeiro, Francisco Faleiro, Pedro de Medina, Diego Gutierrez, Alonso de Santa Cruz, Domingo de Villaroel, Pedro Mexia.

Instruments

The following are listed throughout the volume: compass; chart; marine-astrolabe; quadrant; baculo = balestilla = Jacob's staff; sonda = sounding instrument; nocturnal; sandglass; measurement of the earth as part of chart-making.

Ship types

See Alonso de Chaves, *Quatri Partitu*, p. 210.
"large and heavy ships": esquifes; bateles; barcos; barcas; chalupas; tafurcas; gavarras pataxes; pinacas; carabelas; navios; naos; urcas; galeones; carracone; carracas.
"lighter ships": zabras; bergantinas; galeotas; esquiracas; fustas; galeras; bastardas; galeazas.
There are more types but Chaves will speak only of naos and take as an example a ship of 200 tons.
See also V. Fernández de Asís, *Epistolário de Felipe II sobre asuntos de Mar.*, Editoria nacional, Madrid, 1943.

Terms for ports

Puerto = port; ancon = open road; atracadero = landing for small vessels; bahia = bay; barra, boca barra = river mouth; caleta = creek cove, small bay; embaracadero = port landing, loading; ensenada = cove, bay; estero = tidal inlet, small; creek; fondeadero = anchorage; rada = roadsted; surgidero = anchorage.
The tonnage permissible and the draft for ships which can use these harbors are known.
See Donald D. Brand, *The Development of Pacific Coast Ports during the Spanish Colonial Period*, Estudios Anthropológicos, Universidad Nacional de Mexico, 1956.

Index

8

For Product Safety Concerns and Information please contact
our EU representative GPSR@taylorandfrancis.com Taylor & Francis
Verlag GmbH, Kaufingerstraße 24, 80331 München, Germany

T - #0047 - 160425 - C0 - 224/150/15 [17] - CB - 9780860784739 - Gloss Lamination